FOR THE
GOOD
of the
RIDER

BY THE SAME AUTHOR

Ride With Your Mind: A Right Brain Approach to Riding

Ride With Your Mind Masterclass

For the Good of the Horse

FOR THE
GOOD
of the
RIDER

MARY WANLESS

KENILWORTH PRESS

DISCLAIMER OF LIABILITY

The author and publisher shall have neither liability nor responsibility to any person or entity with respect to any loss or damage caused or alleged to be caused directly or indirectly by the information contained in this book. While the book is as accurate as the author can make it, there may be errors, omissions, and inaccuracies.

First published in the Great Britain in 1998 by
Kenilworth Press
Addington
Buckingham
MK18 2JR

British Library Cataloguing in Publication Data
A CIP record for this book is available from the British Library

ISBN 1-872119-05-0

Typeset in 11/13 Bembo
Illustrations by Christine Bousfield, diagrams by Kenilworth Press
Design, typesetting and layout by Kenilworth Press
Printed and bound in Great Britain by Hillman Printers (Frome) Ltd

QUOTATION PERMISSIONS/ACKNOWLEDGEMENTS
A full list of permissions and acknowledgements can be found at the back of the book.

Contents

Acknowledgements   6
Author's Note   6

Introduction   7
1   The Map is Not the Territory   17
2   Sitting Well: Alignment and Tone   33
3   Plugging in   64
4   Interactive Riding   90
5   Symmetry   120
6   The Challenge of Learning   154
7   Mindwork   185
8   Bodywork   208
9   Fit and Able   235
10 The Zen Competitor   280
    Epilogue   312

Bibliography   323
Useful Addresses   326
Index   328

Acknowledgements

I WOULD LIKE TO THANK Trisha Abrahamsen MSTAT, Adam Nott MSTAT, and Garet Newell (Certified Feldenkrais Trainer) BA, MA, for reading parts or all of Chapter 8 *Bodywork*, I would also like to thank Dr Dave Houlston for reading Chapter 10 *The Zen Competitor*, and Ann Mansbridge for reading everything and being (as always) a great source of support and encouragement. I also want to thank Lesley Gowers and all at Kenilworth Press for turning my manuscript into such a beautiful book.

I am no longer the sole initiator of this work, and would like to thank those of my colleagues who have made significant contributions to our shared body of knowledge. In particular I would like to acknowledge Joani Bolton, Janet Harvey, Alexsandra Howard and Anne Howard MPT in the USA, and Trisha Abrahamsen MSTAT, Clare Bayman and Richard White in the UK.

Author's note

In writing this book it has been my intention to be as international as possible, and to use terminology that can be easily understood throughout the English-speaking world. In some cases it is not possible or necessary to 'internationalise' a word. I trust this will not lead to any confusion nor spoil your enjoyment of the book.

Throughout this book I have generally used 'she' to refer to the rider or trainer, and 'he' to refer to the horse. I do this for ease of writing and in acknowledgement of a predominantly female readership. In doing so I mean no offence to male readers!

Introduction

THERE IS AN OLD IRISH JOKE (which comes with apologies to my Irish readers) in which the protagonist asks an Irishman, 'How to you get to Dublin?' 'Well now,' says the Irishman, scratching his head, 'if I wanted to get to Dublin I wouldn't start from here!'

To me, this amply describes the plight of the average rider, and if I had been able to choose the mind and body I would be born with, I would not have chosen to begin my riding career from 'here'. But whilst some riders spend their lives bemoaning the distance between them and 'Dublin', others are blissfully unaware of just how far away they actually are.

Both types easily fall into the trap of thinking that can have their cake and eat it too. They want to be trained by a successful competitor, preferably a known name, and at the same time they want to work with someone who can relate to a rider at their level, and catalyse the maximum amount of change. What they do not realise is that these two demands are almost always mutually exclusive. For riding well – the forte of the name that they have chosen – is not the same as teaching well. They are two entirely different skills, and the fact that someone can successfully influence a horse, bring him into self-carriage and work him beautifully through the school movements, says nothing about her ability to communicate well with *people*.

Neither is teaching the same as training. Training implies that the person on the ground puts the rider/horse combination through their paces, setting exercises which build on each other and which may well give the rider a new way to arrive at an improved end result. As she works through the movements, she is told that the horse must be more collected, or more bent to the inside. But this feedback does not actually teach her *how* to achieve those results. The trainer may well have very useful experience, gleaned from a lifetime spent training many horses to the upper levels, and he may well be able to pinpoint an approach which suits this particular horse. But he is not teaching the 'how' of riding. He may regard this as beneath him – the province of the instructors who work at the lower levels. But is teaching a lesser skill than training, or is this a way to 'pass the buck' – a cunning ploy which spares him from admitting how little he knows about the way that he (or anyone else) actually does it?

Personally, I think that teaching is a far more complex skill than training, although I willingly acknowledge that at the upper levels of competitive riding, there is no substitute for working with someone who has been there, seen it, and done it. But there is also no substitute for working with someone who can pinpoint the biomechanical problems which limit the rider's performance. These stop the rider from reproducing the text-book interaction with her horse; instead she has spurious effects on him – perhaps he comes more heavily into her right hand, tilts his muzzle, or never quite sits down into collection. All too often these evasions are perceived as the horse's problem: however, there are many occasions when a rider reproduces the same evasive pattern in horse after horse. Then, one inevitably has to question who is the chicken, and who is the egg?

The next question is whether further training will have the same result as previous training – yielding yet more miles of school movements which are marred by spurious effects. But even if the problem genuinely *does* belong with the horse it is still questionable whether teaching or training will be more effective as a way to increase the number of tools in the rider's tool kit, thus enabling her to tackle the problem effectively. Whenever teaching is required, it achieves its result once those spurious effects are gone. Then training is in order, and the two approaches need not be antithetical. They can work very well in concert.

My personal area of expertise lies in my ability to communicate the 'how' of riding to others. I do this at all levels, from club level riders to those who compete internationally. At the upper levels, my clientele is limited to those who have been astute enough to realise that years of training have left some unaddressed flaws in their technique, and that these are affecting both their horses and their competition results. But as time has progressed, more and more people have become willing to make that admission. In addition, a number of well-known competitors have asked me to work with the young riders who are training with them, and who are destined to become some of the best in the world. I feel extremely privileged to have had this influence on the stars of the next generation – there is a wonderful poetic justice in using them to demonstrate the value of methods which have evolved from my own experience as a rider who has had many problems. For I have struggled to do what the talented few do so naturally.

Our society does not validate either the knowledge of the person who has leaned the hard way, or the plight of the talented performer who is forced to teach. For if riding is as natural to you as breathing, how can you teach someone to do it? The talented rider is so familiar with her medium that she is like the legendary goldfish who would never discover water. I am like an interloper in the pond, suddenly submersed in water, perceiving it for what it is, and needing to learn how to swim! This has turned riding and teaching into profound (rather than everyday) experiences, to which I brought the astute mind of a physicist, and a tenacity which few could match. My perceptions have been further enriched by combining them with research into how people learn, and how mind and body interact. As I developed, tested and refined my approach, it gradually became clear to me that my physicist's hunch was indeed correct: the seemingly magical skill of riding really *does* have a structure, with laws of cause and effect which determine just how the rider/horse interaction will evolve. Understanding these laws makes riding far easier (and far more fun) both to learn and to teach.

To date, this has been an eighteen-year research project, which has been peppered with much more than just my experience with horses. In the introductions to my first two books I have written extensively about my background, about how this work began, and about the most important influences on it. But I did not talk so openly about the teachers who had the most impact on me, and on my thinking – people who had probably never been near a horse in their lives.

When I was twenty-five, I became disillusioned with my riding ability and with my life as a riding teacher. So I ceremoniously quit riding, sold my horse (which broke my heart) and spent the 1980s living in London when the 'growth movement' was at its height. After five years of mucking out and teaching I arrived in London in a state of burn-out, feeling physically and emotionally exhausted. I knew that I needed help to strengthen both mind and body, thus enabling me to embark on a more productive course for the rest of my life.

I talk about this now because my credentials for writing this book date back to that time. It was the beginning of an incredible learning process which affected my whole life, and which was initially catalysed by my experience as a client in psychotherapy. I soon became so fascinated with what I was learning that I began to train as a psychotherapist, and I also broadened my horizons to include sport psychology (particularly training with the 'Inner Game' group, and the 'Sporting Bodymind' consultancy), martial arts (T'ai Chi and Aikido), dance and movement therapy, biofeedback, bodywork (including Alexander and Feldenkrais lessons, several forms of massage, Body Harmony and Bioenergetics), and work on learning and creating (particularly Technologies for Creating, Educational Kinesiology, and Neuro-Linguistic Programming).

It did not take very long for my interest in all this to take on the status of a quest, and for my life to begin to revolve around it. I followed up any approach that shed light on the fascinating relationship between the body and its tensions, the mind and its convolutions. I attended workshops, talked endlessly with my peers, and read all the relevant literature I could find. And I did indeed 'grow'; from a very shaky start I gradually gained much more faith in myself and my perceptions – faith that was soon to be put to the test in ways I could barely imagine. I was very strongly motivated, for at last I felt that I was learning something that was really worth knowing – very practical theories that were far more relevant to living than anything else I had ever encountered.

Not only were they relevant to living, they were also relevant to riding. When I arrived in London, I thought I had given up riding and teaching forever, and I started again rather reluctantly, simply because these were the best way I had of funding my quest. Much to my surprise, riding soon became *part* of the quest: it was like a metaphor, a small part of my life in which I could apply and test all that I was learning.

The teachers who worked with me to develop the perceptions of mind and body had far more impact on my riding than any of my riding trainers had ever done, and I firmly believe that the learnings I made away from horses paved the way for changes in my riding that could not otherwise have taken place. The effect of my therapeutic work was to transform my life and my riding both at the same time.

....

Learning about learning

The personal changes I made during this time were hard won, coming – as the most valuable insights so often do – through times of confusion and frustration, and as a result of times when my progress had seemed blocked. I was forced to rethink many of my preconceived notions about myself and the world around me, about the nature of success and failure, and about the development of talent and skill. This was – to say the least – disorientating, and I often found myself dangling between the devil and the deep blue sea: I no longer felt comfortable in my old way of being, but I had not yet fully embraced the new way. Looking back, the early stages in particular seem rather like a 'school of hard knocks'; I had dived right in at the deep end, and had chosen – as I always did – a path which would confirm my notion that life was difficult.

In one particularly confronting time during my training as a psychotherapist, I realised that the difficulties I was having in learning were a complete mirror of the difficulties I had had in learning to ride. During therapy classes our trainer would demonstrate in front of our group, doing a complex and often brilliant piece of work with someone. She then expected us to go and do the same. I never seemed able to manage – despite the fact that most of my peers gave the impression that they could. Was I stupid, or were they kidding themselves? Were the expectations I had of myself far too high for someone who was in reality only a beginner? Was this method of teaching one that ought to work, or was I (as a teacher myself) more aware of the difficulties of the learning process than either my peers or my trainer? I realised that I had to change tack and find the answer to these questions. I left that particular school, and took a more gentle path that enabled me to learn much more about learning.

This entire learning process was an intense, exciting and confronting time, shared with some very special people, who I am sure will be friends for life. Most of my peers took further training and eventually specialised, becoming psychotherapists, psychoanalysts, bodyworkers, business trainers, and movement teachers of various persuasions. Although I gained a variety of certificates and qualifications, I became something of a 'Jack of all trades' in the field. (I do, however, believe that I have finally gained some mastery in the thorny area of communication skills.) My passion became the application of this new knowledge to riding.

....

Learning through doing

Now that I was no longer the 'serious' rider I had been during my days as a full-time professional, I felt much freer, and much more able to experiment. Instead of 'trying to do it right', I started utilising some of my 'growth movement' learnings – focusing my attention simply on perceiving my body and discovering *how it is now*. I knew from my experience in other fields that this would inevitably lead me out of my previous impasse and into positive change. This new emphasis filtered through to my teaching, and I soon realised that I could no longer happily follow the traditional practice of telling riders to keep their heels down.

I found myself questioning everything I had ever been taught. But more importantly perhaps, I had to question the way that I had been taught it. As my own riding started to improve, I began to understand more about the biomechanics of the skill I was attempting to teach – and also to realise how little my own teachers had understood it – brilliant though they may have been as riders. It was tremendously validating when I discovered research which showed that the most talented individuals in any sphere were invariably rather bad at describing their skill in words. It was reassuring to know that the discrepancies I was uncovering between theory and practice were not unique to riding, and to know that riding is not the only field in which you are rarely able to have your cake and eat it too.

You pay a price for working with a known name, especially if you cannot match his level of innate skill; for he will work from the premise that you are like him, and in his training sessions he will instruct you to ride the movements he would ride on this particular horse. When this does not produce the results for you that it would produce for him (since you are not a goldfish, and you have to discover water), you reach the limits of his knowledge. This is the point where he is likely to become impatient, 'shout louder at the natives', and ultimately to lose his temper. When you work instead with a rider who has struggled, you may lose out on kudos – especially as you are identifying yourself not as a protégée of the great, but as a rider with some biomechanical problems. But since your new teacher has learned that skill from scratch, and has staked her reputation on her ability to communicate it, you will gain far more in skill formation.

I honed my teaching skills through communicating to others the 'water' I had discovered in my own riding. As I did this, I soon began to feel that I was stumbling around in uncharted territory: I was thinking on my feet, experimenting wildly, and learning through doing. Self-confidence had never been my strong point, and the truth of the matter is that many of the teaching methods I developed during this time only came about because I had to perform miracles in order to believe that I and my riding lessons were worth anything!

In the hope of teaching better, I brought to my lessons everything I was learning in these other fields; as I found out about communication skills, my ways of talking to the riders in front of me changed. The more I discovered about how people learn, the more I began to streamline my methods, so that they fitted in with the brain's natural learning processes. Coupled with my developing understanding of the biomechanics of riding, this approach was tremendously powerful. It did not take long for the results – as measured by the change in my own riding and the progress of my pupils – to far outstrip traditional expectations.

Although I was no longer 'serious' about my riding, it had – paradoxically perhaps – taken on a new significance in my life. To suggest that learning to ride a horse could become a metaphor for living, or a spiritual quest might seem rather far-fetched; but this did indeed happen. It became like learning a martial art, with all the reverence and discipline that these traditions carry, for implicit in them is the knowledge that one is learning far more than a certain set of behaviours. It is really the attitude and the perceptiveness with which those behaviours are carried out which makes them worth doing, and these are what the Zen Master aims to teach. They are couched in a form that becomes meaningful and effective as one strives for, and ultimately demonstrates, a certain way of being – what the Bible would call 'a state of grace', what athletes call being 'in the groove', and what modern-day martial artists might call 'centred'.

It gradually became apparent to me that the bottom line in riding lay not, as I had once thought, in the aids for half-pass, or a canter transition. Neither does it lie – as I had later come to believe – in the ability to sit really well. Instead it lies in the ability to perceive one's body accurately, to focus the mind in the present moment, and to interact cleanly with another living being in a relationship that can so easily go wrong. I needed to learn these skills away from horses, and the contention of this book is that you may need to as well. The chips are down when one starts to train a horse, for it places an incredibly precise demand on a mind and body that may well not be finely enough tuned. The stakes are high because one so much wants the horse to go well, and (as with spouses and children) one is tempted to use all sorts of dubious means to get the desired response. Either that, or one gives up, and becomes resigned to a life of ineffectiveness.

....

Writing and research

Right back in 1980, I knew that the discoveries I was making had the potential to transform the experience of many stuck and frustrated riders, and I knew that the only way to let them know that was to write a book. I began by writing articles, and then a book outline. After a fair few rejections and one false start, I finally found a publisher who understood what I was trying to say, and could coach me well in how to say it. My credentials for writing lay primarily in my inability to learn through conventional means, and also in my experience of two apparently disparate fields that no one else had attempted to marry. I had no medals, no big competitive wins, no famous pupils, and only the dubious status of a British Horse Society Instructor. To make it worse, on the literary side I could also only boast O-level English, chronic difficulties with spelling and grammar, and a passion for writing illegible journals!

Sometimes I think that I did my therapy three times over; once in therapy sessions, once in my riding, and again through my writing. Given my starting point and the enormity of the task I had set myself, it is perhaps no surprise that writing that first book became a mammoth learning experience! It demanded huge changes in my attitude, for I did not want my writing to be contaminated by the anger and bitterness I felt about the way my riding instructors had frequently treated me. Over seven long and frustrating years, I often found myself praying that this phase of my life would soon be over: but the truth of the matter is that I needed all of those seven years (and all the help I could get) both to develop my ideas, and to become the person who could stand behind them.

That first book was finally published in Britain in 1987 as *Ride With*

Your Mind and in America in 1988 as *The Natural Rider*. Obvious though many of the ideas in *Ride With Your Mind/The Natural Rider* may seem, in retrospect, many of them only became clear to me through the act of putting them on paper. In 1990 the development of my work was again aided by the demands of writing *Ride With Your Mind Masterclass* (published in the USA as *Ride With Your Mind – An Illustrated Masterclass in Right Brain Riding),* and I began to feel that I had created a fairly cohesive theory. In the intervening eight years I feel that I have made it very cohesive, and in particular, I have reached the bottom line in understanding and correcting asymmetries. I have also proved to myself and many others that my ideas work extremely well in practice. Essentially, I have healed myself of my fatal flaw: my lack of talent as a rider has demanded so much learning that it has truly become my greatest gift.

I consider myself the most serious researcher worldwide into the biomechanics of riding. When I was in the second year of my physics degree, I realised to my chagrin that I did not have the brain-power to become a contributor to the field, and I mourned the fact that I would never do original work. I could not foresee a future in which my original work would be performed in a very different field! Riding is a puzzle which has – until now – remained unsolved since the time of Xenophon. It has foxed the great riders of history (who, despite their brilliance as performers, never discovered 'water') and has also foxed some of the experts on biomechanics who operate within the sport science departments of major universities worldwide. (They can easily work out the biomechanics of the horse's movement, since he moves his limbs, and they can measure angles, angular momentum, etc. But how do you do this on a virtually static body?) However, my preliminary talks with some of them have already begun to confirm my own discoveries, and future research will, I am sure, soon validate and extend the theories I have evolved.

Whilst I claim originality in this work on the biomechanics of riding, it has become abundantly clear to me that all I have done in the development of my teaching skills is to reinvent the wheel. I am now undergoing an academic study in coaching, and am mixing with some of the foremost researchers in sports science. So I now know that the coaching techniques I derived from learning all I could about the bodymind and from 'thinking on my feet' are unbelievably similar to those used by the top sports psychologists. They and I have very different theoretical backgrounds and we have learned our crafts in different ways, but it is the same craft that we have learned.

....

In *Ride With Your Mind/The Natural Rider* I wrote predominantly about my own experience, and at the time I was still struggling to reconcile the immense changes I was making to my riding with those years spent sitting at the feet of the great master, doing my best to follow his instructions, but failing to imbibe his skill. I still felt very raw about this, and was – quite frankly – shocked at the enormity of my discoveries, and their complete U-turn from conventional theory. By the time I wrote '*Masterclass*' I was no longer in shock, and felt much more sure of myself; I had suffered the same fate as the child in the story of 'The Emperor's New Clothes', and was willing to shout my truth from the roof tops! Through its format – an illustrated account of ten private flatwork lessons and a group jumping lesson – I found a very good way to bring the theory to life. It slips down very easily when presented through stories – just as a historical novel teaches history without the dryness of the textbook. (However, I am told that '*Masterclass*' carries all the dangers of a medical text, and reading it can convince you that you have the symptoms of all the riders!)

A further eight years of experience embellish this book, and the tremendous response to my previous works has enabled it to be peppered with stories of many different riders, which again make the theory more palatable. They come from three different continents, and are at levels of experience which extend from 'average' to the very top. Some of these stories encapsulate a moment in time which triggered profound learning; others follow that rider over time as she unravels parts of the puzzle of riding.

This book is also enriched by a large number of off-horse exercises which illustrate the biomechanics of riding and make it far easier to learn. When I included exercises in *Ride With Your Mind/The Natural Rider* I did not expect many people actually to do them; but I have been extremely pleased to hear that many did. Most of the exercises in the riding chapters are a 'must' if you are to understand the text; whilst the chapter 'Fit and Able' can be thought of as an appendix of exercises for those keen to learn. If you do not do them, you will miss a lot – but you may find them easier to assimilate if you refer to the videotape 'A Rider's Guide to Body Awareness'.

As its title suggests, this book is also a sequel to *For the Good of the Horse* – in fact the two books were originally envisaged as one, but the project ran away with itself and had to be reorganised. So this book is based on the same ethos as its partner: 'the map is not the territory'. Both books make clear that we carry in our heads undrawn maps through which we make meaning of our experience. Many people only need to know 'sit up tall, stretch your legs down and push your heels down' to think that they have a viable map of riding, and I am always shocked at some people's

Development over time

reluctance to redraw maps which are not written on tablets of stone and which can hardly be regarded as rigorous! What I have done is to create a new map, charting the territory, marking the blind alleys, and delineating the stages of learning. I have also made it clear that redrawing your maps so that they are more accurate and workable renderings of the territory triggers far more profound learning than continuing to chart your course from a map which is inaccurate. It is *teaching* which catalyses the most profound changes in the maps that people work from. Rarely does training seek to create such fundamental change.

The last eighteen years have forced me into the uncomfortable conclusion that hear-say and half-truths are often the basis of the maps which people cling to with unbelievable stubbornness. They are also the means through which knowledge is disseminated – including the knowledge which I put into the world. Very few people latch onto an idea, work with it, study it, and make it their own. Even fewer go to its source and make sure that their knowledge comes 'straight from the horse's mouth'. Instead they take an idea, use it out of context, flavour their half-truth with someone else's hear-say, and twist it into meaninglessness before they reject it. But in contrast, some people have used my books and tapes to do wonderful work on their own before they sought me out and checked their perceptions against mine. Others have put their heart and soul into learning this work, coming on many clinics, and training as teachers. So I am now blessed with a number of colleagues who have done their homework so thoroughly that they too have become contributors to the field. I no longer tread this path alone.

Although I and my theories are highly pragmatic, I have a more spiritual perspective on riding than most of my colleagues, many of whom are competitive riders whose ultimate aim is not only mastery; it is to *win,* and to help other people win. They base this on fostering correct biomechanics in the rider, and a good attitude towards the horse and his work – just as I do. However, learning to ride well often becomes a journey of personal discovery, whether or not you want it to, and I am well aware that my taste for treating it as such may not suit you. Like all riders, you are free to use your riding in any way you wish: it could be a means of making friends, developing a social life and having a good time; or a way to win ribbons and impress your neighbours. It might be a way to commune with nature – to 'switch off' and escape from the pressures of work and home. More rarely is it a metaphor or quest, undertaken with the express knowledge that one is learning far more meaningful lessons than how to sit to the trot. Knowing, as I do, that the rewards of this are well worth the effort involved, I shall spell out its benefits; but the ultimate choice will be yours.

CHAPTER ONE

···

The Map is Not the Territory

···

THE MAP is not the territory. This sounds like a simple enough idea – obvious in fact – but as soon as we think beyond our everyday use of road maps, it is actually not nearly so obvious as it sounds. Maps come in unusual guises: a menu, for instance, is a map that portrays the meals you must choose from. It may be verbal description (anything from 'steak, fries, and mushrooms' to 'medallions of lamb marinaded in a herb and peppercorn sauce and served with Dauphinoise potatoes'), or it may be glossy pictures of full plates. But either way, you would not mistake the map for the territory and eat the menu! But 'eating the menu' is precisely what we do whenever we think that *we* (the consciousness that lives behind our eyes) have direct knowledge of the territory (the world out there, which exists in front of our eyes).

Our differing
maps

It is very sobering to discover that our supposed interactions with the world are not with the world itself, but with the *map* or representation of the world that we each create inside our heads. This means that the way in which we perceive the world is *not* the way the world actually is, and remarkably few of us realise that we navigate through life using undrawn (unconscious) maps which determine all our actions.

Each species makes its maps differently, and as I pointed out in *For the Good of the Horse,* horses and dogs – with their more finely tuned senses – make very different maps to people. In effect, they live in a different world, which is barely imaginable to us. Meanwhile, the world of bats and snakes has virtually no overlap with our own, since their sense organs operate in the range where ours sense nothing.

We human beings share neurological and genetic constraints which have a tremendous influence on our map-making abilities: the human ear, for instance, cannot detect sound waves below 20 cycles per second or above 20,000 cycles per second. Our eyes can only detect light waves that lie between 380 and 680 milli-microns. The phenomena that we call 'sound' or 'light' are but a small portion of the range in which these physical phenomena exist. So, as information from the world – the 'reality' or 'territory' outside of us – comes in through our senses, these act as filters, screening out some pieces of information, and letting others through.

Not surprisingly, our ancestors believed that sound or light lying within the limited range of our senses was all there was to detect; but the limitations of human perception have became increasingly clear since scientists began interacting with the physical world using machines. These sensed phenomena which lay outside the range of our senses, and detected differences that were too subtle for our ability to discriminate. Geiger counters, oscilloscopes, and thermometers, for instance, sense these phenomena and then represent them as signals which *do* fall within our sensory range. As Richard Bandler and John Grinder state in their book *The Structure of Magic,* our nervous system, with its genetic constraints, 'constitutes the first set of filters which distinguish the world – the territory – from our representations of the world – the map.'

Individual preferences mean that even within the rather fixed boundary conditions imposed by our neurological constraints, there is room for tremendous individual variation in map development and subtlety of perception. The upper range of *your* hearing might be higher than mine because I am older than you, and your hearing might be more acute than mine because I am – compared to the average sensitivity expected in human beings – slightly deaf. But I may have trained my ear to make far more subtle distinctions than yours. I might know, for example, when someone is singing very slightly off pitch, and might be able to distinguish between two different recordings of the same piece of music which would sound just the same to you. I might feel delight in listening to bird song which you do not even notice, for we have both picked out and deleted different facets of our environment – the foreground and the background are different for each of us.

However, your sense of touch, or your awareness of your body, might be far more refined than mine, especially if you have a hobby or a job which appealed to you precisely *because* it utilised your natural preference. Your taste 'map' may allow you to savour a vintage bottle of wine that would not register with my senses as anything special, simply because I cannot make the distinctions used by a connoisseur.

Depending on the richness of our maps, we can both experience the world as a bland, unexciting place, or as an abundant source of delightful sensory experience. Some of us might watch dressage and find its nuances unbelievably fascinating, whilst others yawn and declare it to be 'like watching paint dry'.

One of the reasons why you and I are such different individuals stems from our different ways of mapping the world. For whilst you may have mapped one variable, I might have mapped another, paying scant attention to the one which you perceived as important. I was talking recently with one of my older brothers, who remembers our childhood family holidays as tortuous occasions, consisting mostly of fraught arguments between my parents, and fights between us kids in the back of the car. When prompted, I recall these aspects too (especially as I, the youngest and the only girl, usually ended them in tears!). But for me our holidays are remembered as delightful experiences which instilled in me a love of the wild and beautiful places that we visited. I was in heaven when I was playing by rivers or climbing mountains, and I inherited from my parents a love of the countryside which somehow passed my older brother by. Through our selective memories, we each developed unique maps of ourselves and the world – maps whose orientations underpin the differences which still exist between us today.

Alternatively, you and I may have mapped the same variable in different ways, and on different scales. In the various endeavours of life, you might feel happy to proceed with only the barest minimum of information – in fact, you might forge ahead without even looking at the map – and if you do, you probably pay the price! Many people find that they best understand a map when it is shown and explained to them, and only as a last resort will they read about it. (One of my pupils runs a computer software company, in which the exasperated people in the customer service department have a set of abbreviations 'RTFM' which they wish they could repeat to customers. They stand for 'Read The F★★★★ Manual'!)

With a minimum of information, some people are willing to label themselves as 'experts', whilst others feel that only an in–depth understanding of an unusually detailed map will earn them rights to the same title. Others become the kind of people who question maps on principle – having discovered that the hear-say and half-truths which form so many peoples' maps are not a reliable guide.

....

Using our senses

The filtering process through which we delete information stops us from being overwhelmed by a mass of sensory data. But repeated scientific research has shown that our unconscious mind records *everything* that ever happens to us, and that these memories can be evoked through hypnosis. This means that *almost all* of what you could potentially perceive or remember at any moment in time has to be shut out from consciousness, and only a small and particularly useful selection is allowed through. As Aldous Huxley states in *The Doors of Perception,* 'To make biological survival possible, Mind at Large has to be funnelled through the reducing valve of the brain and nervous system. What comes out the other end is a measly trickle of the kind of consciousness which will help us to stay alive on the surface of this particular planet.'

In her book *Influencing with Integrity*, Genie Zaborde gives us a metaphorical explanation for how this happens. 'It is as if each of us were an elaborate television set with five recording devices tuned to pick up five different stations. One station transmits only sound, another only pictures. One sends feelings, and the last two stations send tastes and smells. We have only one screen for our conscious minds. We switch from station to station, favouring one at a time over the others. All the information from the other four channels is being recorded, but not attended to consciously.

'Inside this TV set is a little robot who decides what to do by watching and listening to the conscious mind's screen. The conscious mind's decisions are also affected by all the information on all the four recorders – information it may never have consciously seen, heard, smelled, felt or tasted.'

The presence of this hidden knowledge means that you know far more than you think you know – and realising this has tremendous benefits if it encourages you to trust your instincts. For (as part of 'normal' rather than 'extra-sensory' perception) you call on your unconscious knowledge whenever you follow an intuitive hunch, or pay attention to a nagging feeling that something is not quite right.

All of us have a preferred sense that we use more than the others for recording our conscious impressions. From the way I have spontaneously written this sentence, perhaps you can guess mine: 'impressions' is a kinaesthetic word, i.e. it relates to feeling. The language that people use gives us literal information about the sense they are using to consciously register the input you are giving them, and incorporate it into their existing map. 'I see what you mean!', they say, or 'I can't get a handle on this,' or 'That rings a bell!' Unconsciously, they have access to information from all systems, but consciously their map is dominated by one, which they have preferentially developed since childhood, and which they trust more than the others.

For skills like riding, we need to use our kinaesthetic sense preferentially to vision, which is most people's most dominant sense. So it helps if you begin with a well-developed kinaesthetic sense. However, even this can be a handicap to the rider who simply relies on her feelings of 'rightness' and refuses to change her technique because doing anything new feels so alien. As we shall see, *our bodies lie to us,* with our habitual contortions becoming so familiar that we do not recognise our 'home' for the tumbled down edifice that it is. Thus you could be quite convinced that you are sitting straight, when all around you know that your body is a human imitation of the leaning tower of Pisa!

It is when we compare our own kinaesthetic map of our body and our riding with an outsider's visual map that we gain the most information, and *two descriptions of the same territory will always yield far more information than one.* Skill development requires that we both notice *and* question our kinaesthetic sensations. We need to become much more discriminating, and aware that familiarity breeds amnesia – the 'sensory motor amnesia', which leaves us no longer noticing the oddities of 'home'.

I shall never forget the time when I was beginning to understand the importance of our sensory preferences, and still did not quite believe that language really *is* such an obvious reflection of our preferred sensory mode. I was teaching a man whom I had always found hard to get through to, and in my explanation of how he needed to use the muscles on the underside of his thigh, I had reached a stage of desperation where my thumb was digging (I mean digging) into them.

I was explaining, 'John, it's down here. You've got to feel some tightening in the muscle just here.'

'I still can't get a picture of what you mean,' he told me, as I dug my thumb in even deeper, and realised with a shock that my teachers had not been kidding me!

I was reaching the conclusion that I was somehow going to have to find a visual way of presenting this information (and was beginning to wonder if his thigh had any nerves in it at all), when he said, 'Oh, you mean *there*! I think I feel it.' I resisted the temptation to further refine his 'feel' by giving him one last poke.

....

Because of our selective deletions you and I will probably both remember the the same event in totally different ways – just like my brother and me. If you just read my least sentence as 'remember the same event' you too have used a deletion, for it read 'remember the *the* same event'. By doing this you were able to make sense out of what you saw: you literally deleted the piece that did not fit.

Deletion, distortion and generalisation

As an example of this, one of my pupils recounts the story of how she had rested her Grand Prix horse over the winter while he recovered from injury. Her first competition the following spring was a big one, in which she did well – and afterwards one of the judges came up to her, fired with enthusiasm. 'You fixed it! he said, referring to an age-old problem which was now no more. 'What did you do?'

'Well,' she replied, 'I've spent the winter working on my body.'

'Yes, but what did you *do*? he asked again.

'That's it,' she said. 'I've been working on my body!'

'Yes, yes, but what did you *do*? he asked again, sounding progressively more exasperated.

It then began to dawn on her that 'working on her body' was not a process that he would ever validate. Since it was not part of his map of training horses, he had dismissed (i.e. deleted) her explanation, whilst he kept searching for an answer which *would* fit.

As well as deletions, our maps utilise generalisations. These too help us cope with the world, for once you have touched one hot stove, your ability to generalise stops you from repeating the experience. This allows you (and your horses) to learn many new behaviours much faster than you could if you had to begin each one from scratch, so it is a tremendous blessing. It underlies our intellectual abilities, too, for generalisation allows you to take a word-symbol, say, 'chair', and apply it to many different forms with the same function.

My favourite generalisation, which I continually attempt to instil into people's maps, is the idea of 'learning how to learn'; for if I can show you how to learn – as opposed to showing you how to ride – you can go away and learn *anything* because you know the principles involved. You just generalise them to the appropriate context.

But generalisation is also a curse. It takes only one fall for many people to make the generalisation that riding is far too dangerous an activity to continue. Riders who do continue, and who become really 'serious', often find themselves using generalisations which leave them feeling despondent (although they rarely realise that they are doing so). For within any one work session they generalise from *one* bad transition to 'I can't ride transitions'. They then progress down the slippery slope of generalisation to 'I'm having a bad day', and then to 'I'm a bad rider'. The point from which they can fall no further is 'I'm a bad person'.

Generalisations and deletions can work together: supposing your riding has been so criticised that you have made the generalisation that you will never be any good. You may then literally not hear (i.e. you delete) any positive feedback that comes your way. The opposite could also be true, and you might be so convinced of your ability that even constructive criticism rolls off your ears like water off a duck's back. In fact, a number of known British trainers have had the experience of a renowned Continental trainer working with some of their protégées and advocating the exact same corrections that they themselves had repeatedly suggested. But their pupils had, in effect, deleted them – until a higher authority delivered the same message.

Along with deletions and generalisations, we also make distortions as we create our maps of the world, and we do this by changing our experience of sensory input. Children at play do this all the time, and great artists manipulate their perceptions of reality to create something different – whether it be water lilies as seen by Monet, or the sky as seen by Van Gogh. When you enjoy their works, or read the words of a good novel, you use distortion too. From symbols written on a page you create scenes and characters in your mind's eye – you may even *become* the heroine, and experience life through her eyes.

But our distortions are not always so creative. When your boss compliments you on a job well done you may find yourself thinking, 'I bet he's only saying that because he wants me to do something else.' As each person's life experiences are unique, so are our maps, and as well as allowing us to create and learn, they all too easily blind us and cause us pain. To quote Richard Bandler and John Grinder again: 'A person's generalisations or expectations filter out and distort his experience to make it consistent with those expectations. As he has no experiences which challenge his generalisations, his expectations are confirmed and the cycle continues. In this way people maintain their impoverished models of the world.'

Our language reflects and reinforces the limitations of our maps – and to break out of this mould is extremely difficult. It requires the invention of new words. For instance, one Native American language contains words for only three colours – the world is experienced (approximately) as red, green-blue, and yellow-orange-brown. Since we make more distinctions in our own language, this seems impoverished to us, and we find ourselves asking 'surely they must see more?', but they do not.

Yet our experience of snow is equally limited by our vocabulary, which makes only a few distinctions – nothing like the *seventy* which are detailed in the Inuit language. This enables the Inuit people of the Arctic to have a sensory experience far beyond our perception; they know where to build igloos, where to dig holes, and where not to walk. Mastery of their environment has required them to fine-tune their perceptions and their language, thus ensuring that they – and their children – will survive where we would die. By comparison, they put us riders and our perceptual/linguistic endeavours to shame.

At least within any one particular culture, our maps are similar enough that we can agree on 'consensus reality' – that which we have all agreed, within our families, culture, and institutions, to accept as *real*. Within this, it is as if we all have on a certain pair of glasses that screens out any information which does not match our existing beliefs. Thus anyone who questions that consensus map will probably be met with stone-wall silence and disbelief. As this happens her offerings will be deleted (as in the story of the dressage judge above), distorted (into hear-say and half-truths) and generalised. I came face to face with a new student once who was riding rather a lazy horse, and when I asked her if there was a particular reason why she did not have a stick, she looked me straight in the eye and said: 'But Mary Wanless doesn't allow riders to carry a stick.'

'Really?' I said. 'Well, I *am* Mary Wanless and that's news to me!'

Someone, somewhere had probably been half asleep, watching from the gallery when I had taken a rider's stick away (perhaps her horse had been rather nervous, or she was too slap-happy) – and my listener had assumed that this rule applied to *all* riders on *all* horses! I should perhaps just be grateful that the map-makers of today are not imprisoned like Galileo, or burnt at the stake like witches.

....

Refining our perceptions

In our day-to-day life, we all continually make sense of our perceptions in any moment by comparing them with the stored memories contained in our maps. A skilled rider, for instance, has a very rich store of 'feelages', and as she rides she constantly compares the feeling she is getting now with the feeling she wants to get – something a novice cannot yet do. You use a similar strategy whenever you see someone and find yourself thinking, 'I know you. Where did we meet before?' You search through your store of visual memories and discover if you do indeed have this face on file.

One pupil recently told me how she returned to a house that she used to visit regularly in her childhood, but had not been to for over thirty years. Recent renovations had removed a small step that used to be in one room, and she consistently found herself tripping at the precise spot where she expected it to be. This behaviour was generated from her stored memories – her kinaesthetic map of how to manoeuvre around the house – which, although unreferred to for thirty years, did not immediately update itself, even when new information from the 'territory' was registering in her body in a not-too-pleasant way.

Travel is one of the ultimate experiences through which we can recognise the limitations of our maps, for it helps us to experience the world through the eyes of a culture with values and priorities which differ from our own.

Crocodile Dundee, hero of the highly successful film, was transported to the streets of New York, leaving behind his life as an Australian bushman. When he declared 'These people must really like each other to all live together like this,' he gave us an unusual perspective on the life of a city-dweller! Part of the success of the film lay, I suspect, in the way it allowed us to see ourselves from a different perspective, and to laugh at ourselves – along with the attitudes and behaviours that we otherwise take for granted.

If we compare the way that horses make maps of people with the way that people make maps of horses, it is undoubtedly true that they sense far more about us than we sense about them. It has suited us to think of them as inferior creatures (a map which is well worth updating, given that it deletes their heightened sensory perception) but in only a few moments they can read us like a book. As we walk towards them with the saddle they are responding to our body language, and whilst we are still settling ourselves into it they have recognised our strengths and weaknesses, our skill level, our asymmetry, how much commitment we will expect, and the easiest way out.

No horse needs to go on a training course to learn this. But if people are to read horses like horses read people, they *do* need to go on a training course. The cowboy culture of the west coast of America has yielded trainers (like Monty Roberts, John Lyons and Pat Parelli) who teach people to read horses from the ground, and to interact with them through the language 'Equus'. My own work is designed to teach riders how to read the horse when mounted – this time using his and our kinaesthetic language, and not relying on vision.

I believe that training can develop the refinement of the rider's feel to the point where she can read the horse almost as well as he can read her. This is a long way down the road for the average rider, but nonetheless, it marks the point when she begins to ride the horse, instead of allowing him to ride her! Whether we are on the ground or in the saddle, the pay-off from 'speaking Horse' is enormous; for when the trainer's signals and behaviour become recognisable within the language and the map of 'Horse', the refinement of her skills is such that she becomes able to create changes which the average person working from the average map would find mind-boggling.

....

A number of my pupils have given me wonderful examples of the way in which our beliefs can rigidify and become our 'mind-sets'. This is more or less impenetrable in each individual – and education, quite often, serves only to entrench it more. Debbie had had three lessons with me, and several with a very capable instructor who had trained quite extensively with me. But neither of us felt that we had really got through to her. She actually looked quite good on a horse, but despite this she was a rather timid rider who was convinced that she knew much more than she did. Indeed, she should have been very knowledgeable – she had ridden for many years with an eminent classical trainer – but she rode with a very strong contact and a hand whose backward traction was much more dominant than the push forward she generated in her body. (This idea will be explained in Chapter 2.) Her trainer had focused on teaching her to ride the school movements (as best she could) and had never really challenged Debbie's use of her hand and body.

Both myself and my colleague had done all we could to firm up her

Mind-sets

body, and to get her to lighten her hand and ride 'as if she was pushing a baby buggy'; we had lectured her about the evils of riding her horse 'from front to back', and had showed her how to lighten her hand and to ride the horse forward. Debbie took her second set of lessons with me as a guinea-pig rider on a teacher-training course, so twenty young instructors watched me try to win her round, increasing the strength in her body so that she could finally take off the handbrake.

During her second lesson I stopped her, and in desperation I took hold of the reins near the horse's bit. 'What would be a normal contact for you?' I asked. She took up the reins and pulled hard against my hands, just as she would normally have pulled against the horse. I then took hold of one of her hands, and discovered that her wrist was so completely locked that I could not wiggle her hand around on the end of her arm! Her fingers made a death-grip so strong that the tendons in the inside of her wrist showed white through her skin.

It took some considerable wrist-wiggling to get her to release this tension, and persuading her to sustain the release was even harder. I worked with her in halt for over fifteen minutes before I could hold the reins near the bit, ask her to take up a contact, and have her shorten the reins without pulling back, so that she made a light connection with my hand. I kept testing that her wrist would wiggle freely, and that her fingers did not sneak back into the death-grip.

When I thought she really understood, I asked her to walk on. But I soon realised that she had yet more tricks up her sleeve. Now she knew that tightening her fingers and drawing her hand back towards her stomach were not viable options, she began to make a stronger contact by turning her wrists over so that her thumbs pointed downwards, and by rounding her wrists and pointing her thumbs towards each other. When I challenged her about this, she stopped, looked at me in astonishment, and asked, 'But how am I supposed to pull?'

Debbie's mind-set ('I have to pull on the reins to be in control') was so strong that it defied everything that I, and everyone else, had done with her up to this point. When I said to her, 'Debbie, you don't pull. That's the whole point,' she was literally in a state of shock! It was as if I had taken the ground out from under her feet, and with her apparent security gone she was a very unhappy rider.

Soon after she moved off again I realised that I would have to teach her a new way to ride halt transitions – it was apparent that until she felt she had a way of stopping the horse which worked well, she was not prepared to go anywhere! She actually learned this very easily, and she came up to me after the lesson looking almost tearful. 'You're the first person who's ever made me understand,' she said. What she really meant was that I was the first person to have knocked so hard at the brick wall protecting the map in her brain that I had finally brought it down.

Most of us inhabit a more middle-of-the-road mind-set. But whenever we marvel at stories like this, we forget that for everyone who inhabits one of the extremes, there will be someone who believes the opposite. One of my colleagues told me the story of a woman who arrived for her first lesson on a difficult, flighty horse which – despite my colleague's attempts to keep her safe – did indeed take off with her. My friend found herself yelling, 'Stop – somehow! ... Shorten up your reins and run him into the wall.' But the rider did nothing to stop him, and from having both hands on the front of the saddle she graduated to having one on the front and one on the back. Inevitably, she bit the dust; but she emerged smiling: 'I didn't pull on the reins!' she said, with an obvious sense of self-congratulation!

Gina, whom you may have met in the *'Masterclass'* book, is a much more insightful rider than either of these two, and she had a very dramatic learning experience one day as a participant on a teacher-training course. Each of the trainee teachers was taking it in turn to ride for a short time in front of the whole group, whilst we discussed how we could best work with this person's problems. Gina already felt rather nervous about riding in front of her peers, and as soon as she mounted, she realised that she was sitting on a 'motorboat' type of horse (see page 105 and Fig. 4.5).

He had just been ridden very well by another course member, but Gina was barely in the saddle before he began to speed out from underneath her, and this (coupled with the knowledge that she *should,* like her friend, be able to ride him well) pushed her 'panic button'. It took her quite some time of walking, breathing deeply, and riding transitions to halt before she was able to 'take him' and could dare to work in trot. Even though she eventually rode him quite well, she felt humiliated in front of the group, and was very shaken by the whole experience.

It took a while for her to digest what had happened, and, more importantly, to come to terms with the enormity of her feelings about it. For she had come face to face with the harsh reality that, despite all the improvement she had undoubtedly made, she was not as invincible as she thought. Although her riding and learning had seemed to be becoming easier all the time, she began to doubt herself completely, and to question whether she had made any progress at all. (In other words, she began to delete and distort her previous positive learnings as she made generalisations from this one incident.) The experience had a familiar ring to it, because many of her previous most important learning experiences had come through situations which she had perceived as being so humiliating or so stressful that they had often ended in tears. Once Gina had really worked out what happened, she sent me the diagram you see in Fig. 1.1.

Whenever the rider's mind-set, or 'ability shell' as Gina called it, is widely disparate from her 'core of knowledge' one of two things will happen. Either she will not learn – as happened for so long with Debbie – or she will learn only through experiences that are traumatic enough to crack the shell. Unlike Debbie, Gina had always been aware of the enormous stress involved in both her learning and riding, and it was her suspicion that something was wrong which had brought her to me in the first place. Like all of us, she carries in her mind a map of her ability, and the more accurate this is, the easier life becomes for both her, her horse, and her teachers. When there is a marked discrepancy, everyone is bound to suffer – for the distortions in our maps come at a price, impinging on the much smoother course we could otherwise take through life and learning.

But let us consider how Debbie's or Gina's experiences could have arisen. Supposing I give you a map of Chicago (unnamed), and let you

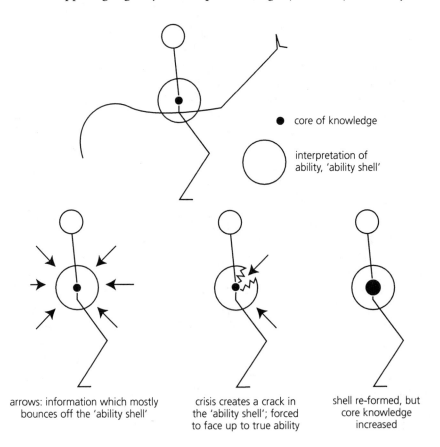

● core of knowledge

○ interpretation of ability, 'ability shell'

arrows: information which mostly bounces off the 'ability shell'

crisis creates a crack in the 'ability shell'; forced to face up to true ability

shell re-formed, but core knowledge increased

Fig. 1.1 Gina's learning process, which was catalysed when circumstances made it clear that there was a discrepancy between her 'ability shell' and her 'core of knowledge'.

loose with it in New York. The grid pattern and the street names might be similar enough to confuse you for quite some time. You could expend a tremendous amount of energy as you tried to find your way – you might get really het up and frustrated, and you might even end up in tears of confusion. Or perhaps you have been to so many seminars about the advantages of positive thinking that you manage to wipe out any negative, defeatist thoughts, and to carry on enjoying being where you are whilst ignoring the fact that you are lost! Most people would take the eminently sensible step of asking someone for help; but few, I suspect, would have the presence of mind to diagnose the real problem.

I firmly believe that riders have been given a map which is so vague, and at times so wrong, that it is extremely difficult to navigate with. But we have all been brought up to trust our maps implicitly – beginning from all the maps we were given by various authority figures both at home and at school. So many people, in response to their predicament, decide that they are stupid, that they do not have talent and will never be able to ride. (Unfortunately, this solution fits very neatly into their maps of themselves!) I was pushed into that corner too, until one little breakthrough (bearing down, which will be explained on page 57) set me on the road which finally led me to stand up and say: 'Hey, this map does not work too well, and that's why we're all finding it so hard. Perhaps we can make a better one.'

....

Some time ago, when I was feeling rather disappointed about the time it was taking for my own map of riding to make any significant inroad into mainstream thinking, one of my more insightful pupils said, 'Don't worry, I think you're right on target. Any new way of thinking must go through the stages of being dismissed, ridiculed, and then only grudgingly accepted before it becomes mainstream.' At the time I was unaware of the fact that any new idea usually takes about forty years to become accepted – and by this time scale, I was probably doing quite well! And, of course, it is helpful for me to realise that any flak aimed at myself or any other map-maker is always sent by those who would rather delete us than study the map and discover if it really is a useful depiction of the territory.

Consensus reality

Try the following for size. Fig. 1.2 (overleaf) shows a duck. Or does it? Look again, and see if there is more to it than first meets the eye.

In Fig. 1.3 (page 31) you will almost certainly see a cube. But try to see it as if it portrays a two-dimensional pattern: imagine it, perhaps, as a mosaic of floor tiles. As you begin to see it like this, do other patterns become possible, and can you move between each one? When you look at these puzzles, it becomes less surprising to discover that vision is 96 per

Fig. 1.2 This drawing shows a duck. Or does it?

cent a 'learned phenomena', and that only 4 per cent of it stems directly from our eyes. So we see only what we have *learned* to see, and we rarely look for the other possibilities which our mind-set precludes.

So it is with riding, and if you and I stood together and looked at a rider/horse combination, I doubt that we would see the same interactions, and describe them in the same way. (If you are still struggling to see anything more than a duck in Fig. 1.2, I will give you a clue: the other creature it depicts is looking to the right.)

Within the population at large, the vast majority of us operate within 'consensus reality' and almost all of us experience tremendous mistrust of anything so new that it lies off the edge of our established maps. We see ducks as ducks, not rabbits. But inevitably, our consensus maps vary in their usefulness, and in theory (although rarely in practice) our trust in them should vary accordingly. A good map will explain and predict far more than a bad one. It will offer more detail and will remain valid under more different conditions. But we stubbornly maintain tremendous faith in maps that do not stand up to scrutiny.

Two notable exceptions are the faith that most people have in weathermen and economists, who have been notoriously bad at predicting the next fine day or the next recession. Here, at least, we have been astute enough to realise that their maps are not very good! But we now have 'chaos theory', one of the latest scientific advances which shows that even these seemingly unpredictable phenomena do in fact follow definable patterns. We are learning how to map the predictability that lies beneath the surface of their apparently random behaviour.

As a venture outside the bounds of consensus reality, take the story (fictitious, I think) of the man who woke up one morning believing he was a corpse. His poor wife was horrified by this and tried to convince him otherwise, to no avail. There followed visits to doctors, and eventually psychiatrists, who all failed to convince him that he was under an illusion. Finally one rather innovative psychiatrist asked him, 'Do corpses bleed?'

'No,' the man answered.

So the doctor found a pin and pricked him with it. As a small drop of much less at the mercy of outside forces; we can become leaders or teachers, who empower others by helping them to develop the same map-making capability. We do not settle for simply telling them what to do.

This book really concerns three kinds of maps. Firstly, there is a specific map of riding. Then there are maps of the mind and the learning process — in effect, a map of our brain — which serve to equip us with a 'user's manual' (a worthwhile exchange for the 'loser's manual' that most of us grew up with). Thirdly, there are maps of the body — showing how its functioning differs in different individuals, and suggesting ways of bringing it back into sync, making it a far more subtle and effective tool for riding horses.

But most important is the map that emerges from all of them, about the development of the human senses, and the ability this gives us to fine-tune our perceptions. For this opens the door to very rich and delightful experiences, including the greatest gift that riding can give us if we choose to take on its challenge — the melding of the human and equine spirits into a whole far greater than the sum of its parts.

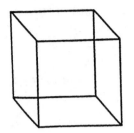

Fig. 1.3 This drawing shows a cube. Or does it?

blood appeared, the man looked shocked.

'My goodness, I don't believe it,' he said, and, as his wife and the doctor began to smile with relief, he continued, 'Corpses *do* bleed.'

The distortions in this man's map were so enormous that I am sure you would have no difficulty diagnosing him as crazy. But his story is not so far removed from that of a pupil who admitted she had spent years thinking, 'Why can't the glove manufacturers make the right glove as strongly as they make the left one?'

Only when she had finally admitted to herself that she did an inordinate amount of pulling and fiddling with her right hand, did she put two and two together! So even within 'consensus reality' we maintain the distortions in our maps in exactly the same way that this man did. Debbie and Gina (as well the pupil with a draw full of pristine left gloves) deleted and distorted input. Inevitably, the distortions in our maps will limit us; but when we work from maps that are good representations of the territory, we do not need to develop all the compensatory emotions and strategies of someone who has been let loose in New York with a map of Chicago. For it is our interactions with the world that help us to generate our maps of ourselves – and who can feel capable and powerful when they are struggling to follow the wrong map?

Living from good, accurate maps increases our personal effectiveness far more than attempts to change our attitude or behaviour *within* an existing, inaccurate map – in fact, all attempts to do this will have very little effect, however much effort we invest in them. But, paradoxically, *once you have a good map, your attitudes, behaviour and the way you apply yourself will make a tremendous difference to where you end up.*

Good mapping brings our values (our map of how things should be) into line with our map of how things are (our read-out on 'reality'). With our values and actions in sync, we 'walk our talk', and become much more congruent, powerful, and at peace with ourselves. We work with, rather than against, the natural laws of the universe – and if life begins to feel rather like trying to push a boulder uphill, we begin to question why this is. With this combination of common sense and inner strength, we are

CHAPTER TWO

··

Sitting Well: Alignment and Tone

··

I AM ONE OF THOSE bull-headed individuals who is extremely reluctant to look at a map. When I drive my car in territory which is unfamiliar and badly signed I often get lost, for I prefer to keep going rather than stop and assess where I am. I get myself into dire trouble whenever I put together equipment designed for home assembly because I am far too impatient to look at the instructions. Finally desperation drives me to do so, but then next time I forge ahead blindly, without seeming to learn my lesson.

Complacency, or respect for tradition?

Essentially, there are two kinds of maps which help us navigate through life – those we know we use, and those which govern our behaviour even though we are blissfully unaware of their existence. These maps are so powerful that they send us unquestioningly through life, running on 'auto-pilot' along pre-programmed routes. (Thus my own internal map which tells me not to bother with the external map continues to reign supreme even though my experience repeatedly proves the need for change. Next time, however, I just might slow down enough to override it!) Despite our blind faith in both types of maps, few of either type really stand up to scrutiny. Even at the most rigorous end of the spectrum, the differing opinions of the experts within any field gives enormous potential for 'map battles'.

In *For the Good of the Horse* we examined some radically different (and apparently contradictory) maps of the human body, and of medicine. We also reviewed the maps which have guided – and more recently changed – the ancient arts of farriery and saddlery. But it is within the medical field in particular that our maps have undergone many radical revisions, and the history of Western medicine documents phenomenal stories of the time, effort, concern, and human ingenuity which have gone into making them. Lives and reputations have been staked on them: medical researchers have raced each other to the winning post, repudiated each other's findings, and waged personal wars over their differing beliefs. In recent years, fortunes have been made and lost both by individuals and by drug companies; but human curiosity has always been the driving force behind the struggle to understand the fabric of the human body, and even of life itself.

By comparison, just think how little effort has gone into making our maps of riding, and how little curiosity we have shown. 'Sit up straight, stretch your legs down, push your heels down, relax, keep your hands still, more leg' – these phrases are heard in riding lessons and training sessions all over the world, uttered by instructors who were told them by their instructors, who were told them by their instructors, who were told them by their instructors ....

Respect for the traditions of the past is one thing – but to me, this smacks of complacency. I find it no surprise that, historically, breakthroughs in many different fields have come from outside that field; for those who are firmly entrenched within its boundaries tend only to repeat the established wisdom. Thus Alexander Fleming, who discovered penicillin, was not a physician but a chemist; and the Wright brothers who performed the first powered flight were not aeronautical engineers – they were bicycle mechanics!

Even at the top levels of dressage, the map is no better defined. I recently heard the story of a renowned dressage rider who was having a lesson with a top international competitor. She requested help with her piaffe, and was instructed to ride the piaffe/passage tour from the Grand Prix test.

'And when you get to the first piaffe,' said the trainer, 'do nothing.'

So when she arrived at that point, she did nothing, and her horse stopped.

'Why has your horse stopped?' he asked.

'Because I'm doing nothing,' she explained.

This was bound to provoke a rather heated response, and it came in the form of the command: 'Do nothing-SOMETHING!'

If we consider this logically, it gives us four distinctions: nothing-nothing, nothing-something (which may or may not be the same as something-nothing) and something-something. But these do not create a map which could teach anyone to ride – not even the rider who is already working at international level.

From my perspective, it seems almost unbelievable that our traditional system of teaching has continued unabated to this day, and that it shows every sign of continuing into the future. As a description which allows us to navigate the territory of riding, our traditional map is extremely limited. The sad truth is that a viable description of the 'how' of riding has eluded us for centuries, and this perpetuates the gap between the 'talented' rider (who instinctively knows the 'how') and the 'average' rider (who does not). The only way we can close it is by becoming more precise.

Fig. 2.1 A possible rendering of the traditional pie of riding.

I think of riding as being like a pie, whose contents are hidden by the pie crust. This is marked into sections, and each one is labelled with one of our standard phrases, like 'stretch your leg down'. (See Fig. 2.1.) These are supposed to describe the contents of the pie. What I have done, over eighteen years, is to strip away the pie crust, sort through the *actual* ingredients of the pie, work out what they are, and re-label it. So instead you will read terms like 'bear down', 'pinch', and 'use the thigh like a lever' (the meaning of these phrases will become clear later, and a possible redrawing of the pie is given in Fig. 4.8 on page 116).

I think of these as the ABCs of riding – its fundamental elements or highest organising principles – the underlying 'how to's' which actually make it work, regardless of your age, shape, sex (and the amount of money you paid for your horse). After all, we can reasonably expect that everyone who follows a sufficiently clear and accurate map to a certain destination should arrive at the same end point.

Redrawing the map of riding does not, to my mind, constitute a threat to the traditions of our art, for *it is not an attempt to change the territory*. Good riders of all cultures and schools always have used, and always will use the same biomechanical strategies – but they have rarely been able to clone riders, who can reliably reproduce these same skills. Thus most training establishments – regardless of where they are in the world – have one really good rider at their head, and perhaps one or two talented members of staff who have also 'got it'. But the vast majority of pupils do not 'get it', however many lessons they take.

Inevitably, it is the professionals within the field of riding who are the first to discredit any new map, implying that it must surely be a threat to our traditions. However, since the majority of them have given the map only a cursory glance, and have not tried to navigate from it, I suspect they may well mean that the map is a personal threat to *them*. For whilst it has the potential to increase the skill of their pupils, a sudden upsurge of new knowledge concurrently has the potential to close the gap which sets them apart from the masses, thus threatening their superior position.

Yet in my mind, redrawing our map of riding is simply a way to make Rome (the biomechanics of a correct rider/horse interaction) more accessible to more of the people more of the time. We all need more signposts to delineate the roads which lead to Rome – as well as signposts which warn us of those that do not! We also need a way to recognise when we have indeed arrived, so that we can all agree on what and where Rome is. If we had more effective ways of learning to get to Rome, we would surely pay far greater homage to the traditions on which riding is built. We would move beyond the limit of simply paying them lip service.

The written word is, in my experience, by far the most difficult way to communicate this map, which is a vibrant, three-dimensional way of describing the ever-changing interaction between two living beings. So a linear, static description has inevitable limitations. Give me a camera (as in the *'Masterclass'* videotapes) and I can do a much more thorough job, encapsulating a thousand words in one frame. With you in front of me, I could tailor the map exactly to your needs: I could put in a marker which says 'YOU ARE HERE', giving you a perspective on your position, and then showing you where to travel. If we had riders in front of us (as we would in a lecture-demonstration or on teacher-training course) I could point out to you how the map works in practice, training your 'eye' so that you too learn to see biomechanics in action, to interpret – and even to predict – how the rider/horse interaction will evolve.

But we have to settle here for the written word, and to make the map as alive and applicable as possible, I have included a series of questions at the end of each section, which help to summarise and simplify it. These are designed to help you assess your starting point, and how to begin your journey.

Unfortunately, the written word makes the map seem far more complex than it actually is, and I can already hear those highly skilled riders who have (metaphorically speaking) already reached Rome dismissing the map by saying, 'Why bother with all this? It's so unnecessary. Just get on and ride the horse.' But if you already lived in Rome, why would you want to spend hours pouring over the map? It hardly seems relevant – except when you need to give good directions to someone else who has not yet arrived.

I have presupposed in these chapters that I do not need to convince my reader that the skill of riding lies in drawing the horse's back *up*, and not in pulling his head *down*. This is an enormous assumption, which may only be valid for the few riders who have had good, classical teaching, as well as for those who have taken my previous work to heart. But having spent two books and much of my working life explaining, justifying – and even pleading – with riders to focus on their horse's back and not his head, I would like to take this as read.

I am also presupposing that I do not need to justify my basic working premise: that changing the rider is the most effective way of changing the horse – that the way the rider sits *matters*. To suggest (as some dressage judges have done) that it is really of no consequence as long as the rider does not hamper the horse, is to state your ignorance of the horse's sensitivity to the rider's weight, muscle tone, asymmetry, and ability to match the forces which his movement exerts on her body. I can barely begin to tell you how much this matters, how precisely each horse 'reads' his rider, and how cleverly he organises his evasive system around her weaknesses.

The horse is like a tennis player who discovers a weakness in his opponent's backhand and makes a point of serving to it. This response is such an inherent part of his 'horsonality' that he does not need to go on a training course to learn how to do it! Humans, however, need an immense amount of training if they are to read horses with anything approaching the equivalent sensitivity.

It is the lack of awareness of our own bodies which inhibits our ability to read and influence our horses. How can we possibly hope to usefully change their balance when we ourselves are out of balance and out of alignment (especially when we do not even realise it)? And how can we possibly control our horse's body when we are not in control of our own?

Yet within the prevailing ethos we do not even think about this; instead we endlessly practise the same old school movements whilst we are (unknowingly) riding in a way which forces the horse to contort his body. I hope it is obvious that this has to be counter-productive, regardless of how easily this mistake is made and how common the practice may be.

This version of the map is less detailed than those presented in *Ride With Your Mind / The Natural Rider* and *'Masterclass'* – and if you find that you do not have enough information to translate theory into practice, I hope you will feel inspired to use those books (or my videotapes) as alternative descriptions of the territory. The map I am presenting here is really a resumé; it includes new elements, some new ways of explaining the basics, and a more cohesive overview of asymmetries. It is less philosophical than my previous writings, with less reference to the thrills, spills, and emotional challenges of the learning process. That comes later in the book. Many of the exercises in Chapter 9, 'Fit and Able', build on the map, and because they involve your body in a similar way to riding, they are a more unequivocal way to describe the territory.

Ultimately, all these descriptions are designed to help you embark on a learning process which will eventually enable you to become a map-maker in your own right. For the territory of riding can potentially yield many different maps (just as any piece of land can be mapped to show rainfall, population, geology, or any number of variables, and each of these maps can be more or less precise). Some variation between individual maps is inevitable – so I and my colleagues may each approach the same issue in slightly different ways. Two conventional trainers may also suggest different exercises which are equally effective (whilst less skilful practitioners may offer suggestions that are next to useless).

Given the possibility of inaccurate mapping, I hope you will take the precautions which guide those of us involved in this work: for we check our new ideas against each other's perceptions, making sure that we are not ardently mapping some blind alley. Given that we all have blind spots, it is a mistake that is easily made.

Whilst I have often thought of my own map as 'alternative', it is perhaps better to follow the wisdom which has termed the new approaches to medicine not as 'alternative' but as 'complementary'. Just as with medical treatment, it is not a case of either/or, so there is room for both systems, and both classes of maps. The important point is that the conventional map of riding works only for people who can translate 'get the horse on the bit' or 'make him straight' into do-able tasks. If they cannot, then you need a complementary map, which works at a larger scale, clarifying the tasks into smaller-chunk pieces which you *can* do (regardless of your apparent lack of talent). By adding these pieces together you eventually reach a stage where you can work from a less detailed map. In effect, you then translate from one system to another.

Thus when your trainer tells you to 'grow up tall' or to 'flex the horse to the inside' you will know exactly what to do. (In fact, he will probably not need to tell you these things, for since you know how to do them, you will have done them already!) You can then follow in the footsteps of one of my most successful pupils, who is heading for a career as an international competitor. She says that, 'When I ride with my conventional trainer it is as if you are sitting on my shoulder, telling me what to do in response to his words.' She continues to use both systems to their maximum advantage, and could not have become a Grand Prix rider without them.

....

Alignment   My understanding of the biomechanics of riding begins with physics. In order to be in balance herself, the rider has to have her centre of gravity

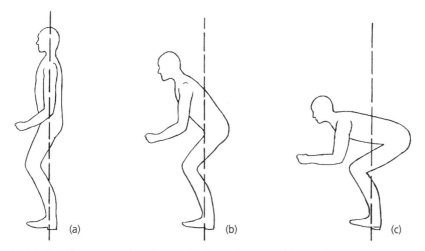

Fig. 2.2 The rider's centre of gravity over her base of support: (a) in 'on-horse' dressage line-up; (b) in one of any number of places in which she can be in balance before she finally reaches (c) and is folded down as she would over a fence.

over her base of support. In a dressage seat, this means that her backside must be over her feet, and that she must display that mythical shoulder/hip/heel line. But she has many more options than this, as you can demonstrate to yourself by performing the following experiment. (See Fig. 2.2.)

Stand in an 'on-horse' position, and begin by noticing where on your feet your weight is taken. Is it predominantly on the balls of your feet, or on your heels? Then gradually bend your knees so that you fold down into jumping position, lowering yourself until your back is horizontal and your backside out behind you. Now where on your foot is your weight supported?

Make this movement slowly, several times, noticing how the weight-bearing area changes. I expect you will notice – as I have done – that it moves back every time you fold down (and you can, in fact, balance in this position supported only on the back edge of the heel of your shoe). If you reverse your concept of cause and effect, this means that changing the weight-bearing area from predominantly on the ball of the foot to the back of the heel necessitates a complete change in body position, from the upright position of dressage to the fold-down that you show over fences.

This immediately explains why many jumping riders find it so hard to adjust to a dressage balance: they are used to pushing their weight down into their heel, and this forces them to make one of two compensations. Either they 'water-ski', leaning back and using the reins as a counter-balance for the down and forward heel, or they lean forward. The latter at least allows them to lighten their hand. But it gives them a 'homing

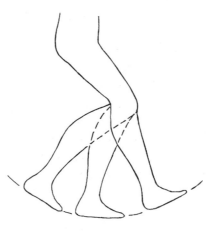

Fig. 2.3 How the position of the heel changes as the foot is rotated about the knee.

instinct' towards jumping position – a situation which will continue until such time as they take their weight out of their heel, and let it rest on the stirrup and the ball of the foot.

This changes the place to which the heel points: for instead of pointing down and forward towards the horse's knee, it now points back towards his hock. But this is much harder to achieve. If you stand on one leg and push the heel of your free leg forward as if you were jumping, your heel is bound to look as if it were down. If you then rotate your lower leg about your knee so that the heel is now under your hip, your heel will look level with your toe, or possibly even up. (See Fig. 2.3.) Yet nothing has changed in the ankle itself, and making the heel point towards the horse's hock requires much more flexibility in the ankle than that which is needed to make it point towards his knee.

This suggests that the phrase 'push your heels down' is of dubious value to the dressage rider. For if she pushes them down by pushing them *forward,* she compromises her whole balance, and she loses far more than she gains. Moreover the act of pushing down has other by-products, for according to Newton's Third Law of Motion ('every action has an equal and opposite reaction'), your push down will generate an equal and opposite push *up.* This has the effect of straightening your knee and hip, locking your joints, and pushing your backside up and out of the saddle. So by this simple action, all your best attempts to sit well can be rendered ineffective. (This is why so many people prefer to ride sitting trot without their stirrups.)

One of my American pupils confessed recently that in her attempts to be an obedient pupil and a good rider, she had pressed down so hard into the stirrups that the soles of her feet went numb when she was riding! To add to this, she woke every night with pain in her right foot – a situation which stopped (thank God) very soon after I made her lighten this pressure.

The rider's push down and its equivalent push up elongate her body, so as well as 'stretching her leg down' she finds herself 'growing up tall'. Few people realise the folly of the posture which most riders aspire to; yet I can usually reduce a group of workshop participants to peels of laughter by standing in a martial arts T'ai Chi position, and growing as tall as I can. (See Fig. 2.4.) Everyone immediately sees the 'wrongness' of this position – so when I then move only my hands and imitate a rider they are left in a quandary. For if I had been on a horse, they would have been *impressed* by my tallness, and would not have appreciated how comical and ineffective this position actually is.

In our fetish for growing up tall, we have trained ourselves not to see the obvious, and by comparison to the grown-up-tall rider, a martial arts posture has a much shorter upper body. For instead of the ribs being pulled up and away from the hips, the chest is more dropped and the back less hollow.

This stance is stronger and more resilient, and the power of the pelvis is available to the whole torso – not cut off from it by a ring of tension around the waist area. All good athletes operate from this posture: it protects your back when you are lifting heavy weights, and adds power to

Fig. 2.4 (a) When a martial artist hollows her back and pulls up her ribcage it is obvious that she is not centered and grounded. Moving her arms as in (b) puts her into the riding position. Yet very few trainers see this as wrong, and the rider who is trying hard to 'grow up tall' believes that she must be doing the right thing.

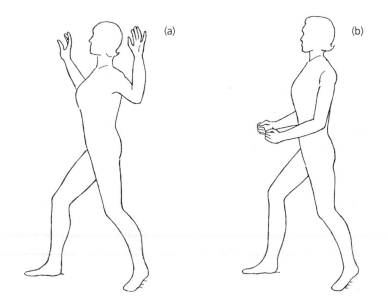

(a)   (b)

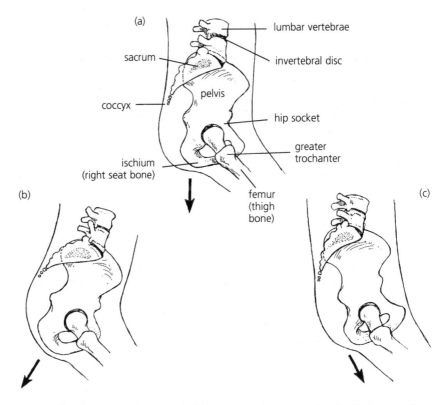

Fig. 2.5 The alignment of the pelvis. In (a) the rider's seat bones point directly downwards, which aligns the spine and pelvis correctly. In (b), in which the rider has a hollow back, they point backwards. In (c), iwhich shows a rounded back, they point forwards.

your tennis shots.

To fully appreciate the contrast, grow up as tall as you can whilst reading this (do it now), and you will feel the effect on your seat bones, your back, your stomach, and your breathing. I hope it is immediately obvious that anything which restricts your breathing this much cannot be a good idea! Neither is it helpful to concentrate solely on the vertical plane (stretching up and stretching down), for *the horizontal plane,* which riders usually never think about, is even more important.

The appropriateness of the curves in the spine is such a major issue that we will return to it on page 246 in the chapter 'Fit and Able', when we discuss the concept of 'neutral spine'. Meanwhile, you can reach a good approximation of this by ensuring that your seat bones point *straight down.* (See Fig. 2.5.) A hollow back makes the rider too tall; she sits predominately on her crotch, raises her chest, and points her seat bones backwards. A rounded back makes her too short; she sits predominantly on her buttocks, her front caves in, and she points her seat bones forward. (Slowly move between these two extremes as you sit on your chair. Which posture feels more familiar to you? Sitting on your hands as you do this will make the change in your seat-bone positioning more obvious.)

Whilst the round-backed position is the stronger and safer of the two, it has the disadvantage that the rider *cannot* hold a shoulder/hip/heel alignment, and her leg will inevitably creep forward into the 'armchair seat'. Riders who do not realise this become frustrated with their inability to hold their leg in place – the inevitable result of addressing the symptom instead of the cause.

Whilst the round-backed rider is doomed to sit in the 'armchair seat', the hollow-backed rider can more easily keep her feet back underneath her. As she makes her thigh almost vertical, she may be congratulating herself on the degree to which she has opened the angle at her hip joint. But she is under an illusion, for if the seat bones are to stay pointing straight down, the spiral-shaped ligaments which surround the neck of the femur (see Fig. 2.6) prohibit more than about a 140° angle between the leg and the body. When the angle at the hip joint reaches its limit the only other place that can give is the small of the back, and it is the *hollowing of the back*, along with the accompanying rotation of the pelvis, which allows the long, vertical thigh. Many people define this as good, but (as I will explain later) the thigh at this angle no longer has the leverage to lift the horse's back. The rider with such an open angle at the hip joint is often thought of as 'supple'; but in reality the hollow back is often a cause of back pain, and (as I will again explain later) it significantly reduces the rider's shock-absorption.

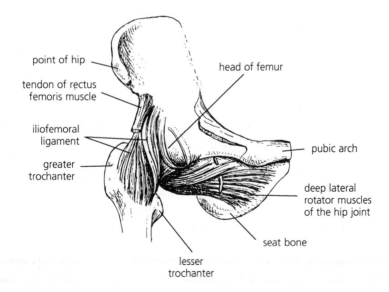

Fig. 2.6 The iliofemoral ligament which spirals around the hip joint and limits its range of motion.

About fifty per cent of riders are naturally round-backed, and fifty per cent are hollow-backed – but they are concentrated in different places. I have seen more hollow-backed riders on the east coast of America than anywhere else in the world. These 'uptight' riders are in contrast to the round-backed riders (the types who 'let it all hang out') who seem to have migrated to the USA's west coast! In Britain, riding schools are mostly inhabited by hollow-backed riders, whilst the round-backed riders are found riding event horses. Usually, they are the more competent, for 'growing up tall' is such an ineffective posture that it is all but impossible to ride well.

The curves of the spine, the direction in which the seat bones point, and also the shoulder/hip/heel alignment of the body are always my starting point with a new rider. As I adjust these, I check that the foot rests lightly on the stirrup, with the stirrup on the ball of the foot. I often ask the rider, 'How would you land on the riding arena if we took your horse out from underneath you by magic?' and 'Would you balance on a diving board?' When her kinaesthetic 'yes' matches my visual 'yes', we are well on our way; but this can take a while, for the adjustments she makes to reach this point can make her feel as if she is sitting very oddly.

The rider who used to 'grow up tall' now feels (by comparison) as if she is slouching, whilst the rider who used to round her back now feels as if she is hollow-backed. The rider who used to push her feet forward now feels as if they are back around the horse's stifles. The changes feel so extreme and the potential for confusion is so great that the rider can find herself reeling, before her horse has even moved!

....

Seeing is believing   It can be extremely disconcerting when the changes you make in your alignment do not feel the same as they look. I have seen many riders struggle with this, and I particularly remember a pupil I met in America, who had been taught for some time by one of my student teachers. Despite the teacher's best efforts Donna was still growing too tall, and riding with her stirrups too long; and she was extremely reluctant to shorten them. My colleague felt that she had dragged from Donna as much change as she was willing to give – and told me that Donna had repeatedly used the words 'short, fat, and ugly' to describe how her body now felt. Given this, her reluctance to change did not seem surprising!

Teacher and pupil had reached an uneasy compromise; but I quietly insisted on further change, repeatedly telling Donna that she was going to have to feel 'even shorter, even fatter, and even uglier'! (These precise words were important, since they were the 'trigger' most likely to evoke the right feeling.) In effect, I had to sell Donna the idea that the benefits of these strange feelings would outweigh their apparent disadvantages. By the end of three days her horse has shown her that they did; but in reality, her reluctance to change had cost her dearly – not least in money.

The major problem here was that within Donna's kinaesthetic map of her body, she was being asked to make changes which felt unbelievably weird. Furthermore, the contortions seemed to conflict with the theory of riding that she had (perhaps unthinkingly) promised to love, honour and obey. This put her in a terrible bind. Yet from the teacher's visual perspective there is no conflict, and once the goal has been achieved the pupil appears beautifully aligned! The teacher (who is often very pleased with her handiwork) denies the *pupil's* conflict at her peril – for when she does so, riding sessions can degenerate into 'map battles'. Inevitably, the rider will believe her body more than she does her teacher, and as she succumbs to the pull of 'home' the arguments begin:

'You're in front of vertical.'

'I'm not.'

'You are.'

'I'm not!'

'You are!'

Or,

'You've got to feel more slouched.'

'This can't be right.'

'It is.'

'It can't be.'

'It is.'

'It can't be!'

Yet the battle is rarely fought openly; most often the rider is passively resistant to the teacher's suggestions – and the teacher leaves the lesson feeling that yet another pupil 'just didn't get the message'.

The fastest, most painless solution to the discrepancy is a mirror or a video camera, which quickly convinces the rider that seeing and feeling are two different phenomena. Visual feedback was, in fact, extremely helpful to Donna, for it helped her to understand that changes always *feel* much bigger than they *look* – just as a lost dental filling or mouth ulcer feels to your tongue like a yawning great chasm, but looks in the mirror like a tiny little pin-head.

This discrepancy between feeling and seeing is, I believe, one of the most significant reasons why riders do not learn and improve as much as they otherwise might; for they censor the amount of difference they are willing to feel. By definition, the answer they are seeking always lies outside the range that feels normal; but it also lies way outside the ten per cent margin within which they are expecting to change. (I had intended to say that fifty per cent would be a more realistic figure for how much change they need to make. But talking this through with pupils they unanimously said, 'No, no! It's much nearer 100!'

Most riders enter a lesson expecting to be shown how to do what they already do better. But learning actually arises from *doing it differently*. Often, when a pupil discovers this, it is as if she says to the teacher, 'Well, yes, I had thought I wanted to ride better, but I didn't realise I'd have to pay the price of feeling this weird. So I'm about to reconsider my options!'

There is no doubt that when it comes to one's own body, seeing is believing. But even when the rider becomes convinced of the value of change, *adjusting* to the new alignment is a different issue entirely (as we shall see in Chapter 6). For making it your new 'home' can be a long drawn-out process. One unusually determined rider I know taught herself to recognise her new shoulder/hip/heel alignment by fixing a weight onto a piece of string, and pinning it to the shoulder seam of her T-shirt. Then, she could drop the weight down to check if it hung by her ankle joint, and hoist it back up again, putting it in her pocket whenever she was worried about it swinging! If you decide to do this, however, please appreciate that I am not recommending it, and I will not be held responsible for your safety!

....

'Hunt the Right Feeling'!
Experiences like Donna's are such an integral part of learning to ride that it is worth telling another story, this time concerning Jackie, who is a much more advanced rider. She had attended one of my teacher-training courses, and because she wanted to actually ride with me, she invited me to teach at her barn. Most of the course participants were her pupils, who had all joined together to pay for her to cross America and attend that course. Given this small amount of original input, I was impressed by Jackie's work with them, and felt that she had amply repaid their investment. Her own riding was also extremely good, and her horse was nearing Grand Prix level. But to my eye, she was breaking one of the fundamental rules which she had seen and corrected in her pupils but not in herself: her shoulder/hip/heel line was good, but she was growing up tall and stretching her legs down, interpreting that saying – as so many people do – in a way which is *not* its intended meaning. So I asked her take up more of a martial arts posture: to drop her ribs down towards her hips, to emphasise the angles in the joints of her hip, knee and ankle, and to lighten her contact into the stirrups.

Despite my explanations about the need for this change, I sensed that she made it with some reluctance. But in my usual tenacious way, I refused to let her 'bail out' of feeling so weird. Then, after about ten minutes, the improvements in her horse's carriage and his lightness in her hand convinced her that I was not off my head, and that the change really was worth making. It was later that day, during the dismounted workshop that she confessed, 'When you said that, I thought, "Oh my God, this feels awful; it can't be right. I'll just humour her for a few minutes." So I did, but you wouldn't let me wriggle out of it in the way I'd hoped to ... and then everything changed. And then I realised how I had been preaching the need for open-mindedness to my pupils, and trying to convince them that change will always feel strange and "wrong" at first ... and yet here I was, censoring the changes I was willing to make.'

This difference between theory and practice often shocks even those riders who have loved my ideas on paper, and understood them even better on videotape. For despite this, they still balk when faced with the changes they need to make. (As one exasperated soul once wailed, 'This is like the difference between reading about sex and having sex!') It also makes me sometimes ask the rider if she remembers the book *Watership Down,* which chronicled the adventures of a group of rabbits who fled after their habitat was destroyed. A popular joke at the time said, 'You've read the book, seen the film, so now eat the pie.' Even teachers like Jackie can be shocked when it comes to 'eating the pie'; but this change was, in fact, the one which most challenged her sense of 'rightness' (although others were physically more difficult).

On one of the evenings of the course, Jackie, I, and the course participants all went out for a meal together, and she proposed a toast to me as her inspiration and mentor. I found this extremely moving, and was fighting back a tear as everyone raised their glasses. Then, at the last moment, one of the group members added, 'And may all your rides be weird!' This immediately changed my mood, and sent us all into spasms of laughter. But whilst it expressed one of the fundamental realisations of a group of people all in search of breakthroughs in their riding, the reality is that every ride will *not* be a breakthrough ride, and that even the weirdest of feelings will become normal in time.

Essentially, riding is a game which could be called 'Hunt the Right Feeling' – but as your body adapts, the right feeling changes over time. This can leave you wondering if you have indeed adapted to it, or if you are actually only half doing it – and again it is the objective perspective of an outside observer which most easily resolves the dilemma.

....

As I place the rider in a shoulder/hip/heel line and rebalance her spinal curves, I also check the length of her stirrups. For – as will become clear later – the biomechanics of riding are at their most efficient when the

The hip and knee angles

angle between the front of the body and the thigh bone is about 140°. Many aspiring dressage riders are attempting to ride with their stirrups far too long; for the cry 'stretch your leg down' has tempted them to try and get their knee *underneath* their hip, coming close to a 180° angle (and hollowing their back). Yet successful modern-day competition riders do not do this, and most are seen with the thigh at about 45° to the ground. In contrast, the look you achieve with a vertical thigh went out of fashion several centuries ago – soon after our ancestors took off their armour. You see it illustrated on seventeenth-century woodcuts, where the rider wears long spurs, a pointed hat, and carries the whip vertically. His horse wears a bridle with an evil-looking curb bit, and is usually performing an air above the ground.

Whilst the 140° angle at the hip joint is the average, some strong male riders are able to achieve the equivalent leverage (which we will talk about on page 95) with a more open angle. But the rider who is reorganising the biomechanics of her riding is usually better off initially with the slightly more closed angle of 135°. Her thigh and her calf form a triangle whose third side is the vertical line from the hip to the ankle. If the thigh and the calf (measured from the knee to the greater trochanter, which is the bony knobble at the top outside of the thigh, and from the knee to the knobble at the side of the ankle joint) were the same length, this would be an isosceles triangle. The angle behind her knee would then be 90°. (See Fig. 2.7.)

I had an interesting experience recently, which was almost the antithesis of my interaction with Jackie and her pupils. I was teaching at a riding centre whose owner is a dressage rider of international renown,

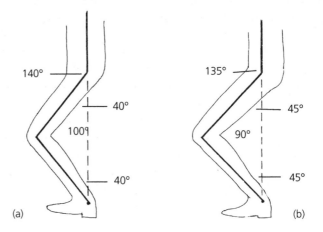

Fig. 2.7 The angles at the rider's joints, assuming that the thigh and calf are the same length, and measuring the hip angle from the thigh bone and not the top of the thigh: (a) more experienced rider; (b) more novice rider.

and who was meeting me for the first time. In her first lesson I took her stirrups up one hole. Her head girl, another talented rider who also rides at Grand Prix, had to take her stirrups up two holes. Most of the other more junior instructors and livery owners needed to take theirs up three.

The 'trickle-down effect' had worked *against* all of these riders, demonstrating that the discrepancy between what good riders do and what they say they do becomes more devastating the further one goes from the source.

But the one striking exception was a young rider who everyone agreed was outstandingly talented. She had already represented her state in young rider competitions, and somehow she had escaped from the usual ramifications of the 'stretch your leg down' scenario. Either she had always ridden so well that no one had ever felt the need to say it, or she had interpreted the saying in a completely different way to the average rider, who is undoubtedly not recreating the 'feelage' which the originators intended to convey.

- *How would you land on the riding arena if we took your horse out from under you by magic? Look in a mirror, take a photograph, use video, or ask a friend for an objective assessment.*
- *Do you have a shoulder/hip/heel vertical line? What direction do your seat bones point in, and are you hollow- or round-backed? Sit on your hands to get a more objective read-out of the change that would bring your seat bones to vertical.*
- *Where does your heel point – towards the horse's knee or towards his hock or stifle? What adjustments do you need to make?*
- *How would you have to adjust your stirrups to get angles of 135° at the hip and 90° at the knee? An observer would then see your thigh lying at an angle close to (but not less than) 45° to the ground.*
  An observer watching you from the side should see a straight vertical line from your pubic bone, to your belly button, to your sternum. She should also see the shoulder/hip/heel line which would enable you to balance on a diving board. She should barely see any curves in your back.
- *How much pressure do you have in the stirrups? Reduce this to 10–14lb (4.5–6kg). Assess the feeling of this by sitting on a chair (or ideally sitting on your saddle on a low saddle horse) and resting one foot on your bathroom scales (or ideally each foot on one of a pair of scales). This is a much lighter contact than most riders have, especially if they are trying hard to 'push their heels down'.*

....

After the rider's alignment, one of the next most important variables is the way she supports her own body weight. To understand this, think of the   **Body texture** difference between picking up a child who wants to be picked up and picking up one who does not. The child who does not want to be picked up makes herself into dead weight, and feels very much heavier. She does this by relaxing completely. This same mechanism is used by the horse who forces *you* to support the weight of his hind leg as you are picking his foot out. I was talking about this in a workshop one day, when a woman reinforced the idea by saying, 'I shall never forget the four days when I carried my sick, feverish four-year-old daughter around on my back in a baby pack. Sometimes I could negotiate with her, and get her to sit still for a while, but there were also times when she wriggled and jiggled, and times when she fell asleep. That was the worst of all, and I'm sure that even if I had had three glasses of beer (which might reduce my co-ordination to the level of the young newly backed horse) I'd still prefer to carry a rider like the wriggling four-year-old than one who mirrors the sound asleep one.'

We all recognise the rider who sits like 'a sack of potatoes', but rarely realise that we are actually seeing too much relaxation! Nor do we appreciate that two riders of exactly the same weight will be perceived very differently by the horse, depending on how effectively each one supports her body weight.

I have several times heard Reiner Klimke say something to the effect of 'One of the things I have learned over the years is that the rider must sit *lightly'*, and I believe he is referring to this same phenomenon – to the idea of being a rider who wants to be picked up, and who in turn can 'pick up' the horse's back instead of squashing it down. He is also referring to the rider's need for high muscle tone.

The only place you could find a completely relaxed horse and rider is flat on the floor of the riding school, for it takes muscle tone to stand, and even more to run and jump. Collection is high muscle tone: whenever your horse is over-excited, dancing and prancing on the spot, you are feeling high tone – and unless you can match it in your own body you are likely to feel extremely unsafe!

Another analogy which explains muscle tone is offered by the 'Superman' movies.* For Clark Kent is a low tone, passive and ineffectual person; but Superman has such high tone that he is all but bursting out of his skin. So the question is: 'Which of them is more relaxed?'

Most riders who are told to relax make themselves more like Clark, choosing what some bodyworkers (Alexander and Feldenkrais Teachers, massage therapists and chiropractors, etc.) call 'dead' rather than 'live'

---

* Since Christopher Reeve's tragic riding accident, I have felt reluctant to use this image; but it is the best description I can find to differentiate between high tone (or 'live' relaxation) and low tone (or 'dead' relaxation).

relaxation. On a high muscle tone horse, riders instinctively recognise their insecurity – so the muscles of their shoulder girdle, arm, and hand step in, making a desperate bid to gain some control. It is this tension which makes most observers judge them as 'tense'. For the rider has to get her feeling of security from somewhere – and if she cannot get it from her pelvis, she has to get it from her hand. Thus it is the lack of muscle tone in the parts of the body that *should* be working which causes 'overkill' in parts of the body that should *not* be working.

Telling the rider to relax the arm or to stop pulling is doomed to leave the trainer feeling like a broken record, and the pupil feeling like a failure; for to address the symptom and not the cause will never work. Before the rider can stop pulling, she needs to be given something else to do instead, enabling her to fix the problem at source – in the low tone of her body.

To use another analogy, the highly toned horse and rider are like brand new stuffed toys, not elderly much-loved playthings that have seen better days. 'Bursting out of one's skin' is one of the best ways to describe the quality of high tone, and when 'Superhorse' and 'Superrider' enter the dressage arena we instantly see their magnificence; but when we call them 'relaxed' we acknowledge only a small part of the overall picture. If there were one change I could make to the ethos of dressage judging, it would be to have judges understand that a still rider is a highly toned rider. We could call her state 'relaxed alertness', but we need to recognise that this is the antithesis of the much more common state of 'dead relaxation'.

If you are one of the many riders whose overwhelming wish is to relax as you ride, you are probably showing the 'dead relaxation' of Clark. Remarkably, the tonal qualities of the rider and the horse tend to mirror each other, so Clark would usually be found on a low tone, passive horse, who will not respond to repeated kicking. Time and time again, I have observed that when the rider 'picks herself up' and adjusts her muscle tone, so does her horse. But until this moment, kicking and shoving will be to no avail. So as you and your horse slouch along together, your instructor may wish she could find an ethical way to put a bomb underneath your tails!

Clark and Superman both have bodies with very different textures, and 'texture' is one of the most important and least recognised variables of riding. On teacher training courses my trainee teachers look at riders, whilst I ask them 'If this person's skin were a bag, what would be inside it?' (My guinea-pig riders are warned in advance that they will be open to such scrutiny, and that whilst everyone is actually on their side, they may discover things about themselves which they would rather not know!) The ideal quality would be something like putty or wet sand. This has the solidity and stability of high tone, without the heaviness of the rider who grinds her weight down into the horse's back, and who might look as if she were full of lead weights (or potatoes). More relaxed riders look limp, as if their skin contained noodles or blancmange, and as their riding improves their body passes through the consistency of bread dough and on towards putty.

The more ethereal types could initially be full of air, feathers, or polystyrene beads. For them to gain the solidity of putty is no mean task, and it requires that they feel much more solid physically – as if they were made of stronger stuff. Ideally, the rider becomes like one of those weighted dolls which cannot be knocked over; but the more ethereal riders are top-heavy, as if all their weight is in their head, neck and shoulder girdle, with very little 'stuffing' in their pelvis or legs. One of the worst case scenarios would be a body so jumbled that the legs were full of air and the torso full of twigs, with the arms and shoulder girdle made of steel. Inevitably, this rider would feel desperately unsafe and unstable.

- *How well do you support your own weight as you ride?*
- *If you try to relax as you ride, are you aiming for the 'dead relaxation' of Clark, or the 'relaxed awareness' and high muscle tone of Superman?*
- *Are you too 'down', with a tendency to treat the horse like a mobile armchair, and to flop, grind or press down onto his back? If so, you are probably round-backed, and sitting in the 'armchair seat'. Or are you too 'up', with a tendency to ping off the top of the horse like a clothes peg? If so, you are probably hollow-backed, and prone to tipping forward and even into the foetal crouch.*
  Even an untrained observer will probably recognise when you have 'up' and 'down' in balance, for you will look like a talented rider. When you have this well, you maintain a full, clear contact with the saddle, but feel almost as if you were levitating in space and did not need a horse to support you.
- *Do you have the tonal quality in your body that easily enables you to give your hand forward? Or do you find yourself pulling back, even though you know you should not do so?*
- *How would you, and how would a friend observing you, describe the texture of your body? If your skin were a bag, what would it contain? Are you more aware of your pelvis, or of your head and shoulders?*

....

'Pushing down the plunger'! The idea of lowering your centre of gravity is intended to help people develop a body with a much more uniform texture, and to have their strength housed in their pelvis. However, in my experience the idea (which sounds great on paper) does not in itself enable people to change the habits of a lifetime. So I regularly use two images which have been particularly successful.

One is to think of your torso like one of those cafétière coffee makers (also known as a French press), where you push down a plunger, pushing all the coffee grounds down to the bottom of the jug once the coffee has brewed. If you have used one of these, you will know that the plunger offers a significant resistance to your push, that you have to push it down *slowly,* and that doing so is a pleasant, sensual experience. Note too that pushing down the plunger does not alter the shape of the jug itself – and by analogy it does not alter the shape of your body (making you round or hollow your back). So, if you had a plunger like this inside you, at what level would it lie? Once mounted, most people can answer this question remarkably easily, and can lower it somewhat simply by paying attention, and slowly 'pushing' it down.

However, the ideal of dropping it down to bikini-line level may not be so easy, especially as the most significant difference between the rider and the coffee jug is that the plunger can lie at different levels in your front and in your back. On one of these (usually the back), it may be far harder to get it to drop down, and it helps to think of each in-breath drawing it down by suction. This requires the use of diaphragmatic breathing, which I will describe in Chapter 9. In contrast, a breathing pattern which raises the chest and shoulders in each in-breath repeatedly pulls the plunger *up* – and I have watched many, many riders struggling to push down a plunger which seemed to have a life of its own!

The key to success lies in breathing, and you really know you have succeeded when you feel as if your brain, your awareness, your weight and your energy are all in your pelvis, and not in your head. (When told this, one of my female students once remarked, 'No wonder men are so much better at riding than women!') The quality that we call 'centred' or 'grounded' is an absolute requirement for riding, and in theory, it should be an inevitable by-product of a training in both riding and the martial arts. Rarely, however, do riders actually learn this – it is either an innate part of their natural talent, or they are taught so ineffectively that it eludes them for life.

Another way of illustrating the same idea is to think of your skin like a plastic membrane which is full of water. You then become what I call a 'water doll'. The doll has a nozzle in the centre of her abdomen at bikini-line level, and water escapes from this with the force of a power-hose. (This is the 'low down bear down', which we will talk about later.) Yet despite this the doll keeps filling up, as if more water were being poured in through her head, and the pressure within her remains high. But sometimes it is as if someone came along with a pin, and put a number of pin-pricks in one or more parts of her body. The water then leaks out, reducing the pressure inside the doll and with it the force of the 'low down bear down'. It is almost as if the rider's power is being drained out of her body. Having explained this, my question then becomes, 'Do you have leaks, or are you water-tight?'

This image is one of my favourites, for it so accurately describes the difference between the average and the talented rider. 'Closing the leaks' is really the same as 'pushing down the plunger', for leaks occur only below the level of the plunger. It is the ethereal, low tone riders (the ones who are full of feathers or polystyrene beads) who leak the most – sometimes, in fact, they are one big leak! These riders need a much stronger sense of their skin as their body boundary: they need to know where they end, and where air begins. The differences that I see (both between different riders, and within one person as she 'lowers her plunger' and 'closes her leaks') relate to the strength and clarity of the body boundary, and this tells me if a rider is 'leaking'. Friends who are more directly involved than me in the field of energetic healing, tell me that I am seeing the body's energy field. But I am certainly not blessed with psychic vision, and my student teachers soon learn to see this too.

At the end of a two-day clinic where I had been doing this work with about eight riders, I once asked thirty non-teaching observers whether they had seen the changes, or had been completely flummoxed. Over twenty responded that they had seen them, and with a little direction it is amazing how subtle our sensory distinctions can become. This was demonstrated too by the riders who had converted my words into subtle but far-reaching changes which they too had perceived – this time through their kinaesthetic sense. The critical factor here is that *the brain learns by contrast*. So you will not become aware of this phenomena until changes are displayed in front of your eyes or within your body; then you might surprise yourself with your abilities.

However, if you think of the archetypal strong male dressage rider (who was far more prevalent in former years) it is inconceivable that he would not know where his body ended and air began, and his energy would be so strong, so stable, and so grounded in his pelvis that he would be completely unaware of any other possibilities! Having never perceived any contrasts, he would probably have no problem declaring that my propositions are crazy. But even he would have to acknowledge that very few people – and especially very few women – have this same quality of power and energy, and that he (lacking the ability to make these distinctions), cannot teach them to have it.

Bizarre and unusual though my language may sound, riders can always understand me – and the difference created when they 'push down the plunger' is phenomenal. The rider who becomes 'water-tight' has such high tone, and so much power stored in her body that she begins to feel both safe and effective – and as she does her 'he-man' imitation, her horse has no choice but to take her very seriously! It is as if the strong rider draws her energy into her body, and particularly into her pelvis. She can then push it out in a very focused and directed way as she bears down.

Most of us, however, have our energy floating around *outside* our skin, and hence we lack power. To understand this concept, think of being in shock, which is the extreme of this condition. Your energy has responded to the trauma by flying outwards – just as you would see the pieces of your precious china ornament fly in all directions if you dropped and broke it. Meanwhile, your core is empty and hollow, and you are left feeling as if you are 'going through the motions' of life. Your friends might even look at you and think that 'all the lights are on, but nobody's at home'.

Many books about healing and energetic health talk about protecting yourself from 'bad vibes' by projecting your energy outwards; for if you do this, your outward flow stops them flowing in. But before you can project outwards, you have to have a strong central core of energy. This is what so many people lack, especially those of us who are sensitive and ethereal.

Healers often suggest that you look at the horizon (especially in a beautiful place) and take twelve deep breaths, imagining that you are breathing in Universal Energy, using it to build and 'charge' your energy field. I described the 'water doll' as being constantly filled up by water which comes in through her head, and this too is a metaphor for the ingress of Universal Energy. Muscle tone is then the key factor which determines whether the boundary between energy and matter is strong enough to enable us to hold that energy in our bodies and project it out in useful ways – or whether we simply leak it away. In general high tone people (whose body has that firmer texture) use their energy well; low tone people do not, and as a result of their 'leaks' even their flesh is less firmly defined. From my own observations, I am even tempted to suggest that it is muscle tone which determines how effectively energy is embodied in matter.*

I have observed these changes in texture, muscle tone and groundedness in innumerable 'average riders' who found that 'pushing down the plunger' and 'closing the leaks' revolutionised their sense of strength and solidity. But it took a long time to clarify these ideas, and I shall never forget a rare moment of exasperation when a pupil was managing to turn my own horse into a convincing imitation of an untrained novice, and when I found myself yelling, 'Nick, you ride like a sieve!' I could barely believe the way my horse was beginning to mirror his energetic state, and was deflating like a balloon before my very eyes. It took several years for me to really appreciate the meaning and the implications of my statement, and to reach the stage where I could teach

---

* *I am still endeavouring to learn all I can about this, and would be extremely interested to hear from anyone who feels that she has a contribution to make to this understanding.*

him how not to be a sieve (and of course, the changes in his riding and his own horse were dramatic).

I have also witnessed these changes in many more advanced riders, including several Olympic contenders. Here, the changes are obviously much more subtle, and I particularly remember one Olympic rider whose 'plunger' came up at the back whenever she rode a flying change. Her control of her body (and her energy) was such that as soon as this was pointed out to her, she could change it, and she then tested her new-found skill by riding some tempi changes. Her ultimate test was a diagonal line of fifteen one-time changes, and she emerged from this saying, 'Wow! I've never been able to keep him so collected and to have so much control of the tempo. He usually dives onto his forehand.'

Amazing as it may seem, her horse had been aware when she had suddenly sprung 'leaks' – and of the opportunity this gave him to fall on his nose. He was then equally aware that she had closed them again.

If you were to insist on using our traditional map of riding, you might say that she had learned to 'use her back'. But this saying does not help many people, and my metaphorical description is the best way I can find to delineate changes in the texture and the quality of the body which we all, as a culture, contrive not to notice – whether we are on or off horses. We do not even have words in our language to describe them, and like the Native American tribe who see only three colours, we see only good, bad and indifferent. If you are dismissive of these descriptions, please realise that you judge them from the confines of a map which is extremely impoverished; you also delete one of the most important variables within the rider/horse interaction, which I guarantee will change your riding (and perhaps your life) more than any other change you will ever make.

- *Think of the analogy of the cafétière coffee jug, and determine what level your 'plunger' would lie at in your back and in your front. Can you find ways of pushing it down lower? Is it easier to push it down in the front or in the back of your body? Is there a place where it tends to get stuck?*
- *Think of the analogy of the 'water doll'. Are you 'leak-proof', and if not, where are the 'leaks' in your torso? Can you keep the pressure inside it high enough to feel as if you could power-hose water out through a nozzle in the centre of your abdomen at bikini-line level? Or does the nozzle become a giant watering-can rose, and your power-hose become a watering-can spray? Or is your power-hose completely non-existent?*
- *How effectively can you change this? If you are struggling either with this or with the plunger, do not worry; you may need to work first with your alignment, with the tendency to 'grow up tall', with bearing down (which follows in the next section) and with your breathing.*

It takes a powerful body to generate, contain and direct the horse's power. **Bearing** The horse's powerhouse is his pelvis, and so is the rider's: but both of **down** them have to be able to disseminate this power throughout their body in a controlled way. The horse must transmit it to his forehand, without blocking it (which he usually does through tightness somewhere between the loin and the wither) and without becoming so unstable or 'soggy' in his back that the impulse dissipates. It could become deviated too – especially if he falls out through his shoulder, thus sending the power and his body in some direction which the rider never intended! The rider too must not deaden, dissipate or block the horse's power – as happens when she is deformed, wobbled or bumped by the impulse. Instead, she must be in control of its effect on them both – from the tips of their toes to the tops of their heads.

In addition to the texture of the rider's body, bearing down – one of the key concepts of this map, and one of the most important hidden elements in riding – plays a huge part in the rider's upper body control as she transmits the horse's impulse.

When I demonstrate its importance to a group of riders in a workshop setting, I have taken to asking one of them to teach the others how to blow their noses. The group is told that they are to follow the instructions to the letter, without improvising, or doing anything that they were not specifically told to do. Within this context, the command 'Put your tissue on your nose and blow' yields some interesting results – but never any mucus!

More assiduous instructors get carried away talking about fingers, tissues and noses (in a way reminiscent of the riding instructor's preoccupation with the intricacies of hand and leg positioning). But everyone to date has left out the most important piece. When I ask the group actually to blow their noses and find out how they do it, the answer is obvious: you blow your nose with your stomach muscles.

During visits to public places, one often sees the mothers of two-year-old children holding tissues to their noses and yelling 'Blow, blow!' The still-empty tissue convinces them to shout even harder, until they begin to sound like frustrated riding teachers! But as the children dutifully expel air through their nostrils, they consistently fail to produce the goods. Fortunately, kids who are armed with their own tissues soon work it out for themselves – and I have heard of only one who did not. ('This is amazing,' said a woman during one of my workshops, 'I can't wait to go home and teach my son how to do it!' He was a twelve-year old boy, who (predictably to me) was the shy, retiring type who hated the rough and tumble of sports: but I never did discover how effectively this revelation changed his life!)

If you clear your throat (do it now) you will again realise how your abdominal muscles engage as you do so. This is bearing down, and good riders do it continually. (Try this again as you sit in your chair, and then hold the muscle use which enabled you to do it.) Most riders almost die of shock when I teach them this, because it feels so alien, and so difficult to do. It is easier, however, when you are actually riding, for it is designed for action. If you push a broom away from you when sweeping you naturally bear down, and the safest way to lift heavy weights is to bend your knees and bear down (rather than leaning over whilst pulling your stomach in).

Bearing down often conflicts with the theory a rider has learned – for if she has been trying to 'grow up tall' she will have pulled her stomach *in* in the process. She then utilises a breathing pattern which I call '*breathing up*', lifting her chest and shoulders (and also her 'plunger') on every in-breath. Nervous riders instinctively do this, and many other people do it because the theory they have heard convinces them that it must be the right. But bearing down requires '*breathing down*', in which every in-breath is drawn 'downwards', filling out the belly much more than the chest. Singers, runners, and people who have played wind instruments already know how to do this, and they bring a tremendous advantage to their riding.

The percentage of the riding population who naturally bear down and use diaphragmatic breathing when riding is very small indeed. (For more help on this, see the breathing exercises in Chapter 9, on page 244.) Paradoxically, they all but die of shock if I show them what everyone else is doing, and they have the equivalent feeling of 'wrongness'.

I did this once with an extremely successful international event rider, who, as a trainer herself, was curious to know how her riding differed from the masses she was teaching. 'You have to be kidding,' she said, as I made her pull her stomach in. 'They do THIS ... it's horrible ... I hate it, and I can barely believe that they manage to ride.'

Returning for a moment to the connection between clearing your throat and the use of your abdominal muscles, realise that this seems obvious once you pay attention to it. But I doubt if it was before. It always interests me that members of the human race who have been blowing their nose and clearing their throat very effectively for a lifetime have no idea how they do it. Even I had not appreciated the connection between nose blowing and bearing down until it was pointed out to me. But this makes me more willing to forgive those good riders who have also been bearing down for years, and who have never noticed that they do so. However, by omitting this from their teaching they leave the rider hugely under-powered.

To my knowledge, the only riders who openly talk and write about bearing down (using the exact same term to describe the same muscle use) are the rodeo competitors of the American West who ride bucking bulls! Bearing down is an established part of their culture, in which they are judged on style as well as their ability to stay on. Bucking bulls are not part of my background (and having seen them, I would not fancy my chances!), but it does not surprise me that this extreme situation should yield conscious knowledge of a fundamental co-ordination which remains *unconscious* for riders whose stability is not so profoundly challenged. Interestingly, the rodeo riders also talk and write about the need to sit across each of the bull's long back muscles – a concept which we will discuss in Chapter 5.

Bearing down constitutes part of the martial arts posture, and the yells of martial artists as well as the grunts of good tennis players are an attempt to increase the power they can harness. One of my fellow instructors who is small and lightly built claims that it is the secret of unscrewing tight jam-jar lids, and this has become one of her favourite ways to impress her friends! I even know people who insist that it makes their old jalopy go faster; but whilst this last claim seems far-fetched, even to me, I do believe the friend who both rides and drives, and who insists that bearing down is also a hidden part of the carriage driver's skill.

I have come to believe that bearing down is the basis of any skill which requires stability on an unpredictable base of support. Riding, wind-surfing and skiing are obvious examples. This became clearer to me after one of my pupils told me the story of taking her family on a wind-surfing holiday. Not surprisingly, she was the one to discover that bearing down was tremendously effective in keeping her body on the board. Her instructor was impressed by her progress, and neither her children nor her husband (who considered himself the athlete of the family) were developing their skills as quickly. She found herself whispering the secret to her kids – who through their riding knew exactly what she meant – whilst showing off her prowess to her husband. Her favourite part of the whole experience, however, was the joy of thinking, 'Shall I tell him now, or shall I leave him to fall off a few more times?'

It is my belief that if we were to change our conventional map of riding *solely* by including the concepts of high muscle tone and of bearing down, we would immediately find a huge increase in the number of 'talented' riders who walked (and rode) our planet.

The story of Sarah illustrates well the change that this could make. She had one of the most low-toned, 'noodley' bodies I have ever come across, and although she had previously had very classical instruction, she was an ineffective rider. Despite all her best efforts, her back and legs wobbled continually, and defied her best attempts to control them. She really balked at the idea of bearing down, and fought it for the first two years that I knew her. I could not convince her that riding well really did require such effort – especially given that good, classical riders appeared to make it look so easy. But at the end of a lesson one day, she made an interesting comment on her experience of riding. 'I wish it was more like picking apples,' she said, 'and less like picking at little wisps of fluff.' It was a brilliant metaphorical description of the frustrations involved in trying to organise a low-toned body.

After this, I did not see her for a further ten months, and then, from the moment I first glimpsed her riding, it was obvious that she had changed. She looked strong and in control of her body – and her horse had improved beyond belief.

'What did you do?' I asked her.

'Well,' she said, 'I got so desperate that I decided to really go for it, and I resolved to bear down for the whole of a long car journey. On the way there, I managed twenty minutes. On the way back, I did the whole three hours. It was a huge breakthrough. By the end, I had worked out how to breathe, and it no longer felt like an effort. So then I could do it in my riding. It's still hard, but at least it feels possible and it makes so much difference.'

At the end of the course I asked her, 'Does riding feel more like picking apples now?'

She laughed, and agreed that it did, for the high tone of bearing down made her body so much more *tangible* that it was well under her control – as was the impulse of her horse's stride.

One of my colleagues told me about two other pupils who would not commit to bearing down. One came round to the idea early in her pregnancy, when it became the only way of keeping her breakfast securely inside her stomach whilst she was riding! She then realised that it had other hidden benefits. Another rider with a less arduous pregnancy had to wait until later, when she could no longer ignore the way that her unborn baby bounced in her womb when she was riding. It began to hit her in the bladder on every 'down'. This was not just uncomfortable – it had other more unfortunate consequences! Bearing down was her instinctive solution to the problem – it held the baby in place, and stopped those embarrassing moments. But it also made her realise just what had been missing from her riding!

I am continually asked, 'Why is bearing down so important?' The answer is, 'Because it makes the body more powerful.' (Without bearing down you do not even have the power to fill your tissue, so goodness knows how you could expect to match the power of a horse and sit to the trot!)

Bearing down is part of a force that the rider must exert within her body from the back towards the front. If the horse were on roller skates, and his legs remained still whilst someone towed him along at constant speed, no force would be required to stay in balance on his back – you could just sit there. But once we are out of the relatively smooth and even motion of walk (which is not so different to being towed along on roller skates) the horse is always either accelerating or decelerating, for the up-and-down motion of trot and canter means that during some phases of his stride he goes forward–but–not–up, whilst at others he goes up–but–not–forward.(See Fig. 2.8.) This continual change in the horizontal and vertical components of his velocity means that a force is acting (and Newton's Second Law of Motion tells us that the force is the product of the mass of the horse and his acceleration). This is the force that we must match. It is as if the horse kicks the rider up the backside with every step he takes.

If the rider is being worked on the lunge in sitting trot, she can usually sit well as long as she holds on to the front of the saddle, exerting a force which acts *from the front towards the back*. But as soon as she lets go, she most probably starts bumping – and she bumps both up and down, and towards the *back* of the saddle. It is as if the horse keeps moving forward in each step, but without using her hands to pull her forwards, the rider cannot match his propulsive force and stay 'with' him.

If she is to stay in place without using her hands, she must change the direction of the force, making a push within her body which acts *from the back towards the front*. But this alternative is far more difficult; it is an awful lot easier simply to pull on the reins.

All too often, the rider does this without even knowing she is doing so. (This is reminiscent of Debbie, whom you met in Chapter 1 – although

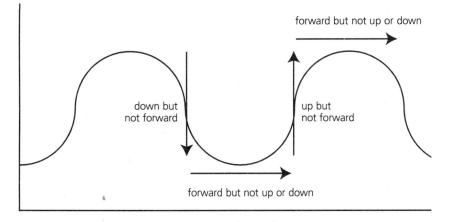

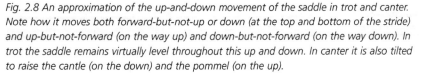

Fig. 2.8 An approximation of the up-and-down movement of the saddle in trot and canter. Note how it moves both forward-but-not-up or down (at the top and bottom of the stride) and up-but-not-forward (on the way up) and down-but-not-forward (on the way down). In trot the saddle remains virtually level throughout this up and down. In canter it is also tilted to raise the cantle (on the down) and the pommel (on the up).

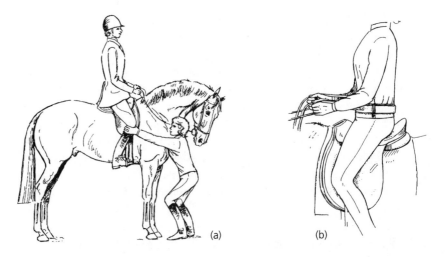

Fig. 2.9 (a) Pulling on the rider's knees to direct the push from her back into her thigh. (b) Wearing the Rider's Belt, which helps her to activate the muscles across her sacrum, and begin her bear down in her back. (Rider's Belts are available via mail order – see page 327.)

Debbie thought it was the right thing to do, and that everyone did it.) It is an inescapable truth that until the rider exerts a force in the forward direction she *cannot not* pull on the reins. This adds new meaning to the phrase 'May the force be with you'!

I have often demonstrated the concept and the feeling of having the force 'with you' by squatting down beneath the horse's neck and pulling on the rider's knees. Ideally, another instructor puts her hand on the rider's lower back, and exerts a push forward, showing her how the force which begins in the back of her body can come out through her 'low down bear down' (the 'power-hose' push forward which acts at bikini-line level) and also pass into each thigh (see Fig. 2.9a). *So the rider who looks as if she is doing nothing, is in fact exerting a force within her body which matches the propulsive force of the horse's hind legs. Thus she stays in place where others are doomed to bump backwards.*

I have recently devised a way to help riders learn to do this far more effectively than most do through conventional means. A soft belt, about 3 inches (75mm) wide, fits snugly around the lower abdomen, just above the greater trochanters of the femur (shown in Fig. 5.10, page 138). It covers the sacrum, and has elasticated over-pieces which ensure that it fits tightly and stays in place. Around the belt is a 'handle', enabling the rider to slip a soft cotton strap under her thumbs, and – quite literally – to pull on her back, increasing the force she exerts in the forward direction. (See Fig. 2.9b.)

Doing this has the added benefit of preventing the rider from pulling back with her hands. The feel of the belt also makes the rider far more aware of the muscles in her lower back, helping her to tone them, to 'begin her bear down in her back, 'close the leaks', and keep her 'plunger' down.

A few minutes with this (which is obviously only safe when used in an enclosed area, on a predictable horse, and in a learning context) is worth hours of sitting trot on the lunge whilst holding the front of the saddle – for this can perpetuate the passivity which accompanies the rider's use of her hand, and may do nothing to instil the right pattern in her body.

This practical way of changing direction of the 'pull' is so simple that I kick myself for not making this leap from theory to practice years ago. (And I thank my colleague Anne Howard, who in desperation one day with a pupil who had never mastered sitting trot, put her sweat shirt around her lower back, and asked her to pull on the sleeves!)

Very often, people who have never sat well to the trot wear the belt and find that they suddenly 'get the message', and it gives me enormous pleasure to watch both horse and rider breathe sighs of relief. In fact, the increased forward force which enables the rider to match the horse's power in each stride is often all that is needed for the many horses who do a convincing camel imitation to drop 'onto the bit' – instantly forgetting the investment they had had in their 'resistance'.

- *Do you bear down when you ride, or do you pull your stomach in?*
- *Clear your throat to show your body what to do, and then maintain that muscle use. Can you breathe easily? If not, does the difficulty lie in the in-breath, or the out-breath? Turn to page 244 for help with this.*
  Realise that if this is difficult for you, you will only become good at bearing down and breathing by practising when you are not riding. Driving your car is a good opportunity for this.
- *Can you match the propulsive force of the horse's hind legs as you ride? Or do you have a tendency to pull back on the rein? Once you have attained 'an independent seat' you know that your bear down is sufficiently strong. Until that time, keep working on it!*

CHAPTER THREE

Plugging In

THINKING ABOUT THE FORCES which act in trot and canter drops the rider so far into the deep end that I want to simplify her task by coming back to walk. Here, alignment, tone, texture and bearing down are joined by the concept of 'plugging in'. This is an important precursor to faster work, and to understand the idea, put your hand on your thigh, and slide it up and down. This mirrors the movement which we commonly see as the rider's seat slides backwards and forwards over the saddle and the horse's back. However, she is usually unaware of the fact that by doing this, she has *disconnected herself from the horse*. To mirror the much tinier movements made by the rider who is plugged in, see how much you can move your hand whilst also moving the flesh underneath it, so that within this movement you are always in contact with the same part of your thigh. Your hand now remains *connected* with your thigh, mirroring the ideal connection between your backside and the horse's back.

Riders disconnect themselves in two ways. Some are too 'flopsy' to plug in, and need to exchange their wobbles for the body control given by higher tone. Meanwhile stronger, more forceful riders (who think, perhaps, that they are 'driving the horse forwards' or 'using their seat') deliberately shove their seat around so much that they too lack the sensitivity and body control which is needed.

As a metaphorical way to describe their antics, think of trying to put an electric plug into a socket in the dark; you could easily find yourself moving it backwards and forwards over the holes until – 'glunk', the connection is made. Once you make the equivalent connection into the horse's back you are *'unignorable'*: his immediate response is to walk at a slower tempo, and this gives *you control of the speed at which he moves his legs*. Often, this change alone is sufficient to bring a hollow-backed horse into carriage.

When the rider is plugged in the outer casing of her body remains *still, relative to the horse*, and an observer does not see it make any movement over and above that which is a mould for the horse's back. As a result of this, she now looks far more like a rider from the Spanish Riding School. She is much more highly toned and causal. ('Causal' means 'having an effect', being pro-active rather than reactive. Do *not* read this as 'casual', a mistake made by many people who avidly read *Ride With Your Mind/The Natural Rider* in which the word crops up repeatedly!) Yet within the rider's backside there is still a small movement of her seat bones, which I call 'bottom walking'. To demonstrate this, sit on the floor with your legs together and out in front of you. Then walk your backside along, moving each seat bone in turn.

'Bottom walking' requires each seat bone to lift up and make a large movement in each 'step'. But as the horse walks, the seat bones do *not* lift up, and it is the backward part of the 'stride' which needs to be emphasised; *so each seat bone in turn moves down and back as the back of the saddle moves down and back on that side.* This happens during the phase in the stride when the horse is propelling his body forward by moving it over his hind leg. Thus your movement matches his, for you too are (in effect) pushing your upper body forward over your seat bone, mirroring the time when you push off your foot in walking. This enables you to stay 'with' the horse – a task which is much more difficult in trot and canter than it is in walk.

I often call the movement 'duck paddle', for if you were to play with a little wind-up duck in your bath tub, you would discover that his feet have to paddle backwards in order to move him forwards, and if they paddled the other way he would in fact go backwards. Some authorities have talked about sitting 'with' or sitting 'against' the horse, and (although their explanations have never been that clear) I believe that they are referring to the options of 'paddling' either forwards or backwards.

In my own riding, I have embraced this new logic, and changed to using the 'paddle' which would move me forwards – with benefits which have shown even more clearly in the faster gaits. Thus the 'down', 'down', 'down' trot has the sense of aiming down and backwards to the horse's hind legs. But in walk most people paddle the other way round, using far too much movement. So I often find myself telling riders to 'halve the size of your seat-bone movement, and halve the "push" that you put into it. Now halve these again ... and again ... and now emphasise the *backward* and not the forward part of the motion.'

The resulting movement may seem back-to-front and surprisingly little – but if you ask someone to lead your horse whilst you walk along beside him and place your hands on his long back muscles, you will realise just how little movement there is in this part of his back. You are not, after all, sitting on his shoulder blades. All that happens is that his back muscle drops down slightly as the hind leg on that side is extended out behind him, and lifts up as the hind leg advances to become weight-bearing.

To help the rider who has way too much movement I often say, 'Think of your spine like the pole which passes through a carousel horse; so instead of ending at your coccyx, it has an imaginary extension down into the horse's body.' I then ask, 'Do the real and the imaginary bits really connect, or are there wiggles and jiggles which separate them?' Although the majority of riders find it hard to eradicate the wiggles, they can usually recognise when they have done so — even if the connection lasts only a step or two.

The ultimate value of plugging in lies, I suspect, in the way that it connects the rider to the horse's *centre of motion*, which is the point in his body which moves the *least* in each stride (and which may or may not coincide with his centre of gravity). It makes intuitive sense that connecting with this would help the rider to be the least disturbed by the horse's movement, and to have the greatest influence on it.

Stopping the wobbles requires increased muscle tone in the muscles lying across the rider's lower back. This gives her a sense of making her back narrower from side to side, and this is the feeling which I have called the 'pinch'. (When I first coined this term I was unaware of the American expression 'Pinch with your knees'. I am advocating a very different muscle use, but unfortunately the term has caused confusion to Americans, who have heard that I advocate 'pinching' and have presupposed that they knew what I meant.) I have described the 'pinch' (which I now tend to call 'narrowing in') by saying it's 'as if there were a bolt connecting the bony knobble at the top of each thigh, and someone were tightening up the nut'. Whilst useful, this description has the disadvantage that it often makes riders 'pop up', over-tightening the muscles which lie between their seat bones and the saddle. (The dismounted exercise beginning on page 247 contrasts this with the ideal way of organising your bones and your flesh.) If you tend to pop up, it can be better to think instead of 'lacing up across your back' — as if you were wearing some kind of corset which could be laced tightly across your sacrum area, narrowing both sides towards the middle.

The people who have the most difficulty 'narrowing in' are the riders (often jumpers) who grip (or, to use the American expression, pinch) with their knees. As they pull them in together, they can feel, subjectively, as if the distance between their knees is less than the width across their back. Given the horse's shape this is actually impossible — but it *is* a convincing feeling. To assess each rider's starting point, it is helpful to think of the line of the thigh bones, which join the knee cap to the bony knobble at the top outside of the thigh (the greater trochanter of the femur). If each line were extended beyond the knees, and back beyond the knobble, they could be parallel, or could be a 'V' whose point lies in front of the horse's chest, or could be a 'V' whose point lies back behind the rider's backside. (See Fig. 3.1.)

The ideal is a 'V' whose point lies about 3 inches (75mm) behind the

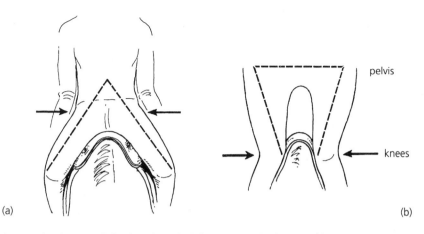

Fig. 3.1 The shape made by the rider's thigh bones can either be a 'V' whose point is behind her, as in (a), or parallel lines, or a 'V' whose point is in front of her as in (b).

rider's sacrum. However, few of the riders who have the 'V' the right way round have the point close enough behind them, and it is often over the horse's croup, or behind his tail. They have to narrow in the whole 'V' shape *without* taking their thigh and knee off the saddle – essentially by narrowing in across their back, as well as between the upper part of their thighs. (I sometimes suggest that the rider thinks of having 'both legs coming out of the same hole' – an expression often used to describe narrow-chested horses – and this puts the tendons at the corners of the pubic bone firmly onto the saddle, activating the inner thigh muscles.) The stability and influence gained from making the body *narrower* can be enormous, and in particular, the increase in the muscle tone in the lower back makes it possible to plug in.

To understand this in practice, stand in an 'on-horse' position, and check the direction that your seat bones point in. Notice that if you hollow your back and make them point backwards, they feel as if they widen apart. If you make them point down, they feel as if they come in closer together. With your seat bones pointing down, aim your left seat bone towards the bony knobble on the inside of your right ankle, and your right seat bone towards the bony knobble on the inside of your left ankle. This should immediately give you a sense of increasing your muscle tone – as if you were bringing your seat bones even closer together and making your pelvis become narrower from side to side.

If you stay in this position for long enough, you may also feel a narrowing across your lower back, which is the sense of 'lacing up'. To exaggerate the feeling, think of pushing your thighs apart – as if you were pushing out against a resistance – and use this to make your thigh bones into a 'V' whose point lies a few inches behind your sacrum. Turning your heels out so that you become pigeon-toed also exaggerates the feeling.

(Riders who ski have likened this to doing a snow plough, except that your skis are set in concrete!) As you stand in this position you may find that you also feel muscles working on the front, inside or outside of your thighs. If you do not feel the strain somewhere (ideally in your lower back) you are not doing the exercise well. Thus it has come to be known as 'the pain exercise'.

Many riders initially find it difficult to plug in and reproduce this muscle-use when riding. Then, when they do, they are convinced that they must be doing it wrong: they tell me that they feel 'stiff', or 'rigid', and that they are not 'going with the movement'. As the horse slows his tempo, they become worried that he will stop – and they often hassle him into action, unplugging themselves in the process. However, when the horse has been speeding out from underneath them, the value of plugging in becomes immediately obvious – because once *you* control the speed at which the horse moves his legs (and you can bear down and hold your alignment at the same time) you no longer feel tempted to pull back on the reins.

This can be even more dramatic when you learn how to plug in in canter, for riders with a big backwards-forwards movement in the saddle unplug in just the same way that they do in walk. They too need to emphasise the down and back movement of the seat bones in each 'down', so the movement of their upper body becomes like a minute fold-down over a jump. This prevents the rider's shoulders from rocking backwards, and is the antithesis of 'polishing the saddle with your bottom' (which most of us learned in Pony Club). It is delightful to discover that by doing this you can control the horse with your body and not with your hand, and the biggest thrill of being causal is the knowledge that the horse is dancing to your tune, instead of you dancing to his.

- *How well do you plug in as you ride? Do you unplug by deliberately shoving your backside about in the saddle, or are you so wobbly that you cannot find enough muscle tone to hold yourself in place and control the duck-paddle movement?*
- *What shape is made by your thigh bones? Are they parallel, or a 'V'? Where is the point of the 'V', and how do you have to adjust your sitting to position this about 3 inches (75mm) behind your sacrum? How high up is it? The point should lie about half way up your sacrum*
- *As you attempt to 'lace up across your back' be careful that you do not 'pop up'. People who tend to pop up (tightening the muscles between their seat bones and the saddle) find this a difficult pattern to break. If necessary, seek help from the dismounted exercises on page 247.*
- *Are you in control of the horse's tempo as he walks? Do not be worried by the way the walk slows when you become causal, and do not immediately send the*

horse forward again. Whilst you may well need to use your leg, take your time, and be careful not to unplug yourself as you do so.

....

Very often, the rider who is learning to plug in and duck paddle also needs to relearn how to use her leg, so that nothing changes from the knee up as she does so. Experienced riders commonly unplug slightly as they use their legs, whilst novices do so in style, tipping forward and/or making a jerk with their backside. The rider may also disturb her thigh position by taking her knee off the saddle – perhaps moving it up as she moves her heel up, and/or bringing it out as she moves her toe out. Or she may squeeze the horse hard with her lower leg, in such a prolonged way that the muscles in her thigh and torso tighten as well. This becomes extremely effortful (as well as inefficient), and I often find myself asking the rider, 'If it takes you this much energy just to make him walk on, how are you ever going to ride a canter pirouette?'

How horses unplug their brains

The rider also needs to ensure that her leg aids retain their meaning. Experienced, professional riders know the importance of this, but many people use their legs repeatedly, *without expecting a response*, and remaining blissfully unaware of the fact that they are training the horse to be dead to their leg! For some, the response (if it ever came) would be frightening – so this arrangement suits them well, and they can convince all concerned that they 'are trying'.

Some authorities believe that the horse cannot distinguish between two stimuli which are given less than thirty seconds apart: but even if this is *not* true, when there is no penalty for ignoring the leg it easily becomes like background music to the horse, who 'switches off' to it. He stops noticing that rhythmic banging on his sides just as you soon stop noticing the soothing music played in a restaurant or supermarket.

To make the lower leg effective, it helps to think of using it as *prevention* (i.e. to stop the horse slowing down) rather than as *cure* (i.e. to make the horse go). This means that somehow, you have to wake the horse up so that he takes notice of you and knows you mean business. Metaphorically speaking, it is as if you get him out of bed. Then, if he threatens to crawl back under the covers you say 'Not with me you don't!' Then you leave him to go on – and the fact that you 'get off his case' becomes his reward for responding. But since the horse is not a perpetual-motion machine, he will not go on forever, and the moment his clockwork begins to wind down you need to be there again, reminding him that this is not acceptable behaviour.

This interaction is totally different from nagging the horse, as if you were saying to him 'You've got to get out of bed,' and he then replies 'I don't want to.' So you say 'You've got to …' – and so the argument goes on, with no resolution, and no real action from either party. To prevent this stalemate, I often suggest that the rider uses her leg *only* when she means it, and if she does not mean it, then she does not use it. She then demonstrates her resolve by imposing penalties (a stronger kick or her stick) on the horse who disregards her.

This may sound simple, but it requires the rider to be extremely strict with herself. The bottom line is that she needs to raise both her own and her horse's adrenalin levels, for they are both in need of a 'wake-up call'. But without this, it is as if the rider uses her leg, and receives in return a pre-recorded message, similar to the messages used on mobile telephone networks. On the horse's behalf, the message replies, 'The cell phone you are calling is switched off. Please try later.' If you were making a phone call, you would hang up in response to this: but the rider never actually hangs up, she just keeps on nagging, hearing the message again and again without taking it in and taking action. Or she may get one small stage closer to actual communication, receiving the message which accompanies the 'call waiting' system: 'Please hold the line, we are trying to connect you. The number you are calling knows you are waiting. Please hold the line, the number you are calling knows you are waiting ….'

The truth is that horses are unbelievably adept at 'doing their thing' whilst pretending to be doing your thing', and most of them do it in such a benign, genteel way that the rider never even realises! Donkeys and mules do not have the same capacity, and this makes them much less rider-friendly. Yet within their feigned co-operation, many horses have their riders sewn up. I often anthropomorphise wildly, and think of them chatting together in their stables at night, asking each other "What shall we do tomorrow? 'Let's go on a picnic,' says one. 'Great idea!' comes the reply, 'but what a drag … I shall have to take Ann.' 'And I shall have to take Judy,' says another. 'Well, never mind,' says a fourth, 'we'll have a good time anyway!' When you go on your ride, both they and you might well 'have a good time anyway'; but the danger of this is that the agreement could well break down – perhaps when you go to a show. The 'party' then becomes so exciting that 'doing their thing' no longer encompasses 'doing your thing'. In consequence, you might even bite the dust.

To use another analogy, riding the 'switched-off' horse is rather like sitting at the breakfast table with your husband, who is drinking coffee and reading the paper, engaged in his own little world. But you are attempting to have a conversation with him – and in response you receive the occasional 'Yes, dear,' 'Uh-huh', and 'Umm'. These half-hearted utterances are intended to keep you happy and throw you off the scent; yet you *know* he is not really listening. In some marriages, this pretence becomes a way of life and appears satisfactory to both parties – as it does in so many rider/horse relationships. Few couples have the integrity to confront each other when one of them stops listening, and to do so with good humour. (Yet the alternative can undoubtedly have its advantages, and you can even utilise the situation by adding 'And you don't mind, do you, dear, if I spend that extra money on a new saddle?')

The horse who is *doing his thing whilst pretending to be doing your thing* will usually have his ears pricked, for he is actually admiring the view, using his focused vision as he interacts not with you, but with the external world. Often he is like a tourist, out for a day's sight-seeing in which he will 'have a good time anyway'. Some see 'ghoolies' in every shadow, whilst others gaze into the distance with a far-away look on their face.

There are many ways in which horses can absent themselves from this game called riding, and some retreat not into the distance, but into themselves, putting layers of anaesthetic between themselves and the rider. (As one of my pupils once remarked, 'Thoroughbreds go ballistic, and warmbloods go autistic.') They then contribute as little effort as the rider will allow – working out your bottom line before you have even mounted. So a rider whose commitment level is a 3 out of 10 finds herself riding a horse who delivers only 3 out of 10. She becomes the victim of his seduction technique, for as he smooches around the school, it is as if he is saying 'I like my rider. She's my friend. We have such a nice time together doing 3 out of 10.' Yet a 10 out of 10 rider (who is willing to risk her popularity) may not even need to raise her stick before that same horse willingly delivers 10 out of 10!

Other horses treat riding as if it's all a dream – as if they are telling themselves 'Any moment now I'll wake up, and find that I'm in my stable eating my hay....' Some go one stage further, and are so 'spaced out' that 'all the lights are on but nobody's at home'. Sadly, this is so common that I have come to suspect that what I call the 'psychic escape route' is most horses' first response when they are dealing with either pain itself, the memory of pain, or a painfully inept rider. Riders who are desperate to get their horse onto the bit can do tremendous damage, forcing him so far down these escape routes that he becomes their 'sacrificial horse'. Their interaction – with its physical and its psychic contortions – becomes painful to watch, and difficult to unravel. (The remedy requires such self-discipline from the rider, and such a change in her map of what riding *is* that when it really comes to the crunch, few people are up to the challenge – even if they do find a teacher who is capable of catalysing the change.) One is then left hoping that the rider might learn enough from experience not to torture another horse in the same way.

For the horses, 'spacing out' is a way of not feeling themselves from the neck back, so before taking action which will bring them 'back on the planet' I like to satisfy myself that there is no obvious cause of pain.

Getting through to these horses may require not that you 'beat their brains *out*' but that you 'beat their brains *in*' – always remaining ethical, respectful, and sensitive to the hidden sensitivity which originally caused them to exit from the rider/horse relationship. Horses who 'space out' may need the most delicate version of 'beating their brains in', and instead of saying 'Hey, you, pay attention!', you may have to quietly say, 'Hello, it's me and it's OK; just listen for a moment.' You have to develop a very stoic, empathetic frame of mind, saying this over and over again, and knowing that if you are *too* strong you will pay the price of 'freaking the horse out' all over again.

However, horses with a 'tourist' mentality are a different kettle of fish, and are often such bossy, opinionated types, that riding them takes a more dynamic form of commitment. If the horse's commitment to looking at the view rates as an 8 out of 10, then you as rider need at least an 8 out of 10 commitment to getting his attention. You use this to make yourself more compelling to the horse than the outside world (and although you may well need your stick, you are wise to remember that your hands are off limits). This can be a very testing ride because of the mental toughness it requires – contrasting with the delicacy needed to bring the more sensitive and 'spaced-out' horse back to reality. This need to operate from different parts of your personality adds to the challenges of riding.

Please appreciate that none of these horses with their various escape routes are malicious or vindictive; they are simply taking the line of least resistance – whatever that may be for them. Thankfully for us, only a few horses cannot even bring themselves to 'go through the motions' of this game called riding. Those who openly react against it may well have an inherited unwillingness to play, and may also be the 'walking wounded', who are suffering the pain of undiagnosed physical problems, and whose reluctance to work has been exacerbated by riders who have pushed them beyond their physical or emotional limits. Sometimes the scars are irreparable – but the options offered by skilled riding, along with orthodox and/or complementary medicine at least mean that 'bute it or shoot it' is no longer the bottom line.

The ideal, of course, is to make riding an experience in which the horse does not need these psychic defences, and as with handling from the ground, his ears are a big key to his mental state. The horse who is engrossed in his work usually has his ears out sideways, whilst the unhappy horse lays them back, and the distracted horse keeps them pricked. So, as a minimum response to the use of your legs, which says 'Hello, pay attention!', they must come out sideways – at least for a moment. During that time the horse is using his peripheral vision, paying attention *internally*, and focussing on you and on his body. He becomes present, instead of 'absent' – and I often insist that the horse is allowed to prick his ears and absent himself from interacting with you only for one second at a time. Whilst mature horses seem able to prick their ears without 'tuning you out' (and are often seen in competition going well, and with their ears pricked) young horses are not so flexible, and I often think that the old adage 'no foot, no horse' should be rewritten 'no ears, no horse'.

I was reminded of this in a very amusing way one day when I was working abroad, and my clinic organiser announced at the end of the day that we had to run an errand on the way home.

'But didn't you ask your husband to do that?', I asked her, recalling a conversation I had overheard in the morning.

'Well, yes, I did,' she said, 'but he didn't have his ears out sideways at the time!'

But whilst she had been fully aware of their interaction, *the rider who repeatedly nags the horse (and who settles for his version of 'absent') is usually just as 'switched off' as he is.* She is giving her aids on 'autopilot'; but somehow she maintains the expectation that her horse should be 'switched on' enough to respond to her. (This has to be some of the most back-to-front thinking I have ever encountered!) So the bottom line is that the *rider* has to become present, committed, and unwilling to 'go through the motions' – for only then can she demand the same of her horse.

This, however, is not so easy as it sounds, and humans as well as horses 'space out'. One of my colleagues, whose concentration has earned her a tremendous reputation in the roles of competitor, trainer and judge, told me about a lesson in which her pupil made a rather characteristic mess-up. In response, my friend asked, 'What happened?'

'I left,' came the reply.

My colleague is rarely stumped for words, but it took her a few moments to think of her next question, which was 'Do you leave often?'

'Yes,' was the reply.

'Do you know how to get back?' asked my friend, and when her pupil again said 'Yes,' she said, 'Then get yourself back here!'

My colleague left the lesson muttering to herself about the strangeness of people, but finally understanding something of how this particular pupil repeatedly got herself into such messes. But the postscript to the story is her own recognition that 'I was riding a very young horse a few days later and he made a bucking match out of a canter transition, and I realised that I left too, just for a few moments ... and I can still hardly believe it!'

So none of us are 'space-out' proof. Concentration is undoubtedly the master art, and it proves an enormous boon whenever you are learning anything. Paying attention when you ride is rather like listening to a piece of music – you don't check in now and again. Instead you listen to the piece in its entirety. Once you and your horse are both engrossed in the same piece of music, magic can happen.

- *How do the horses you ride absent themselves from interacting with you? What do you do about it? Are you tempted to nag with your lower leg, and to accept a non-response? Or do you insist that both of you remain present and committed?*
- *How often do you 'space out' and how well can you pay attention moment by moment?*
- *How would you rate your own commitment level out of 10? (If you are unsure, think about the minimum level of commitment that you are willing to accept from your horse.) Does a friend who knows your riding agree with your assessment?*
- *When you use your legs do you actually mean it? Or are you just passing the time of day?*
- *When you are working your horse, how much of the time does he have his ears out sideways?*
- *Some horses genuinely are more forward-going, more sensitive and more committed than others, and this makes them easier to ride. Only by riding a lot of horses can you appreciate these differences, and understand the particular challenges set by your own horse. Ask a professional for her assessment of him.*

....

Using and stabilising the leg

Once the rider realises how important it is to keep herself and her horse awake and interacting, she has to address the technical aspects of *how she uses her leg*. It is most often used as a series of nudges, or as a prolonged squeeze, and in neither case does it do its job well. It needs to be used as a quick touch, becoming a hard slap if necessary. This means that it makes contact with the horse's side, and immediately releases. Only then can the lower leg be used independently of the rest of the body, leaving the rider free to get on with the business of riding. However, the tonal quality of the leg is also extremely important, for if it is soggy (like limp lettuce) even a biomechanically correct kick will have little effect.

The leg becomes effective when it too has the solidity and stability which bearing down gives to the upper body. So if Superman used his legs, the horse would listen (and you might well hear a resounding thud!). When Clark Kent used his legs not much would happen – and he would probably move his leg back to use it, raising his heel, and turning out his toe. His contortions are an attempt to get more strength – but they make his leg even weaker. Ideally, the rider's lower leg acts like a wooden boot-tree inside her boot, functioning as one unit, and as if she had no ankle joint. It slaps inwards (rather than backwards), and without distortion.

The 'Superman effect' is gained by *pitting opposing muscle groups against each other.* The muscles then work *isometrically*, functioning as if they were pitted against a resistance they cannot move. So attempting to push, say, a large wardrobe would require an isometric use of your muscles, through which they *contract* but do not *shorten*. However, this is not how we commonly use muscles, for to produce movement we contract them *isotonically,* causing them to shorten.

To gain a practical understanding of the difference, sit by a table and put your wrist beneath its top, as if you were holding the reins. Then push up against the table. This is an isometric use of the arm muscles. If you then move your wrist away from the table, you can raise it towards your upper arm by using an isotonic contraction. Only if you have a particular interest in the physiology of riding will you need to explore this difference further; but realise that if you do *not* understand it well (and very few people do), you are not in a position to pass judgement on its relevance to riding (as so many people have).

One of the best ways to learn how to contract your riding muscles isometrically – and to appreciate the benefits of doing so – is to sit on your horse (correctly aligned), and to let someone provide the following resistances. (These are similar to the tendon exercises on page 255, which you can do sitting in your chair.)

Firstly, your partner pushes *down* on your knee whilst you try to lift it *up*. If you then place your fingers in the crease between the front of your thigh and your torso, you should feel a tendon which sticks up and feels like a taut piece of rope. I call this the front tendon; it attaches the large quadriceps muscle at the front of your thigh into your pelvis. (As you do this be sure that you do not 'pop up', activating the muscles beneath your seat bones and putting a thick layer of flesh between them and the saddle.)

Next, your partner places her hand on your lower thigh just behind your knee, and whilst she pushes up, you push down. You must be extremely careful that you do *not* lift or move your backside in response to her challenge, and if you do not, she should feel the tendons behind your knee become taut and stick out. The muscles of the top of the thigh (the quadriceps) are now pitted against the muscles of the back of the thigh (the hamstrings); both have increased their tone without any movement occurring.

Next, your partner tries to pull your knee away from the saddle whilst you try to hold it on. Then you reverse directions, and she pushes it onto the saddle whilst you try to draw it away. 'Try' is one of my least favourite words, since the idea that 'if at first you don't succeed, try, try again' is really a suggestion that you should continue to bash your head harder against the same brick wall. It would be better to realise that your lack of success is feedback that your technique is ineffective, and that it might be wiser to do your task in a different way. But 'try' is absolutely appropriate here, for the whole point of the exercise is that neither of you will succeed in moving your knee.

The muscles of the inner thigh (the adductors) are pitted against the muscles of the outer thigh (the abductors). The muscle groups of the calf work in a similar way, and to stabilise your calf, your partner again exerts four pushes: forward on your heel, back on your toes, and towards and away from the horse's belly. Again, neither of you should succeed in moving your foot. As a minimum response to this exercise, you should feel that you gain much greater control of your leg, bringing your texture much closer to putty or wet dish towels. This amount of muscle work would obviously would not be Clark Kent's forte; but Superman (along with the small proportion of riders who are 'talented') could do it with consummate ease. If you now use your leg to slap the horse's side, you will find that it has much more 'clout'.

However, every day riders are repeatedly told to 'relax your legs'. There are, I believe, two reasons for this. Firstly, the highly skilled rider has such high tone, and is so familiar with this muscle use, that she feels as if she is doing nothing – and even if she *does* feel that she is doing 'something', she is unlikely to feel strongly enough about it to go against the established grain. Secondly, there is an inherent imbalance between the muscles of the inner and the outer thigh. *Eleven* muscles have the action of pulling the thighs in; *two* have the action of pulling them apart – and they are relatively weak, cramping very easily if you hold your legs out away from the saddle. Few riders balance the use of these muscle groups well, and 'relax your legs' or even 'relax your thigh and take your knee off the saddle' are possible (but not entirely appropriate) responses to this imbalance.

I will always maintain that before you learn to use the muscles of the outer thigh, you firstly have to learn to use the muscles of the inner thigh – and that this is not the same as gripping (or pinching) with your knees. For it gives you the appropriate 'V' shape to your thighs, and a constant contact (see Fig. 3.1 on page 67), extending from the tendons at each end of the pubic bone (where the adductor muscles insert into it) down to the knee. Used correctly neither muscle group moves your knee.

One of my pupils came away from her first clinic with me rather bemused by this discrepancy between my teaching and that of a trainer who has always insisted on relaxation. So she went to visit him, and after watching him ride for a while she sheepishly asked if she could touch his thigh. When he agreed, she placed her hand behind it and discovered that it was impossible to slip her fingers between it and the saddle! Although horrified by the difference between what he was actually doing, and what she had tried to do in response to his words, she decided to keep her thoughts to herself, and she left quietly.

One of my fellow teachers took this exploration one stage further during a lesson from a very talented young rider who had trained at the Spanish Riding School. He rode her horse to improve the extensions, and afterwards she asked him, 'So you've been telling me to relax my legs. Are yours relaxed?'

'Yes,' he said.

Having educated her 'eye' through training extensively with me, she was suspicious of this response; so when he brought her horse to halt, she requested permission to put her fingers between his thigh and the saddle, this time from the front.

'Show me how your legs would hang normally,' she said – and the pressure was enough to squash her fingers significantly!

Not yet satisfied, she added, 'Now show me what you would do in extended trot.'

She prepared herself for the onslaught, which did indeed happen, and when she finally extracted her hand, it was squashed and white. This did not shock her; but it obviously shocked him – for he failed to show up for her next lesson, and every time she attempted to arrange another, he was miraculously unavailable!

However profound the use of his inner thigh muscles, it would undoubtedly have been balanced by use of the muscles of his *outer* thigh. Riders who are weak here usually have very wobbly lower legs (running out of 'stuffing' at or below their knees), for it is a sense of connectedness down the *outside* of the thigh and calf which gives 'wet-towel' stability all the way down to the foot. You can help yourself achieve this by pushing your heel out as if against a resistance and activating your thigh muscles as if you intended to take your knee off the saddle. (The 'pain exercise' on page 67 shows this dynamic off the horse, coupling it with the correct 'V' shape of the thighs.)

This use of the muscle chain which I call externals is not easy to do – and for the vast majority of riders, it is the end point of a learning process which begins by activating the muscles of the inner thigh. Yet I am convinced that this connection down the outside of the thigh and calf is the result that the good riders of antiquity wanted from their pupils when they told them to 'stretch your legs down'. It feels like a stretch (yet is so different from the interpretation of 'stretch your legs down' in which you straighten your joints and push harder into the stirrups). It also yields tremendous stability, as well as the look that I and my colleagues call 'German dressage leg'. So here we arrive at a very different understanding of words whose familiarity has made them legendary, and whose misinterpretation is responsible for so many riders' problems.

• *How far down each of your legs do you feel solid and in control? To put it another way, if you were a stuffed-toy rider, how far down each leg would the stuffing go? You are likely to find that this is different on each side.*

- *To ask the same question in a different way, if you think of your thigh bones within your thigh, do they have the strength and stability of iron bars? Is one more iron-bar-like than the other, and where are the 'mushiest' places?*
- *If you cannot get the stuffing or the iron bars to go as far as your knees, you will have problems with your line-up and your balance. Once they go part way down your lower legs you will cope better, but there is no substitute for feeling that you are firm and solid right down to your feet.*
- *When a friend gives you the challenges listed above, how much difference does this make to your sense of solidity? Which ones do you find hardest to respond to?*
- *Can you use your leg without raising your heel or turning out your toe? Do you use it inwards, or backwards? Does it make contact with the horse through a slap, a squeeze, or a nudge? When you begin to make slaps in an inward direction, be prepared for the response! It is then imperative that you 'go with' your horse.*

....

Rising-trot mechanism

In these last sections we brought the rider back to walk and even to halt, using exercises and demonstrations which give her a practical understanding of the biomechanics of riding. However, our last chapter ended by explaining the need for the rider to match the thrust of the horse's hind leg within each step that he takes. Walk minimises the challenge of this, and in trot, it is easiest to learn when rising, for the rider actively makes that thrust by swinging her pelvis over the pommel of the saddle. In fact, rising trot is such an important learning tool that I rarely let people sit until they have mastered it. This once led one of my pupils to complain that she was suffering from 'terminal rising trot'!

In a biomechanically correct rising-trot mechanism, the knee is the centre point of a circle, the thigh is the radius of that circle, and the bony knobble at the top of the thigh (the greater trochanter of the femur) moves on an arc of the circle. The knee cap rotates to point down towards the ground as the thigh moves over it: the lower leg remains still throughout the movement, with the foot barely changing its pressure into the stirrup. The rider could, in fact, be amputated from just below the knee and still perform the movement well – for it is like kneeling on the ground, and raising your backside up off your heels. Rising trot, however, involves small changes to the angle of the upper body: it is inclined slightly forward in the sit, and becomes almost vertical in the rise. This means that the pelvis moves far more than the shoulders (see Fig. 3.2).

Although it is very common for riders to push their feet forward as they rise, the rider can only remain in balance throughout the movement when her feet stay back underneath her. Each swing forward of her pelvis

Fig. 3.2 The biomechanics of a correct rise.

then brings her body to the balance point, where she can remain in place (for as long as she likes) without falling backwards. Pushing the foot forward makes this impossible, for she cannot then swing her pelvis over it.

Most riders are taught to minimise the rise and keep it 'tidy'; so when they first learn to hold their feet back under them, they are shocked by just how far out of the saddle this balance point is. Yet Kyra Kyrklund and Reiner Klimke both show exemplary rising-trot mechanisms in their training videotapes, where the pelvis makes a big sweep forward, and the thrust they make matches the thrust of the horse's hind leg. In fact, they use the thrust forward of their pelvis to *control* the thrust of the horse's hind leg, and thrusting a little more (whilst bearing down a little more) would put him into extension – with minimal use of the leg.

In contrast, using the leg whilst *not* thrusting more would be ineffectual on a lazy horse, and inappropriate on a 'bomby' one, for reasons I will delineate more clearly in the Chapter 4. Suffice it now to say that when your thrust forward does not match the thrust of the horse's hind leg, your centre of gravity fails to reach the balance point at the top each the rise, and by falling behind the horse you become a 'water-skier'. Whilst the lazy horse will give up in despair at this overloading of his hindquarters, the 'bomby' horse will seize the opportunity to whizz out from underneath you and to tow you along. He becomes a motorboat, providing the appropriate counter-balance. Then, however much you may want him to slow down, he will not do so until *you* adjust your balance, catching up with him, matching his thrust, and refusing to water-ski.

The correct way of levering the torso out of the saddle places tremendous strain on the muscles in the thigh, and typically, riders use one of two strategies to avoid this. Some attempt to haul themselves up from their shoulders, chest and abdomen. Each rise then lengthens the front of the body and hollows the back, pulling the rider's stomach in and stopping her from bearing down.

It recently took me two full lessons to change this pattern in a rider who did it in style, even though she had worked previously with several of my colleagues. In fact, her first encounter with my work had been at an adult riding camp, where the teachers have very little time to influence a large number of pupils. When my colleague was unable to make any in-roads into the pattern during the first class lesson, she came to the afternoon's private lesson armed with a role of strong adhesive tape. (This encounter took place in a part of the world where 'anything goes', and was a very un-British solution to the problem!) She asked the rider to wrap the tape around the centre of her bra, passing it down her front, beneath her clothing, and attaching it to an unmentionable part of her anatomy which would hurt a lot when pulled!

Amazingly, even this did not work – although it was enough for the rider to say, 'Ouch! ... I think I get what you mean.' But the pattern was so entrenched that even though her mind understood, her body did not. (What worked in the end was my suggestion that she should tilt her pelvis, keeping her coccyx *down* and her pubic bone *up*.) However, I have subsequently found that the threat of the 'adhesive-tape cure' (which I myself would never actually use) has always worked extremely well! Interestingly, the rider who lengthens her front in the rise finds it hard to clear the pommel of the saddle (with inevitable unpleasant consequences), for even though her pelvis moves *up*, the lengthening of her front drops her pubic bone *down*.

Despite this disadvantage, you can demonstrate how effectively the strategy spares your thighs by kneeling with your backside on your heels,

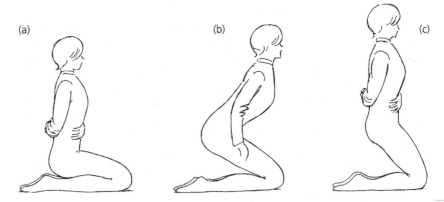

Fig. 3.3 Kneeling up and down. From starting postition (a) you can either lengthen your front, as in (b), which hollows your back and takes all the strain off your thighs, or you can lever yourself up, as in (c), with no change in your torso. The person in (c) would land back in the saddle with her coccyx lower and her public bone higher than the person in (b).

and then raising yourself up by lifting first your chin and then your chest. Notice how this lengthens your front whilst hollowing your back. Contrast it with levering yourself up from your thighs with no movement in your upper body – and to check that you do not cheat, place your hands on your belly button and the small of your back (see Fig. 3.3). This exercise requires so much effort that people rarely want to do more than a few repetitions! It is in fact more taxing than rising trot, in which the horse assists you by 'kicking you up the backside' in each step, and where the change in angle of your upper of body makes it easier. But if you cannot do this exercise kneeling on the floor (or cannot demonstrate a good rising-trot mechanism whilst your horse is standing still) you will be in big trouble when riding trot itself.

A larger proportion of riders avoid levering themselves up off their thighs by pushing themselves up off their stirrups. So each rise pushes the heel down and forward, and straightens the knee. When the rider has her foot this far forward, the rising action is like heaving herself out of an armchair, and then collapsing back into it – and this, of course, makes it tempting to use the reins for assistance. Lazy and run-away horses respond to the rider being 'behind' them in just the same way we noted above; so bringing the rider into balance slows the run-away horse (providing some of the most dramatic changes in a rider/horse interaction that I have ever witnessed), and energises the lazy horse.

To understand the change that occurs to the lazy horse, think of the rider who is behind the correct balance point (in the armchair seat), and who thuds down into the saddle on each landing, squeezing hard with her seat and leg. She expects her horse to go forward in response. But rising trot is rather like bouncing on a trampoline, which provides a rhythmic impulse not dissimilar to the impulse of the horse's hind legs. But if you land on the trampoline and attempt to exert a prolonged pressure on it, what happens? Most people immediately recognise that you deaden its bounce ... and of course, you do just the same to your horse. So the method by which you are attempting to make him *go* actually makes him *stop*. We noted earlier that horse and rider commonly mirror each other's tonal quality, and in this example, they can wind each other into seize-up! Whilst considering rising trot makes the trampoline mechanism easy to understand, the same mechanism generates seize-up equally well at walk, sitting trot, and canter.

The pay-offs for the rider in mastering the rising-trot mechanism are huge. She is bearing down, thrusting forward, and matching the propulsive force of the horse's hind leg. She has control of her alignment and her body weight, so she becomes a minimal encumbrance to him, thus minimising the evasions through which he initially responded to her imbalance. She can then gain control of his tempo – not by rising slower (which tends to make the rise go soggy, thus reducing its thrust) but by *pausing* as she lands in the saddle. She is then controlling the horse with her body, and not with her hand; for she is like a metronome which goes 1-2-1-2-1-2 in a pre-set, unalterable tempo, giving him no choice but to match that tempo. However fast his brain might *like* him to go, the speed of his legs is determined by the rider. She is 'taking him', instead of him 'taking her'.

This difference mirrors the difference between pushing round the pedals of a bicycle, and then discovering – as the bicycle goes down hill – that you can no longer pedal fast enough to keep up! But once you are in charge of the speed at which the legs (or wheels) go around, you can even use the rising-trot mechanism to change the horse's carriage, bringing his back up underneath you – and then you know you are *really* riding.

- *In rising trot, does your thrust forward reach the point where you can balance over your feet? Test this by staying out of the saddle for several beats before you sit again. To do this well, you need to begin with your heel beneath your hip, being sure that you do not move your foot forward as you rise.*
  If you are used to pushing your heel down and forward, you may only be able to hold your leg in the right place by feeling that it is exaggeratedly back and up. If you are struggling, practise balancing at the top of the rise whilst the horse is standing still.
- *How much does the pressure in your stirrups increase as you rise?*
  Minimise the initial pressure, and then minimise this increase, putting the weight that was in your feet into your thighs. (You should not have more than about 10–14lbs (4.5–6kg) weight in your stirrups. This makes many people feel as if they are gripping. If necessary, practise the rising-trot mechanism at a standstill, and without your stirrups, and think about the knee pointing downwards.
- *Does your front lengthen as you rise? Be sure you do not allow it to, and be prepared to take yet more strain on your thigh muscles as you change this.*
  If you are really struggling, it may be that you need to build these muscles. Practise kneeling up and down without letting your front lengthen, and realise that riding well takes far more muscle-power than treating the horse like an armchair!
- *Are you still bearing down throughout the movement?*
- *Can you control the horse's tempo? If you cannot make pauses because the horse catapults you out of the saddle the moment you land in it, you almost certainly have a hollow back.*
- *What direction are your seat bones pointing in as you land?*
- *Can you change this, and make them point down?*
- *How much control do you have of the landing? How many times out of ten can you land in the same place?*

Let us now return to sitting trot, in which it is more difficult to match the thrust of the horse's hind leg. Earlier on, we simplified our discussion by thinking separately about the forces acting in the back/front plane, and those acting in the up/down plane. We must now return to the up/down plane. On the 'up' phase of the stride, rider and horse are usually well in sync; but then, as the horse reaches the top of his arc and begins to drop down, the rider usually keeps on going up! Sometimes she actually leaves the saddle, and sometimes the flesh underneath her backside is so spongy that it expands on the way up, and is compressed on the way down, giving her seat bones much more up-and-down movement than the saddle.

This is especially true of women, who are naturally lower toned and much 'spongier' than men. However, photography which uses 250 frames/second reveals that even exceptionally good riders (who would swear that they do not bump) actually leave the saddle, invisible though this is to the naked eye. All riders need to minimise this discrepancy; for by the time the rider has landed on the saddle, the horse is already on the next 'up' phase, and they are in sync again only until he next reaches the top of his arc. (See Fig. 3.4.)

To sit well, the rider firstly has to let the horse come 'up' underneath her, for if she tries to force herself *down* into the saddle at this point in time her 'down' interferes with his 'up'. When these are in opposition to each other in trot she has a very hard time sitting. In canter, the rider who is desperately trying to sit *down* can drastically limit the period of suspension which marks the horse's *up*. Having 'up' and 'down' out of sync is horribly incapacitating for both parties, and the secret of success lies in turning 'up' into 'down' at just the right moment. At the top of the horse's

The mechanism of sitting

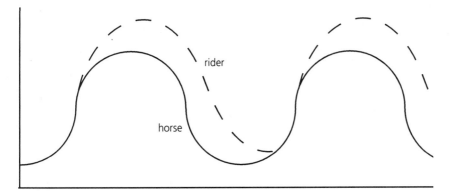

Fig. 3.4 The up-and-down movement of the rider compared to the up-and-down movement of the saddle: slow motion photography shows that the rider always comes down a little late; but there is a lot to be gained by turning 'up' into 'down' as soon as possible after the saddle reaches the top of its arc, and getting your backside in the saddle as the horse's hind leg is on the ground.

arc the rider literally has to *pull* herself down into the saddle – for if she relies on gravity alone she will come down too late.

One of my most effective ways of helping riders with this (assuming that they can already bear down, maintain their alignment, and not actually bump backwards) is to say, 'Think of your body having the shape of a cardboard box, with the two vertical back edges running from your armpits to the back corners of your backside. Then imagine that the buttock muscles which form the back corners of your backside are like two big car suspension springs. In each "down" beat, think of pushing down onto those springs; for if you do not push them down, they will "boing" you up.' (See Fig. 3.5.)

'Pushing down on the springs' also gives you a connection to the springs of the horse's hind legs, encouraging his joints to close whilst his foot is on the ground. When you push his springs *down* on each down beat, you enhance both his gaits and your sitting (as long as you do not break up the passage of the impulse of the hind leg as it passes forward over his back); but if his springs push you 'up' on each down beat you now have two sets of springs both 'boinging' you up!

Riders are often 'boinged' up in rising trot too, especially when their flexor muscles (at the front of the torso and thigh) dominate over the extensor muscles (at the back of the torso and thigh). This means that the weaker, longer muscles at the back of the body are no match for the stronger, shorter muscles at the front. So despite their best intentions these riders have a tendency to fold forward, closing the angle at the hip joint. Attempting to lengthen the shortened muscles and open this angle always has limited success, and it is far more helpful to think of 'pushing down the springs at the back', since this *shortens the longer muscles* and builds their strength.

In the *'Masterclass'* book, I explained the phenomenon of muscle imbalance by likening opposing pairs of muscles to the springs in one of those restaurant doors which can swing both ways. This makes it clear that

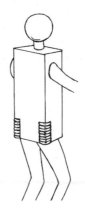

Fig. 3.5 Thinking of your torso as if it is a cardboard box, and pushing down the springs at the back.

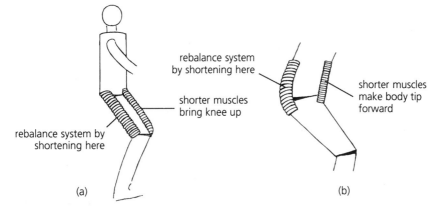

Fig. 3.6 Comparing the muscles to the springs on a restaurant swing door. In (a) the torso is the post, and the thigh is the door. Lengthening the shortened muscle at the front will have limited success; we also need to shorten the muscles at the back. In (b), where the thigh is the post and the torso is the door, the same is true.

we can only bring the system into balance by shortening the longer spring, and cannot fix it solely by lengthening the shorter spring – for it will always contract again to take up the slack. In '*Masterclass*' I used this image to refer to imbalance in the muscles at the front and the back of the thigh, which commonly causes the knee to come up. So we would then think of the thigh as the door, and the torso as its post. (See Fig. 3.6a.) If we reverse this, thinking of the upper body as the door and the thigh as the post, we have the situation I am describing here. (See Fig. 3.6b.) (In reality, though, muscle imbalance in the torso will almost certainly be accompanied by muscle imbalance in the thigh, so both versions are needed – firstly stabilising the knee by shortening the muscles at the back of the thigh, and secondly shortening the muscles at the back of the torso to hold the rider vertical and enhance her sitting).

A somewhat different perspective gives us an even better description of the rider's shock-absorbing mechanism. Many riders 'give' in the middle of the back in sitting trot. In hollow-backed riders it gives forward in every stride, whilst in round-backed riders it gives backwards. Some people even manage to hollow their back on the 'up', and round it on the 'down'! (The discussion of 'neutral spine' on page 246 gives more information about the dangers of this. Also, the 'Rider's Guide to Body Awareness' videotape gives a clear visual understanding of correct and incorrect sitting.) I spent many years cultivating my 'wiggle in the middle', yet top-class riders do not do this. Their give is in the hip joints, and the 'down, down, down' of pushing down on the springs stabilises the middle of their back.

I sometimes put a weightlifter's belt on riders who are having trouble

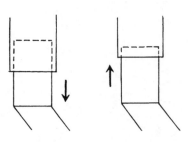

Fig. 3.7 Thinking of the torso like two cylinders, and allowing the top one to slide down over the bottom one on every down beat. This limits the deviation of the lumbar spine, which leads to a hollow or a rounded back on every down beat.

stabilising the middle of their torso, for this holds them so firmly in place that it limits the movement possible. I also suggest that they think of their torso like two cylinders. On each down beat, the top one – which ends at their lower ribs – slides down over the inner one which comes up slightly higher. This mechanism limits the rider to a strictly up-and-down movement, prohibiting any deviation which would make her hollow or round her back. (See Fig. 3.7.)

To understand more about how and where the give in the body *does* happen, think of the vertical back edges of the box as one line (passing down to and also including the gluteal muscles, so that it ends near the back corners of the backside). The top of the thigh (the quadriceps muscle) then becomes another line, and we can think of them being joined by a diagonal line running down and back from the point of the hip. (This is the muscle *tensor fasciae latae*, which joins the gluteal muscle. Both then form a fibrous band which passes down the outside of the thigh. This is activated when you do the 'pain exercise' (see page 67) and think of pushing your thighs out against a resistance.) (See Fig. 3.8a, and Fig. 3.1 on page 67). The lines give us a shape rather like a 'Z' laid on its side, and on each 'down' beat the 'Z' deepens and its angles close. We could make a very simple model of this by taping together three pieces of

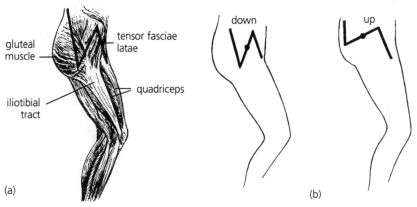

Fig. 3.8 (a) The anatomy of the 'Z'; (b) the 'Z' on the 'down' beat and on the 'up' beat; (c) the 'Z' in the rider with ideal conformation, i.e. a deep pelvis and a short spine, and the 'Z' in the rider with the more difficult conformation of a shallow pelvis and a long spine; (d) the

doweling, and it gives us a good understanding of how the hip joint works.

Do not let this anatomical description frighten you – there are simple exercises which help you find and isolate these muscles on page 255. For now it is enough to understand the theory: that whilst on every 'down' beat the back corners of your backside are moving 'down, down, down', those front tendons are moving 'up, up, up' (Fig. 3.8b). Block this action, and you are in trouble. Learn to use it well, and you have the structure of the half-halt: an extra big 'Z' on the 'down' beat, which puts the back corners of the backside maximally down, and the front tendons maximally up. This pushes down the horse's springs and keeps his hind legs on the ground for longer. Whilst the rider might also simultaneously close her hand and use her leg, note that the half-halt has nothing to do with leaning back, or pulling on the reins. Also note that it is a momentary holding on one 'down' beat (which may then need to be repeated). It is not a prolonged pitting of man-against-horse.

This shock–absorbing mechanism is at its most efficient when there is a large vertical distance between the front tendons and the back corners of the backside. Thus a conformation with a very deep pelvis (and ideally a short spine above it) is very helpful, and German rider Klaus Balkenhol exemplifies this. It is the direct opposite of the most difficult conformation, which is a shallow pelvis with a very long, unstable spine stacked up above it (Fig. 3.8c). But even this can be made to work well, until the rider hollows her back (Fig. 3.8d).

If you do this whilst sitting in your chair, you will realise that it brings the back corners of your backside up, whilst dropping your front tendons down. With no vertical distance between the two, the upthrust and the downthrust collide, and the 'Z's can no longer perform their function.

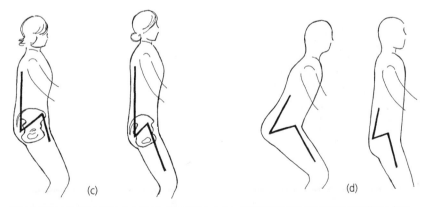

(c)   (d)

'Z' is distorted, and loses its shock-absorbing properties when the rider either hollows her back, or grows up tall and stretches her leg down (as so many people do in a downward transition).

Hence a hollow back reduces shock absorption. Think, too, of the rider who makes a downward transition by pulling the rib cage up to make herself taller, whilst at the same time pushing down into the stirrup. She opens the 'Z' angles and blocks the horse's impulse, making the transition a pull-and-pray affair. The rider who misinterprets the words 'grow up tall' and 'stretch your leg down' holds that state permanently. It is the antithesis of good riding. (See Fig. 3.8d.)

In contrast, 'pushing down the springs at the back' and maintaining the 'Z' angles can make a tremendous difference to both rider and horse throughout trot, canter, transitions, and half-halts. The rider can also help herself to come down into the saddle earlier by eradicating any tension around the knee or any excess push down into the stirrups, for these stop her joints from closing, and effectively they hold her 'up'. One of the primary differences between dressage and event riders is that whilst event riders just cruise along, dressage riders emphasise the 'down, down, down' of each step, encouraging the horse to bend the joints of his hind legs – which keeps them on the ground for longer and encourages him to 'sit down' into collection.

When the rider emphasises the 'down', the change she makes is much more far-reaching than just eradicating her 'spongy' backside. It is particularly helpful on warmblood horses with naturally slow tempos, who tend to dwell (or 'balance drop' to translate directly from the German), giving the trot a passage-like quality. For on them – unlike on Thoroughbreds – you need to *quicken* the tempo. But on any horse, coming down fast enough to keep you as in sync with him as possible *automatically* helps to engage his hind legs where kicking and beating would inevitably fail. There is a lot to be said for having your backside *in the saddle* when his hind legs are on the ground! *

- *How effectively can you sit in trot and canter?*
- *Is there movement in the middle of your spine, and if so, do you become round-backed or hollow-backed? Where do your seat bones point?*
- *Are you 'boinged' up? Does your backside actually leave the saddle, or are you suffering from the 'spongy buttock syndrome'? Begin by paying attention to your alignment, being sure that your seat bones point down, and that your feet rest lightly in the stirrups. If you are hollow-backed, and if you push down into your stirrups, you are doomed to bump.*
- *Before you think about synchronising 'up' and 'down' and 'pushing down the springs at the back', be sure that you can match the horse's power on the back/front plane: that you can bear down strongly and begin that bear down in*

---

* *I am indebted to my colleague the American Olympic rider and trainer Alexsandra Howard, who developed this concept further than I had done.*

your back, keeping your 'plunger' down and your 'leaks' closed. Work with the Rider's Belt (see page 62) if necessary.

- *The series of exercises which begin on page 247 show you how to get a 'square bum' and will help you to 'push down the springs' more effectively.*

- *Remember that it is important to attain a correct rising-trot mechanism before you begin work on your sitting, and that there is no point in attempting to ride sitting trot on the hollow-backed horse.*

....

Our commonly used phrases like 'relax', 'use your seat', 'use your leg', 'use your back', 'sit deep', 'drive him forward', and 'follow the movement' attempt to map and talk about some of the most important variables in riding. But they are open to so many interpretations that obeying them takes riders to some very strange places on the map! The Great Masters, I am sure, never intended them to go there – but without clearer explanations it is easy to get lost. Many people who shove their seat backwards and forwards in the saddle claim that they are 'using' it; and others who press down really hard claim that they are 'driving'. But as we have seen, they are actually creating tremendous problems, forcing their horses into evasive patterns which they then attempt to cure through other, equally dubious, means.

A resumé

Thus far, we have reviewed the concepts of alignment and tone, and of plugging in and bearing down, beginning to get an idea of the forces that the rider must generate within her body if she is to sit well and look (paradoxically) as if she is doing nothing. I meet a fair number of riders who have worked on their own with my ideas, and have done a creditable job of lining up their body, supporting their own body weight, and sometimes of plugging in and learning how to use their leg. But few of them have taken the next step of generating power within that alignment. This does not surprise me, for it is gargantuan task, which will tax their willingness to feel weird, and their capacity for hard work.

When we watch the highly skilled rider apparently 'doing nothing' we are witnessing one of the greatest optical illusions of all time, and it leads many riders – like Sarah (who you met on page 59) – to misunderstand the task they have set themselves. The difficulties of staying 'with' the horse would be almost completely eradicated if we all took to riding toy horses who were towed along on roller skates. But this might not satisfy our needs for a meaningful partnership!

CHAPTER FOUR
Interactive Riding

Bringing 'up' and 'down' into balance

THE QUESTION WHICH ALL RIDERS want answered – and one of the most critical parts of this map – is: 'How, exactly, does a rider change the horse's carriage, and bring his back up underneath her?'

I have a number of ways of thinking about this (all explained in more detail in *Ride With Your Mind/The Natural Rider* and '*Masterclass*') but I gained a rather different perspective on it one day when a spectator came into the riding school half way through my explanation of 'pushing down the plunger'. (I was using the analogy to the cafétière coffee maker which is explained on page 52.) She later confessed that she thought I had been talking about a sink plunger! My initial amusement subsided when I realised that the analogy might have some value; for just placing the plunger over the plug hole achieves nothing, just as placing the rider on the saddle achieves nothing (except, perhaps, from squashing the horse in the middle). This means that wondering why you cannot draw the horse's back up just by sitting on it is rather like wondering why the sink plunger does not work when you simply put it over the plug hole!

One part of the dressage rider's skill is to stay in sync with her horse on the up/down plane, so that she does not fly off the top of his 'up' (as shown in Fig. 3.4). Alongside this she also acts like the sink plunger. But the major difference between her and the plunger is that *she both pushes down and draws up constantly and simultaneously*. It is isometric muscle use which gives her this ability, and it is the primary lifting mechanism when the rider influences the horse's back in walk (with its negligible up and down). Trot and canter can utilise both mechanisms, giving the rider a dual-action which surpasses that of the sink plunger! It enables her both to feel sucked onto the horse, and to suck the horse's back up under her.

At one end of the spectrum, millions of riders never create the upward force of suction; so they do nothing to counterbalance the downward force of their weight. At the other end, I have taught only a few people who had read my first book, taken its message to heart, and decided that they must – at all costs – keep their weight out of the horse's 'mantrap'. (This is my name for the part of the horse's back which lies under the top of your thigh and your backside, and which so easily becomes a hollow.) Their backsides were barely touching the saddle, and as soon as I asked them to bring their weight more onto the horse's back and make the 'down' part of the sink-plunger mechanism, they panicked. For it seemed as if I was making them do the opposite of everything they had read in the book! It took some hard work on my part to convince them they needed to *make contact* with the horse's back before they could indeed draw it up.

Given our concerns about squashing the horse in the middle, it seems paradoxical that the rider – like the sink plunger – has to push down before she can generate suction. To the downward force of gravity, she adds the muscle use which keeps her 'plunger' and her 'springs' down. Pitted against these downward forces are the upward forces which she generates by *supporting her own body weight* – making herself into a rider who wants to be picked up. The alternatives are to flop down into the saddle, to press down into it, or even to *grind* your weight down into it. The mythical rider who looks like a 'sack of potatoes' is making no effort to support herself, and to the horse she becomes 'dead weight'. (As my friend found when she carried her sick child on her back, this may be the more difficult option for the horse than the rider who wriggles and jiggles.) Other riders who pride themselves on 'sitting deep' or 'driving the horse forward' are in reality squashing him.

To understand in practice how supporting your weight can become a lifting mechanism, sit in a chair (with your feet back underneath you if possible). Then without leaning forward or pressing harder on the floor, make the tiniest beginnings of the movement you would make if you were going to stand up. Do this now, and then experiment, making it tinier and tinier until you do not actually move, but feel exactly which muscles are tightening. This will cause changes in the tone of the muscles which lie beneath your thigh and backside. Be careful, however, not to 'pop yourself up', tightening the muscles which would put a layer of flesh beneath your seat bones, lifting them up off the chair. (We shall meet these muscles again in Chapter 10.)

The muscle work which would – if continued – get you out of the chair, serves when you are riding both to keep you out of the mantrap and to bring the horse's back up with you. You lift not only you, but him as well – as if you could lift the chair up with you as you come up out of it! When the rider does this well, she really does look as if picking her up from beneath her armpits would cause the horse to come up too!

This suction effect profoundly affects the horse's lightness into the rein, and to explain this connection between his back and his head, I often liken the horse to one of those hour-glass egg timers which has been lain on its side. One part is the horse's body, and the other part is his head. The horse wants the sand in his head, and wants the rider to hold it up for him; but the rider wants the sand in his body, so that his ribcage is filled out beneath her, and his head and neck remain light. Once the sand is in his head, it is impossible to pull it from there back into the body. Countless generations of riders have tried this, and failed. The secret lies in realising that the sand can only get there by passing through inbetween her legs: so the rider's job is to think of holding it there in his back.

I have said this to a large number of riders who replied, 'That sounds great, but how do I do it?' Then before I could even say, 'Well, you just think about it,' they had amazed themselves by succeeding! When I do not have instant success (and my timing is the key to this), I may embellish the image by suggesting that the rider thinks of her body and legs like one of those mechanical grabs used in car scrap yards. This has four arms, and as it picks up the car, it squashes it into a rectangle. The rider's 'arms' are her legs, and although there is no need to squash the horse anywhere near this hard, the rider does have to *keep hold of his ribcage*. Otherwise she cannot 'keep the sand in his back' and draw it up under her.

Whilst this may appear to present a complex picture of opposing forces, the complexities of the riders who get it wrong are even more daunting. For instance, I recently taught a Grand Prix rider who, in rising trot, squashed her horse on each 'down', 'deadening the trampoline', having a very negative effect on his gait. After we had corrected this she went sitting and I saw just the opposite pattern (which operated in canter as well). For now she was growing up tall, pulling her ribs up away from her hips – and although she was not squashing him in the same way, she was still having no suction effect whatsoever. This proved a much harder pattern to break, for she was not easily convinced that she had to compress her upper body, bringing her ribcage down, and thinking 'down'. (Her pattern may remind you of Donna and Jackie, whom you met in Chapter 2.)

The more she thought about collection, the more she was tempted to grow tall, and I could see her point when she said, 'What you're saying seems so strange when I've heard so much about lightness and elegance, and that's what I want to create.' However, when she *did* create it she knew immediately that she had done so, for her horse did not beat about the bush in his response to her 'rightness'. As his back came up and the contact in her hand lightened, she was bemused by the sensation in her body, which she described as feeling 'like I'm a little worm, trying to crawl into a hole'.

One should never judge a rider's subjective experience (however strange it sounds), for it is so coloured by the pattern she was using previously. But whilst my explanations may make the sink-plunger mechanism seem complicated, the primary problem is that we are not used to mapping these variables, and do not have good language to describe them. However, in practice, I bet you could watch a group of riders and instantly recognise the one who brings 'up' and 'down' into balance. You would instantly perceive her as talented, for she looks very solid and stable on the horse – and whilst appearing to do nothing, she has a tremendous effect on his back. Her posture is similar to that of the martial artist, but very different to the rider who has made the traditional interpretation of 'grow up tall', and 'stretch your legs down'. For this version of 'up' and 'down' pulls the body in two directions, and has no suction effect whatsoever.

- *How well do you support your body weight as you ride?*
- *Are you a rider who wants to be picked up (and who thus can pick the horse up with her), or a rider who squashes the horse?*
  This relates to the concepts of 'live' and 'dead' relaxation, and to the difference between Superman and Clark Kent. It is important to maintain high muscle tone, and to sit as if you were kneeling on a balance stool instead of sitting in an armchair. However, do not make the mistake of drawing your ribs up away from your hips in your attempts to be light. When you can plug in, bear down, support your body weight and maintain your alignment you have a good basis on which to build.

....

Let us now consider the hollow-backed horse, and the additional forces that he exerts on the rider. Gravity causes her to topple down into the hollow in his back, which I call the 'mantrap'; but in addition, the hollow-backed horse exerts a horizontal force which actually *pushes* the rider back. (In thinking about the horse's push back, we are now considering the forces acting in the horizontal rather than in the vertical plane. To consider them separately is to make an artificial split which simplifies our thinking.) It is as if someone has put her hand on the horse's muzzle and pushed backwards, making the horse contract his head back into his neck, and his neck back into his wither. (Some horses – especially Thoroughbreds – appear to have telescopic necks, and when you watch them being ridden it can be hard to believe that they can reach the ground with their muzzle, and are designed to eat grass and not leaves!) The wither then contracts into the back, which drops to form that inviting hollow. Unless the rider is very careful she will simply fall back down it.

When the horse is above the bit, sitting well in trot and canter becomes very much harder than it is when his back is rounded and his neck reaches into the rein. The horse's movement becomes less 'sittable-on'; his shock absorption is reduced, and he throws the rider around more. The angst and tension involved can easily tempt both parties into battle, for it is

The hollow-backed horse

highly likely that the rider who is determined to get him onto the bit will resort to using the reins, and pulling his nose towards vertical.

However, only an equine contortionist can combine a hollow back with a vertical nose. Some horses admit defeat and do their best to oblige: however, whilst their nose may be vertical, they will look as if they have a big head rammed backwards into a short neck, and their movement will be cramped and short – a far cry from the freedom and power of the archetypal dressage horse. Other horses have much more integrity. They will try and force their noses upward, tossing their heads or coming strongly against the bit. It is as if they are saying, 'Hey, dummy, horses can't do this. Haven't you realised?' Yet the 'dummy' rarely gets the message; she prefers to label the horse as 'resistant', and to torture him even more.

To counteract the horse's push back, the rider has to generate a push forward within her body, which is firstly, big enough to match the propulsive force of the horse's hind legs, and secondly, bigger than his push back. Only then is she free of the temptation to pull back with her hand. This is reminiscent of our discussion about riding on the lunge (see page 61), only now we have added a stronger temptation for the rider to pull back (pulling the horse's head in) and the need for a stronger push forward (equal and opposite to the horse's push back). Matching both the horse's thrust and his push back is a big strain on the rider's muscles – a long way from 'just sitting there' – and wearing the Rider's Belt (see page 62) helps many people discover how to do it. Once achieved, the rewards are enormous; for when the rider's push forward becomes bigger than the horse's push back, the result is that the horse stretches his head and neck down and away from her, joining her in pushing forward, and lifting his back in the process.

- *Does your horse push back at you – and if so, can you push forward bigger than he can push back?*
  The three possibilities are: that he works with his back raised and his neck reaching away from you so that the contact remains light; that he has 'sand in his head' and comes heavily into your hand; or that he moves in the hollow-backed posture which brings his ears towards your chin.
- *What is the shape of his back: does it feel as if you are sitting on top of a flat surface, on a little mound, or down in a hollow?*
- *Have you ever felt a change in the shape of the horse's back? To demonstrate to yourself how his back can lift, place your fingers under the mid-line of his stomach whilst you are grooming him, and tickle him there. Keep a close watch on his hind leg in case he kicks out; but also notice how his back changes. Whilst some horses are very supple, others may appear to be set in concrete! Do this regularly, and if possible have someone else do this to him whilst you are mounted. Then you can feel as well as see the difference.*

• *When riding, do you think more about changing the position of the horse's head or more about changing the shape of his back?*
Once your hand becomes dominant, you ride the horse 'from front to back', encouraging him to either pull against you or to contract his neck even more. Riding him 'from back to front' requires the push forward of your bear down to be stronger than your hold on the rein, and stronger than his push back.
If you find this difficult, keep working on bearing down and breathing, and on 'pushing down the plunger' whilst plugging in, supporting your own body weight, and keeping your vertical alignment.

....

It was the Swedish trainer Lars Sederholm who said, 'The rider's role is to be a framework around the horse, and not a load on top of the horse.' To be a load (i.e. dead weight down the horse's mantrap) is so easy and comfortable (for the rider) that she is often reluctant to give this up; but she unknowingly ensures that the horse's back will stay hollow until such time as she gets her weight out of the hole he has made for her. This is true regardless of how much she twiddles on the reins, and regardless of what she thinks she is 'teaching' the horse about coming onto the bit. For the change she wants him to make is not just a question of obedience to a set of commands: the horse's hollow is a *reflex response* to the concentration of all that weight in the middle of his back, and exchanging the hollow for a lifted back must also be a reflex response. The horse *cannot not* respond to the positioning of the rider's body, and it is impossible to replace these reflexes with something that the rider 'teaches' and the horse 'learns'. She can only lay one level of contortion over another – a dismal fate for both parties.

Only when the rider's body becomes a framework around the horse can she begin to fit him into that ideal round-backed shape. The key is the way that she redistributes her weight, taking more of it down her thighs and using them as levers. To help you understand this, stand in an 'on-horse' position with an angle of about 140° at the hip. You will not have to stay there very long before the large quadriceps muscle at the front of your thighs begins to hurt! The muscle work involved is considerable, for your body weight is stacked up above your pelvis, and if you are not just to collapse to the floor it must be counterbalanced by your thigh. So the rider sits in the saddle as if she were kneeling, or as if she were standing with her knees bent, and *not* as if she were sitting. When you are riding, you have your inner thigh muscles against the saddle, and they can also help you to counterbalance your body weight. What this means in practice is that they can now feel the strain too!

Figure 4.1 (overleaf) shows four ways in which average riders

Staying out of the mantrap

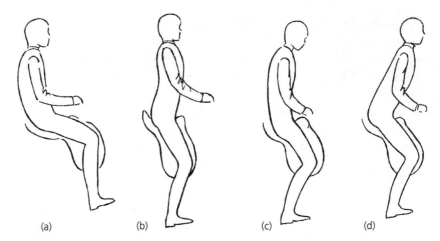

Fig. 4.1 Four ways that the rider can fall down the mantrap: (a) by being in the armchair seat, with her weight in her backside, her knee coming up, and her foot pushed forward; (b) by riding with her stirrups too long and having a vertical thigh – many people think of this as the 'dressage seat'; (c) by caving in below the sternum so that the front of the body becomes 'C' shaped; (d) by folding forward from the hip joint so that the angle between the leg and the body closes and the rider's backside slides backwards.

completely 'lose the plot' and fail to create this leverage. Most common is the armchair seat in which the rider makes no attempt to support her own weight. The knee comes up and the thigh is not used as a lever. Then there is the straight legged 'dressage' seat, in which the rider – who is usually riding with her stirrups too long – is attempting to get her knee underneath her hip. The vertical thigh *cannot* be used as a lever. Thirdly, there is the rider whose front caves in and becomes 'C' shaped, as if the horse's push back overpowered the strength of her middle. Lastly comes the rider who – although she does not mean to – closes the hip joints and folds forwards towards a jumping balance. She may be prone to the 'foetal crouch', she may be in the habit of pushing her heel down and forward, and/or she may have some major muscle imbalance, developing shortened flexor muscles at the front of the thigh and the abdomen, and very long muscles at the back of the thigh and in her back. (See Fig. 3.6, page 85.) Without the help offered by 'pushing down the springs at the back' she will feel completely helpless as she slides, backside first, down into the mantrap.

These are also the ways in which riders who are attempting to do a good job will be overpowered by the horse who suddenly increases his push back. Like the proverbial chain which breaks in its weakest link, the rider gives way in her weakest place. So she may topple back into the armchair seat (with her shoulders falling back and her knee coming up), may collapse below her sternum and become 'C' shaped, or may fold forward from the hip joint. When riding the hollow-backed horse, the rider's thigh, pelvic and abdominal muscles have to work overtime to make her counterbalance effective; for the odds are stacked against her – and whilst some horses seem relieved to be ridden well, others seem determined to compromise her framework.

It makes me think of one in particular – a spectacular Thoroughbred owned by a pupil of mine – who I think wins the prize for persistence. It's as if he saying, 'Take that ... and that ... and that!', throwing tirade of rotten tomatoes, bad eggs and general abuse in her direction. Pushing back becomes a good game to the horse who can knock the rider off balance – and to make this particular horse stop doing it he has to be made to feel as if he is bashing his head against a brick wall! The rider has to become so stable that the front of her body does not give way whatever he does. This was a hard-won skill which has changed his rider's life, and by anyone's standards, it is no mean achievement.

Thus the answer to the question 'How, exactly, does the rider bring the horse's back up underneath her?' lies in the question, 'How does the rider stay out of the mantrap?' For just by virtue of *refusing to fall back down it*, she is exerting leverage which draws the horse's back up. Once she has done this, and the horse has begun to agree to use his own muscles to hold it there, riding him becomes very much easier. It is a cruel truism that the art of riding lies in making the horse easy to ride. This gives most of us a huge mountain to climb before we can sit there and claim that 'it's easy'.

There are a number of conformation issues for the rider, which make climbing this mountain more difficult. For instance, the rider's seat bones are, in effect, the end of the lever arm of the thigh, so if they are rather forward within her backside her centre of gravity may be back *behind* the end of the arm. This makes the counterbalance extremely taxing. It is difficult too (as we saw on page 87) for the person with a shallow pelvis and a long spine, and for the person with shortened flexor muscles, and/or a hollow back. However, since these last two involve muscle use and are not written in bone they – at least – are alterable.

At the other end of the spectrum a small percentage of strong, skilled, riders with a favourable conformation succeed in shaping the horse despite not sitting in the most effective way. A rider with her feet in front of the ideal shoulder/hip/heel line can still ride well, but needs to be unusually strong to do so. For with her body weight behind her feet it takes more muscle work to counterbalance it, and only when she has achieved this much can she go one stage further – generating suction and pushing forward more strongly than the horse can push back. With her thigh too close to vertical her leverage is again reduced. Many good riders could ride even better if they realised that the laws of physics are always operating, and that *they* determine the style of riding which is biomechanically the most efficient. Indeed, the vast majority of us will only ever succeed by maximising our chances, and co-operating with them fully.

Whilst biomechanics is the bottom line in riding, we cannot isolate it from the emotional issues which impact on us all. *Anyone* who has a history of focusing on the horse's head position and attempting to pull it down will become her own worst enemy until she trusts the new skills she is learning. For she will be tempted to lower her hand, to pull back, and to tip her shoulders forward the moment things go wrong. This makes her pelvis slip back into the mantrap, increasing the hollow in the horse's back precisely at the moment when she most needs good leverage (to hold herself out of the mantrap) and a strong push forward (which has more power than the horse's push back). The biggest task facing her is to inhibit her panic reactions and to substitute useful ones. Underlying this is the understanding that her job is to influence the horse's *back* and not his *head* ... a concept which will only have real meaning for her as she begins to succeed.

- *Do you think in terms of 'teaching the horse to come onto the bit' or in terms of positioning your body so that you can draw his back up, and push his neck away from you?*
- *How do you fall down the mantrap? Are your stirrups set at a length which puts your thigh at about 45° to the ground, or is your thigh so close to vertical that it cannot form a good lever?*
- *Do you fall into the armchair seat, collapse your front and go 'C' shaped, or fold forward from the hip?*
  The cure is different in each case, and you need to address your own specific weakness.
- *Do you tend to panic when the horse's head comes up, and to try to pull it down again? If so, you are undoubtedly becoming your own worst enemy ... try to resist this instinct, and to trust that bearing down and sitting correctly will work well once you have sufficient strength, and enough pieces in the puzzle.*

....

The girder over the horse's suspension bridge

When I was abroad recently, I heard a discussion about how another foreign instructor enjoyed teaching at a certain venue because the riders there had warmblood horses who were capable of working on the bit. Previously he had taught at a venue with less skilled riders and mostly Thoroughbred horses, and had felt that his visits there were a waste of time because the riders and horses could not produce the results he wanted. To my mind, the trainer was actually saying that he could not break the skill of riding into small enough pieces to help these riders. So when 'Get the horse on the bit' failed to achieve its result, he had little else he could say.

Most of the riders I know would love to own more expensive and talented horses; but we all have the horses we have, and rather than consigning them to the scrap heap, I would rather teach riders the baseline skills which will influence the horse, whatever his make and shape, and which will also serve them well – and make their riding much more precise – when they do eventually graduate to a more talented horse. So this next technique is for use on the horses who feel as if their bodies are set in concrete, and who push back for a living!

Riders who bear down well and can push forward very strongly from their back can go one stage further than stopping themselves from falling back into the mantrap: they can span it. This is similar to the way that climbers go up or down a chimney – a narrow crevasse which they span by placing their knees and calves against one wall and their back against the other. The value of this for the rider is that by spanning the mantrap she holds its edges apart, stopping the collapse which deepens the hollow in the horse's back.

In 'Masterclass' I likened the mantrap to the hollow that would be formed if the stanchions on a suspension bridge were to collapse towards each other, making the wires which hold up the bridge go slack, and making the bridge itself hang down. (See Fig. 4.2 overleaf.) The ligaments which hold up the horse's spine are analogous to those wires, and they pull the vertebrae beneath the twist of the saddle towards the wither, and those lying further back towards the croup. Thus the wither and the croup are the stanchions of the bridge. Since the rider can really only influence the length of the horse's back which lies between her knee and her hip, I like to think of *these* points as the stanchions, and to imagine that the rider's thigh could act like a girder, placed in between the stanchions so that the bridge cannot collapse.

Making the thigh into 'the girder over the horse's suspension bridge' requires both of the rider's thighs to have the high muscle tone which makes them strong and solid instead of weak and mushy. High tone makes the thigh bones themselves feel more defined, so I often suggest that the rider assesses her starting point by thinking of her thigh bones like iron bars, and determining whether one is more 'iron-bar-like' (i.e. more highly toned) than the other, and whether one or both have soggy bits. This would mean that her girders would have some compressible places. A little thought usually enables the rider to firm them up.

Another way to think of this is that the rider is using her thighs like buffers. (This translates into American as bumpers, and Americans are much less familiar than Europeans with the structure at the end of a railway line which would stop a runaway train.) Good jumping riders

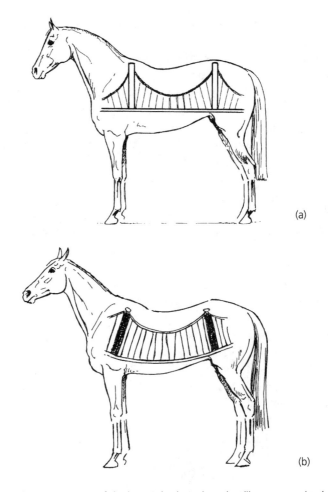

Fig. 4.2 The ligament system of the horse's back works rather like a suspension bridge, whose stanchions are the wither and the croup. In (a) the ligament system is working well, but in (b) it and the stanchions have collapsed.

have very effective buffers, and their more horizontal thigh makes this an easier strategy for them. It is can also save their lives, for if a good rider is riding a horse into a big parallel and he begins to stop, she utilises the buffer and braces into her knee. This enables her to maintain the position of her upper body whilst she uses her lower leg and stick. Other less effective riders do not have this brace, so they topple forward as the horse stops, with their thigh becoming vertical. When this happens, their lower leg also moves back, and it is as if their whole body pivots about a point in the middle of the thigh. (See Fig. 4.3.) Riders who look as if they are permanently toppling forward (even on a horse who is not about to stop) often lack good buffers, and this strategy is enormously helpful for them.

To use a different analogy, once the rider's thighs are working well they are like the elastic in a catapult (or slingshot), which has been pulled into a long, thin, narrow 'V' shape, with the muscles under tension. This is a far cry from the short, fat, soggy 'V' shape which would be so much easier to maintain. When the rider has lengthened out the 'V', she will feel as if she has brought her seat bones and her upper body *further back* in the saddle. Now that her thigh spans the mantrap, the push forward of her bear down begins from further back because her torso is further back. It is as if she has taken a step back around the horse, sitting round his barrel in a place which now puts more of him 'in front of her'.

I often help the rider get a sense of this 'feelage' by crouching under the horse's neck, grabbing hold of her knees, and pulling on them (as in Fig. 2.9, page 62). But at the same time I ask her to *pull back against me*, and ask an observer to check that she does not round or hollow her back. When the rider finds the right feelage, I feel the tendons behind her knee stick out (see Fig. 9.8, page 256), and she feels a strain in her thigh muscles, often on the inside and the front of the thigh. She can help herself by digging her knees into the saddle, and then pushing back off them. (This strategy requires strong use of the inside thigh muscles, although once the horse has agreed to hold his stanchions apart the outer muscles may become dominant.)

Another method to help the rider intensify her push back was invented by a pupil of mine who – despite every explanation I could think of – was still not getting the idea. So she spent a short time in the lesson working on her own and experimenting. She then came back to me saying 'Is this it?' She had put the heels of her hands on the pommel, and then used them to push her upper body back, without letting herself lose her vertical line-up. (If you are sitting reading this on a chair by a table,

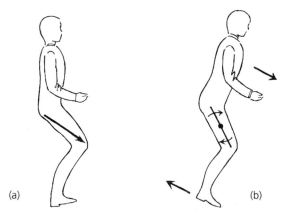

(a) (b)

Fig. 4.3 The thigh operates either as a buffer, as in (a), or as a pivot, as in (b). Whilst the buffer stabilises the rider and enables her thigh to act like the girder over the suspension bridge, the pivot results in her tipping forward.

try lining your body up well, putting the heels of your hands against the edge of the table, and pushing back off them. You should feel changes in the muscles of your front, if not your thighs.) This new use of her muscles helped to lengthen out her 'V', whilst also helping her front (which had been very weak) to become much more strong and 'leak-proof'. It put her horse so much more 'in front of her' that the results were dramatic.

The following exercise shows more clearly how you can change the quality of the thighs. To understand how firm they can become and how effectively they act as a buffer, sit on a hard chair facing not forward, but at an angle of 45°. Place your more forward seat bone very close to the edge of the chair, and place your hand about an inch in front of your knee. Then without moving your torso, reach your thigh forward until your knee touches your hand. Having done that, retract your thigh back into your hip socket, taking your knee away from your hand. Do this several times, realising just how much your thigh can move into or out of your hip socket. Then, keeping your knee against your hand and your thigh pulled out of your hip socket, push *back* off your knee. Feel your seat bone on that side roll back over your flesh (whilst still pointing straight down). If you sit in this position for a while, you should find that the quadriceps muscle along the top of your thigh begins to feel some strain. When the rider does this mounted, it is almost as if she subjects herself and the horse to the medieval torture of the rack – a primitive machine which stretched the body until its unfortunate victim confessed.

I have met riders who used the strategy of bracing into their thigh very well when jumping, but who abandoned it whilst riding dressage. For the belief that they should 'stretch their legs down' stopped them from discovering the value of good buffers. These have the triple function of stabilising the rider, enabling her thighs to become the girder over the horse's suspension bridge, and putting more of the horse 'in front of her'. It is a strategy which stops her from toppling forward; but since she must still match the forward thrust of the horse's hind leg it demands in return an increased push forward from her back. The pay-off, however, is that the more she increases both her push forward *and* her push back, the more immovable she becomes on the back/front plane. This now gives us a fuller understanding of the forces which act in the back/front plane, and we can write these as an equation:

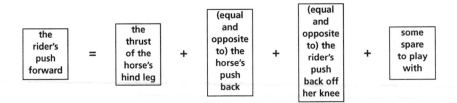

- *Making your thigh into the girder over the horse's suspension bridge is a more advanced strategy which you may not yet be ready for. But if you tend to topple forward, it may help your stability to think of your thighs like buffers, or like the elastic in a catapult.*

- *Firstly think of your thigh bones like iron bars, and give each of them numbers out of ten for stability. Which parts of each thigh are most compressible? To strengthen these, work in walk, and think of extending the 'iron-bar-ness' from the areas of strength inch by inch into the areas of weakness. Then endeavour to hold this in trot and canter.*

- *If one thigh is significantly weaker than the other, you may not be able to change it that much until you work with the asymmetry corrections in the next chapter.*

....

Each of the explanations I have offered here places much of the function of lifting the horse's back in the *thigh,* the abdominal and the back muscles, and not in the calf. In my youth, the general assumption seemed to be that if you held on to the front end and kicked the back end, then the horse's hind legs would be activated so much that they would step more underneath him, thus elevating his forehand. I find it more useful, however, to think of this the other way around: that when you have lifted the back, there is then room for the hind legs to advance further under the belly and to engage. You can demonstrate this in your own body if you stand with a hollow back, lift one of your knees, and attempt to hug it against your chest. It will not come very close. But if you remove the hollow from your back, your knee will come much closer to your chest. So it is with the horse.

Nowadays, more people subscribe to the idea that the function of your calf is not so much to activate the horse's hind legs as to lift his belly. Many even suggest that the thigh should be taken off the saddle in this process (which I believe, as I said on page 76, is a misunderstanding of the function of the chain of muscles which I call externals). It is certainly true that the horse's belly muscles are involved in the lifting of his back, for they are like the string on a bow, which tightens to pull the wood into an arc. (See Fig. 4.4 overleaf.) The horse's sternum and his pubic bone then come closer together – as do the hollow-backed rider's. This in turn affects his ribcage, and if sitting on the hollow-backed horse is like sitting on the pointed end of an egg (with a large width of belly dangling downwards), the ideal change in his carriage causes the shape of his ribcage to invert so that the rider now feels as if she is sitting on the rounded end of the egg. This makes it much easier for her to get her legs around the horse.

When the horse changes his carriage, he too bears down, gaining

The rider's thigh and calf; the horse's back and belly

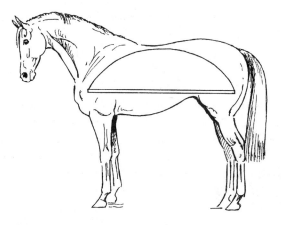

Fig. 4.4 The horse in carriage can be thought of like a strung bow.

tremendous strength and support from the use of his stomach muscles. This explains why horses often snort, grunt and groan when they first come onto the bit – and one colleague of mine has a big, hefty Grand Prix horse who can only do a decent canter pirouette when each stride is accompanied by a grunt! (This is rather like the tennis players who grunt as they serve, bearing down to give their shot more power.) But whether this whole back/belly process is activated from the thigh or the calf is open to question. Some literature refers to the 'magic spot', a ganglion of nerves just behind the girth, which stimulates the back to lift when touched by the rider's lower leg. Whilst this may well exist, I do not believe that it is the fundamental lifting mechanism, and if it were, more people would succeed just by kicking. I am convinced that there is much more to it than this.

....

The water-ski/ motorboat dynamic

Understanding how the rider stabilises her body and shapes the horse puts us in a position to understand the mechanics of acceleration and deceleration (which means that we are thinking again about the back/front plane). Let us consider, first of all, what happens when the horse accelerates without warning. This is essentially the same as if you were standing on a small rug, and someone tried to pull the rug out from under your feet. You would almost certainly topple backwards; but if the rug was on a polished floor, this would make it go out from underneath you even faster! The same dynamic takes place in skiing. The moment you decide that you would prefer not to go down the mountain you instinctively retreat from the challenge by leaning back; so your skis speed out from underneath you, and you go down it even faster! Paradoxically, committing yourself to going down the mountain keeps your body more perpendicular to your skis and helps to control your speed.

Using yet another analogy, the rider who topples back as the horse accelerates falls into the 'water-ski' position. If she then attempts to stop by pulling back on the reins, she water-skis even more. In response to this, any horse with a forward-going attitude will – like the rug or your skis – go out from under you even faster. (See Fig 4.5a.) Another version of the same dynamic is the horse who jogs when asked to walk on. He is coupled with the rider who tips back each time she gives a 'walk on' aid. She may either fall back unintentionally, or be trying to stop the jog; but either way she pays the same price of perpetuating the water-ski/motorboat, pull-and-jog dynamic.

Through jogging, even lazy horses (who would not normally run away from the rider who water-skis) fulfil their allotted role in the water-ski/motorboat scenario. In essence there are two types of horses: those who respond to the rider's 'wrongness' with frenetic evasions which maximise their energy output, and those who respond with evasions designed to minimise their energy output. (Thus the slow jog is *less* effort for these horses than walking on.) I call them Type A and Type B horses, mirroring the classification used in people. Not surprisingly, it is Type A people who die of heart attacks! So where a Type A horse whizzes out from under the rider who water-skis, lazy Type B horses *minimise* their energy output, and may even 'give up the ghost' in response to this extra loading of their hindquarters.

However the Type A horse is in no doubt that every water-skier needs a motorboat, and as he tows the rider along they together form a *system,* balancing each other like two sides of an equation. Think of two people

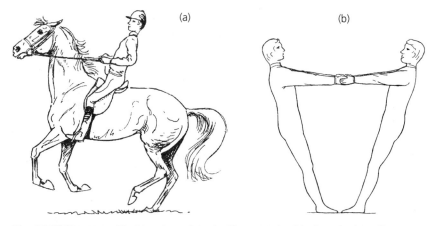

Fig. 4.5 (a) The water-skier/motorboat scenario. The more the rider leans back, pulling on the reins and pushing into the stirrups, the more the horse speeds out from underneath her. The dynamic of this is very similar to that of (b), in which two people hold hands and lean back against each other, counterbalancing each other's weight.

who link hands and lean back against each other (see Fig. 4.5b): it would be ludicrous for one to blame the other for pulling, yet some riders who are water-skiing place the blame entirely with their horse. What they have failed to appreciate is that the horse would be equally justified in blaming them!

Since the horse will not volunteer to change the status quo, the only way out of the problem is to refuse to water-ski: for when you give up *your* role, the horse cannot sustain his. This implies that you must refind vertical, stabilise your torso, and ideally give forward one hand. (There is an art to doing this without also giving away your body, allowing it to lose tone and crumple forward.) In our analogy of the two people who lean back against each other, this is equivalent to one partner bringing her shoulders forward to vertical and thus bringing her hands forward. This forces her partner to take a step back, obliging her to bring *her* body to vertical, and to take responsibility for balancing herself.

But whether you were on the rug, on skis, or on a horse, it is far better to pre-empt the whole scenario by *staying in place* as the rug/skis/horse accelerates. In riding, this requires an increase in the force of your bearing down, matching the increased propulsive force of the horse's hind leg. This is a particularly important solution for people who feel that they dare not stop pulling because they are convinced that the horse will take off with them. I usually change their mind-set by working with transitions between walk and halt. The first challenge is to stop the horse without leaning back or pulling; for as soon as the rider leans back, she begins to water-ski, and the horse inevitably begins to motorboat. Whilst they both keep pulling, the horse keeps moving – in a scenario which one of my pupils has described as 'perpetual motion'.

The secret to an immediate, precise halt lies in remaining vertical and bearing down. (Making the sound 'Sssssh' can help here, since it ensures that you bear down and breathe out.) You then stop your seat-bone movement, and as you do so, the horse (once he has been retrained) stops moving too. The last factor is the hand, which offers a passive resistance. This is different to pulling, and it requires that the rein is short enough for the rider not to need to draw her hand back to take up the slack. It works best when the rider holds the rein between her thumb and her first finger with the middle joint of her thumb up. Then all she has to do is to press harder with the thumb. As long as she bears down and remains vertical – and as long as she does not need to draw her hand back to take up the slack in the rein – she gets a very different feeling in her hand to the one she gets when she pulls.

When riders are making mistakes here – but are actually quite experienced and have a good sense of humour – I have been known to crack jokes with them. For the horse will want to perpetuate the status quo by beginning to motorboat (after all, this has been his agreement with the rider) and this tempts the rider to water-ski, with the inevitable pull on the reins. It is as if the horse says, 'Go on, just one little pull. It really won't matter. Go on, spoil yourself ... it'll all work out fine.' But underneath he knows that 'once you have eaten from the tree of knowledge of good and evil', you will be truly enslaved to him. You will become his water-skier, and then he has you just where he wants you.

Once you can ride the halts well, you then have to maintain your balance in the move-off. To stay 'with' the horse you have to ensure that you stay upright, without letting your shoulders jerk backwards. This is rather like riding on an underground train, standing through the sways and jerks without holding on! It requires you to hold a constant angle between your leg and your torso so that the 'Z' angles do not change (see Fig. 3.8, page 86) and this is much easier if you have good use of the front tendons (see Fig. 9.8, page 256) and can keep them sticking up.

- *Do you ride a Type A or a Type B horse?*
- *How easily to you get caught in the water-ski/motorboat dynamic?*
  Think when you ride of the analogy to the two people who lean back against each other. Are you and your horse doing this? If you cannot easily get him to be light into your hand (without fiddling or pulling), be suspicious that there might be a subtle water-ski/motorboat dynamic in place.
- *Can you ride crisp, clear halts, or do they drag on, as if the horse were a clockwork toy that is winding down?*
  It is very important to master the walk/halt mechanism, for this is a microcosm which demonstrates so clearly the effects of correct and incorrect riding.
  The most common mistakes are having your reins too long, leaning back, pulling your stomach in, and growing up tall whilst pressing harder into the stirrups. Once you can maintain a martial arts posture throughout the halt you will achieve a very different result.

....

How the rider mirrors the horse

One sees the water-skier/motorboat scenario acted out at all levels of riding, in flatwork as well as in jumping, and for some riders, water-skiing is a way of life. Many riders and horses survive water-skiing with little more than a strong contact and a 'downhill' horse to show for it, and the more subtle end of the spectrum is peopled by riders who continually lean back in an attempt to motivate (or motorboat) a lazy horse. This is one of the best ways to ensure that the horse will have 'sand in his head', for it creates a counter-balance in which he *has to* lean into the rein. Alternatively if the horse suddenly dives onto his forehand he can, quite literally, pull the sand into his head, whilst (in effect) pulling on the rider's seat bones so that they rotate forward. This pulls apart the angles of her 'Z', causing her shoulders to lean backwards, and channelling her energy towards the horse's shoulders and front legs. Thus she dumps him even more onto his forehand. But regardless of which partner first 'lost it', lightness is impossible without some major rebalancing – not of the horse, but of the rider.

Yet more subtle is the rider's response to the horse who would like to take each step in a movement pattern which lengthens his underneath and hollows his back. (I call this 'doing an arabesque', naming it after the classical dance movement.) This lengthening of his abdominal muscles acts like an acceleration, tending to tip the rider back so that she lengthens her front – the equivalent part of her own body. Often, she does not even know that she has done this, and only if she can maintain her vertical posture (holding her ribs dropped down towards her hips and refusing to lean back) can she cause the horse to take each step by reaching over his top line.

There is an even deeper significance to this mirror relationship between the rider who lengthens her front and the horse who lengthens his underneath. Regardless of who is the chicken and who is the egg, both are using a strategy which some of my colleagues have named 'extension pattern'. Its converse, 'flexion pattern', keeps the rider's strength in her pelvis, and keeps the horse 'sat down'. By staying vertical the rider is able to maintain control of her 'Z' angles, and 'hold the sand in the horse's back'. If she is foolish enough to mirror the extension pattern of the horse who wants to tow her along, both of them are left with their strength coming from their forehand/upper chest, and with minimum involvement of their pelvises. The horse pulls himself along with his forearms, and the rider pulls back with her forearms.

The most dangerous end of the water-ski/motorboat spectrum is inhabited by the few horses who really are crazy runaways. However, they always calm down when the rider masters the walk/halt transitions, and gains the courage and the skills to bear down, plug in, align her body, breathe deeply, and maintain her high tone as she gives away her hand. This was the task that faced Gina, who you met in Chapter 1. The rider who is water-skiing is never fully in control (and Gina was extremely sensitive to this – although many riders happily water-ski their way through a day's hunting or a 50-mile endurance ride!). For when the horse 'takes the rider' she has *lost control of the tempo*. (Remember our analogy to riding a bicycle on a downhill slope, and discovering that you can no longer pedal fast enough to keep up. The bicycle – like the horse – then 'takes you'.) In contrast, controlling the speed of the horse's legs gives you control of the whole horse. It is important to realise that when the horse attempts to accelerate, *you match the thrust of his hind leg*, whilst holding your body vertical (so that you do not fall backwards on the rug). But paradoxically, *you do not match any increase in his tempo.* Instead you keep control of your seat-bone movement, so that your body beats time like a metronome, and you retain control of the speed at which he moves his legs. Being able to do this on a highly strung horse yields a tremendously reassuring feeling.

- *Do you and your horse utilise extension pattern or flexion pattern, i.e. does your horse take each step by lengthening his topline, or by lengthening his underside? If the latter, you can be virtually certain that you are lengthening your front. You can discover this by halting, and seeing/feeling how he then takes the very first step of walk. He will probably take each subsequent step in the same way. If he lengthens his underside – which will bring his ears back towards your chin – be absolutely sure that you do not tip back during that first step of walk. (Be sure too that you do not tip forward.)*
- *How do you react to that first step of walk? Do you stay vertical, or do your shoulders flip back?*
- *Whilst some horses have a very apparent extension pattern, creating an obvious water-ski/motorboat dynamic, others are much more subtle. You may find that you are unknowingly leaning back and lengthening your front, thus encouraging the horse to lengthen his underside. Regardless of who is the chicken and who is the egg, realise that you can only rebalance your horse by rebalancing yourself.*
- *Can you control the horse's tempo through controlling your own seat-bone movement? If not, be suspect that you might actually be water-skiing.*

....

In its most obvious forms, water-skiing is one of the first patterns that novice teachers learn to recognise – although its subtle forms are endemic and rarely diagnosed. (In fact, they masquerade as good riding, and I would dearly love to see the posture of water-skiing recognised as the atrocity it actually is.) As far as I am aware, the world record for early diagnosis is held by a fledgling teacher who is only five. Her mother, who is a pupil of mine and a very capable teacher, was forced by circumstance to take her daughter with her when she went to assess a prospective purchase for a client. The horse was stabled with a local 'he-man' trainer who was not renowned for his finesse. As mother and daughter sat together at the side of the arena, the youngster piped up rather loudly, 'M-u-m, he wouldn't land on his feet.'

'Sshh,' came the reply, 'not now, be quiet.'

But the little girl was not to be silenced so easily. 'M-u-m, he's really water-skiing!'

This was met with more demands for silence. But as he came round

Maintaining flexion pattern

again, the daughter could not resist. 'M-u-m, someone's really going to have to keep their eyes on him!'

Whilst water-skiing was undoubtedly this rider's preferred style, it is very difficult *not* to water-ski on a horse who sets you up to do so. I have extremely clear memories of one of my most profound experiences with this. I was riding a pupil's horse during a clinic one day, after it became clear that I would get limited improvement from them both unless I did so. I needed to discover if his pattern felt as entrenched as it looked, and give his young rider more chance of success. The horse was one of the most 'spaced out' creatures I have ever seen, gazing from glassy eyes into the distant horizon, with his ears pricked and his back so hollow that they were not very far from his rider's chin! The pattern was so strong that I feared its origins might lie in pain; yet he was a successful show jumper, and was the ultimate 'point-and-shoot pony', producing fast clear rounds for his capable teenage jockey (whilst her mother held her breath!). But the youngster was – not surprisingly – flummoxed by dressage.

My first task was (as always) to plug in, to get his attention, and to make a push forward which was bigger than his push back. His 'stanchions' were so collapsed that it was not easy to lengthen out his back: his ability to hold that contraction was at least as great as my ability to make my thighs into the girder over his suspension bridge! In fact, I was struggling to have any impact on him at all. But whilst I needed to galvanise all of my muscle-power, I also needed to tread very carefully, for although he was a willing soul with no malice in him, he was potentially so sensitive that he had to be brought back onto the planet respectfully – honouring the impact of the experiences that had driven him down this escape route.

Working on one rein yielded slightly more chinks in his armour than working on the other, and from two-thirds of the way up his neck he kinked it slightly to one side, making me suspect that there might be damage which would benefit from manipulative treatment. In my bid to make him pay more attention and to find a more rigorous challenge to his carriage, I resorted to walk/halt transitions – and I soon reached a point where he halted with a much rounder back. He then stood there shaking his head, momentarily bringing his back muscles up underneath me, and then taking them away again each time he tossed his head up.

By this point, his ears were continually held out sideways, and his attention was rivetted on me. All I needed was for him to take at least one step forward in this rounded carriage – but I could not persuade him to do it. He could step sideways and stay round, or step backwards and stay round; but every time he took a step forwards his ears suddenly flipped back towards my chin and his back dropped away from me. (Had he been less of a gentleman, he might have used rearing as the ultimate escape route – but he was far too honest for this.) Each time he did this I felt my front lengthen and my shoulders jerk back – despite my best attempts to stay in place. I was as well prepared as I could possibly be; but each time he caught me out, until I decided that his message ('I simply cannot do this') really should be taken seriously.

I dismounted, describing to his owners that I felt discretion to be the better part of valour. It was as well that I did, for he was lame the next day. This might, of course, have been coincidence – but it provided further evidence for my suspicion that his 'spaced out' attitude and his hollow back were indeed a defence against pain. (His family were very concerned to do their best for him, so I gave them the names of practitioners who I thought might help. I do not, however, know the outcome of the story.)

This horse had one of the strongest extension patterns I have ever seen, and highly strung runaway horses are usually much easier to ride than he was. Another very different version of extension pattern is the horse who does not necessarily speed off, but who (before you have even taken a step) pulls into the rein as if he were pulling a cart. I know one horse who must be the ultimate exemplification of this pattern, and who does in fact both ride and drive. Driving is far more his forte than dressage – and to remain in flexion pattern on such an extension pattern horse really takes some doing! But it *is* possible to bring his back up and have him light into the hand, and whilst he is desperately trying to plough his energy towards his forehand and front legs, the rider must redirect it towards his hindquarters and his hind legs. The key is to maintain the 'Z' angles (and to plug in and bear down with a strength you might not have thought possible!), deliberately aiming your seat bones towards his hind legs in each down beat. (This is not, however, an invitation to hollow your back; it simply keeps the up-and-down mechanism of the two cylinders described by Fig. 3.7 on page 86.) This stops you from being pulled into the water-ski position, and encourages him to flex his joints, and to sit down more.

People who do not understand the biomechanical difference between flexion pattern and extension pattern often talk about it as 'timing', since it relates not only to the direction of the rider's 'down' but also to its speed. This is well illustrated by a conversation recounted by one of my colleagues. She was teaching someone who is herself a teacher, and who was bemoaning that 'All my pupils seem to ride canter in Moz-am-BIQUE, and I want them to ride it in tre-MEN-dous. But they don't seem to get it.' 'I'm not even sure you want that,' said my friend, 'I think they'd be better off in CAN-a-da.' Getting the rider's 'down' to coincide with the horse's first canter beat helps her sit both of them down into flexion pattern, thus transferring weight to his hind end.

But the rider in 'Moz-am-BIQUE' is being dragged by the horse into extension pattern, and as the horse's weight falls onto the leading foreleg, so her shoulders rock back and her backside slides forward. I fear that the old Pony Club advice to 'polish the saddle with your bottom' actually promotes this way of sitting – and the rider does better by thinking of a slight rock forwards of her shoulders during the canter stride, almost as if she were folding down for a jump. The better her canter, the more upright she stays and the smaller this movement is; but skilled riders rock from vertical to forwards (maintaining flexion pattern), never from vertical to back (which puts them into extension pattern).

As with the revised way of 'bottom walking', which emphasises the backward movement of each seat bone (see page 65), this also helps you to match the thrust of the horse's hind legs, and in effect to pull your torso forward over your legs.

Whilst most riders are blissfully unaware that their riding style is based on extension pattern, they *are* aware of using it to ride extensions. For by leaning back and bringing their centre of gravity *back behind the horse's* they make him speed out from under them. Some of the more classical trainers question this strategy, as it will inevitably encourage the horse to mirror the rider, lengthening his underside and falling onto his forehand. These classical riders prefer to keep their centre of gravity 'with' the horse's (maintaining flexion pattern), and I believe that they get better quality extensions as a result. In practice, however, riders who utilise the water-ski/motorboat dynamic get away with it as long as they can bear down so strongly that they match the thrust of the horse's hind leg, and do not need a backward force from their hand to keep themselves in place; but its ethos is questionable.

However, the most interesting question concerns what then happens at the end of the extension. Many people, as they want to collect the horse, *lean back more*, only to discover that the transition becomes a pulling match. But according to the laws of physics it must, for the rider has forced the horse to motorboat more by bringing her centre of gravity back and sending her energy towards his shoulders. So instead of leaning back she must realign her body (just as she would on the runaway), coming to vertical again, and *advancing* her centre of gravity to reposition it over the horse's. This means that many dressage riders need to rethink their strategy both for the half-halt and the downward transitions – and I have taught a number of international competitors who have valiantly done this, despite years of believing that they could lower the horse's haunches by leaning back. They have all marvelled at the pay-offs.

* *Do you utilise extension pattern when you ride extensions, or do you keep your centre of gravity 'with' the horse's?*
* *How do you then ride the transition to the working or collected gait? Do you lean back more, or do you come forward to vertical? I recommend that you pay*

attention to bearing down, the angle of your upper body, and the 'Z' angles (described in Fig. 3.8 on page 86). The temptation to lean back may be overwhelming; but if you can instead think of an extra big 'Z' on each down beat (which brings the back corners of your backside more down, and your front tendons more up) you will revolutionise your understanding of half-halts. This change to flexion pattern may not be easy to make – but the pay-offs are enormous.

. . . .

Whilst many riders think that they *should* have their centre of gravity behind the horse's, everyone knows that it is not good to have it ahead of his. We often think of this as the posture of novice or nervous riders; but a surprising proportion of more advanced riders do not keep their centre of gravity far enough back. To state the obvious, the rider's centre of gravity is most likely to come in front of the horse's when the horse stops suddenly – perhaps in front of a fence. This is the extreme opposite of the runaway: it is as if someone suddenly pulled the rug out *backwards* from beneath the rider's feet. (See Fig. 4.6.)

When the horse's centre of gravity comes behind the rider's

As we have seen, good jumping riders counteract this by bracing into their knee as the horse slows down, and using their thighs as buffers. This enables them to keep their upper body upright and their centre of gravity back over the horse's; they do not make the more novice rider's mistake of letting the thigh rotate towards vertical, so that their upper body topples forwards. (See Fig. 4.3 on page 101.)

Fig. 4.6 Surprisingly often the rider comes in front of the horse so that much of his body is behind her. Her thigh is not acting as a good girder, and her low down bear down does not land at the breastplate (see also page 115).

The more subtle version of the stopping horse is the horse who does not want to go forward – the nappy horse, who is, in effect, trying to crawl out backwards from between the rider's legs. (It's as if he says, 'Bye bye, have a nice time trotting round the arena. I'm not coming!') Most people's concern when they see a rider ahead of the horse is the extra weight that is placed over his forehand; but this is one of the less important problems that it generates. For whilst Type A horses will run to catch up with you – advancing their centre of gravity to bring it under yours – Type B horses maximise the discrepancy which already exists. (The runaway horse also maximises the existing discrepancy when he pulls the rug out from under your feet as you lean back.) Type B horses can fox even advanced riders, for they have discovered that *as soon as the rider's centre of gravity is in front of theirs, they have made her powerless.* The way they play on this can make them extremely difficult to ride, and sometimes these horses use more energy in *not* going than they would use if they did indeed agree to trot willingly round the school!

The rider on the nappy or stuffy horse must keep her centre of gravity *back* by using the jumping rider's strategy of bracing into her thigh. When she does this, it is almost as if her body makes a step backwards around the horse, thus putting more of his barrel 'in front of her' – an important concept which we will elaborate later. At the same time, she becomes able to span the horse's mantrap. The more skilful the rider is, the better she controls the positioning of her centre of gravity, and this makes it increasingly hard for the horse to knock her off balance. (She gains this stability by intensifying both sets of opposing forces noted in the equation on page 102, i.e. because she is pushing back more, she must also push forward more.) The moral of the story is that she always needs to be able to respond to each horse and to circumstance – especially if the horse she is riding is a 'quick change artist' who can vary his evasions without notice.

Once the rider gains sufficient control of her own centre of gravity, she easily learns to control the *combined rider/horse centre of gravity*, and to bring it back when she wants to sit the horse down. If she maintains the correct alignment, she does this without water-skiing or falling down the mantrap, i.e. *without separating her own centre of gravity from the horse's.* It is this which generates collection, producing half-halts which are not half-hauls.

- *Do you ride horses who want your centre of gravity in front of theirs? Are you able to stay 'behind them', or do they get you to topple forward and become powerless?*
- *If necessary look again at page 99 and Fig. 4.3 on page 101, and review the concept of using the thighs like buffers.*

When the horse is 'in front of' the rider, she has her centre of gravity precisely over his. She knows that she is in the right place when her low down bear down (the push forward that she makes from her lower abdomen at the level of her bikini line) lands where a breastplate would lie, just in front of his wither. If she is positioned too far forward in the saddle it will overshoot, landing somewhere further up his neck, or aiming into outer space. Then, he is no longer in front of her, and her thighs are not functioning as buffers (or as girders over the suspension bridge, see page 99 and Fig. 4.2 on page 100). To sense this, she needs to be able to make her bear down powerful, focused, and directed: it must have the quality of a power-hose, not of a watering can spray. She can only achieve this when her 'plunger' is down, and her 'leaks' are closed (see page 52 *et seq.*).

This concept is an extremely useful one, *for it tells the rider where to sit.* It also provides an explanation for the extremely misleading term 'between hand and leg'. For the horse is really held within two triangles (see Fig. 4.7). These are made up firstly of his crest (giving a slightly curved side), the cheek piece of the bridle, and the rein; then also of the line of the low down bear down, a vertical line through the rider's body to her seat bones, and the line of the horse's back from beneath them to the breastplate. The novice rider who is struggling to get her horse onto the bit has somehow to create these two triangles. The more experienced rider can use them as a guideline throughout the school movements:

Between hand and leg

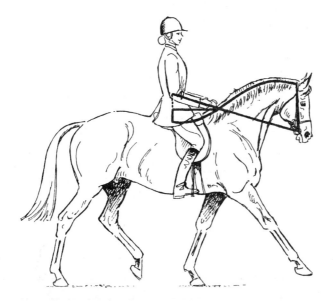

Fig. 4.7 When the rider is correctly positioned, and the horse is 'between hand and leg', he is held between two triangles as shown.

keeping them in place can save her from the contortions which become so tempting when one is not quite sitting well enough to make a difficult movement seem easy.

Everything we have talked about so far has been the build up to producing these two triangles. For to do this successfully, the rider has to be able to fulfil a large number of requirements. Firstly, she must keep the horse's attention, using her lower leg as necessary, so that his ears are out sideways. He is then paying attention inwardly, and not looking at the view. The rider must be able to sit still and plugged in, at the appropriate level of tone, so that her push forward matches the propulsive force of the horse's hind legs, and is bigger than his push back. It is important that she takes the horse, so that she is in control of his tempo. At the same time, her lower leg generates sufficient energy to keep him motivated, creating that fine balance between tempo and impulsion.

But this activity (both hers and the horse's) must not disturb her sitting. Simultaneously, her thigh must counterbalance her body weight and act as a suction device, holding her out of the mantrap and lifting the horse's back. Then, her hand and the rein must act like the lid on the end of a toothpaste tube – not letting the toothpaste leak out, but not scrunching the horse/tube backwards from the front. She can make her thigh even more effective by thinking of it as the girder over his suspension bridge.

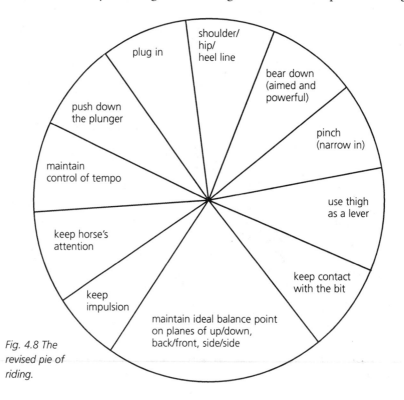

Fig. 4.8 The revised pie of riding.

As she does this, she makes her low down bear down land at the breastplate. (See the revised pie of Fig. 4.8.) Only then, she is in a good position to make a creditable attempt at riding the school movements.

I recently read an article in which an American dressage rider of some renown was talking about her training with a top German professional rider. After he had ridden her horse, she would get on again to find that the basic carriage and the advanced movements were in a different class. 'How do you do it?' she asked. 'It's just riding,' he replied, shrugging his shoulders, and no more information was forthcoming! His teaching skills were undoubtedly not commensurate with his riding skills, and my contention is that he – like other top-class riders – had unknowingly fulfilled all the above requirements supremely well. He then used them to retrain the Grand Prix movements.

....

- *Is your low down bear down focused and powerful like a power-hose, or is it weaker and more diffuse, like a watering-can spray?*
- *Whereabouts would it land on the horse's neck, or does it aim over his ears? It is extremely important to be able to give it power-hose quality, and to aim it to the horse's breastplate. This change may sound esoteric when you read it on paper, but the vast majority of riders can make sense of it. Just thinking about it can help a lot, but you may also need to move back in the saddle, whilst keeping your torso vertical (rather than leaning back).*
- *Your bear down will only become powerful and focused when you can push your 'plunger' right down to bikini-line level, and 'close the leaks' in your front. To review this, you might want to look back at page 52 et seq.*

....

We have now outlined the basic structure of the rider/horse interaction, and given ourselves another way to understand the half-halt. Our discussion of the 'Z' angles on page 86 focused on the up/down plane, and the need to deepen the 'Z' rather than using the much more common strategy of growing up tall, leaning back, stretching down into the stirrup, and pulling it apart (see Fig. 3.8). By focussing on the back/front plane, we are now viewing the same moment from a different perspective. As the rider elongates the horse's back to keep it functioning like a suspension bridge, her knee and her hip are kept maximally far apart. But let us suppose that the horse's back is working well, with no tendency for his stanchions to collapse: we then have the possibility that if her knee and her hip come *closer together*, the back could change its shape to become like the Sydney Harbour bridge, or like a strung bow, rounding up even

The half-halt

more in the middle. (See Fig. 4.9.) But if the rider attempted to bring her knee and her hip closer together *before* the horse had agreed to lift his back, the ends of the bridge/back would scrunch together – like crinkling a table cloth.

When the rider brings her knee and her hip closer together she simultaneously pushes forward from the back, and back from the knee. This reduces the width of the 'Z' from back to front, which concurrently closes its angles, giving an increased vertical distance between the quadriceps tendon and the seat bones. (See Fig. 3.8, page 86.) So in the half-halt there is an increased 'down' in the back corners of the backside and an increased 'up' in the front tendons. Imagine the ultimate extreme of this, in which the pelvis would be *hung* from the tendon of the large quadriceps muscles as they attach below the point of the hip. Just think of the tremendous lightness and shock absorption this would give the rider.

However, it is a very small percentage of riders who push back off their knee in a half-halt, and instead, most riders push themselves back from their *foot*. They brace into the stirrup – and by Newton's Third Law of Motion (see page 40) the increased downward force which accompanies 'stretching their legs down' generates an equal and opposite force which pushes them up out of the saddle. It opens the 'Z' angles, making the rider's thigh more vertical, and tempting her to lean back into the water-ski position. The result is a half-haul, not a half-halt. Biomechanically, it is as if the thigh has rotated about a pivot point at its centre and thus become too vertical. (See Fig. 4.3 on page 101.) This is one of the most pervasive mistakes that riders make in half-halts and downward transitions.

When riders change their tactics from 'pivoting' and water-skiing to 'buffering' and closing the 'Z' angles, they find an effective way of bringing the combined rider/horse centre of gravity back, and they no longer generate the evasions which accompany water-skiing. But they

(a)   (b)

Fig. 4.9. The half-halt: making the horse's back round upwards. From the flatter carriage of (a) it is as if the middle of the horse's back has been drawn up, creating the shape of a more tightly strung bow. Note also how the abdominal muscles have shortened.

need to think of their thigh remaining out in front of them, and having the buffering action of a jumping rider's thigh. To people who have learned to stretch their leg down, the idea often comes as a shock. Note too that the hand and leg have little to do with the half-halt: the 'lid on the toothpaste tube' may become momentarily stronger, and the leg may reinforce the impulsion. But to say that a half-halt is done with the hand and the leg completely misses the point; and to attempt to do it before the horse's back forms a good suspension bridge is courting disaster.

- *Can you set the horse's back up well enough for half-halts to become a viable option, or are you trying to do them prematurely? If so, you will only create more evasions.*
- *I meet many riders who think that their half-hauls are half-halts. Are you one of them?*
- *Do you pivot about the thigh, open the 'Z' angles, grow tall, lean back, and pull on the reins? Or do you use your thigh as a buffer, remain vertical, keep your ribs dropped down towards your hips, and keep the 'Z' angles closed?*

  When you have performed a good half-halt you will always know, because the horse's response is so instantaneous and correct, and so little hand is required. But you may not know how you did it, and may not be able to repeat it.

  Whilst you are learning, letting them happen as lucky accidents is often better than deliberately trying to do them, since this is so likely to access the wrong pattern. Be patient, pay attention to the basics, keep these ideas in the back of your mind, and wait for your skills to develop.

The fencing-lunge position

AS A RIDER who has spent many years learning how to mitigate the effects of quite a marked asymmetry, I have been told to 'sit straight' many more times than I care to remember. I brought to the problem great determination and a strong desire to become straight; but it soon became clear that willpower alone is not enough. The correction of bringing my inside hip towards the horse's opposite ear (which I wrote about in *Ride With Your Mind/The Natural Rider* and *'Masterclass'*) was a giant leap forward, as was the understanding that the rider needs to keep two equally weighted seat bones, with her hips and shoulders parallel and lying on the radius of the circle she is riding. (I will briefly justify this later; if it contradicts the theory you have learned and you need to understand the reasoning behind it, I refer you to *Ride With Your Mind/The Natural Rider* and especially *'Masterclass'*, where I explained it in great depth.)

The exercise of sitting on someone's back (explained more fully in *Ride With Your Mind/The Natural Rider* and on the 'Symmetry and Circles' videotape) makes it clear that facing your body in the direction of the turn only persuades your 'horse' to twist about her axis, bringing her shoulders towards the inside and her backside towards the outside. (See Fig. 5.1.) Riders unfamiliar with my work and doing this exercise for the first time *always* face both their shoulders and their pelvis in the direction of the turn – regardless of the theory they have learned. I do not think I have encountered anyone who has proved the exception to this rule, and I suspect that the mechanism of facing to the inside is so instinctive because it replicates the way that we turn on our feet.

In contrast, the fencing-lunge position (with your outside shoulder, seat bone and leg behind their counterparts on the inside) enables you to turn (rather than twist) your 'horse'. (Note, however, that whilst your hips and shoulders are parallel, your hips and seat bones are actually positioned on different axes. If you stand in a slight fencing-lunge position, with your outside leg behind your inside leg, and your hips and shoulders parallel, sticking your arms out directly sideways makes them lie on the radius of your circle, just like your hips and shoulders. But if you then use your

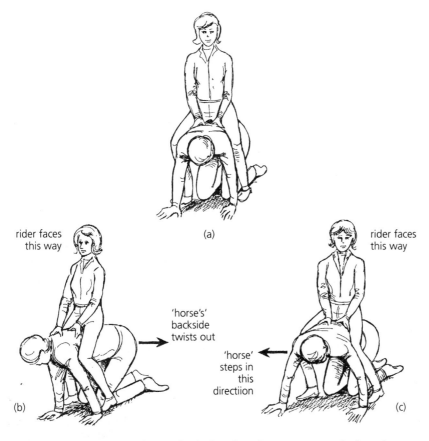

rider faces
this way

(a)

'horse's'
backside
twists out

'horse'
steps in
this
directiion

rider faces
this way

(b)

(c)

Fig. 5.1 Sitting on someone's back makes it clear that when you turn your body to the inside, as in (b), your 'horse' twists about his axis. However, by taking up the fencing-lunge position of (c), he can easily be made to take a step in the required direction.

fingers to feel for your seat bones, they lie on a completely different axis, with the inside one much more in advance of the outside. This will become even more clear if you then stick out your arms so that they lie on the same axis as your seat bones.)

The fencing-lunge turn begins from your outside thigh and seat bone, creating the fencing-lunge impulse which moves diagonally through your body, as if someone were pulling on your inside knee. This causes your horse (whether real or improvised) to take a step with the inside foreleg, thus moving his/her whole forehand in the direction of the turn. Further evidence for the value of the fencing-lunge position comes from realising that this is also how an ice-skater goes around a circle – pushing off one foot and then gliding on the other, with her body facing away from the direction of the turn.

I have used this analogy for many years, but have only recently had the chance to discuss it with an accomplished skater. By chance, I met a man who had been an extremely successful professional. He had thought much more deeply than most about the biomechanics of his sport, and was clearly a very innovative teacher. In his experience, conventional teaching rarely tackled the issue of keeping the skater's body on this axis (and of persuading her to stay with the weird feelings that this position generates). The forces acting during a turn or a spin tend to turn the skater's shoulders towards the inside – and if she succumbs to them, she loses control of the movement. The maintenance of the fencing–lunge orientation is the primary way to mitigate this, and was one of the cornerstones of his teaching.

Our discussion confirmed that the issues of asymmetry affect the skater much as they affect the rider. Virtually every skater does her figures more accurately to one side than to the other, and this is primarily because when going in one direction she cannot so easily resist the forces which tend to turn her upper body inwards. The jumps and spins, however, are considered so difficult that skaters are only ever expected to do them to one direction – and only a few of the great skaters of history have been able to do them both ways. My new friend bemoaned the fact that the decreasing influence of figures in competitive skating (which now weigh much less heavily than the freestyle) has reduced the emphasis on this basic need for symmetry, and on the drive for accuracy which had played such an important part in the training of his youth.

To return to riding, the exercise of sitting on someone's back helps novice riders visualise the possibility of steering the horse by positioning his wither with their pelvis and thigh, rather than by positioning his nose with their hand. The problem experienced by most novice riders is both intellectual (since pulling on the inside rein makes such instinctive sense) and physical (since so many factors make it difficult to find and maintain the correct pelvic positioning). Yet attempting to steer the horse's nose with your hand is actually no more effective than pulling on the inside

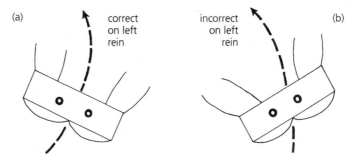

Fig. 5.2 The position of the rider's pelvis on a turn: (a) shows the position which is correct on the left rein but incorrect on the right rein; (b) shows the position which is incorrect on the left rein but correct on the right rein.

handlebar of a bicycle, or grabbing at the inside handle of a wheelbarrow. Finding a viable alternative, however, is not so easy – and without one, there is an inescapable temptation to ride 'handlebar turns'.

The concept of the fencing–lunge position becomes easier to grasp when the rider imagines herself sitting on a clockface with twelve o'clock positioned towards the horse's head. This delineates the ten to four position as a basic rule of thumb for the positioning of the seat bones on the left rein, and the ten past eight position as the basic orientation for the right rein. (See Fig. 5.2.) It has since become clear to me that these positions are not written in stone, but they are a useful guideline, especially for more novice riders who have the tendency to lose their outside seat bone. They then need to know where to find it. In most cases it has floated too far forward and too far out, and they can bring it into contact with the saddle by placing it further back and closer to the horse's spine, i.e. closer to six o'clock.

In this fencing–lunge mechanism it is the outside aids which initiate a turn by bringing the horse's outside shoulder away from the wall. So without a functioning outside seat bone and thigh, the rider cannot begin the turn, and she has little choice but to pull on the inside rein. Riders soon discover that attempting to steer the horse's nose causes them to lose control of his wither, for usually he '*jack-knives*', and as his nose comes to the inside his wither falls to the outside and the circle becomes larger. (See Fig. 5.3.)

Yet this concept is difficult to grasp intellectually, and the realisation

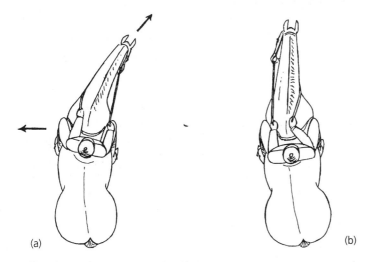

(a)   (b)

Fig. 5.3 The jack-knife seen from the top. In most cases, this is much more marked when the horse falls out as in (a) than it is when the horse falls in as in (b). This is primarily because the rider's instinctive response of pulling on the inside rein shortens the inside of the horse even more as he falls out.

that the wither and the nose go in opposite directions surprises many riders. I often find myself asking 'Which way is the nose going?' and 'Which way is the wither going?' and receiving replies which do not match reality. It can take some time before a rider's preconceived idea of what should be happening crumples in the face of what is.

On the opposite rein the horse's wither usually falls in, so he looks to the outside, and the circle becomes smaller than the rider intended. Whilst the horse falls out on one rein and in on the other, what remains constant is that his weight is directed onto one shoulder – he is like a ship with a list to port. Unless the horse is extremely green or 'wooden' the falling in is rarely as marked as the falling out, but usually it annoys the rider more. Here she *knows* she has a problem – although in reality she has an equal and opposite problem on the rein where the horse falls out. But this often goes undiagnosed. (This is despite the fact that the rider's instinctive response of pulling on the inside rein makes him fall out even more, thus compounding the problem!) Few riders appreciate that when the horse falls in he is at least going in the direction they wanted (which he is not if he falls out) – and only if they are novice enough to pull on the outside rein will their interventions make the tendency to fall in become worse.

On the 'stiff side', where most horses fall in, the horse may instead pull against the rider's pull, making a strong contact into the inside rein and refusing to turn at all. When this is the case, suspect that he may have sustained an injury that has left him in need of manipulative treatment. On the horse's 'soft side', where he jack-knives and falls out, the rider is often very happy because she has satisfied the traditional criteria for a correct bend, for she can see the horse's inside eye. But she has lost control of his wither – which actually means that she cannot steer.

I often point this out to riders by asking them if they could keep the horse's forelegs stepping along the line of a circle drawn on the surface of the riding arena. Few could, even though they had been congratulating themselves on their horse's 'bend'. The confusion between a jack-knife and a correct bend seems all but universal.

The jack-knife shortens the inside of the horse, and lengthens the outside of the horse, and this makes the inside long back muscle go 'soggy'. Ideally the horse turns not like an articulated lorry (known in the USA as an eighteen-wheeler), but like a bus, with his whole forehand turning around his hind end. This is reminiscent of a turn on the haunches. His body then remains much more symmetrical through the turn, and his wither is displaced in the direction in which he is going – *not in the opposite direction*, as one so commonly sees.

This turning mechanism keeps a much more even tension in the two long back muscles, and we can envisage each one as part of a chain of muscles, which functions like two long elastic bands. (See Fig. 5.4.) These

Fig. 5.4 *The horse's muscle system on each side of his mid-line is like a long elastic band reaching from the hock to the ears. The jack-knife makes the inside elastic band go soggy.*

pass all the way from the horse's hocks, over his croup, under the panels of the saddle, and up the crest of his neck to his ears. Both of these elastic bands must be under tension, or the impulse of the hind leg does not travel through this circuit. Thus it does not pass over the back on the soggy side of the horse. Even in mild cases of 'scrunch' this connection is lost.

To counteract this, I often suggest that the rider imagines the inside of the horse's body strapped onto a board, which miraculously passes from the top of his neck, past his shoulder blade, and under the saddle to his flank. Then as the rider turns, she must keep his body against the board. (See Fig. 5.5.) Pulling on the inside rein would make the board and the

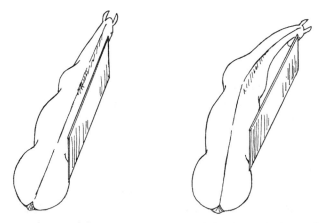

Fig. 5.5 *Thinking of the inside of the horse's body as if it were strapped onto a board can help the rider keep his wither moving in the direction of the turn or circle, and stop it from falling to the outside as it would if the horse jack-knifed.*

horse part company in the area of his wither – so this is off-limits. In extreme cases of a soggy inside, the rider might even need to think of counter flexion. For only then can she keep the inside of his body *lengthened* enough to hold it against the board, thus holding the horse's wither on her imaginary line. The concept of *lengthening the inside of the horse* surprises many people, since it seems such a blatant contradiction to our commonly held concept of bend. Yet it only exists as an antidote to the all-too-common jack-knife.

- *How have you been taught to position your body on a turn? Is this what you actually do? If you pay close attention to the positioning of your shoulders, hips and seat bones, you are likely to find that they are different on the two reins. (Thus, whatever theory you subscribe to, you are likely to contradict it on one rein!)*
  Do the exercise of sitting on someone's back to help you understand the fencing-lunge mechanism. Be careful to support some of your weight on your feet, so that you do not squash your 'horse'.
- *On which rein does your horse jack-knife, and how marked is this? When it happens, are you tempted to pull on the inside rein? At this point, what has happened to your outside seat bone?*
- *How does he turn on the opposite rein? If he still jack-knives, it is likely that you have pulled on the inside rein so much in each turn that you have taught him this strategy. If he falls in, does he do it to a greater or a lesser extent than he falls out? Or does he pull on the inside rein and attempt to go straight on?*
  See if you can find your way out of the jack-knife by being sure to keep your outside seat bone. Think of initiating the turn with the outside of your body, and then imagine the inside of the horse's body strapped against a board.
  Realise that the moment you pull on the inside rein, you have become part of the problem instead of being part of the solution.

....

The bulge of the horse's ribcage

Most people now know that the horse cannot bend in his spine in the same way that we can (creating creases down one side of the body). So the articulation which enables him to turn takes place primarily in the area of the shoulder blades, and in the loin area. Yet the ribcage can tilt one way or the other, giving the illusion of a bend. However, in a correctly executed turn, its bulge remains remarkably even on both sides. This surprises many people, since our instinctive logic suggests that it should bulge to the outside. Also, pictures in books which show bird's-eye views of horses going round a circle suggest that if the horse is not bending as we bend, then his ribcage must surely be bulging.

When the horse's ribcage does bulge to the outside, his centre of gravity is displaced that way, making him fall out on the circle. His inside long back muscle then all but disappears from under the rider's inside seat bone (or, more accurately, from under the neck of her femur – see Fig. 5.10 on page 138). It then becomes harder for her to stabilise her leg and body on that side. Yet the converse is also true. When the rider has her pelvis less well arranged on one side – and has a non-existent seat bone and/or a wobbly thigh – the horse's ribcage and long back muscle will not be correctly positioned underneath her. So by default, she will be tempted to steer by using her inside hand. In this situation – where riding on one rein will feel 'good' whilst the other feels 'bad' – we are left wondering who is the chicken and who is the egg? Did the rider make the horse crooked, or the horse make the rider crooked? Since nothing is nature is symmetrical, this scenario affects every rider, and in truth, each brings to their union an asymmetry which may be either rearranged or reinforced by the other's.

But regardless of how this interaction occurs, I am convinced that no rider will ever work effectively with her horse's asymmetries unless she can work effectively with her own. Many experiences have shown me that within the rider/horse system, the effects of carrying an asymmetrical burden are almost always greater for the horse than the effects of his own innate asymmetry. The exceptions to this rule are provided by horses who are in need of chiropractic treatment or who are lame – and their asymmetry (which could, of course, have been induced by a very crooked rider) will be extremely marked. Its most obvious symptom is a very strong contact on one rein, which makes it difficult to turn that way at all. This degree of muscular 'holding' is extremely difficult to ride through; however, in the vast majority of cases, it is all too easy for the asymmetrical rider to label the problem as the horse's, and not to recognise it as her own.

I have very clear memories of some of the more pivotal experiences through which I peeled off the layers of my own asymmetry, allowing this realisation to dawn. For as I changed the horses underneath me, I was forced to acknowledge that the original problem must have been my own. Watching that process of change in other riders has also been highly significant, although some of my most profound learning experiences have involved me riding pupils' horses when they were having problems on the left rein. Within a minute of me arranging myself in the saddle, it became clear that my problems were primarily on the *right* rein. On the first occasion when this happened I was really shocked; as it happened again and again, I began to realise how quickly I can put my stamp on a horse – and how quickly we all do so (for better or worse). It is as if the rider were a container and the horse were a liquid, automatically taking up the shape of the container he is put in.

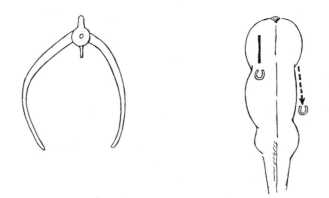

Fig. 5.6 The bulge of the horse's ribcage can be very uneven. Along with this, the two long back muscles may become very different, with one seeming to disappear, dropping downwards, or tucking itself in under the horse's spine. The step of the hind legs is also affected: the one on the side of the bulge carries more weight but cannot step forward so far; the other has room for a freer swing forward, but carries less weight.

Yet I also remember occasions when this change did not happen. For instance, one pupil's horse had a pronounced ribcage bulge to the left, with the left side of his body lengthened to such a degree that he was completely set against the left hand. Concurrently, it was hard to find a place to sit on the (virtually non-existent) right long back muscle, and extremely difficult to persuade him to take any contact into the right rein. (See Fig. 5.6.) I know that my asymmetry tends to make horses bulge more to the right; so he was clearly not reflecting me. (If the bulge had been in the opposite direction I could not have been so sure that I was not implicated – although in this case the pattern was *so* marked that it had to have its basis in a physical problem.) When I began questioning the rider, she remembered that she had recently gone down to the stable one morning and found him hanging upside down with one foot caught his hay net .... the kind of trauma which is almost guaranteed to leave the horse in need of manipulative treatment.

The vast majority of horses are naturally 'C' shaped, although a few contort themselves into an 'S' shape. Then, even though their shoulders fall outwards, their ribcage bulges inwards – and in my experience, these horses are in particular need of bodywork. (The most effective strategy for riding them is to think of their body like series of blocks which are misaligned, and which must be lined up from the quarters forwards.) I believe that the bulge of the ribcage *defines* the horse's asymmetry, for if its side-to-side swing in each step is not even, the hind legs cannot step evenly. The leg on the side of the bigger bulge carries more weight, but cannot swing forward so freely since the ribcage is in the way. The other carries less weight in each step, but has room for a freer swing forward. Only when the rider controls the bulge of the ribcage and can position it where she wants it does she truly have control of the side-to-side balance of her horse.

Whilst novice riders are always tempted to try and steer the horse's nose, thinking of steering the wither is a huge improvement on this – especially when the rider realises that she can do this by making a narrow corridor with both thighs, and channelling the wither down it. This reduces the role of her hand; yet to be truly successful she has to think even *further back on the horse*, becoming aware of the asymmetrical bulge of his ribcage. It is almost beyond my comprehension that this has gone virtually undocumented in our literature. In fact, the only reference I have ever found to it is in Tom Dorrance's book *True Unity*. Perhaps it took a very talented cowboy to be so unconstrained in his thinking that he could describe what he was feeling without recourse to the trappings of (dressage) convention.

• *Is your horse 'C' shaped or 'S' shaped? Imagine his quarters, loins, ribs, shoulders, lower neck, upper neck and head as a series of blocks. Are they lined up one in front of the other?*
• *Can you detect the displacement of your horse's ribcage? To do so, imagine that you and he were bisected down the middle. Are you sitting on a symmetrical bulge, or does one seat bone and one thigh have a wider base of support? Is there a flat bit of horse to the right of your right seat bone and to the left of your left seat bone, or does one side fall away more than the other?*
If it is harder to feel one seat bone than it is to feel the other, this may reflect an asymmetry of your own, and/or it may reflect the way that the asymmetrical bulge of your horse's ribcage gives it less of a base to rest on. It is worth considering chiropractic treatment for both yourself and your horse, so that you know you are both starting from the cleanest slate possible.

....

Functional symmetry

The most obvious asymmetry which the horse brings to the rider/horse system is a tendency to fall onto one shoulder. The asymmetrical bulge of his ribcage displaces his centre of gravity, making him fall *out* on the circle where the bulge is to the outside, whilst falling *in* on the circle where the bulge is to the inside. ('S' shaped horses obviously present a more complex picture.) The rider brings to the rider/horse system a tendency to both lean and twist to one side. (See Fig. 5.7a overleaf.) The majority of riders form a simple 'C' curve, with their shoulders, neck and head leaning over, with creases between their armpit and their pelvis on the shortened side. The bottom line – for both parties – is the displacement of the ribcage, and once we can correct this we are making significant moves towards what I term 'functional symmetry'.

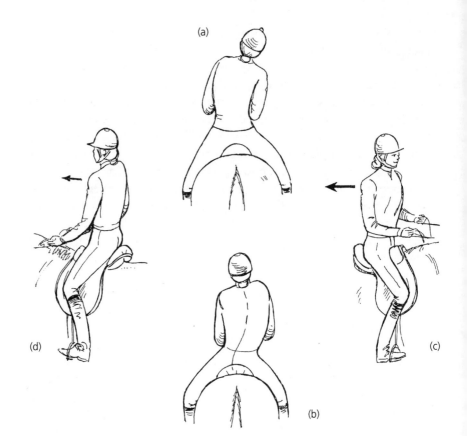

Fig. 5.7 (a) Shows the most common type of collapse, in which the rider has a 'C' curve. Usually, the inside seat bone is heavier in this case; but some riders draw it up into their backside making the outside seat bone heavier.

(b) Shows the 'S'-shaped rider seen from the back. Her inside shoulder will be the higher one, and instead of having creases around her waist on the inside, she now has them beneath her armpit on the outside.

(c) Shows either rider from the inside. An observer in the centre of the circle sees the rider's chest, her inside hand behind her outside hand, and her inside leg coming forward.

(d) Shows how an observer standing on the inside of the circle would see the rider if she were working on the other rein. If her asymmetry is marked, the observer may not see the body in profile (as is ideal) but would see more of her back. However, the inside leg and hand are both steadier and in a more correct position than on the other rein.

Chiropractors believe that the 'C' curve so commonly seen in the rider is always accompanied by a twist, which advances the shoulder on the side of the body which has lengthened. This is certainly borne out in my observations. To understand it more clearly, collapse to one side as you sit in your chair, and notice how natural it is to advance the higher shoulder. If we collapse then we twist; but it is also true that if we twist then we collapse. This makes turning the shoulders into the circle a dangerous (as well as an ineffective) policy – even though we so commonly hear that we should place our shoulders parallel to the horse's shoulders and our hips parallel to his hips. (Later I will explain why I think this idea is so prevalent.) On the rein where the rider's body (like the skater's body) is more vulnerable to the effects of the centrifugal force, the twist is soon accompanied by a lifting of the outside seat bone, thus generating the collapse to the inside. A secondary issue is that the body is vulnerable to damage when the spine is twisted, and bodyworkers of all persuasions frequently warn against this.

The twist and collapse cause unequal weighting of the seat bones, and a lean to the inside. (One very rarely sees someone leaning to the *outside* of a circle; so on the other rein the rider usually remains on the vertical axis, and to a superficial glance all seems well.) This explains why I consider equal weighting of the seat bones to be so important – even though riders are often told to weight the inside one more. But whenever one becomes lighter, the other becomes heavier (and vice versa), with the inevitable result that the rider loses her vertical axis.

In the majority of cases, it is the inside seat bone which becomes heavier, whilst the outside one lightens or disappears. However, a few people collapse to the inside by *lightening* the inside seat bone and drawing it up into their backside – a pattern which I took many years to recognise, since it is the opposite of my own. Its external manifestations, however, are virtually the same.

Whilst most riders lose their vertical axis by becoming a 'C' shape, a small proportion of riders show the more complex 'S' shape – a pattern which I have termed 'break dance', since it mirrors the displacement of the ribcage seen in that dance form. (See Fig. 5.7b.) The 'S' shape is sometimes the rider's natural pattern; but it often evolves out of the 'C' shape when an instructor tells the rider to drop her outside shoulder. (Try making a 'C' and then dropping the higher shoulder; then you will understand what I mean.) By addressing only a symptom of the pattern and not its *cause,* they have produced another more complex contortion.

Since every horse and rider are unique, there are many variations on the theme. But in all of these cases, a trainer standing on the inside of the rider's circle will see the rider's inside hand behind her outside hand, and a twist to the inside which reveals her chest. (See Fig. 5.7c.) (The ideal would be to see her body in profile.) She will also see a sogginess in the rider's inside leg, which indicates a lack of tone, and will see her inside knee tending to ride up, with her foot coming forward. Viewing the rider from the back, she would see her spine coming off axis to the inside, showing either the 'C' or the 'S' shape discussed earlier.

On the other rein where the rider can maintain her spine on (or much closer to) its ideal vertical axis, she contributes much less to the overall rider/horse pattern of asymmetry. If her twist to one side is so marked that she now faces too much to the outside of the circle, the trainer standing at its centre will now see too much of her back. (See Fig. 5.7d.) Yet the rider's inside hand is rarely pulling back, and her leg position is more stable. Often, both rider and trainer define this rein as 'good' and the other as 'bad'. However, their conviction that the rider should turn her shoulders to the inside may make them ignore the improved performance of the horse and define this rein as 'bad'. As we shall see, a closer inspection reveals that both reins have their problems, and that a difficulty which shows up clearly on one side of the body inevitably involves the other side, requiring a correction which encompasses both.

Achieving 'functional symmetry' requires both horse and rider to make different corrections on the different sides of their bodies. The net result should look symmetrical, and on one level it will feel it – since the horse steers in a far more symmetrical way. But on another, it will be very clear that this symmetrical result comes at the cost of 'conscious asymmetry'. In contrast, doing what comes naturally – i.e. working within your 'unconscious asymmetry' – could erroneously convince you that you are acting symmetrically, for 'home' is so familiar that it may well masquerade as 'right'. Yet it will yield a very asymmetrical look, and the sense that you are steering an inherently asymmetrical creature.

I shall never forget one rider who had a marked 'C' curve to the right. Yet when I asked her 'Does your spine go straight up, or does it veer off to one side?' she replied with no hesitation that it went straight up. Her asymmetry was so marked that the audience gasped (and I hope they learned a lesson about the difference between feeling and seeing). I then backed away from the issue, and asked the same question later. When I had received the same reply several times I asked her, 'Is your chin over the horse's mane?'

This sent her into confusion; so I stopped her, manoeuvred her spine to the vertical, and said, 'Now this is straight.'

'Oh my God,' she replied, 'I feel as if I'm falling off to the left.'

Yet she could *see* that her chin was directly over the horse's crest, and moving between the two positions eventually convinced her that her feel sense was not to be trusted.

This is an example of one of the basic premises of Chapter 1: that changing the map you work from (redefining your understanding of straight versus crooked) yields far more change than any attempt to change your behaviours within your existing map (which does not question your perception of straight).

It is impossible to change any asymmetry before you have diagnosed your starting point. So ideally work with a friend as you both answer the following questions, working on a circle firstly in walk on both reins, and then in trot on both reins.

Your friend should observe you from both the inside of the circle, and from behind, assessing whether your answers match her observations. Once you have agreement, it may be helpful for her to write them down.

- *Do you have equal weighting of both seat bones. If not, which is clearer, and how much weight out of 100% does each carry?*
- *Is one seat bone further forward and one further back? Imagine you are sitting on a clockface, with twelve o'clock pointing straight ahead, and work out what time they say.*
- *Does one point more forward (i.e. towards the horse's front foot) and one point more back (i.e. towards his back foot)?*
- *Are your stirrups the same length? Check them if necessary, but if they are uneven do not adjust them yet.*
- *Is one stirrup more weighted than the other? Rate these weights out of 100%.*
- *Is one heel more down, and one more on tip toe?*
- *Does one knee stay in place more easily than the other, and function more effectively as the centre point of a circle in rising-trot mechanism? (See Fig. 3.2.)*
- *Does one thigh rest more snugly against the saddle than the other?*
- *If you think of your thigh bones as being like iron bars, is one more strong and one more soggy than the other?*
- *Think of your body as a waterfall, or as a pipe with water going down it, and imagine that when the water gets to your pelvis it divides, with some going down each leg. How much water goes down each leg? Rate each one out of 100%.*
- *Do both thighs point in directions that are mirror images of each other? If twelve o'clock were straight ahead, do they point towards five-to and five-past, ten-to and ten-past, etc.?*
- *Think of the bony sides to your pelvis (the pelvic wings, which have your points of hips as their most forward part). Is one more solid and stronger than the other?*
- *Is your chin over the mane? If your body is off axis, which side are you leaning to?*
- *Do you have creases on one side between your ribs and your hips?*
- *If you are 'C' shaped, they will be on the inside, at waist level. If you are 'S' shaped they will be on the outside beneath your armpit. Which pattern do you fit, and does your assessment match with your friend's observations as she looks at you from behind? Double check – which seat bone has become heavier?*
- *Does the axis of your shoulders lie on the radius of the circle you are riding, or are you facing in or out of that circle?*
- *To clarify this, imagine you were wearing a milkmaid's yoke. What direction would it point in? Would the inside arm aim towards the centre of the circle you are riding, behind the centre, or in front of the centre? Does your assessment match the assessment of your friend as she stands at the centre of your circle? Is she seeing your body in profile, seeing more of your front, or more of your back? It may help you to caricature your asymmetry, exaggerating it so that it becomes clear to you. Ideally have someone video you from the back and side as you move between this and straight (or as straight as you can get).*

The spine as a flexible mast

I heard recently of a great success story which made me appreciate the value of these corrections. It came from a relatively novice rider whose horse napped to the right whenever she tried to turn left. Unable to change this whilst riding, she resorted to sitting on her saddle on a strong saddle horse, with a copy of the *'Masterclass'* book in one hand, and a pencil in the other. She then imagined herself riding on each rein, and answered the questions in a list similar to the one above. This made her realise that whilst her right leg lay snugly on the saddle, her left leg dangled off to the side, especially when it was on the inside. She discovered that lying it on the saddle required great effort; but the next time she rode, she reproduced that same feeling the moment her horse began to nap to the right. Her response was a little weak and little late; but it was enough to cause her horse to change his mind, and to come around to the left 'like a bus'. Within a week she had the problem solved.

Despite successes like this, I have also found that I cannot necessarily get a rider to maintain her vertical axis (and make the adjustments needed to straighten her horse) just by getting her torso stacked up above two equally weighted seat bones, and then making her aware of the way she tends to lose that alignment. My initial approach (as put forward in my other two books) generated more viable changes than any other system of thought, but still was not entirely convincing. So I began looking beyond it, driven by an instinctive feeling that there had to be some kind of overview which would fit the myriad problems of asymmetry into a simpler whole.

It took an extremely good book on bodywork to help the penny drop. In *Bodywise,* Joseph Heller and William A. Henkin put forward a convincing argument that the spine is like a flexible mast, held up by guy ropes. Thus telling a rider to 'sit straight' is doomed to fail because however much she *wants* to sit straight, her spine will soon be pulled out of true by the unequal tension in the ropes! So obedience and will power will inevitably fail. It can, however, be helpful for her to regularly check that her mid-line is over the horse's mid-line with her chin over his mane, her seat bones equally weighted, and no extra creases on one side of her torso. But doing so cannot hold her straight indefinitely – however aware she becomes of the inherent asymmetry in her body.

It then became important to understand more about the guy ropes themselves. I was already well aware of the importance of the rider's psoas muscles, which affect her stability both in the back/front plane, and in the side/side plane. Initially I thought of these as the guy ropes, but I now think that they are just one part of the way the spine is pulled off its ideal vertical axis. I often call them the *internal muscles*, since they are hidden in the body cavity (along with your guts). They begin on the bottom rib, and have connections into each of the lumbar vertebrae, becoming thicker

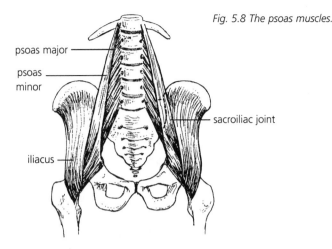

Fig. 5.8 The psoas muscles.

psoas major

psoas minor

iliacus

sacroiliac joint

and stronger as they pass down through the abdominal cavity and then forward through it, reaching the front a couple of inches above and to each side of your pubic bone. (See Fig. 5.8. Also, the psoas stretch in Fig. 9.18c on page 276 may help you to feel them, especially at this point. The psoas test in Fig. 9.10 on page 260 may also help.)

At this level, the psoas muscles are joined by the iliacus muscles, which cover the inside of the pelvic wings: so if you put your hands on your hips, they cover the inside of the bony ridges you are resting on. The muscles (known now as iliopsoas) then follow a path which ends with them attaching to the underside of the bony knobble (the greater trochanter of the femur) which you can feel at the top outside of your thigh.

Iliopsoas is normally described in anatomy books as 'a principal flexor of the hip joint'. To quote from *The Anatomy Colouring Book* by Wynn Kapit and Lawrence M Elson, 'It may play a role in balancing the torso during sitting. In standing, there is evidence that iliopsoas functions to counteract the tendency of the torso to fall back of the line of gravity, which passes somewhat behind the hip joints. It is certainly an important postural muscle in aligning the lower limb with the body trunk.'

Thus the iliopsoas muscles stabilise the rider, stopping her from falling backwards, aiding her as she holds 'flexion pattern' and refuses to water-ski.

Their importance in riding was validated recently for me by a pupil who is an emergency room physician. A senior surgeon told her the story of a quiet day when the staff had been watching horse racing on television. A well-known jockey fell, and was trampled badly. Knowing that he would be brought to them for treatment, they prepared the operating room. X-rays and scans confirmed the need for surgery, and to the surgeon's amazement, opening him up revealed by far the largest iliopsoas muscles that he had ever seen!

In anatomy books the muscles are drawn as neat, symmetrical structures. But texts which show actual pictures of cadavers reveal a different story. One may be much thicker than the other, and they may follow very different paths within the abdominal cavity. For instance, the 'C'-shaped rider may have 'C'-shaped psoas muscles, with one much longer than the other. The 'S'-shaped rider may have muscles with a step in them; but in every asymmetry these muscles are implicated, and inevitably, the problem can never lie in just *one* of them.

....

The boards exercise

Experience has convinced me that explaining how to hold the spine on axis when riding on both reins is best done through the following exercise. To understand this, you have to do it – the words on their own have little meaning.

So sit on a chair with your legs slightly apart, making a 'V' shape between your thighs. This 'V' should be symmetrical, and its point should lie on your mid-line, beneath your pelvic floor and further back than your seat bones. (See Fig. 5.9a.) To give you a sense of the psoas muscle on one

(a)   (b)

Fig. 5.9 The boards exercise: (a) shows the rider sitting on a chair with a symmetrical 'V' between her thighs; (b) bringing the right board towards the mid-line advances that side of the body and that thigh, making the 'V' asymmetrical.

side think of a line joining your nipple and the corner of your pubic bone; better still, think of a *board* which follows this line and goes through you from your front to your back. (This does not quite approximate the line of the psoas muscle, which makes me think that many more structures are involved. In fact, the front and back of the boards follow the edges of the muscles in your front and back which have vertical fibres. To the outside of these are muscles whose fibres run crossways, virtually parallel to your ribs.)

Then *move the board towards what was the mid-line of your body*, and feel how it becomes a more solid entity – you really should now feel as if you have a board inside you. This movement will advance the hip and shoulder on that side, twisting your body towards the opposite side (Fig. 5.9b). However, it is not just a twist of your shoulders, since it also involves movement *within* your skin, pushing your 'stuffing' against the board.

The thigh on the advanced side should now feel longer and stronger than the other; it should also look longer. The seat bone on the advanced side becomes more prominent, and the 'V' shape made by the inside of both thighs becomes very asymmetrical. The arm of the 'V' on the side you have advanced will be clear and strong, right back to the point of the 'V'. This is now displaced towards the *opposite* side, for the other arm of the 'V' has become shorter and fuzzier. (A few people initially find that the opposite thigh becomes stronger. If this is the case, you have almost certainly brought the other side of the body back, instead of bringing the side you intended to move forward. Experiment with this, until you discover a way to make the thigh on the same side become the longer, stronger one.)

If you hold this position for a while, the quadriceps muscle running along the top of the advanced thigh may well feel some strain. (This is reminiscent of the exercise on page 102, which showed you how the thigh can be used as a buffer.) Also, the tendon of the inside thigh muscle on the active side will become prominent, and when you are riding, it will come onto the saddle, making your thigh lie more snugly against it.

Next, return to neutral, and reverse the positioning, thinking of the line (or board) on the opposite side, and moving it towards your mid-line. Already, you may have a sense that the two sides are very different. Repeat this slowly and mindfully a number of times to each side, maintaining each position for a while, so that you feel how your seat bones roll over the flesh in your backside with each movement, and how the 'V' shape of your inner thigh becomes asymmetrical in opposite ways.

I have tested this explanation on hundreds of people, and most people can easily make sense of it – at least on the side of their body which gives them clearer feedback. (You will almost certainly have chosen to do this side first.) However, it once took two days for a rider to 'get it', with

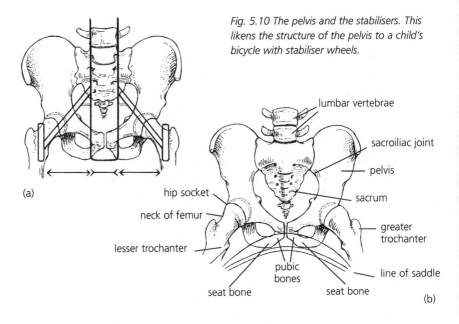

Fig. 5.10 The pelvis and the stabilisers. This likens the structure of the pelvis to a child's bicycle with stabiliser wheels.

(a)

lumbar vertebrae

sacroiliac joint

pelvis

sacrum

hip socket

neck of femur

greater trochanter

lesser trochanter

pubic bones

line of saddle

seat bone

seat bone

(b)

lunch-times, coffee breaks, and the evenings in the pub all given over to explanations and experimentation! But this was an exception – and if you feel similarly flummoxed keep experimenting, and perhaps ask a friend to join you. When you get it, I think you will be in no doubt that you did.

Next comes the punch-line. Advance the weaker board, bringing it towards your mid-line, and making it as strong and clear as possible. Then advance the stronger board as well. You will now feel that your way of sitting is no longer in the range of 'normal', for it has made you so narrow from side to side that you would never choose to hang out like this! It is as if you are pushing both sides of your body in towards each other (reinforcing the sensation of narrowing in which you get from the pinch). As you sit in this position, notice that you have been bearing down – probably without even realising that you were doing so – and that the 'V' shape of your thighs is now narrower, stronger, and symmetrical. Also realise that you are sitting not just on your seat bones, but to the *outside of them*, with a broader piece of flesh resting on the chair. This is highly significant, for this muscle, which lies under the neck of the femur, must lie across each of the horse's long back muscles. (See Figs. 5.10 and 5.11a.) This is a theme that we will return to in the dismounted exercises of Chapter 9.)

Whilst this way of sitting is not normal, you might well sit in a chair with *one* side advanced – and I suspect that many people with a stronger right board drive their car like this. My contention is that the vast majority of riders ride in one of these asymmetrical positions, with one psoas column (or board) virtually over the mid-line of the horse, and the other dangling ineffectually off to the side. I call this 'one side on, one side off'. It explains why so many riders only connect well with one of the horse's long back muscles: for they always have one seat bone (or, more accurately, one neck of the femur) resting, as it should, on top of the horse's long back muscle, with the other one falling off its counterpart on the other side (Fig. 5.11b). So the bottom line of any asymmetry correction must be to get both boards functioning well, making the rider so narrow that her pelvis fits *across* the horse's back in the ideal way. But until a rider discovers her boards, this can seem impossible – as it did to me for many years.

The 'one side on, one side off' positioning also explains why the steering on one rein works well, whilst the other so easily degenerates into pulling on the inside rein. For when the rider has *her inside board over the horse's inside board* all is well (for reasons I will clarify later). (See Fig. 5.5, page 125.) But when her inside board is soggy and out of place she will inevitably resort to pulling on the inside rein. This also explains the way that a rider will go to a trainer who rants and raves about her difficulties in riding one rein. So by hook or by crook, she finds a way to fix the problem, and she goes home euphoric. Then a few days later she 'comes to' and realises that she is now having problems on the *other* rein.

What she has in fact done is to reverse her pattern of 'one side on, one side off', making what was the 'bad' rein 'good', and what was the 'good' rein 'bad'. But in either case, only one side of her body is functional, and she only connects well with one of the horse's long back muscles. The reversal may not happen again for weeks, months, or years – and many riders spend their entire riding life 'ping-ponging' between these two positions. Given that the 'both boards on' position is never a part of our everyday life, I find it no surprise that so few riders ever find it.

When I need to work with these issues in a less complex way, I often ask the rider about the 'V' shape between her inner thighs. If she were sitting symmetrically with both boards on, the 'V' made by her inner

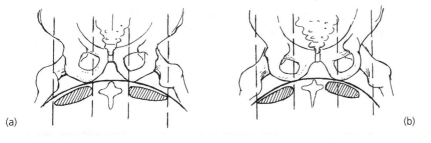

(a) (b)

Fig. 5.11 Ideally, the neck of the femur on each side rests across the horse's long back muscle, as in (a), but more often, one side is on and one is off, as in (b), so that the rider connects correctly with only one of the horse's long back muscles.

thigh muscles would also be symmetrical, with two strong arms meeting at a point which lies on the mid-line shared by her and the horse. But as the above exercise shows, any asymmetry in the boards will show up in the 'V', and in practice, I have yet to find a rider who does not have one weak arm. Commonly, this fizzles out before it joins the other, and the point of the 'V' – if there is one – is rarely on the combined rider/horse mid-line. (I have also met a few riders whose 'Vs' had arms which were at different angles, and which could never meet until the higher one was brought down. Bringing them to a point has corrected asymmetries which had defied everything else I could think of!) Persuading the arms of the 'V' to meet at a point forces the rider to make changes to her boards (or at least to the bottom of them), strengthening the weaker side, and bringing it more distinctly onto the saddle.

Some riders find that they can only get one board to function at a time, in which case I teach them how to bring the *inside* board strongly into place on each rein (this is usually a much bigger challenge on one rein than it is on the other). My original idea of bringing the rider's inside hip towards the horse's opposite ear on the rein where she leans and twists inwards went some way towards engaging the inside board. It faces the body to the outside, and brings the bottom of the front of the board (the adductor tendon at the top inside thigh) onto the saddle. This concurrently changes the 'V' shape of the inner thighs. But the correction will not necessarily make the *whole* board strong (and of course it does not address the board on the outside of the body). With it, I had found part of the map, and not the whole map. Yet I still use this correction with people where I am short on time, or if I sense that doing the above exercise on their horse (which takes much of a lesson) would put them into overload.

Since you are highly likely to be one of the millions who has an asymmetrical 'V' and who rides with 'one side on and one side off', I suggest that you practice alternating between the two positions when riding, repeating the exercise you did on the chair but with your horse in walk. This makes the unconscious conscious: one position will be 'home' – and now, you can recognise how grossly asymmetrical it actually is! The other may be very hard to get into, and may feel extremely strange: yet it is actually the mirror image of the first. (You will do this exercise more easily once you have shared Denise's struggle with it in Chapter 6.)

Ride the exercise as you warm your horse up, and do it every day for three months. Your strengths and your weaknesses may change, so be prepared for your preconceived notions about yourself to become outdated.

If you do lateral work reasonably well, leg yields in walk may help you clarify your sense of the boards. All of the lateral movements degenerate into push-pull battles unless the board in the direction of motion is functioning well (although the rider does a much better job when she has both). If you have not been able to ride the movements well, you now know why – and I now feel that it is pointless to teach them unless the rider has her boards well in place. When you work with the movements anew you will have a very different vantage point – although you will doubtless still struggle until you can get your weaker side to function so well that it ceases to be a limitation!

If you have previously ridden the movements well, you have a useful resource you can draw on (at least on one rein). Take the exaggerated clarity of the board which you get within the lateral movement and *keep that feeling* as you ride the horse on one track.

Within any session, do not be in a hurry to put 'both sides on'. Wait you have done the 'one side on, one side off' exercise a number of times on both reins, and can easily get into the position which puts your weak side 'on' and your strong side 'off'. Then use this as a basis for putting your strong side 'on' too; but do not let it push the weak side off. As you add in your strong side, notice what effect this has on your 'V' shape. Once you can hold this in place, and keep it symmetrical, you will be well on your way to a more symmetrical functioning throughout your body.

- *Do the boards exercise sitting on a chair. Once you understand this well and can find both positions, do the same exercise whilst riding your horse at walk, taking lots of time to alternate the two positions before you put 'both sides on'. Repeat this every day as you ride out, or warm up your horse on a long rein. Do not be surprised if the 'one side on, one side off' positions make him head off in some seemingly strange directions!*
- *Which board gives you the most trouble? How can you strengthen its weaknesses? If you need to, strengthen it by deliberately riding with this side on and the other side off.*
- *Can you sustain the 'both boards on' position in walk, rising trot, sitting trot, and canter? Do not expect this to happen overnight; but do expect to get some dramatic improvements each time you succeed!*
- *Can you make the 'V' shape of your inner thighs symmetrical?*

....

Errant boards

For many riders first learning this, the primary difficulty becomes the need to process information from both sides of the body at once. Almost certainly, these people did not cross-crawl as babies, for moving the opposite arm and leg both at the same time is an essential developmental stage which programmes both brain hemispheres to work together. If instead the child shuffles along on her bottom, or crawls as a horse walks (i.e. right hind, right fore, left hind, left fore), then one brain hemisphere is always switched off whilst the other is switched on. This way of processing then tends to be maintained throughout life, and this is the underlying problem in many children who are labelled dyslexic. (The bibliography lists some simple and extremely helpful books about this.) For riders, changing this pattern is a challenging and important task, which is all but inescapable, for the fundamental answer to all asymmetries lies in putting 'both boards on'.

One of my favourite descriptions of this was suggested by a pupil who called it 'the whole body pinch' – as if the laces which make you narrower across your pelvis (see page 66) now go all the way up your back. One (rather large) rider who got it well once said, 'I've heard you say that riding well is like wearing a corset around your pelvis which holds your muscles more firmly. But now I feel as if you've wrapped me up like an Egyptian mummy!' Other descriptions have included: 'like two people, both fighting to sit on the same bar stool, only neither of them must push the other one off'; and 'like putting both legs into the same sock'. One of my student teachers likened the action of the boards to using two pieces of wood to scoop up autumn leaves.

The variations on the theme of errant boards are enormous, and I have yet to meet a rider who has two functioning boards on both reins. A small proportion of riders get this far on one; many have soggy places, missing bits, or kinks in one or both boards. I have met one (but only one) rider who always had her *outside* board strong and her inside board soggy, and this accounted for the difficulty I had had in stabilising her inside leg and hand whichever rein she was on. In fact, with both boards on, her reputation as an ugly duckling – an ardent trier with no talent – quickly came up for renewal!

I have also met a handful of riders (including Kate, who you will meet in Chapters 6 and 10) who had managed to always have her inside board in place, and thus to ride rather well on both reins. But then she had been an international competitor – and although she found it extremely difficult to bring the outside board into place, one has to admire her guts for even attempting it now that she is well into her sixties! Only one rider has ever failed to understand the concept, and asked me not to continue with it. (She did not give me long, however, to try and get it across to her, and since she had been working alone for the three years since her last set of lessons, she had a long agenda of her own!) No one has ever found that it made no difference. In fact Denise (who you will meet in Chapter 6) probably struggled with it more than anyone else has ever done, and the stories of miraculous transformations are legion.

Two that stick in my mind concern rather novice riders, whom I had wrongly felt might be too inexperienced to benefit from the idea. One was extremely crooked (with the 'C' curve to end all 'C' curves), which she attributed to her previous addiction to tennis. Her trainer had sent her to me in desperation, and I began by using awareness questions that would clarify the pattern for her, asking 'Which is the heavier seat bone? Which one is further forward and which is further back?' etc. The idea of keeping her chin over the horse's mane and the correction of bringing her inside hip towards the horse's opposite ear, helped somewhat; but I had the sense that however hard she worked with these ideas, her attempts to stay straight were doomed.

So I dived in at the deep end and taught her about the boards. Her 'C' curve to the right made her right-hand board go soggy in the middle, and she realised that she had to find a way both to strengthen it, and to keep it away from the edge of her body. Her right-hand third (between the board and the edge of her body) had to become wider, and more stuffed – a very common scenario. (See Fig. 5.12.) This difference immediately helped her to find her outside seat bone, and to stay much straighter (if not truly straight) around each corner. She also gained control of her inside leg and hand. But what inspired me most was the way that she began to mutter under her breath as she was riding. 'I think I can do this. I really can. Come on, Sheila, you can do this. It's really making a difference ... I can do this!' Amazingly, she kept this up for several circuits of the arena. This implied, of course, that everyone's previous attempts to make her straight (including my own) had not been things she felt she could do, or things that made a difference – and *this* implied that we had come very much closer to the nub of the problem.

The other story concerns a relatively novice rider who was in desperation about her inability to steer. There was an immense

Fig. 5.12 A 'C'-shaped collapse to the inside occurs in part because the rider has so little stuffing in her inside third. The collapse brings the board (which has already gone soggy) far too close to the edge of the rider's body.

Fig. 5.13 The turning aids work correctly when the rider has her inside board over the horse's inside board, and her inside third well 'stuffed and stacked', and positioned over the horse's long back muscles. They then both turn as one; but as soon as this connection is lost, and either or both boards become soggy, the rider is forced to pull on the inside rein.

discrepancy between the theory she understood, and the practical difficulties she was discovering. So I taught her to make an inside board on each rein (but did not go so far as to getting her to put 'both sides on'). I also explained the idea of 'as if the inside of the horse's body were strapped on a board', and suggested that the answer to steering lay in keeping her board over the horse's board. (See Figs. 5.5 and 5.13.) This soon enabled her to ride very good 10-metre circles in both directions in walk, without using her inside hand at all.

In fact, it was one of those changes which was so easy, and so quick that I found myself thinking. 'This isn't fair. She shouldn't be able to do it this easily. She hasn't suffered enough yet.' Inwardly, I was comparing her learning with my own, realising how futile those years of wrongness had been – and I had to steel myself to spare her from suffering the same fate! In the early days when I was first learning and teaching the basic biomechanical patterns of riding, my magnanimity was regularly tested by similar situations. But when this particular experience occurred I had not felt that way for years; the memories of my frustrations had faded, and I had grown to expect that I would create profound changes in riders. To revisit this feeling so unexpectedly made me realise that I had reached a fundamental truth about turning.

- *Find your own image, which best describes the feeling of having 'both boards on'.*
- *If all you can manage is to ride with your inside board in place on each rein, think of keeping your board over the horse's board, so that you both turn together.*
- *Is one of your outer thirds less 'stuffed' than the other? Does this affect the strength and the straightness of your boards? What happens when the less*

'stuffed' third is positioned on the inside and on the outside of the circle?
* *Can you increase the amount of 'stuffing' in this third? Think of keeping the board away from the edge of your body, and of filling it out so strongly that you cannot get kinks or creases in either.*

....

To begin a turn, riders need to have their outside seat bone clearly positioned on either four or eight o'clock (see page 123). For novice riders, this presents the primary problem, as it can go missing in so many different ways. Then, with the outside of their body 'floating', they have no way to initiate the turn – so they pull on the inside rein. But once it has been found, the problem of the more advanced rider is that there needs to be not only something to *push round from* but also *something to push into*.

The rider's board over the horse's board

To understand this, think of riding a horse without a bridle. Unless you were an exceptional rider, you could not keep the horse in carriage for very long – for there is nothing to push the 'stuffing' up into, and it would soon begin to leak out of the front. In the turning aids, the 'something to push into' is the inside board, which is positioned over the horse's inside board. As long as there is a connection between the rider's inside psoas muscle and the horse's inside long back muscle, horse and rider, as one, will move to the inside. But when either one of them loses the solidity of the board, or loses its connection with the other, the turn or circle is compromised. There are, in fact, five options:

(1) Neither horse nor rider has a functioning board.
(2) The horse does but the rider does not.
(3) The rider does but the horse does not.
(4) Both do, but they are not stacked one over the other.
(5) Both do, and they are stacked over one another.

Often the more advanced rider who has the outside of her body well in place can think of creating the fencing lunge, and galvanise so much strength that she pushes herself *off* the inside long back muscle. Even if her inside board was strong and connected to begin with, this displaces it (and could also make it soggy). Either way, the rider's initial impulse has lost its effect on the horse. In the worst case scenario it becomes rather like pouring flour through a sieve – so again, she has to resort to pulling on the inside rein. This explains why lateral movements become a struggle when the board in the direction of motion is not positioned over the horse's long back muscle, and able to receive the rider's 'push'.

This connection between the rider's inside psoas muscle and the horse's inside long back muscle is the critical ingredient in a turning aid. With the inside board in place, virtually everything else works well (although the outside board is also needed before you can reach perfection!). Once the rider is correctly connected to the inside of the horse she can ask with the fingers of her inside hand for the horse to look to the inside. In response he will maintain the even bulge of his ribcage and the positioning of his wither, whilst he replies 'Yes, I'd love to do that.'

This, of course, is exactly what it says in the books – but the great Masters who wrote them presupposed this connection between the rider's inside psoas muscle and the horse's inside long back muscle. They did not realise just how much could go wrong – and what sins the rider would inevitably commit with her hand – as soon as that connection was lost.

The feeling of having the inside board in place has, I suspect, been rather dubiously described as 'lengthening your inside leg' (for it gives such a strong connected feel to the inside leg, which will otherwise tend to go soggy) and/or as 'weighting your inside seat bone'. To me, it is no surprise that these descriptions do not help the rider to 'get it'. In fact, they can lead her up a gum tree, encouraging her to collapse to the inside. For the map is then so far removed from the territory that only the most talented riders can use it to navigate well.

- *Do your steering problems lie in initiating the turn from your outside aids, or in pushing yourself off the horse's inside long back muscle?*
- *Analyse your interaction with him on both reins in terms of the options listed above, e.g. do you have a weak inside board on the right rein, whilst his is strong? You are more likely to find that if yours is weak, his is weak, and that by strengthening yours you can begin to strengthen his – assuming, of course, that you can keep yours stacked up above it.*

....

'Stuff and stack' If your brain is reeling from all these new ideas, you might want to skip the rest of this chapter – for you certainly have enough information to work on. But if you want to understand the whole picture, read on. For even in my own map, which uses boards and 'V's to help us counteract asymmetries, we do not yet have the complete answer. To reach it, we have to extend the boards up to the point on the rider's shoulders where a shoulder strap would lie. The boards, which follow the line taken by braces (known in the USA as suspenders), divide the rider's body into thirds. Pupils have suggested thinking of them like the divisions in a water bed, which are made of strong plastic and are known as baffles. This might well be a better analogy; but since they feel so solid when positioned well (and since I and most others have little knowledge of water beds) I continue to refer to them as boards. The boards/baffles comprise part of the chain of muscles which I call internals. This continues on down the inside of the thigh and calf. When the boards are well in place there is much less strain on the adductor tendons at the top inside thigh, for the body itself is narrowing in and they are no longer struggling to combat its width. The middle third of the body does very little riding: essentially it is squashed towards the mid-line (by the boards) and pushed forwards (through bearing down). The *outer two thirds* are the critical ones, for by keeping them firmly stuffed, and by stacking them over the horse's long back muscles, the rider ensures that her spinal axis cannot leave vertical. She has not only equalised the tension in the guy ropes which hold that flexible mast, she has built a scaffolding tower to each side of it!

However, to 'stuff and stack' these outer two thirds takes some doing, for one third inevitably contains less stuffing than the other – and when the rider has a tendency to become 'C' shaped, this difference can be dramatic. Like my tennis-playing pupil, the rider has to fill the weaker third with so much stuffing that the board and the edge of her body are held apart, spanning the width of the horse's long back muscle. The third must be stacked not just in its centre, but for its entire length. When its bottom is in place, the neck of the femur lies across the horse's long back muscle (see Fig. 5.11, page 139), and when its *top* is in place, the distance from where a shoulder strap would lie to the edge of the shoulder also lies directly over the horse's long back muscle (see Fig. 5.13, page 144). When the middle does not deviate either, the whole third is stacked.

The rider's legs are best thought of as *continuations* of the outer two thirds, and the tone in each one is hugely influenced by the tone in the third that is stacked up above it. So it should be no surprise that when the rider tends to twist and collapse to the inside (losing tone in that inside third), her knee on that side rides up, and her foot comes forward. (See Figs. 5.7a and c on page 130.) Attempting to correct this by focusing on the leg itself (as I did for many years) is relatively ineffective for it addresses the symptom and not the cause. Firming up the rider's inside board automatically activates the chain of internals and improves the tone in the inside of her inside leg, helping her to maintain the ideal shoulder/hip/heel line-up. It is even more effective to increase the stuffing in that whole inside third, and to make sure that she does not have a 'rag doll' crease between her torso and her thigh which prevents the stuffing from going down into it.

When the chain of internals is working well, our next concern becomes the chain of muscles which I call *externals*. The most important of these is latissimus dorsi (see Fig. 5.14 overleaf) and if the rider is to have maximum effect as she 'stuffs' her inside third, this has to become involved. (Doing this would have made even more difference to my tennis-playing pupil, but was beyond her brain-power at the time.)

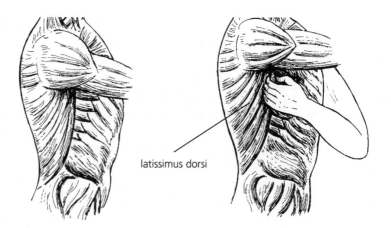

latissimus dorsi

Fig. 5.14 Finding latissimus dorsi. Feel for the front edge of the muscle, which bulks out like a broom handle.

Latissimus dorsi is a large, flat triangular muscle, originating from a fibrous sheet which attaches into the spinal vertebrae (and extends from T6 down to the base of the sacrum). Its fibres lie across the back, covering the shoulder blade, and finally attaching into the front of the humerus – the bone of the upper arm. The third side of the triangle runs down the side of the ribcage, from the back of the armpit all the way down to the pelvic crest and sacrum. If you pull down your shoulder and elbow and then reach around with your opposite hand to feel just beneath the back of your armpit, you can feel the edge of this muscle bulk out. However, in most riders it is so weak that by the time it reaches one hand's width below the armpit there is no more bulk! But if you practise pulling down the shoulder and elbow (both on and off your horse), you can strengthen it until it will (eventually) bulk out all the way down to the pelvis.

When the rider's boards and her latissimus dorsi are all functioning well, the outer thirds of her body both have two strong, unbendable boundaries. It becomes impossible for the rider to either twist or collapse – for it is almost as if someone had strapped a broom handle onto each side of her torso. However, if one of the rider's boards goes soggy, latissimus dorsi on that side (lying as it does on the inside of the 'C' curve) will become even soggier. Conversely, strengthening latissimus dorsi on the weaker side makes it easier to keep the board on that side strong, to increase the stuffing in that third, and to maintain its ideal position stacked up over the horse's long back muscle.

Ideally, latissimus dorsi holds the rider in place so that the top of each outer third – from where a shoulder strap would lie to the edge of the shoulder – has to remain over each of the horse's long back muscles. When a collapse becomes marked, one side will pull the other side off so that neither third is aligned at the top; but quite often, one side remains aligned whilst the other shoulder deviates from the ideal stack. (Almost all of us carry so much tension around the shoulder blades and the base of the neck – especially on the side of our dominant hand – that this is not surprising. See Fig. 5.15.) To 'stuff and stack' so that the entire length of each third stays in place over the horse's long back muscle, many riders have to make tiny adjustments to the tone in the muscles beneath the shoulder blade on one side, and in the area of the shoulder strap – differences which I cannot begin to delineate on paper, but which add enormously to the precision of her stack.

'Stuff and stack' is the critical ingredient of straightness – the end result of a process which gives the rider the ideal connection with each of the horse's long back muscles. He may still have some evasive patterns up his sleeve, but the rider who can hold herself in place has eradicated all those evasions which were responses to her asymmetry. She then has every chance of ironing out those which are solely his.

When you can 'stuff and stack' you can steer, and whilst there might seem little difference between this and the idea that you should 'sit straight' there is – in practice – all the difference in the world. For as the rider narrows in her boards, activates her latissimus dorsi and stacks herself correctly, these changes in muscle tone reorganise guy ropes and rearrange stuffing to such an extent that 'functional symmetry' is the result. All of the muscle changes involved would *not* happen if she just thought of keeping her chin over the mane.

- *Can you find your latissimus dorsi as described above? Is one side weaker than the other? How far down the side of your body does the muscle bulk out? Practise pulling down your shoulders and elbows to activate the muscles. Since you will need more practice than you will get from riding, do it when driving your car.*
- *Can you get an equal amount of stuffing in each of your two outer thirds? Is it*

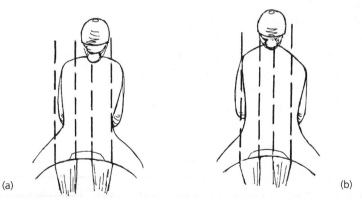

(a)   (b)

Fig. 5.15 When the rider is not 'stuffed and stacked', the tops of both outer thirds may be misaligned, as in (a), or one side only may deviate from its ideal position, as in (b).

more difficult with the weaker third on the inside or the outside of your circle?
- *To what extent does the stuffing in each third go down into your leg? Do you have a rag-doll crease which stops it on one or both sides it? How effectively can you change this?*
- *Do you have the neck of the femur lying across each of the horse's long back muscles? Are both thirds still stacked by the time you reach the bottom of your ribcage? How about up by your shoulder straps?*
- *To assess this, think of the horse's long back muscles as they pass beneath the panels of the saddle and extend back towards his croup. Then think of the distance between your shoulder strap and the edge of your shoulder. Is this above the back muscle? Is one side stacked and the other not, or are both out of place? What adjustments do you have to make to change your stack up?*

....

'Twist and twist again'
The chain of externals runs all the way from the armpit to the ankle. Below latissimus dorsi are the pelvic wings, which are covered by muscle both on their outside (gluteus medius, gluteus maximus, and tensor fasciae latae – see Fig. 9.3 on page 248) and on their inside (iliacus) – Fig. 5.8 on page 135. The tone in these muscles makes the bone within feel more or less defined, and sogginess on one side weakens the chain and contributes to the collapse. For years I routinely asked riders whether one thigh bone felt more like an iron bar than the other, but it never occurred to me to ask them whether one side of the *pelvis* felt more bony than the other. For making the soggy side feel bony activates both sets of muscles, and brings us closer to completing the chain of externals.

The chain continues down the outside of the thigh, and is activated by thinking of bringing your knee away from the saddle and turning your heel away from the horse's side (which has been mistakenly described as relaxing your thigh and taking your knee off the saddle). We can only presume that whoever first told us to do this already had the chain of internals functioning well. But even so, her woolly description of engaging the external thigh muscles is far from useful, and is not a timely intervention for riders who are not yet using the chain of internals well.

However, people with wobbly lower legs and toes which habitually turn out find that activating their externals is a life-saver – for whilst completing the chain requires thought and effort, it gives maximum stability to the lower leg. I have stated earlier that activating the external muscles is the true meaning of the words 'stretch your leg down'. To this we can now add the feeling which I believe has been described by the words 'stretch up tall'. For when the chain of externals functions fully, there is length, solidity and connectedness from the armpit to the ankle – a 'tallness' which has neither lifted the rider's ribs nor hollowed her back.

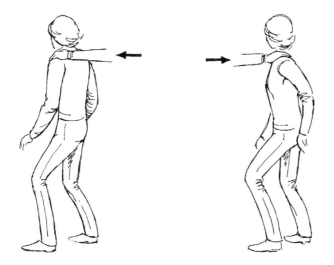

Fig. 5.16 The fencing-lunge exercise, showing the position from which the tester (who would be standing so that she faces and obscures the subject) offers her challenges.

To test the effectiveness of this, and to make yourself one stage stronger, stand in the fencing-lunge position, ideally with a partner who can test your stability. She does this by standing to the side of you and pushing the shoulder which is advanced forwards (with her hand cupped behind it) or back (with her hand cupped in front of it). (See Fig. 5.16.) If you just hang out in this position, you will probably be quite wobbly – although one of the fencing-lunge positions is likely to be more stable than the other, mirroring the greater stability which enhances your riding position on one rein. Next, deliberately activate latissimus dorsi on the forward side (testing it with your hand if you need to), and have your partner test you again. You should be significantly more resilient, with one of the fencing-lunge positions again giving you more stability than the other.

Your partner will now do a third test. But before she does so, slightly turn your body towards your rear leg. Then think of turning it *back the other way again*, but use your latissimus dorsi on that side to prevent you from actually turning. There is enormous strength in this position (which I call 'twist and twist again'). To add even more to it, push your thighs out as if against a resistance, and aim to feel that the advanced side is really well stuffed, with your board in place and a strong sense of connectedness in the whole chain of externals. Yet again, you should withstand your partner's test much more easily, and should also be able to mitigate at least some of the weakness of your less developed side.

In riding terms, the position of 'twist and twist again' does not actually face your shoulders towards the inside of the circle. It is *as if* you would face them inward, *but you stop yourself from doing so*. Thus the attempt to turn becomes an isometric use of your muscles. Again, the confusion between this muscle use and the isotonic use which creates movement almost certainly explains how one school of thought can suggest that you should face to the inside of a circle whilst, another says that you should keep your shoulders lying on its radius. In a sense, both statements are true.

Finally, let go of all these muscles, and ask your partner to test your stability again (or if you are doing this alone, get a sense of how it has changed). The difference should be significant – and you may now feel (by comparison) that you can be pushed around like a rag doll. There will probably be a significant difference, however, between the two fencing-lunge positions, and when the *stronger* side of your body is advanced, this letting go may only make your shoulder girdle move in response to your partner's challenge. However, when the *weaker* side is advanced, letting go may make that whole side of your torso give way, rocking forward or back from the pelvis upwards.

Discovering this makes it easy to appreciate that when you are riding it has probably never been securely held in place on the inside of a turn. Then, when it drops behind the ideal line-up, the horse is compromised by the fact that your centre of gravity is too far back on the inside. His struggle to carry you becomes worse as you become tempted to get some stability by pulling on the inside rein – and so layers of wrongness are built on each other, creating the tensions and compensations within the rider/horse system which are commonly known as 'evasions'.

When you can replicate the feeling of 'twist and twist again' on your horse, it gives you phenomenal stability, enabling you to 'stuff and stack', to keep the back of each board strong, and to *push forward from their whole length*. During lateral work and the other advanced movements, this can make a huge difference to your ability to maintain the correct balance point and the ideal connection with each of the horse's long back muscles. In fact, one of my pupils who is riding at Grand Prix rang me from America to tell me how much her flying changes had improved, now that she could activate latissimus dorsi on the new inside! She had also miraculously solved the problem of her horses drifting to the right in piaffe – it had simply stopped happening as their response to her new line-up. But if your horizons only encompass basic work do not decide that this is not for you: the improvement you can get in your horse's gaits and through circles and turns can be astounding, and well worth the effort it takes to get it.

• *Can you feel a connection down the whole chain of externals, from your armpit to your ankle on both sides of your body? If you can, congratulate yourself, for you are functioning far more effectively than most riders!*

- *Think in turn of your latissimus dorsi on each side, of the bony sides of the pelvis, and of your outer thigh and calf. Where do you lose the most strength, or is the whole chain soggy? Which side is stronger, and which leg is more stable? If lower leg stability has been a big issue for you, know that the solution lies in activating this chain of muscles.*
- *Once you have done the above exercise in the fencing-lunge position, take the idea of 'twist and twist again' into your riding. How much difference does it make? Were you already doing it on one rein?*
- *Every time you are tempted to pull on the inside rein, realise that your inside third is behind the correct balance point. Instead of pulling back can you advance your hand, advance that third, and push forward from the back of the board?*

....

To ride well, the rider must be in balance in three planes: up/down, back/front, and side/side.

Without high muscle tone this is all but impossible, for the body cannot be stabilised enough to be capable of such fine, precise positioning. Also, the horse has his own agenda: for he knows that he can perpetuate his favourite evasions as long as the rider can be persuaded (say) to water-ski, stay up off his back, and sit off to the right. Each horse sets us a different challenge, and overcoming this requires different body parts to be emphasised: the ingredients in the recipe stay the same, but their relative proportions vary. The horse both suffers from – and at times plays on – each rider's idiosyncratic weaknesses, so the variations on the theme of how it can go wrong are endless. But when it goes *right* – when the rider gradually brings the biomechanics of her riding closer to the classical ideal – her improvements are reflected in the horse, who finally has no choice but to take up the biomechanics of correct movement. As a result, they both show the classical silhouette – making each individual horse and rider look (and feel) the same. But within this process of change lies the pivotal question of riding: will the organised rider organise the disorganised horse, or will the disorganised horse disorganise the organised rider?

Conclusion

CHAPTER SIX

··

The Challenge of Learning

··

Cybernetic learning ONE OF THE BASIC TENETS that underlies my teaching is the idea that if a skill is possible for somebody, then it is possible for anybody, and it is only a matter of how. (This is actually one of the presuppositions of Neuro-Linguistic Programming – an approach to cognitive psychology which has influenced me enormously.) All of my experiences in teaching and learning lead me to believe that this is indeed true, and that 'HOW?' is the big question which the learning rider must answer.

Sport psychologists support this idea by differentiating between *declarative knowledge*, which is essentially about the 'what' of any given skill, and *procedural knowledge*, which delineates the 'how'. If you think of the phrases we so commonly hear in riding, ('relax, keep your hands still, get the horse on the bit', etc.) they are all declarative statements, which tell you nothing about how to do them. We lack procedural knowledge because our traditional map of riding is so incomplete. The ethos is that either you have talent (which is innate procedural knowledge) or you do not – in which case, very few trainers have knowledge explicit enough to help you.

Even though I stand by my presupposition, it does not even matter if riding well *is* possible for anybody – it only matters that we act 'as if' this is true. For whether I am the teacher or the pupil, this attitude opens doors. The rider with a body which has not taken to riding like a duck to water will probably never match the skill level of the talented rider – for she has lost too much time barking up the wrong trees, and she loses even more time eradicating the scars this has left her with. If I chose to say that a rider had no talent, I would place her in a dead-end and doom her to mediocrity. As her teacher, I would then not regard my job as that of generating learning and catalysing change, and would be all too likely to take on the role of 'baby sitter' – keeping the rider amused and occupied whilst she spent her allotted time in the riding school.

I like to think of learning like a journey, in which I – having mapped the territory and travelled one of the paths it contains – can act as a guide for others who also wish to travel. But in 'baby sitting' we go nowhere: it is not learning, and it is not teaching, for it dooms the rider to keep repeating her mistakes as she clocks up yet more miles of riding experience. This happens at all levels of riding, and whilst novices scour their local area in search of a trainer who can really make a difference, top-class riders scour the world. Since more than seventy per cent of riders would tell you that they are 'stuck on a plateau', one is left presuming that their search rarely yields the procedural knowledge they need.

Consider this analogy: if you go into a room where there is a certain smell, you smell it very strongly for the first few minutes. Then you habituate to it, and do not smell it any more (regardless of how pleasant or how foul it was). To become aware of the smell again, you have to go out of the room for several minutes and then return to it. It is the same in riding. If you always do everything in exactly the same way, and your horse always does everything in exactly the same way, your body habituates to the point that you soon cease to feel anything – for everything is perceived as sameness. You have to *leave the room* and *do something different* in order to re-awaken your kinaesthetic sensitivity. From this point, learning can start afresh, and it will continue for as long as you do not fall into the same trap again. Perceiving only sameness is deadly to the learning process, since *the brain learns by contrast*. The way to keep learning is to keep developing a progressively more refined awareness of what 'is'. This means that learning is essentially a perceptual task.

Some time ago, I spoke to a wealthy woman who has two outdoor arenas on her property. One is situated out in the fields, and the other is right beside her house, so if she works her horses here she can have the radio playing the background. 'I much prefer this,' she said to me, 'it takes away the boredom of riding all those circles.' In that simple sentence she told me exactly why her money, her good horses, and her good trainers, had not brought her a significant level of skill and competitive success. Despite all these, she had never paid sufficient attention to the process of riding to start noticing differences. To her, it was all sameness, and hence it was boring. So she never asked herself why one circle worked well whilst another went wrong; never even noticed that all of her horses lent more heavily into one rein, and therefore never stopped to wonder why. The answers to these questions may not be easy to find – but until you ask them you have no hope of even entering the process which could one day offer solutions.

In contrast, anyone who learns well is – whether they know it or not – operating a cybernetic learning process. (I discussed this at great length in *Ride With Your Mind/The Natural Rider* and *'Masterclass'*; but the principles are so important that I make no apology for repeating them here.) It was Maxwell Maltz, a plastic surgeon, who introduced the

Fig. 6.1 Cybernetic learning: homing in on a goal through trial and error.

concept of 'psychocybernetics', suggesting that the brain is a goal-striving mechanism, designed to home in on goals rather like a self-guided torpedo homes in on the hull of the ship it is aimed at. The torpedo recognises its goal through a metal detector in its tip. If it is heading straight for it, it keeps doing what it is already doing; but if it gets feedback that it is off course, the rudder automatically comes in and changes its course. It may well over-correct, in which case a further adjustment is made, and so the torpedo gradually homes in on its goal through trial and error, making more and more refined corrections as necessary. (See Fig. 6.1.)

This is the brain's natural way of learning, and all of us used it as very young children whilst we gained control of our bodies, learned to walk, and began to discover our world. But all of this exploration soon gets us into trouble. My generation had their in-born learning mechanism stifled by discipline, but the children of today can also have theirs drugged out of existence by television, videos and computer games. Although we rarely realise it, the effect on our lives can be devastating. My own problems have always lain in how to learn, and the will to learn has never been in question. However, I realise more and more that this cannot be taken for granted, and it is *the will to learn* as much as the *how to learn* which is the subject of this chapter. But however motivated we may or may not be, we will not get very far in riding (or in any other skill) without deciphering its 'how' through the cybernetic process.

The techniques I use in teaching are all designed to facilitate this, so that the rider becomes clear about her goal, and is able to process and understand the feedback which tells her that she is 'getting hotter, hotter still, cooling off a bit,' etc. (If you are around my age, you will have childhood memories of playing 'Hunt the Thimble', which is the ultimate cybernetic party game.) When left to themselves, many riders have a hazy or even wrong perception of the goal, and few focus their attention well enough to register the small changes which tell them if they are getting it or losing it. You only have to be looking at the view, thinking about something else, worrying about the people who are watching you, or be overly concerned about the position of your horse's head, and you are guaranteed to miss that feedback – possibly for a lifetime.

It is when we lose track of the cybernetic process that things go wrong with our riding. Then, we each become our own worst enemy: so some people panic, some give up, some seize up, and some blame the horse. Keeping the pupil on track can be one of the teacher's most demanding jobs, and I shall never forget a pupil who was one of the world's great panickers, despite riding and competing at quite a high level. Working with me gave her a much more stable sense of herself than she had had before – and between my annual visits to her country she regularly crossed the world for more input. But when things went wrong she would 'lose it', and she had a very subtle way of making me feel responsible for her problem. I would carefully talk her through the corrections she needed to make until her brain began to function well again; but all along I had the suspicion that I was being 'hooked' into playing a game which was not actually serving her well.

During one of my visits to her area, she rode as a guinea-pig rider on a teacher-training course, and one of the participants volunteered to do some work with her at the other end of the arena. Not long afterwards, I heard the familiar screech, 'I've lost my seat bones ... it's all going wrong, and I can't find them ...'

I then heard the slow Australian drawl of her teacher, who calmly said 'So what are you going to do about it?'

There was a long silence, after which a much less panicky voice replied, 'Well, er ... well ... er ..., I think they're pointing backwards and I have to bring them forward again. I think I ... that's it ...'

I chuckled inside at this interaction, which showed me exactly the mistake I had been making. Asking 'So what are you going to do about it?' had thrown the ball right back into the pupil's court and completely avoided the need for a rescue mission. When I next taught her, I entered the arena armed with my new phrase. I never needed to use it.

This pupil, like many others, took her riding far too seriously. But others do not take it seriously enough. These latter are under-focused, with their brain operating like a badly adjusted camera lens which sees a whole load of information as a blur. (Often, these folks do not know what commitment really is, and they rate their commitment level as an eight-out-of-ten, whilst I think they are riding on a three!) Under-focused riders rarely have goals, and they wander around aimlessly without ever embarking on a journey of learning. In contrast, there are people who operate permanently on 'overkill'. They are 'over-focused', in the state where they cannot see the wood for the trees: this conditions them to believe that *more must be better*, and to substitute willpower and increased effort for simply paying attention. This dooms them to become some of the world's great triers.

The breakthrough, when it comes, can be a shock. Pat is one of my regular pupils, and although she had undoubtedly made great improvement, she was still struggling with some fundamental issues. The ultimate crunch came one day when she was riding an extremely lazy horse, and in response to my statements that 'He needs to go more forward' I could see nothing happening. I found it hard to believe that Pat could not diagnose this lack of impulsion for herself – and even harder to believe that she was not willing to do anything about it. When I began to question her commitment, and even to get impatient with her (a very rare occurrence) she was deeply upset.

'But I *am* trying,' she said, 'and I *am* committed, and you're being so unfair ....'

She was almost on the point of leaving the arena when I realised what was happening: all of the trying and activity was happening *inside her head*, and its only outward manifestation was a tendency to look anguished and to topple forward. There was no use of her leg, and no use of her stick; but mentally she was working hard.

I was able to explain our dilemma by saying, 'It's as if your energy and your commitment is like a search-light. But instead of shining it outwards towards the horse, and indirectly towards me, you're so busy shining it inwards and thinking about what's happening that neither of us see it at all. So the horse barely knows that you're there, and I don't see you being committed even though you feel that you're working so hard.'

Thinking is indeed one of Pat's strong points, and she is a university lecturer who has made her name in the academic world. So I encouraged her to analyse less, to talk to herself less, to react quicker, and to focus her energy outward.

The real breakthrough came on the next course she attended, when I realised that every time she began to think hard, she pulled down her sternum. This was the way that her mental intensity became reflected in her body, and when I stopped her from doing it, her mental state changed too. There was an instant change in her horse (thank God, because without this she would never have believed me), and she said, 'But I'm not doing anything.'

'Keep doing nothing,' was my inevitable response, as Pat gradually came to terms with the idea that all the 'somethings' she had been doing had really been wasted and misdirected effort.

'But I thought this was bearing down,' she said, pulling her sternum down again, 'and I thought it was supposed to be really hard ... I don't believe it can be this easy!'

Let your horse be the judge of that,' I said. 'What's his verdict?'

The answer was obvious; but it took Pat some time to reach the realisation that trying had become a way of life, and that as a child, she had been rewarded for effort.

'The only thing my father ever praised me for,' she said, 'was trying ... and I'm still trying to please him now.' When she stopped trying, she felt that she was being 'bad' – although her riding really became very good. ('Keep being bad,' I said, 'and see if you can get a thrill out of it.')

Another contrast to the triers are the competitive riders with big goals. Instead of becoming over-immersed in detail they try to gloss over the surface, and to run before they can walk. They desperately long to 'arrive', and take some convincing that journeying is not just half the fun, it is all there is. In truth, we are each driven by our own maps of riding, of the learning process, and of ourselves – and these can stop us from engaging with the subtle feedback which makes riding such a demanding and sophisticated skill. Its delicacy and refinement adds enormously to the challenge – so sometimes a good moment seems to flash past in the blinking of an eye, and you are left thinking 'I know that was right, but what the hell happened?' To extract the learning from these situations is rarely easy. Even if we get the kind of help we really need, and we succeed in staying on the track of the cybernetic process, we have embarked on an exceedingly testing journey.

....

Maintaining the cybernetic learning process

When I first presented the cybernetic model of learning to riders, I had the naive expectation that everyone would immediately see its benefits, and would become as enthusiastic about the learning process as I had become. I had seen its tremendous effectiveness in practically everyone who was willing to engage in it; but I did not find queues of people on my doorstep. It was too weird (in 1980) for people to stomach.

Some riders have found it too demanding, and despite the tremendous improvements it catalysed in their riding, they abandoned it later. I suspect that many of them relinquished their commitment because of peer pressure. ('Why won't you talk to me any more when we're hacking out?' 'Why do you spend so much time in walk?' 'Why are you thinking so much about this?' 'There's no way I want to work that hard.' 'You're no fun any more.') But being the odd one out is also no fun, and without friends to support you, learning can be a very lonely task.

The famous American show-jumping trainer George Morris has frequently said something to the effect of: 'I'm not interested in riders with talent. They are two a penny. But give me a rider with the three Ds:

dedication, determination, and discipline. Without these, the rider won't get anywhere.' He is certainly right that many riders with talent do not have these – they expect to rest on their laurels, and when they reach the level where this does not work any more, they often fall by the wayside. But many riders *without* talent do not have them either. Neither do they have the two Cs – concentration and commitment – which are my preferred way to describe the qualities that are needed. Unlike Mr Morris, I believe that riders with natural talent are extremely rare; but riders with the two Cs and the three Ds are apparently even rarer! Sadly, there seems to be a limiting factor built into human nature: we all want it to be easy.

We think of childhood learning as simple; but how many times did you fall over before you finally mastered walking? How intense was your concentration as you first tried to draw your house? How many times did your food go all over your body before you gained the skills to put it consistently into your mouth? As adults, we forget that there is far more to learning than 'I'll tell you what to do, and you'll do it.' Indoctrinated by parents and teachers, we abandon trial and error, sell out on concentration, and expect improvement to 'just happen' as a result of practising our sitting trot or the school movements.

From my position now, I find myself scratching my head to understand the mentality of the average rider, who seems content to drip water on the rock, and to wait forever for improvement. Perhaps she is in the state where ignorance is bliss – where she does not know what there is to know. Or perhaps she become resigned to her plateau (to whatever level of riding her habit patterns automatically produce). This becomes tempting when the commonly used approaches to learning do not yield enough small (or large) successes to keep her motivated.

In Chapter 1 I noted that when you are struggling to find your way from an inaccurate, incomplete map, it makes very little difference how hard you work; so why bother? But if this same rider were presented with a more useful, workable map of riding, would her interest be rekindled? If riding became more learnable, but that learning required continued dedication, determination, and discipline, would she want to do it? Would she want to do it even if it required her to go against our cultural norms, and even if her friends thought she was crazy?

Even with the very best teaching, improvement will never be a straight-line path, and since no one can do it for the pupil her use of the two Cs and three Ds are the most important factors that determine her success. Inevitably, she will be tested by times when the pay-off does not seem to justify the effort, and this is especially true for anyone who is working alone for long periods of time.

With no external feedback to keep the cybernetic process on track, there is always the danger that you will *think* you are doing what you know you need to do, when actually you are kidding yourself, and settling for only a vague approximation of the goal. As your body habituates to the feelings involved it can be hard to decide if the new way is simply beginning to feel normal, or if you are no longer doing it! You may happily let your new feeling fade out of your repertoire, or you may be one of those extremely zealous people who always over-corrects – like one Australian friend of mine, who returned home to her arena in the bush after her first clinic with me, and worked exceedingly hard to change the habits of a lifetime. She came back on my next visit one year later, only to have changed from being one of the most hollow-backed riders I had ever seen to being one of the most round-backed riders I have ever seen!

When people over-correct they understandably find it very upsetting to be told that their efforts have been in vain, and that they now have to do the opposite of everything they were told to do last time: so when I met this woman for the second time, I took one look at her, and wondered how I was going to break the news. Since she was a teacher herself, I stood her and her horse in front of a large mirror, and asked her what she saw. She had no trouble diagnosing what had happened, and we dutifully began the process of getting her back on course again. (As she walked out of the lesson, her friends enthusiastically asked her 'How did it go?' 'Ah,' she said, focussing her attention on one of the most positive comments I was able to make, 'Mary really liked my new boots!')

She had probably spent the previous six months heading in completely the wrong direction, yet she took this with good humour and learned an important lesson from it, realising that she somehow needed to get some external feedback to gauge her progress by. (When video cameras or mirrors are beyond your budget, you can at least get a friend to shoot a role of film for you.) A few years later, when this same person was working on far more sophisticated changes, I received a postcard from her which read, 'So glad you're coming out in March. Think I passed through "just right" a few days before Christmas and I can't seem to find it again!'

The success of some of the world's best young riders is based on several factors. Firstly, their talent naturally points them towards the right feelings and enables them to concentrate well. But this is coupled with the support they get from teachers and mentors who see them every day. These sessions – common in Continental Europe – are essentially 'supervised riding', where the riders are given occasional feedback and encouragement whilst they are left to develop their skills. (Ideally, learning should take place both in intensive one-to-one sessions, and in supervised sessions. Typical British riding lessons are not a good format, and neither is 'clinic hopping' – moving from clinician to clinician – which seems to

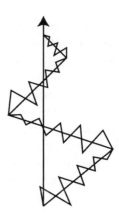

Fig. 6.2 When the cybernetic process is less streamlined and there is confusion about the goal, the learner maps a much larger area.

common in America.) But the essential factor is that someone is always there to catch these riders before they stray very far off the straight and narrow, and much of the time that could have been wasted in barking up the wrong trees is put to good use.

Because their progress is so well monitored, problems arise when very talented riders set out to map the territory of riding. For the map produced by any rider will inevitably only include the area covered by the trial and error deviations that she makes (so the talented rider will produce a map not unlike Fig. 6.1). But if our map-maker is *not* talented as a rider, she makes so many corrections and follows so many different paths that she begins to find her way around a much larger territory, and to map out the many possibilities which are not encountered if her path is simply one straight line. (See Fig. 6.2.) My friend in Australia has become an extremely good teacher largely because of all the over-corrections she has made, and all the myriad ways of doing it *wrong* which she has experienced in the process of learning how to do it *right*. So when she sees them in front of her, she recognises them, and she knows what to do. Her brain has learned an enormous amount through experiencing so many contrasts.

One of my favourite stories concerns the scientist Thomas Edison, famous for his invention of the light bulb. It took Edison about one thousand attempts with various substances before he hit on tungsten as a viable filament for the bulb. (One version of the story recounts that he even tried peanut butter, not because he thought it might work, but because broadening out his thinking to include the impossible often stimulated creative insights which did eventually lead somewhere!) After his great success, a journalist asked him, 'So what about your nine hundred and ninety-nine failures? Didn't you get horribly bored and frustrated?'

'Not at all,' replied Edison, 'I discovered nine hundred and ninety-nine ways to make a light bulb not work!'

Like Edison, the rider who has discovered many ways of making it not work has been able to map a tremendous amount of territory. The talented rider who does *not* do this produces a map which can take a rider with similar talent to great heights. But its base lacks scope and depth. For our rider will presume that factors which are actually unique to her and other good riders are shared by everyone – that they come automatically as part of the package we all receive when we are born. So these would not appear on her map. They are unknown, like the smell in the room you have been in for a while.

....

Most people are familiar with Macbeth's famous speech in which he asks, 'Is this a dagger I see before me?' He is about to murder Duncan, and the thought is – quite literally – making him crazy. As his speech progresses it becomes clear that he sees the dagger but cannot feel it; but he still believes his eyes more than his hands, until blood appears to spurt from the blade and he then *knows* that he must be hallucinating. Riders too need this double-check between their kinaesthetic and visual senses, and whose who do not have it hallucinate wildly about the visual counterparts of the feelings they are creating. This tendency makes it extremely easy to go astray.

Seeing, hearing and feeling

During a training session, the rider's developing kinaesthetic map of riding is refined and expanded through comparison with the trainer's visual map of riding. This gives two descriptions of the same territory, which (as we said in Chapter 2) will always be better than one. Even 'the powers that be' have realised that they can enrich our maps by drawing on our dormant senses, and if our primary sense is becoming dulled, they utilise another to increase the impact of their message. Thus the 'rumble strips' and other altered road surfaces which mark the entrances to speed restrictions are designed to feel and sound different, giving a 'wake-up call' to the driver who is not paying attention visually.

But although it is vision which gives us riders confirmation of our feelings, we do not always see clearly. Think of the anorexic, who can look in a mirror and see herself as fat. This must be the ultimate in distortion – and we all distort reality to a greater or lesser degree as we look in the mirror and see only the best or the worst in ourselves.

When riding, the process of looking in the mirror is even more difficult, for you have to do it on 10% of your attention, maintaining your peripheral vision, and leaving the other 90% to keep on riding. Otherwise you suffer the fate of one well-known competitor whose riding disintegrates each time he passes the mirror. Sadly, he never gets to see how good he really looks!

Following her massive over-correction, my Australian friend bought herself a mirror; but she soon reached the point where seeing her bad habits displayed in glorious technicolour became so distressing that she was ready to cover it over, and end its role as the bane of her life. She then realised that she could use it constructively if she halted in front of it, and asked herself out loud, 'Now, Clare, what would you do if this person appeared in front of you for a riding lesson?' Then she would tell herself the answer, put the correction into effect, and proceed on her way.

Seeing and feeling are more complexly linked than perhaps even she realised, and most teachers are familiar with the pupil whose hands are, for instance, unlevel. 'Look down at your hands,' you say, 'and tell me what they're doing.' So the rider looks down; but before she has done so, her hands become level. 'They look fine to me,' she says, as you groan inwardly. A few minutes later, you seize your next chance ... and the same thing happens.

I shall never forget the pupil who, as a Cambridge graduate and managing director of her own computer software company, is undoubtedly highly intelligent. She was fiddling horribly with the reins, but every time I asked her to look down, her hands became miraculously still. Eventually she caught on, and caught herself at it. 'They don't want to show me!' she wailed, sounding like a six-year-old whose best friends are keeping a secret.

It is not just struggling riders who are this unaware of their habit patterns. The whole trial-and-error process of learning can happen so unconsciously for the talented rider that she too does not know what she is doing. So let us suppose that a talented rider has a tremendous feel one day, and then attempts to teach this to her pupil. She then puts that feeling into words. This is the first place where slippage can occur, since her verbal description may be inaccurate. It may leave out some vital pieces of the puzzle which she did not notice, and it may presuppose some skills which are inherent in her but not in the pupil. I call this the 'Do X' phenomenon – the teacher's command works perfectly if you (like her) are doing A,B,C,D, etc. But if you are not, you are doomed to fail – and almost inevitably, she will have no clue as to why that is.

But even if there is no slippage in this first stage, the pupil may hear the teacher's words and misunderstand them. So here – between the saying and the hearing – more slippage can occur. You will know this from the surprisingly high proportion of everyday conversations which later require post-mortems! One of my pupils once gave me a poster which summed up the problem; it said, 'I know that you believe you understand what you think I said, but I'm not sure you realise that what you heard was not what I meant!'

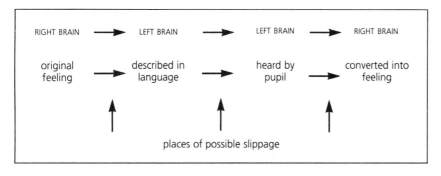

Fig. 6.3 The communication process between teacher and pupil, and the places of possible slippage.

As an example of (precisely) this my editor told me the story of riding on a London bus when a passenger asked the conductor to tell her when it arrived at London Bridge. The conductor went to look at the timetable, and came back saying 'Nine thirty-six.'

'No,' said the passenger, 'I want you to tell me when we arrive.'

'It's nine thirty-six,' said the conductor, continuing a misunderstanding which went on for quite some time – to my editor's amusement – until the conductor realised that the passenger wanted her to say, 'We're here now' as they arrived!

In riding lessons, the last stage of the process – which occurs with more or less slippage – happens as the pupil attempts to convert that verbal information into a feeling (see Fig. 6.3). How high are the chances that the pupil will reproduce the feeling which the instructor originally intended to communicate? And will the instructor be astute enough to know whether or not her communication had succeeded?

Extrapolate this scenario to encompass countless generations of teachers and pupils, and you have the situation we are in today, where the stock phrases used in riding can be interpreted in a multitude of different ways, with very few of them bearing much resemblance to their original meanings.

Most people would have to admit, albeit sadly, that they do not have the good fortune to be the supremely talented rider whose learning comes so close to the straight-line path. Nor do they want to be the average rider who remains on her plateau, and never goes anywhere. The only viable option that lies between the two requires concentration and commitment, dedication, determination, and discipline. Yet most riders expect to improve without ever having to engage their brain, and without suffering the indignity of changing what they are doing. Contrary to popular belief, your riding will not improve automatically by spending more time in the saddle. For as I have said so many times, practice makes perfect not what you *think* you are practising, or what you *ought* to be practising, but what you are *actually* practising, and this makes it the best possible way of perfecting your mistakes. (Or to put it another way, only perfect practice makes you perfect.)

But perhaps perfection is not the issue anyway, and I recently read a religious column in a newspaper which suggested that it might be better to think of God commanding us not to 'be perfect', but to think of Him wanting us to 'be present'. This makes concentration and commitment even His bottom lines, and takes a lot of pressure off us – for it is far easier to 'be present' than it is to 'be perfect'. Or perhaps in reality the two are the same, for it is when we are fully present that we most perfectly express our essence. Only an illusory promise of perfection is held in that redundant practice which lacks awareness. When you exchange this for a cybernetic learning process you change not only your riding but also your understanding of learning, and your feelings about yourself as a learner and a rider.

....

Becoming dextrous with the pelvis
The first challenge in each cycle of learning is to find out *how* to ride that bit better, and the next step is then to groove that response so that it becomes part of the body's natural functioning. But in doing this, we as riders have a specific handicap, for the skill we are wanting to learn is not a part of the body's natural repertoire, as are the hand/ball/eye co-ordinations which underpin skill in ball games. The rider's ability does not rely – indeed must not rely – on manual dexterity; yet the expectation of the bodymind is that almost all of the problems we ever encounter in life can be fixed with our hands. In our everyday lives, we use them continually to put our world to rights.

It is because of this that a relatively very large part of both the motor cortex and the sensory cortex in the human brain are dedicated to manual dexterity. The motor cortex is the part of the brain which sends neurological messages to the muscles causing them to contract. The sensory cortex receives information from the muscles, telling it about the body's position in space, and about sensation or pain. In effect, your brain has etched into it a map of your body, and the amount of space that any specific body part takes up on the map does not relate to its size. Instead it relates to its sensitivity – to the number of movements that part can perform, and the number of skills it is involved in.

Interestingly, the neural area representing the thumb is one of the largest of the whole body, for the role of the thumb is crucial to any movement involving the hand. The lips and mouth, too, are very well represented, for they get busy whenever we eat, drink, talk, or laugh – and

Fig. 6.4 The homunculus, or 'little man', which illustrates how the surface of the body is represented in the somatosensory cortex.

on a minute level there is probably some activity in them whenever we talk to ourselves, or subvocalise when reading. The fact that we can imitate different accents shows the degree of subtlety that is available to the mouth area, and also to the muscles of the throat. Try it – and make yourself aware of the tiny kinaesthetic differences which create such significant variations in the sounds you make. As you do so, realise that each of the people you are imitating (whether they be from the north or the south of the country) habituated years ago to the way they use their mouth and throat – as you have done in your own speech. They no longer feel what you are feeling now, for you are perceiving this only by contrast. It is like the smell which can only be recognised by contrast.

Traditionally, the way in which the surface of the body is represented in the sensory cortex has been illustrated by the homunculus or 'little man'. (Fig. 6.4.) Inevitably, it does not look much like a normal human being; yet to your brain, this is who you are. Your hands, mouth, and eyes are huge, for so many different messages need to pass between them and your brain. Your feet are also quite large, and whilst they do not have the sensitivity of the hands or mouth, they are very important as a source of feedback about the environment. But despite the relatively enormous size of your actual thigh, pelvis and abdomen they are scantly represented, for they perform so few movements – and those which they do perform are fairly simple and gross, with very few variations on the theme.

When I first looked at this, it became clear to me why our traditional textbooks talk so much about the positions of the rider's hands and feet, and why so little has ever been said about the centre of the body. We define the aids in terms of inside hand and outside hand, inside leg and outside leg; concurrently we 'sit deep' and 'use our backs' but rarely do we even attempt to delineate what these expressions actually mean. It is tacitly assumed that any rider who is armed with information about the correct position for her limbs ought to be able to ride well. The fact that such a high proportion do not suggests that this might not be true.

Unfortunately, the Great Masters who wrote our classical texts were no exception to the rules of neurology, so inevitably they talked about the parts of their body which were clearly represented in their cortex. This would be particularly true in the talented rider, who so naturally stumbled on the pelvic positionings which are involved in doing it right. He cannot contrast these with all the myriad variations involved in adjusting one's body – changing it from a pelvis which naturally does it wrong to one which eventually does it right. The rider who has been through this process has, like myself and many other teachers, a much richer set of contrasts. To continue to speak in just one accent has proved itself fruitless; so we opted for a learning process which would transform us into mimics.

Looking at the homunculus, it is also immediately obvious why it is so tempting to try and solve all the problems of riding with your hands – even though you know you are not supposed to – and so hard firstly to learn about the positioning and the changes in muscle tone which are needed in the pelvic area, and secondly to choose to act with this as opposed to the hand. For the ultimate challenge of riding is to overcome the way we are naturally 'wired', to reduce the dominance of the hand and to become *dextrous* with the pelvis – ultimately, to have as much sensitivity and as many choices in how to position it as we have with our hands. Inevitably, this cannot happen over night.

It was once thought that the 'cortical maps' through which we define ourselves were stable, remaining unchanged for an individual's lifetime. However, experimental work done in the late eighties and early nineties has revealed that this is not the case. The cerebral cortex is incredibly plastic, and in the newly blind, the constant use of one finger for reading braille leads to a huge expansion in the area in the cortex which represents that finger. When the newly deaf are learning sign language, large areas of the auditory cortex are reallocated for visual processing. These dramatic re-mappings within the brain prove that 'you've either got it or you haven't' cannot be the final truth. Learning to be dextrous with the pelvis is essentially a neurological task, requiring an increase in the amount of 'brain space' that is dedicated to this area of the body. Our task is not dissimilar to the learning undertaken by some disabled artists, who produce intricate and beautiful paintings by holding the brush either in their foot or their mouth. But they at least start with a part of the body which is already well mapped in the cortex. We, as riders, do not.

On average, we are thought to use about one in ten of the possible neurological connections that lie within the brain itself, and about one in three of those within the body. The proportion used has been described by the American researcher Paul Goodwin, using the term 'activated neural network density'. The idea of *density* implies that the pathways in any chunk of the brain or body would look like a bundle of fibres which are more or less tightly packed. We activate these networks according to how many possible options we use: crude repetitive movement utilises very few, whilst subtle and refined movement, with many variations on the theme, utilises more of the possibilities available within the network.

With increasing neurological refinement comes an increasingly subtle perception, and the ability to make finer and finer distinctions: in other words, the rider develops 'feel'. But her learning will be immeasurably easier if she has access to an interpreter who can help her decipher the horse's feedback, showing her how the cause/effect rules of riding are working either for or against her in each moment. Putting two and two together is very much easier when there is someone there to tell you that 'You just lost the holding in your thigh muscles and fell back down the mantrap. That's why the horse hollowed his back and lifted his head.' Or that 'The horse just backed off because he's coming up to the corner, and your right side went soggy as you came "in front of him".' Or that, 'He's bound to accelerate as he comes to the long side of the arena, so be ready for him, and don't let him tip you back as he pulls the rug out from under your feet.' The feedback which finally enables you to lead the dance – and to read the horse in the way that he reads you – is not writ large for all to see.

....

Changing our wiring

The cause/effect rules which underlie riding are the same worldwide; but every horse and rider is unique. There is tremendous individuality in the way we each develop our neurological wiring, and like our anatomical make-up, this has a huge bearing on our individual strengths and weaknesses as riders. For instance, one pupil of mine who is a Grand Prix dressage rider had always known that her left side was weaker and less sophisticated than her right. Through our work together, she had gained much more sense about how to use it, strengthening her muscles, and – more importantly – activating more of her neural network. But the light really dawned one day when she had to walk a horse who had been off work, and she decided to make this a productive exercise by focusing very specifically on her weaker side. She did everything so slowly and mindfully that she felt how her intention to increase the tone in her *left* leg actually became an increase in tone in her *right* leg. Somehow, the message from her brain got diverted, and went to the wrong leg! She then realised that every time she had deliberately placed her weak leg more clearly on the saddle, the other one had also increased its tone, keeping the differential between them the same.

This discovery made her appreciate that she had to establish a much better communication system between her brain and her left leg, activating wiring which would function without her right leg getting in on the act. (Her plight reminds me of the way that children always ask, 'Mummy, how does the pill know which leg to go down?') Some time later she was having lessons with a teacher of the Feldenkrais Method (which is discussed in Chapter 8), who was keen to get to the bottom of this pattern, and who asked her more about her history. She had had a forceps birth – and she still has the dent on the left side of her skull which proves what a struggle it was. As a result of the damage she has never seen clearly through her left eye, although both eyes together have virtually perfect vision. The dominance of her right side mirrors the dominance of her right eye. This is, apparently, a very common developmental pattern.

So now, whenever she makes a correction to her left leg she has to check on the right, and release it if it has also joined in. Otherwise the right side of her body will overwork forever. But to really get to the bottom of this, she will also need to tackle it in the rest of her life as well, for her right leg undoubtedly does more than its share of the work in standing, walking, and everything else she does.

More obvious mishaps can disturb our wiring and our development. One of my pupils, for instance, fell out of a tree at age eight, and broke her arm. The break did not heal well, and complications kept her wearing a sling for the next year. She is a talented rider whose performance is marred by an unusual and deep-rooted asymmetry which does not follow the usual 'C' or 'S' shapes. Its origins and its form became very clear to me when I realised that as far as her brain is concerned, her arm is still in that sling.

Denise is pupil of mine who rides quite well but at the lower levels. She had only just begun to tackle quite a marked asymmetry, in which she collapsed to the left. Her horses mirrored her 'C' shape by also bulging their ribcages to the right. She could live with the jack-knife this created on the left rein, but the heavier contact into her right hand became a real problem on the right rein – along with her horses' tendencies to fall in on the circle. She arrived for her third course saying, 'I used to be relatively immune to what was happening, but even though it's better than it used to be, it's bugging me so much more that I'm beginning to hate working to the right.' Since the time I had previously seen her, I had honed my theory that the root of this kind of problem lies in the asymmetry of the iliopsoas muscles (and other muscles of the trunk) and not just in the offending seat bone or thigh. So in my work with her, I used the idea of the boards (see page 136).

The bottom of Denise's left board was very strong, and in fact her left adductor tendon (at the top inside of her thigh) was actually stopping her from falling off to the right! But higher up, the strength of the board was compromised by her 'C' curve to the left. She was one of the minority who produce the 'C' by lifting and lightening the seat bone on the inside – so she had a heavier right seat bone which was falling off the right side of the horse, and a lighter left seat bone which was probably closer to its ideal positioning on the inside edge of the horse's long back muscle (see Fig. 5.11 and page 139). Her whole right side was lengthened, so in effect she was stretching her leg down and growing up tall. Meanwhile her left side was compressed, and she was twisted to face that way.

Many people who show an approximation of the same pattern actually dislike this rein more (which just goes to show how idiosyncratic each person is!). But Denise's starting point was particularly complex, and whilst she had the disadvantage of not being correctly 'plugged in' on either side, her disconnection with the right long back muscle left her feeling more compromised on this rein. However, if you, as an observer, were to ignore the stronger contact in her right hand, you would probably judge her right side as the better one; for whilst her left inside thigh muscles were working overtime to stop her from falling off to the right, the rest of her left side lacked tone. The 'sogginess' in her lower leg and thigh was extremely obvious. Her foot came forward and wobbled about; but this was *symptom* and not a *cause* of the problem.

I know from experience that to go directly from this starting point to the ideal of having 'both sides on' (i.e. both seat bones sitting on the inside edge of the horse's long back muscles, with the necks of the femur lying across them as in Fig. 5.11, page 139) is all but impossible. So to make Denise aware of the pattern we did the boards exercise described on page 136. Since she was closest to the position I call 'left side on, right side off', I began by helping her to get her left board strong for its entire length, with her left third much more 'stuffed'. Her upper body came much closer to vertical, and the creases in the left-hand side of her waistband all but disappeared. I then wanted her to reverse the pattern, and find the position I call 'right side on, left side off', which meant that she had to bring her right side much closer to the horse's mid-line, and let go with those left adductor tendons. But they took their job extremely seriously, and it was hard to make them budge.

She sat for a while in the best approximation to 'right side on, left side off' that we could find. We then reversed the pattern again, which brought her closer to her old 'home'. Then came the long, slow process of reversing it again. My plan was to do this a number of times before we began from the position which was most unfamiliar, and then put 'both boards on', so that both seat bones were plugged in, and her outer thirds were aligned and 'stuffed'. But during this particular lesson we never reached that point, for when Denise was sitting in the unfamiliar way I began hearing a very quiet, uncertain voice: 'I feel really weird. This is not like me at all. You've made me feel like someone else. I can't recognise me in this. In fact, I'm starting to feel dizzy.'

Denise had worked with me enough to appreciate that no learning takes place without a sense of 'weirdness'. For if the rider is to change how her body operates she has to *do something different*, and the new pattern will inevitably feel strange. But this was beyond her usual appetite for 'weird', and was such a dramatic re-wiring that it elicited the most extreme reaction I have ever experienced from anyone. Whilst we did not back off completely, we had to ease our way into the new pattern very, very slowly.

The next day I brought two sets of identical bathroom scales into the dismounted workshop, and Denise, along with the other course participants, stood with one foot on each of them so that we could gauge how she carried her weight. Her right leg carried 3 stone (42lbs or 19kg) more than the left. Denise was horrified, but retained her usual good humour as she contemplated the implications of all this. 'That's it,' she said, 'I'll just have to spend my working day walking round the hospital like this ...', and she demonstrated what she thought was a walk with more weight carried on her left foot. But she got it the wrong way round. Her neurology and her habit patterns tricked her into weighting the right leg even more!

The kind of change that turns 'me' into 'not me' is the most difficult of all, for we *are* our memories and our habit patterns. To change them is to change our map of who we are. This explains part of the reluctance of many people to take on the challenge of learning, for to leave 'home' and to feel weird is threatening. We are programmed for homeostasis – to ensure physical and psychological stability whatever happens in the external world. This is why the trap of 'sameness' is so strong, and instinctively so tempting: it is almost as if we are engaged in an archetypal battle, sameness versus contrast, *survival versus learning*.

....

Sameness vs contrast

Collectively, those of us who teach this work have become extremely adept at persuading people to choose learning over sameness, and to change the habits of a life-time. But left to themselves, remarkably few people make that choice, and selling a new co-ordination to the pupil is a skill in itself. The art lies in convincing her that we understand how strange she feels in her new way of sitting. We have to empathise with its weirdness, whilst being sure she appreciates that (like the ulcer in your mouth) it feels so much bigger than it looks. We then avoid any possible map battles between our visual sense of rightness and her kinaesthetic sense of wrongness.

But sometimes empathy fails, and when the rider still balks at these apparently enormous changes, one of my more strident colleagues has taken to saying, 'Oh, so you mean that you want to look like Nicole Uphoff Becker, but to feel like you've always felt?' Or, if the pupil is desperately addicted to her old way of sitting we might question its value by asking her, 'So in this way of riding, are you part of the solution to the problem your horse is setting you, or are you part of the problem?' Another 'hard sell' is to wait until the pupil is reeling from the weirdness of the feelings involved in the change she has made and to tell her, 'Now *this* is what a German dressage leg looks like!' (which we would only do, of course, if it really did).

We need to get creative as we take people beyond their self-imposed limitations – showing, explaining, demonstrating, convincing, and sometimes even asking for an act of faith – for, as riding coaches have proved time and time again, when you simply put information in through the ears there is absolutely no guarantee that it will come out through the a—e!

Our greatest ally in this is the horse, for he will soon respond to the changes the pupil is making, and he, in effect, will 'sell' them to her. But the time-lag – short though it is – is too long for some people. In effect, each of us has within us a 'wall', which represents our personal limit of 'weirdness' and of attention to detail which we are not willing to go beyond. Sadly, the pull of homeostasis is so strong that there really are very few 'no limits' riders, who will redraw their own personal maps of riding (and of themselves) in whatever way the development of their skill requires.

Experiencing contrasts is the key to crossing the wall, to doing it differently, and thus to learning. By analogy to the room with a smell in it, Denise had to 'leave the room' in order to appreciate where she had indeed been living. For the brain could only perceive it for what it was by contrast. The first step in learning is this initial change, and often it is a quantum leap. This is where the idea of gradual improvement becomes exposed as a myth, for to do something different is a *discrete* and not a gradual change. Initially our bodymind is continually doing the same thing in the same way, functioning like a scratched record which is stuck in a groove. When you change the pattern, you 'jump' out of the old groove and into a new one. The next challenge is to stay in it.

....

I was giving a talk to a riding club one evening when a woman asked the question, 'What happens when you have had a fantastic ride, and you go out the next day and you can't do it again. Where did it go?' The reaction of the audience attested that she had pin-pointed one of the most

Linguistic markers

tantalising and frustrating aspects of learning to ride. I used to talk about those magical rides as if they were a gift from God, but one of my colleagues recently suggested that perhaps they come from the Devil. To lose that state of grace is so devastating, and the desire to get back to it is so strong, that the experience can bring out the devil in each of us!

I answered this woman's question (I hope) to her and the audience's satisfaction. But it was only when thinking about it the next day that I realised how she had really asked the wrong question. For the right question is not, 'Where did it go?' but ''Where did it come from?'

If the woman concerned could have answered *that* question, she would have been able to go out and ride the same way again the next day. For she would have known exactly what to do, and the pattern would have been reproducible. But most people, when they have one of those fantastic rides, float around on cloud nine, and (although their middle-class upbringing might preclude these words) their thought process rarely goes much beyond 'Wow, man!' Then, they fall into the trap of thinking they have 'got it', only to exchange their euphoria for disillusionment in their next ride. This makes it abundantly clear that some lucky quirk of fate had dropped that magical ride into their lap as a one-off experience.

The first important step in making this magic reproducible is to switch on the analytical part of your brain as you are riding; so instead of becoming 'blissed out', you have to ask yourself, 'How am I doing this?' (This is not so easy to do, however, for bliss is such a tempting experience!) Your answer to this question will pin-point some of the important and obvious aspects of the feeling, and will allow you to describe and name them. This gives you a 'linguistic marker' for the experience, which helps you to understand it, and to find it again. Some people think in terms of body parts, saying, 'Well, there's a stretch down the front of my thigh and it's rotated in more than I'm used to ...' Others think in terms of images, and pupils have told me that they feel like they are sky diving, like a meringue, like frozen cheese, like Quasimodo, like a 'Barbie' doll, or like they are made of concrete. The greater the contrast they are experiencing, the more extreme their imagery tends to become – which is fine by me, as long as it works!

These images are a gift, too often ignored by trainers. A new pupil who was quite an accomplished rider once told me that she knew she leant forward, and that she had tried with all her might to break the habit. But she always felt as if there was a magnet on her forehead and another on the horse's poll, creating a constant attraction which pulled her forwards. She had been told to keep her upper body back for years on end, but no amount of will-power could overcome that fatal attraction. So my course was obvious. I made a convincing show of taking the magnet from her forehead and placing it under her backside. That was all I needed to do (and to understand the change she really made, you may want to consult the Ki Aikido exercises in Chapter 9). For crazy as this may sound, it completely altered the way she perceived her body, which in turn altered her sitting. With a few reminders about 'Where's that magnet?' she was a changed rider.

I am utterly convinced that this metaphorical use of language is one of the most effective ways of enhancing the learning process, but it has often got me into trouble. It seems that dressage judges and other important people always insist on visiting my clinics on the last day, by which time my pupils and I know exactly what we mean when we talk such apparent rubbish. The dressage judges, however, do not; so they mutter to themselves and walk out! I am never sure if it is worse for them to find us talking about 'being like frozen cheese', or to find me telling the rider to be 'rigid' or 'perched' – words which have been used by pupils who had initially been too floppy and not supporting their body weight. But despite the controversy of this language to someone who is not 'in the know', realise how cleverly my pupil and I have avoided the trap of Fig. 6.3 (page 165). By working through the sequence from right to left we have removed the slippage which occurs when the *teacher* sets the agenda.

During one clinic, I myself experienced the shock which so horrifies the dressage judges. I was teaching a pupil in the presence of her usual teacher – who had herself trained with me – when she interrupted me to ask the pupil, 'Kathy, has this blown your reverse banana?' My brain was reeling so hard in the attempt to work out what 'blowing her reverse banana' could possibly mean that I barely heard Kathy's reply! But it transpired that 'banana' was her code name for how she used to sit, with her upper body rounded forward. 'Reversing her banana' had brought her upright – but the inevitable had happened, and I was unknowingly challenging the way that she had reversed her banana too much! With our terms now clear, and the progression of Kathy's learning understood by all concerned, we were able to proceed.

Images can encapsulate a tremendous amount of information in a few words, and when we think about body parts we are in danger of clocking up an endless list. But some people need to process information in small chunks, sifting through all of these small pieces until they finally put the big picture together and get a more holistic feeling. Others are overwhelmed with all of these details; they prefer larger pieces, and will arrive more quickly at a big picture (which is less well filled in). Some people are much more precise than others in their use of language, and one of my colleagues stands out in this regard. She came to me as an almost unteachable pupil, who had fallen foul of a number of teachers. I too was sometimes hard pushed to stop her from running out of our lessons in tears. Her downfall lay in her need to be tremendously precise, and in the panic which overtook her when this need was not met.

Over the years, she has become much more teachable, and a very good rider. But we were working together a short time ago when the trigger phrase became 'I need to keep my seat bones feeling closer together and to drop them down more.' This change made all the difference, and the work was so good that we soon had to rest and walk on a loose rein. As she gathered up the reins to begin again I said, 'Now remember to drop your seat bones down and keep them feeling closer together.'

'No, no, no!' she said. 'It's not that. I have to make them feel closer together and *then* drop them down more!'

She then noticed how extreme her reaction had been. 'Oh dear,' she said, 'I haven't really changed much, have I?'

It was a beautiful moment of self-reflection, which left both of us chuckling about one of the foibles that makes her so uniquely who she is.

....

Ten thousand repetitions   Doing all of this without a teacher to help you is, of course, the ultimate challenge – and although it is far from the ideal of intensive training and 'supervised riding', it is the inevitable plight of many riders. I find, for instance, that summoning up the best linguistic markers I can muster rarely gets me right to the root of the new pattern. Even with the skills I now have, I can rarely reproduce the clarity of that first experience – where the feeling of contrast was so obvious – and the next day is usually a disappointment. So instead of ending that first ride saying, 'I've got it! I've got it!' I have trained myself to say, 'Now that will be an act to follow!' This makes me much more level-headed – a mind-set which helps me enjoy the time that I will inevitably spend tracking down the origins of the feeling, so that it truly becomes part of my repertoire.

Nowadays, this happens much quicker and easier than it used to, for a higher proportion of my neurological connections function well, and the pelvic area of my body is better represented in my sensory cortex. Since I can build on past experience, it may now only take a few days for me to feel that the new co-ordination is up and running. But it has been known to take me *six months*, during which I get it and lose it, and get it and lose it, and discover more about it until I reach its 'bottom line', and am no longer struggling to make myself 'do X'. I use mental rehearsal to help me maintain the clarity of that original feelage (see Chapter 10, page 290), and sometimes I dream about it at night. But the key issue is that instead of longing to arrive, I now enjoy the journey.

Sometimes I have lost the feeling for weeks on end, and have started to get lazy about it. So I have pulled myself up by my boot straps (it works well for me to tell myself, 'You wouldn't let one of your pupils get away with this!') and gone searching for the feeling again. What is really happening here is the search for full answers to the two key questions that catalyse learning: 'What's happening now?' and 'What do you want?' Paradoxically, knowledge of the final goal (the 'What do you want?') is contained *within the understanding of the present*. Once you know 'what is happening now', you have unpacked the etiology of the change you need to make, and you have a starting point for your journey. Without this, you cannot begin to travel.

Think of Denise, or any of the riders whose stories have served as examples, and realise how their learning fits this pattern. Their journey towards a more sophisticated level of riding began with the discovery of the wobbly right side or of the hands that fiddle and move. Once aware that A, B, and C are the mainstays of your repertoire, you can choose to stop doing A, do more of B and less of C. But without this initial realisation you cannot move, for you have not 'smelt out' your problem.

'What's happening now?' and 'What do you want?' are deceptively simple questions which the rider must return to again and again, for only *they* have the power to fill in the blanks in her map, revealing hidden information about the 'how' of riding. That initial breakthrough takes you from being 'unconscious of your incompetence' (where you do not know what you do not know) to being 'conscious of your incompetence' (where you discover what you do not know). But you have much further to travel, passing through the stage of being 'consciously competent' before you arrive at 'unconscious competence'.

Research done some years ago in Japan with gymnasts showed that it can take about two thousand repetitions of a new co-ordination before you stop just doing the old one on automatic-pilot. This means that on two thousand occasions you have to catch yourself, and realise 'Oh-ho, I'm doing it wrong again.' Then you make the correction – assuming, of course, that you have worked out what it is, and can find it without too much groping. But it takes a further eight thousand repetitions before your response becomes so streamlined that you are able to do the new way on automatic pilot.

More recent research has thrown these figures into question, but I continue to quote them to riders because they are (in my experience) a reasonable working assumption. In the Los Angeles Olympics, gymnast Mitch Gaylord successfully performed a dismount from the high bar that he had done only twice before and that no one else had ever done before. However, we do not know how many repetitions he had performed in mental rehearsal, and we can rest assured that he has one of the most sophisticated nervous systems on the planet. So whilst ten thousand repetitions is a good rule of thumb for the average rider, it undoubtedly is a limitation which can be overcome.

Most people contemplate ten thousand repetitions and groan at the enormity of the task – and it is indeed daunting. But in one teacher-training workshop, I presented this information, only to discover a few minutes later that one member of the group had immediately set about calculating that if you were catch yourself twice a minute, you could be through the whole process in eighty-three hours and thirty-three minutes! (Someone else in the group, which was made up primarily of Americans, could not resist pointing out that the calculation was the endeavour of the only German in the group!)

But to catch yourself twice a minute would be a super-human achievement, needing you to be able to pay attention far better than most people do. Once I am reasonably adept at the new correction, one of my favourite ways to keep myself hot on its trail is to work my horse on a slight slope. For any new co-ordination will almost certainly be lost on the downhill, and will be easier to regain on the uphill. I then have a built in opportunity to make the correction at least once on every circle!

Most riders hate to work on a slope because they abhor the fact that their riding and their horse's carriage will, almost certainly, deteriorate on the downhill. Their only interest lies in producing their best work, and in sustaining it for as long as possible: thus they are rating performance much higher than learning.

When they lose that (high) level of performance some riders so hate to acknowledge their mistake that they pull their horse's head down in a dramatic attempt to sweep it beneath the carpet. Others barely notice: they 'come to' about ten minutes later and wonder what has happened. Instead of getting straight back on track (like the cybernetic mechanism) most of these riders get side-tracked. They berate themselves for their lack of commitment, swear at their body for being so inept, or decide that they'll never be able to do it. They punish the horse for their own mistake, and hassle him into more evasions. The potential to get lost, and to lose track of the cybernetic learning process, is huge. For at this point – when constructive analysis has given way to panic or self-criticism – the rider is no longer on track of the new pattern and is not even engaged in overly large pendulum swings. She has abandoned the learning process.

If we were to draw a graph of the learning process, as applied to one particular breakthrough, it would look like one of the variations in Fig. 6.5, and very rarely would you see the ideal of Fig. 6.5d that we all fantasise about. The initial change is a quantum leap – a jump from one groove to another – and this has to happen to set the rest of the learning process in motion. The line representing the ten thousand repetitions needed to ingrain the new response could look very different according to the individual concerned, and how easily she either gives up, or homes in on the new correction (as in Figs 6.5b and 6.5c). She may never go

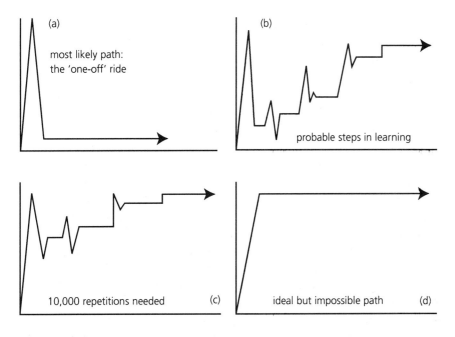

Fig. 6.5 The initial breakthrough experience may come to nothing as in (a), or may go through more or less streamlined a process of ten thousand repetitions before it becomes ingrained, as in (b) and (c). The ideal path of (d) is virtually never realised in practice.

back to where she was; or she might be straight back there again tomorrow (as in Fig. 6.5a). If she bites off the task of tracking down the origins of her breakthrough, her dedication, determination and discipline, her concentration and commitment, will probably be tested to the full. I and others like me can engineer tremendous breakthroughs for riders, and can change their riding in ways they had not thought possible. It is not so hard for us to lead the horse to water. But we cannot make it drink.

....

I reckon that most people can have two or three of these changes in process at once, each at various stages. Some breakthroughs will inevitably be harder to track down and more elusive than others, but with experience, ingraining these changes does become easier. With enough repetitions under your belt you are ready to test the new pattern – by riding more difficult combinations of the school movements, and maintaining your new alignment as you work on circles, on changes of bend, through transitions and in the lateral movements. For these are not just training exercises for the horse, they are training exercises for *you*.

However, when done by rote they are the antithesis of training, for you practise your mistakes and your horse practises his evasions ... until you

Learners and performers

both do them perfectly. So if you think of the school movements as tests of your technique, and as an ongoing way to monitor your progress, you will use them much more wisely. But of course, one of the ultimate tests is riding in competition. For by the time you are concerning yourself with a dressage test or a jumping round, you need to be producing many right patterns on the automatic pilot of unconscious competence.

In a dressage competition, when the judge marks each movement you ride out of ten, she is assessing how close you have come to perfection. If we think of the basic rider/horse interaction, and consider the rider as *cause,* and the horse as *effect,* it is the discrepancy between *effect* and *ideal effect* which causes you not to receive a ten. Trainers, like dressage judges, usually aim their comments at this gap between effect and ideal effect, saying 'The horse must be rounder', or 'Make him more impulsive.' In doing this, they assume that you already know how to make this difference – which, of course, you may. But if you do not, it is the underlying link between cause and effect which needs to be addressed. (See Fig. 6.6.) This is the 'how' of riding – the declarative knowledge which is the subject of much of my work.

In *'Masterclass'*, I presented the TOTE model (Test, Operation, Test, Exit – see Fig. 6.7) as another way of explaining how the rider uses her brain in riding, and this is worth repeating here since it also illustrates some of the stages in learning. If the rider is going to do anything other than simply accept what the horse gives her, she has (in effect) to regularly ask herself the question, 'Does the feeling I am getting match the feeling I really want to get?' So she makes a *comparison* between the current reality and her 'reference feeling' – the best feeling she has had to date for the kind of work she is doing (which – given her limited experience – may not necessarily be perfection). This is the first test, and if the feelings match, she has nothing to do. But if they do not, she has to enter into an *operation,* which will hopefully make them match.

The rider who has just had a breakthrough experience will be involved in operations much of the time, as she gropes her way back to that feeling

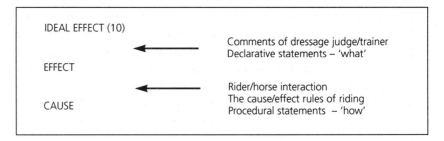

IDEAL EFFECT (10)

Comments of dressage judge/trainer
Declarative statements – 'what'

EFFECT

Rider/horse interaction
The cause/effect rules of riding
Procedural statements – 'how'

CAUSE

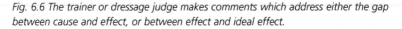

Fig. 6.6 The trainer or dressage judge makes comments which address either the gap between cause and effect, or between effect and ideal effect.

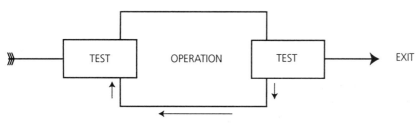

Fig. 6.7 The TOTE model.

and clocks up her ten thousand repetitions. Initially, the operations may be hard to do – or even unsuccessful – but they become more slick over time. When the rider successfully re-establishes her reference feeling, she is able to exit the TOTE – until the next time it goes wrong.

The skilful rider spends much more time out of the TOTE than in it, for there is rarely a discrepancy between her current feeling and her reference feeling. When there is, she can (in theory at least) perform the right operation in a moment, and exit from the TOTE again, leaving her brain free to think about riding the movements of a test. (And unfortunately, the whole operation is probably so refined that she will not have the faintest hope of being able to tell you how she did it!) The learner and the performer – one of them in, and one of them out of the TOTE – are in very different states. This makes the good performer a much better trainer for other performers than she is for learners.

I often draw an analogy between learning to ride, and learning to sail a boat. But this boat has leaks, and water is coming in fast. So should you be trying to sail it, or should you be bailing? Very often the trainer is attempting to teach you how to sail, without realising that bailing would be much more appropriate (after all, her boat does not leak, and if she has failed to realise that you are different to her, she will not have noticed your plight!). Sailing represents riding the school movements, and bailing represents fixing the 'leaks' and problems in the biomechanics of your riding which stop it from functioning well. The difference between the two is the difference between having exited the TOTE, and being inside it, refining the operations which will ultimately let you out.

Many people who consider themselves as performers (rather than learners) are functioning at a much less sophisticated level than they could do if they were willing to make more stringent tests, to become learners, and to re-enter the TOTE. Golfers and tennis players realise the need to constantly refine their skills: we frequently read in the press about top-class players who are working on their swing, or their volley. So they are cycling through the TOTE again and again, clocking up their ten thousand repetitions of each new pattern before they take it into competition. But few riders see the need to keep learning the new operations which enable their body to activate more neural networks, and to work in a more subtle yet effective way.

Those who *do* soon become captivated by the lure of success. Let us suppose that you are working on fixing your most obvious leak: you may be aware of others which are waiting for your attention, or you may have plugged so many already that you are happily thinking to yourself, 'Boy, once this is fixed I shall be able to sail really well!' So you fix it, and you sail well for a while, and then you realise that your dreams of perfection are not coming true: for you discover yet another leak, which you had not noticed previously. When you were busy bailing, its effects were irrelevant; but now that all those other leaks are fixed, this becomes the important one to work with. So you fix it, thinking, 'Once this is dealt with I shall be sailing so well ...'

With each leak you fix, you think you are solving the ultimate problem, and with great excitement, you fantasise that you are about to 'arrive'; but your excitement is always short-lived, for there is always another leak lying just around the corner and waiting to be discovered. If you are a teacher, you run the risk of becoming 'faddy', and of assuming that your 'ultimate problem' is everyone else's problem too. For suddenly you see it in other riders (this is rather like buying a blue Ford car, and suddenly realising that the roads are full of the exact same model, many of them blue) for what was once part of the *background* has just become part of the *foreground*. This can tempt you to believe that you alone are in the position of being able to offer all of these riders the 'ultimate fix'!

One of my student teachers gave an amazing demonstration recently of the importance that fixing one's current leak can take on. She is a small, slightly built rider, who was riding an enormous, fresh, recalcitrant horse, who resented being transformed from a hunter into a dressage horse. She did a fantastic job of banishing the evil thoughts in his brain, and of bringing him into carriage. Her riding remained very correct throughout, with remarkably few biomechanical flaws – and everyone watching was spellbound by such a virtuoso performance. But at the end she was hugely disappointed, because in the midst of all the evasions he was throwing at her, she had been unable to keep track of her current leak. (This was a lack of upper body strength which left her chest collapsed. The 'fix' opened her chest and made her look more elegant – but even in her struggles, she did not become unduly round-shouldered.) 'It felt like Monty Python's Flying Circus,' she said, commenting on the rather crude responses she had been forced to make to his extremely crude evasions. It was a Herculean piece of riding, which she should, in theory, have been very pleased with; but it failed to satisfy her personal criteria for 'good'.

This means that the rider is in danger of seeing 'good' around each next corner, and of feeling that she can never quite reach it. So we all need to think back – to realise that we now easily do what was unknown and impossible a year ago. Then (when we are ready) we need to test ourselves against other people's definition of 'good'.

Another colleague who has put her heart and soul into learning recently found that she was passing this test, receiving good results in competitive dressage. But surprisingly, she was not celebrating the fact that she now had enough free attention to work more with the school movements, to use them as challenges for her and her horse, and to show them in public. Instead, she found herself saying, 'What I'm doing doesn't feel like riding anymore. There's something missing.' She had at last become able to exit the TOTE for much of the time. Having been through innumerable cycles of ten thousand repetitions, she had fixed the major problems in her body, and was riding her horse well. But she was missing the time she had spent groping around trying to make her operations work in the hope that she could one day be able to exit the TOTE!

Her experience is extremely unusual, and commonly, people are not reluctant to leave the TOTE, they are reluctant to enter it. In his book *The Case of Nora*, Moshe Feldenkrais wrote about his treatment of a patient who had been hugely incapacitated by a stroke, and who – through his patient work – learned to read and write again, and to orientate herself in space (she had previously bumped into furniture and walls). He says of such patients, '...unless they can do the recovered act without thinking about it, they do not feel they are "cured". They want simply to have the intention and do the action without knowing what and how they do it. In short, people are so ignorant of the way they learn to do things that they believe any awareness of a conscious effort is an indication that they are not normal. To most people, life is something that works automatically, and if it does not, they have to be cured.'

To many people, riding is the same, and the story of Kate illustrates this well. She is an older woman, who in her day was one of the best event riders in Australia. She was renowned for her verve and dash across country, and like all good event riders, the mechanics of her jumping functioned extremely well on 'unconscious competence'. But her flatwork had always let her down, and when she began riding with me several years ago, she began undoing the patterns of a lifetime. In the particular lesson I remember, she had just worked out some of the mechanics of sitting in a way which drew the horse's back up underneath her. The change in her horse's carriage was impressive; but the type of concentration it required and the attention she had to pay to her body were a new experience for her.

As I looked on at the change that Kate had made I was feeling rather pleased with myself; but it soon became clear that she did not share my enthusiasm. Suddenly she let out a wail, 'But you've just spoilt riding for

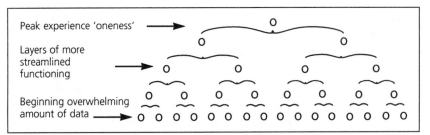

Fig. 6.8 The process of chunking: as the rider encapsulates two separate co-ordinations or body parts into one feelage or image, she is able to work her way up the pyramid to the experience of 'oneness' with her horse.   **O** = a chunk of information

me!' She had always ridden on the flat as she did across country, 'by the seat of her pants': but the 'seat of her pants' – although good enough to make her one of the best over fences – was not good enough to produce worthwhile flatwork. (We met Kate in our discussion of asymmetries (page 142), and will meet her again in Chapter 10, where we look in more detail at some typical personality differences between event and dressage riders.) Kate made the choice to focus and to keep learning; but not without some regret.

Most people want to be performers, not learners, feeling that riding – like life – should happen automatically. We all know that the beginner cannot hope for this; she is forced to try and process an overwhelming amount of data about her backside, thighs, calves, hands, and feet etc. (and very soon she is expected to steer her horse as well!). Gradually, the brain becomes able to 'chunk' two pieces of information into one, and another two into one, giving more free attention to take on new and more sophisticated pieces (see Fig. 6.8). (Images serve a very useful purpose here, for suggestions like 'Ride as if you were Isabel Werth' can encapsulate a very large number of pieces.) Gradually, the pupil arrives at that breakthrough ride which gives her that magical experience of oneness with her horse.

Her choices then are either to mourn its passing, or to re-enter the TOTE, discover its origins, and make it her own. The existential choice is to ride automatically, or to reach our potential. But even if we were all familiar with the language which best describes learning, I doubt that anyone would ever look at a really good rider and say, 'Wow! I can't wait to engage in a cybernetic learning process and find out how to do that!' We just say, 'Wow! I want to ride like that!' Our sights are set on the goal, with no thought for the process of getting there. We simply want to arrive, without ever submitting ourselves to the journey. So our discussion leaves one unanswered question about skilful riding, which each individual has to answer for herself: 'Is it worth what it takes to get it?'

CHAPTER SEVEN
Mindwork

MINDWORK IS, quite literally, the management of your brain, and the maps it contains. It requires you to step back one stage from your everyday experience – rather like operating the 'File Management' option on a word processor. Analogies are frequently drawn between the brain and a computer, and it is often said that the sheer complexity of the brain and its capacity for learning far outstrips that of any computer which ever has been or ever will be produced. But the brain does not come with a user's manual. This means that it can be used in a huge variety of ways, and as it selectively pays attention, it makes the links and forms the beliefs which create your internal maps. Through the mechanism of your unconscious mind, these maps drive your behaviour.

Freud's postulation of the unconscious (he was the first to suggest its existence) was a great stroke of genius; but he made one big mistake in his 'talking cure'. For who you turn out to be is not so much a factor of what happens in your life, regardless of whether your mother hit you when you were three, or whether you have survived a concentration camp. It is more a case of how you *respond* to what happens in your life, for your future decisions and feelings are determined by the maps you made in the light of circumstance about yourself, the world and others.

The internal maps which influence our riding and our lives as riders, are much more far-reaching than our maps of the behaviours which constitute skilful work in the saddle – important though these are. They themselves are encased in our maps of what riding *is*. (Is it trail riding, barrel racing, show jumping, dressage, or western pleasure classes? Does it take place in show rings, or in muddy fields?) Concurrently, we inherit or develop our maps of the ways in which horses should be treated, kept and worked. Then, there is our map of how we do things: do we expend a minimum of effort, expect to find it easy, or expect to struggle whilst operating from the belief that 'anything worth doing is worth doing well'?

Our maps of how to learn, how much to 'go for it', and of the nature of concentration are extremely important. So are our understandings of success and failure, and the value of competition. Since learning to ride touches all of these issues, it is obviously a much more far-reaching enterprise than simply sitting on a saddle.

The way we set goals, and set about doing everything we do, is undoubtedly influenced by many aspects of our background. But regardless of individual factors like wealth, poverty or ambition, the brain always functions as a cybernetic, goal-striving mechanism. This is inescapable, and without a goal it (and you) are like someone trying to balance on a stationary bicycle – you topple over and have very little fun going nowhere. But as soon as the brain has a goal it faithfully heads towards it, *with absolutely no concern about how useful or appropriate that goal is*. It performs on cue without judgement.

It is this mechanism which underpins the self-fulfilling nature of our thoughts. I had a wonderful example of this recently. It happened some time after one of my friends had ridden my horse whilst I was away, and had found herself working in the outdoor arena alongside a field of cows that had recently calved. One of the cows (she subsequently discovered) had suffered a paralysis of her hindquarters following the birth, and the farmer had been rolling her over regularly to stop her from getting sore. But the time had come to move her to a new piece of grass, so he fixed up a sling, and somehow managed to suspend her from the bucket of his JCB excavator, and to drive her across the field close by the arena! My friend had seen all this out of the corner of her eye (wondering what the hell was going on) but had kept my horse's attention throughout, working her continuously with her ears out sideways. It was no mean achievement.

After I had heard this story I told it to riders during my workshops, since it was such a good example of focused attention from both rider and horse (especially given that my horse is quite spooky). Then one day my friend and I took the same horse to the same arena to give each other some feedback about our riding. As I worked him in, I began saying, 'You know, I've told that story about the cow and the JCB to so many people. It's such a good example of concentration ....' As I spoke, I was riding up the long side towards a pile of jump stands which were stacked outside the arena. I continued, '... and it's even more impressive, given that this is the type of horse who would spook at those jump stands.' My horse spooked at the jump stands!

The most dramatic examples of our prophetic abilities occur whenever we find ourselves thinking about negative outcomes and dire results. For we are – quite literally – forming them as goals, and programming ourselves to manifest them. The brain cannot code a negative, so if I say to you 'Do not think about a pink elephant,' you have to think about a pink elephant in order to know what it is that you are not supposed to be thinking about! Thus as soon as you think 'I hope we don't stop at the ditch' you are in fact thinking about stopping at the ditch ... and programming your brain to do so. (The knock-on effects of this are such that your brain will have no trouble programming your horse!) In acknowledgement of the power of thinking, one popular psychology book is entitled *You Can't Afford The Luxury of a Negative Thought.* You do not need to be ill, in crisis, or in the cross-country start box for this to be true. It is preventative medicine at its best.

Captain Mark Phillips is one of the few trainers who appreciates the importance of what you think when you ride, and when he discusses the effect that larger fences have on the rider he talks about 'the worm in the brain', the part of you that begins to fantasise about all the awful things that could happen. If they have happened before, this becomes even more tempting, and it is here that our functioning so easily begins to differ from that of the self-guided torpedo. For this *remembers its successes and forgets its mistakes.* If what it is doing is already working, it keeps on doing it. If it is not, it simply changes course. It never tortures itself by thinking 'I hope I don't do that again', giving *that* the status of the goal, and sending us head-first towards another repetition of our mistake!

Jane Savoie's book, *That Winning Feeling*, builds, like much of my own thinking, on the work of Maxwell Maltz, suggesting techniques that specifically programme the brain for success. But very few people do this naturally, and the huge majority — if they ever stopped to think about it — would realise that *their brain runs them.*

....

Riding in flow

Whenever I think about learning, I always remember a pair of ten-year-old twin girls I taught when I lived in London. One of them, Linda, was lithe, confident, well coordinated and brave. Her sister Susan was fatter, timid, and prone to the 'foetal crouch'. (Soon after their birth Susan had been hospitalised for some time, and when she came home she was no longer the lively, content baby she had been before she went in.) Linda was a natural rider — to keep challenging her I had to get quite inventive about the exercises I set. But despite this I had the feeling that riding was still somehow far too easy. In contrast, Susan was challenged just by the fact of being on a pony, and she worked very hard to organise her body and act as if she was brave. Within this, I had a strong sense that she knew — somewhere in her being — that she was doing something very important for herself, although I am sure she could never have said so. But her mother telephoned me one day to report, 'Susan is changing so much. She's far less clingy and much more outgoing than she has ever been before. Of course we can never be sure, but I can only put it down to her riding.'

Soon after this the sisters moved away, and I lost touch with them, so I have no idea how their riding progressed. But I suspect that Susan will finally become the rider, and that her talented sister may well give up. For, with their different starting points, riding had tremendously different meanings for each of them, and its value to Susan in terms of the change that it could catalyse was far greater than its value to Linda. There was very little actual learning involved for Linda; riding was within her 'comfort zone', and therefore it lacked the challenge of any 'stretch zone' activity.

To 'hook' somebody, riding has to be not too easy, and not too impossible or scary. To keep them 'hooked', it has to become (if only occasionally) what Mihaly Csikszentmihalyi calls a 'flow' activity. In his book of the same name, he defines this as 'the state in which people are so involved in an activity that nothing else seems to matter'. In his work at the University of Chicago, he has made an extensive study of the 'optimal experience' of both highly skilled performers and the general public. He has discovered that according to his subjects, 'the best moments (in life) usually occur when a person's body or mind is stretched to its limits in a voluntary effort to accomplish something difficult and worthwhile.'

In the flow experience there is a sense that, 'one's skills are adequate to cope with the challenges at hand .... Concentration is so intense that there is no attention left over to think about problems. Self-consciousness disappears, and the sense of time becomes distorted. An activity that produces such experiences is so gratifying that people are willing to do it for its own sake, with little concern for what they will get out of it, even when it is difficult, or dangerous.' His book abounds with examples from rock climbers, skiers, sailors and surgeons; from chess players, mathematicians, musicians, painters, poets – and even the members of a motorcycle gang. But sadly, not a single rider graces its pages.

Csikszentmihalyi presents the diagram opposite to describe the progress of someone learning a skill (see Fig. 7.1). In it, skills are plotted against challenges, and when the two are fairly evenly matched the player can be in what he calls the flow channel. At point A1, our beginner might be riding on the lead rein, or simply hitting balls over the net in tennis. Her skills are so basic that these activities will be sufficiently challenging to stimulate flow. But she will not stay in this state for long. As her skills improve she will soon get bored with this minimal level of challenge, and her response is represented on the diagram by position A2. But let us suppose, in contrast, that she is made to ride a horse who is far too difficult for her, or that she is pitted against a tennis player whose skills outweigh her own. She may suddenly realise that there is much more to this activity than she had thought, and she may become anxious about her obvious lack of skill. This is represented in the diagram by position A3.

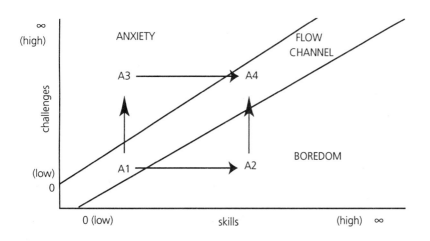

Fig. 7.1 The flow channel (courtesy HarperCollins Publishers). For an explanation of A1, A2 etc., see text.

Our fledgling rider or tennis player will not want to remain in either boredom or anxiety, so she will strive to return to the flow experience. Alternatively she may give up (unless, of course, she is a youngster whose parents are forcing her to continue). If she is bored, then she needs to increase the challenges she is facing – by playing tennis against someone slightly better than herself, or perhaps by riding on the lunge, on her own, or on a hack. If instead she is anxious, she needs to increase her skills in order to return to the flow channel and position A4. In theory, she could also *reduce* the challenges she is facing at position A3 down to the level of those at A1. In riding, her safety might require that she does this; but in practice it is quite difficult to down-grade into a flow experience. For once one is aware that new challenges exist, it is hard to feel satisfied whilst ignoring them.

Both positions A1 and A4 are flow experiences, but although both are equally enjoyable, A4 is the more complex experience, involving both greater skills and greater challenges. Further learning will, ideally, take the person on up the flow channel, and ultimately, perhaps, to the level of international competition. For rarely can we enjoy doing the same thing at the same level for very long, and because we want to enjoy ourselves, we seek to increase our skills, or to utilise existing skills in more challenging situations. But this is often not so easy to orchestrate – particularly in riding – since horses and the challenges they set are less predictable and less easily changed than tennis partners.

Money is a factor here too, for in contrast with many flow activities, riding does not come cheap. I shall never forget one of my friends who was struggling to afford to compete in eventing: she looked so utterly miserable as she said, 'I wish I could still get excited by the thought of jumping a fallen log in the woods.' At the opposite end of the spectrum, the technical and fitness challenges presented by endurance riding have come to the rescue of many a bored rider, who had fallen from the flow channel and given up on the quest to increase her biomechanical skills. The flow channel lies at the boundary between boredom and anxiety or frustration – in the space where a person's capabilities are well matched with the challenges set. To stay in it throughout one's riding career is, perhaps, the greatest challenge of all.

Flow is only possible within a structure that has distinct goals, a clear system of rules, and immediate feedback about one's progress: sports, games, music, and many intellectual activities fit the bill well. People in every walk of life regard flow experiences as the best moments in their lives – they are, in fact, addictive, bringing out the best and the worst in human nature. Society suffers greatly when a significant proportion of its youngsters find them only in the challenges of petty crime.

The American spiritual teacher Ram Das tells the story of one of the first public talks he gave, in which he was, in effect, extolling the virtues of the flow experience. For society teaches us that if only we were rich, famous and good looking, then surely we would be happy. Meanwhile, if we can earn more money and buy a bigger house, a smarter car, or a better horse, we will certainly be well on our way. But many a mid-life crisis has been sparked off by the realisation that this is not true. For selling your soul to the company and consumerism can leave you feeling hollow and empty, regardless of whether you have made your millions, or kept yourself in poverty – spurred on in your endeavours by the thought of some future gain (which inevitably never comes). During his talk, he noticed a little old lady in the audience, who kept nodding and smiling, giving every indication that she completely understood. She came up to him afterwards, and told him how thrilled she was to hear him say all this. 'You see,' she said, 'it makes perfect sense to me because I crochet'!

Crochet might well not strike you as challenging enough to provide the ultimate flow experience. But regardless of the medium that we experience it in, the value of flow is that it enables us, for a short time at least, to control the contents of consciousness and therefore to control the quality of our experience. If you have ever tried to meditate (sit in inner silence) you will know how difficult, and how powerful, this can be. As Csikszentmihalyi makes clear, the result of practising the Eastern disciplines – or any other skill – is that they make it possible 'to free inner life from the threat of chaos, on the one hand, and from the rigid conditioning of biological urges, on the other, and hence to become independent from the social controls that exploit both.' With this, one realises the folly of society's belief that the flow experience can be bought, and it becomes clear that it may or may not accompany winning. For it is when we act freely, *for the sake of the action itself rather than for ulterior motives*, that we experience flow.

The value that flow has for us is tremendous, and the person who looks back on her flow experience is *not the same* as the person who went into it. When immersed in the activity we temporarily forget who we are, for we are not aware of ourselves as separate from the action we are performing. Since we are not preoccupied with ourselves and our (frequently petty) concerns, we are able to *expand* our sense of self. By increasing our skills and moving through barriers we become self-transcendent – and when we reflect on ourselves again, the person we reflect on has been enriched by the acquisition of new skills and fresh insights. She may even have excelled in ways which could not even have been imagined sometime previously. The self has become more *complex* through this activity, and it is this growth of the self – the real subject of Ram Das's talk – which makes flow activities so innately compelling.

If instead you invest your time in eating, drinking, resting, sleeping, watching television, and surrounding yourself with all the comforts and luxuries that money can buy, you may well feel *pleasure*, but you have not increased the complexity of the self. You have also invested very little psychic energy – and although you might expect that a passive stimulation of the senses will make you feel happy, the satisfaction that it generates is bound to be transient. In fact, as you feel it wear off, you develop the need for *more*, and (if you do not stop to wonder 'More what?') you can easily become caught in the treadmill of rising expectations.

Comfort and luxury are society's *symbols* for happiness; but to consume the symbols – as so many people do – is to make the same logical mistake as the mythical gastronome who eats the menu! To believe that you have 'arrived' and to indulge yourself with the symbols of happiness is often the kiss of death for, as soon as you stop striving to achieve your goals, you 'fall off your bicycle'. The same sentiment is expressed in an old Chinese curse, which says, 'May all your dreams come true.' When asked at the age of eighty about the secret of life, the sculptor Henry Moore replied, 'The secret of life is to have a task, something you devote your entire life to, something you bring everything to, every minute of the day for the rest of your life. And the most important thing is, it must be something you cannot possibly do.' Given this, it is perhaps not such a surprise that lottery winners are given counselling!

I feel extremely grateful that my life has yielded three flow activities, for riding, teaching and writing all put me very easily into that state. And the down-side is, of course, that one becomes tempted to shun the more mundane experiences of life, with their relative ambiguity and chaos. (In practical terms, this used to boil down to frequent and impassioned cries from my ex-partner, who wanted to know, 'Where are my clean socks?'

and 'When are you going to cook supper?'!) I was probably better at washing socks and cooking meals in the days when I had not achieved such a good balance between skills and challenges in quite so many areas of my life. But the struggle to do so has occupied much of my time, and only in teaching has this balance been easily achieved. For there I am a 'natural'. In my other skills I have never been prone to boredom, but I have certainly experienced more than my share of anxiety and frustration.

....

Trying vs flow

I wrote in the last chapter about the woman who asked me, 'What happens when you've had a fantastic ride, and you go out the next day and find you can't do it again? Where did it go?' She – like all of us – had undoubtedly been tantalised by the occasional ride which does indeed generate flow. That exquisite sensation of 'oneness' with a horse always leaves us clamouring for more ... and with this comes the inevitable frustration of trying to catch a will-o'-the-wisp. Csikszentmihalyi talks little about the experience of not-being-able-to-find-flow, preferring to focus on the psychology of optimal performance. We touch on it in this book, and in *Ride With Your Mind/The Natural Rider* I wrote at length about the trials and tribulations of the struggle to ride well, and about the fears and anxieties which arise.

Two of my favourite authors on this subject are Eloise Ristad, whose beautiful book *A Soprano on Her Head* gives guidelines not just for musicians, but for 'life and other performances'. Similarly, Denise McCluggage's *The Centered Skier* is an extremely far-reaching book. Also useful are Timothy Gallwey's *Inner Game* books, in which he gives many tips for heightening concentration and exchanging the tyranny of 'Self 1' – the critical disparaging voice in your head – for the flow experience of 'Self 2' – the part of the brain (often thought of as the right brain hemisphere) which is adept at focused attention and physical skills.

It is when riding becomes 'serious' that trying, frustration, boredom, and anxiety begin to dominate the rider's experience (and I am very happy to have taken so many people out of these dead ends and back into the flow channel). As we saw with Pat (page 158), trying involves *excess muscular tension* which – in riding as in many other skills – usually involves the shoulder girdle, neck, jaw, hand and arm. It also involves *focused vision*; so instead of using peripheral vision, and taking in everything whilst looking at nothing, the eyes stare, usually at the horse's ears. By taking on this limited visual perspective the rider sees only one tree whilst missing the entire wood: not only does she become a danger whilst working with others in the riding school, she also fixes her brain in visual mode, so that it cannot 'tune in' to the 'channel' which registers feelings.

I gave a very rewarding lesson some time ago to an event rider who had a 'thing' about canter transitions, despite riding well the rest of the time. She dreaded the transition, and repeatedly messed it up. She was convinced that nothing she did would work, so she resorted to 'overkill', leaning back and kicking frantically. Then, if her horse *did* canter (instead of trotting faster) she was so far into water-ski mode that *he had to take off in motorboat mode*. My primary intervention was to ensure that she kept her peripheral vision into and through the transition. I also suggested that she gave the aid as if she believed it would work, and that she asked herself, 'Am I well enough in place to "keep up with him" on the first canter bound?' (She condensed this into the short reminder 'keep up with him'.) She then realised how far out of balance she had been – and how greater desperation had inevitably led to greater 'wrongness'. She also realised that contemplating the transition had suddenly caused her to focus her vision, and to start talking to herself ('Oh God, do we have to do this? I bet I mess up.')

The change she made was dramatic, and to the relief of her horse she was soon producing neat, clean transitions. She had completely by-passed the self-fulfilling ways in which she had set herself up to go wrong. By consciously thinking about her *vision*, she was able to maintain the focused attention of flow, and to stop that critical voice in her head. The three components of trying (excess muscular tension, focused vision and internal dialogue) all have the effect of limiting sensory input. Thus listening to the voice in your head is the same 'hiding to nothing' as focused vision, since your attention is held in your auditory 'channel', and this stops your conscious mind from being able to register feelings (remember Genie Zaborde's description of this on page 20). The rider who tries and the rider in flow, have each picked out and deleted different facets of experience; the effects of this are so huge that whilst one would be following instructions in the (non-existent) user's manual, the other has exchanged it for a *loser's* manual.

A person's best performances inevitably take place in flow, and sports psychologists often use the term *interference* to refer to the difference between these, and her everyday level of work. Much of this interference is the result of internal dialogue: 'You ought to be able to do this by now,' 'It's about time you learned how to ride the corners properly,' and the even more insidious versions like 'I must stop talking to myself'! These voices yatter on on the edge of consciousness, half heard, and largely disregarded, but still devastating in their effects. But even if you *did* listen and you *could* obey their dictates they would still not work well for you: for internal dialogue takes so long that by the time you have reminded yourself how to ride the corner, the corner has come and gone!

To make one's internal dialogue useful it firstly has to be condensed into shorthand, and a few trigger words. These linguistic markers help you to access a particularly useful feeling, and can be worth their weight in gold. To trigger the feeling from a visual image is probably even better; but since people who specialise in internal dialogue often find it hard to work from pictures, it is easier to modify the dialogue. Do *not* let those words become sentences, or have a disparaging, critical tone. They must be short, helpful reminders, delivered in an enthusiastic, caring way – just as you would like your teacher to say them. Some of my pupils tell me that they use my voice, which is fine by me and a very sensible option, since I come much cheaper this way than I do in the flesh!

If this change is hard for you to make, you may need to change tactics and pay more attention to the voice instead. Whose voice is it? Is it yours, your mother's, or an instructor's? Whereabouts in your head does it come from? Is it in the centre, the side, the back or the front? Try moving its location within your head – often that will cause it to change its tone, and if you shift it to the mid-line of your skull it may suddenly become less believable. Give it an accent: have it make its demands as if it were Agatha Christie's Belgian detective Hercule Poirot, or as if it were Chinese. Or have it sing to you in opera. Imagine the volume adjustment on a radio or a remote control and turn down its volume. Get creative, and instead of automatically feeling victimised, realise that the owner of this voice does not carry a shotgun. Contrary to its demeanour, it is *not* the world's greatest authority on riding.

If you are still having trouble, imagine the character who does indeed own this voice – let's call it your inner judge. Put him or her out in front of you in your mind's eye, and see what he (or she) looks like. Is he one person, or is there a committee? Is this person angry, and frustrated at you for ignoring his advice? Let him rant and rave for a while, and actually *listen*. Does he have any good ideas, or is he just full of hot air? You could negotiate with him or them, tell him that you really do want to ride well, and ask if he is willing to make his suggestions in a different way – as occasional reminders of the pertinent points – so that you really could take them on board and learn from them. If he is, then this could be the beginning of a very fruitful partnership.

If he is *not* then you will have to ham him up some more. As Eloise Ristad suggests, you could imagine him as a cartoon figure. Dress him in judges' robes, have him grow a long nose and long gnarled fingers, and have him read to you from official-looking scrolls. Or you could strip him naked, and watch him shiver with cold and embarrassment as he runs for cover. To gain even more respite from him, hum or sing to yourself as you ride – for it is impossible to hum and talk both at the same time. To understand him better, you might want to read Richard C. Carson's book *Taming Your Gremlin*. But the major point is to realise that you do not have to believe his accusations and his tirade of supposedly good advice. He is not God.

....

Young children – having not yet fallen prey to the tyranny of their internal dialogue – practically live in a state of flow, and unlike the vast majority of the population, good performers have retained their childhood ability to learn and perform in flow. (As we shall see in Chapter 10, this also relates to their brain-wave pattern.) I have particularly enjoyed teaching a number of world-class competitors, and seeing the ease with which they learn, and how quickly their skills develop from just a few pieces of input. Their most important but least recognised attribute is their ability to pay attention; but without *knowing what they know* they cannot pass on this skill to others. As one of them said to me, 'I now realise more and more that this is something I actually have to teach. I was completely unaware of that before. I thought everyone else concentrated just the same as I did, but I couldn't have been more wrong.'

Identity vs behaviour

It is their ability to *concentrate* which allows these riders to perceive the feedback that makes their cybernetic learning process so efficient. But there is another important factor at work here, and whenever that feedback is not indicative of success, they do not take it personally. In contrast, people who struggle with learning commonly believe that *negative feedback is failure*, and as such is a personal statement about their identity. It is this which stimulates the trying, the frustration, and the devastating need to get it right.

Organisations, too, can experience the same confusion; but healthy ones do not. As a registered instructor I have to retrain in first aid every three years, and I am always impressed by the trainers, and by the way that their knowledge moves on. As we are taught new procedures which have proved more effective in saving lives, there is no embarrassment about having been wrong, and no loss of face. No one's ego has been laid on the line and found to be lacking. In Britain, the Royal Yachting Assocation have been similarly open to learning, and they retrain their instructors every *five* years, passing on new knowledge. This implies a healthy organisation for which change does not carry a stigma. In contrast, an organisation cannot promote new learnings if *admitting to having been wrong* would imply a loss of face.

Unlike Thomas Edison (who revelled in his nine hundred and ninety-nine ways of making a light bulb *not* work) most of us hate to fail. So we either settle for mediocrity, or if we do strive for success we do not admit to our mistakes. Thus one of the primary tenets of Neuro-Linguistic Programming is the idea that 'there is no failure, only feedback'. Thinking like this makes the learning process much less risky, and it may help you re-evaluate the meaning you ascribe to success and failure.

I first heard this statement at a time when I hated myself for having failed, and since I knew that I needed to change my mind-set, I repeated the phrase over and over. But unknowingly I turned it around, telling myself, 'There is no feedback, only failure ... there is no feedback, only failure ...'! However much thought I put into getting it right, it always seemed to come out the wrong way round. My brain had an uncanny ability to distort the statement in a way which reinforced its existing map!

In essence, this happened because I was not able to make the appropriate distinction between *identity*, and *behaviour*. The statement 'I rode a bad transition' is about behaviour, and is a very different to 'I am bad rider'. Sadly, most of us grew up staggering from one admonition of 'Bad girl!' (or 'Bad boy!') to the next, and it does not take many of these to create the internal map which says 'I am bad.' In fact, we more often split ourselves into two, creating the inner judges who side with our accusers and say '*You* are bad'. Then, as a cover-up, we also develop compensatory strategies, designed to prove to ourselves and the world that this is not the case – that really and truly we *are* 'good'. We become much more complicated people than we were, in essence, designed to be.

But despite all our efforts to be 'good', we tend to selectively notice things in the world which reinforce our underlying sense of being 'bad'. Thus we both delete and distort information (as I did so cleverly) in ways which reinforce our negative self-image. As a result, many people spend their time in the riding arena hurtling down a slippery slope which begins with 'I [or 'you'] rode a bad transition'. They then pass through 'I'm having a bad day', move on to 'I'm a bad rider', and finally end up with 'I'm a bad person'. Many teachers and trainers also reinforce the belief – for they seem to specialise in leaving the pupils they are *supposed* to be helping in a far worse state at the end of the lesson than they were in at the beginning! But, whether 'You are hopeless' is actually uttered or only thought, the pupil's antennae and her inner judges will pick it up, and use it as further reinforcement of her plight.

It is a rare teacher who can make this separation, commenting on *behaviour* without incriminating the person. This is like insisting (against the weight of our cultural presuppositions about more and less skilled performers) that a rosebud really is no worse than a rose. I was once extremely impressed when I heard the Irish show-jumping trainer Iris Kellett use her beautiful, soft, lilting Irish voice to tell one of her pupils, 'That was one of the most diabolical show-jumping rounds I have ever seen in my life. Now go and do it again and this time make sure that you ....' Her voice conveyed no criticism of the person, and was simply a statement about the way she had ridden. It was a pleasure to hear her say it, and she spoke in striking contrast to the trainers whose whole ethos is that only after they have reduced their pupil to pulp will they consider rebuilding her (if indeed there is anything left to salvage), creating someone who thinks and operates in their own image and likeness.

I have ridden abroad many times, and only once has a leading Continental trainer said to me, 'You may find this horse quite difficult. He hasn't been ridden well for a while and he's bound to be quite evasive. Just do the best you can.' (Effectively she was saying, 'This is going to be difficult, and I will not judge you by the results.') On almost every other occasion when I have gone abroad to train, I have met both extremely evasive horses and an attitude of, 'Why haven't you got this horse working perfectly by now?' This attitude may be born of ignorance (both of the state of horse and of the power of implied or actual judgement). But in my view, feeding the pupil's sense of inadequacy is an unforgivable sin which can (quite literally) scar her for life.

The really frightening thing about this confusion between identity and behaviour is that each transition, each jump, and even each step the horse takes, becomes so loaded with meaning. For it has the potential to *prove* that the rider is a bad or hopeless person. Recently, Julia, who is a fairly long-standing pupil of mine, provided me with a powerful example of someone entrenched in a behaviour/identity confusion. She is a regular participant on my two-day courses, and her lessons always used to follow the same pattern. On the first day she would ride well, demonstrating that she had done her homework diligently since her last visit, and each time during that first lesson she was ready and able to take on some new input.

At the end of the lesson she was extremely pleased with herself. But she would come out the next day thinking 'I've got it now', only to discover that she had indeed *not* got it. Inevitably, this second lesson was a disappointment – and as we discussed previously, there is a certain inevitability about this. But Julia's experience was extreme, and time after time I could not get her close to the skill level that she had demonstrated the previous day. The critical factor was that I could not get her to pay *the same quality of attention*: she somehow expected to begin this second lesson as she had ended the last one – even though she had only clocked up a measly few of the ten thousand repetitions she would ultimately need! The Devil was doing his work, making her extremely reluctant to begin again at the beginning, and to go through all the necessary steps needed to achieve her aim.

On the second afternoon of one particular course she was feeling less despondent than usual, and suddenly she became aware of the pattern that had been repeating itself. I chose that moment to tell her, 'You know, the sense of failure that you so often feel at the end of a course is just the opposite side of the coin to the euphoria you feel on the first day. If you want to lose all this doom and gloom as a feature of your learning, you also have to be willing to let go of the heroics. For the 'I've got it, I'm so brilliant!' will always give way to 'I'm useless, I'm awful, I'll never be any good.' You can't have one without the other.' The realisation that not taking her failures personally also required her not to take her successes personally set her thinking, and she left saying 'I understand what you mean, but I'm not sure I'm willing to lose all those good feelings and to pay the price.'

By the time I next saw her she was indeed much more level-headed, and much less identified with both her successes and her failures. Her riding had been through a low patch in between courses, and she had decided that letting go of her 'I'm brilliant' self-image was indeed a price worth paying in order to lose the 'I'm awful' one too. This does not mean that she cannot congratulate herself when she rides well; but to say 'That was well done' as a comment on *behaviour* is to feel good in a very different way to her original euphoria. It is softer, quieter, and more enduring. It also allows her to say, 'Wow! That'll be an act to follow,' when she rides exceptionally well, and to say 'I blew it there,' when she makes mistakes. This relative lack of emotion is an acquired taste – and Julia, like everyone else, will peel away the pattern in layers, as her concept of who she is gradually becomes independent of how she performs.

The knock-on effects of this change can be tremendous, and if your inner judges comment only on behaviour and do not make identity statements, they will no longer function as judges. Instead they can become allies, who help and heal. One of my pupils in Australia offered a wonderful example of the effects of this change, and amused me greatly when she told me about the improvements in her riding and her life since I had taught her for the first time the previous year. 'My husband used to come home from the office in the evening,' she said, 'poke his head around the door, and ask 'How did the horse go today, dear?' Only then – with the appropriate prompt as to how he should behave – did he dare to set foot in the house! But when I ride badly it doesn't bug me anymore, and I don't get cross with my horse and the world any more, so my riding *and* my marriage are really much better, and I'm having so much more fun!'

....

The need to win   Another variation on the theme of identity and behaviour was demonstrated to me by Andrew, a rider I had taught many years ago, and whom I met again recently. It was obvious that both he and his horse were highly stressed, and every time he went into trot or canter it would be ages before he would stop again. I could see his horse becoming more and more tired, and with that, more and more resistant, yet still he would not stop going round and round on the same circle. All the while, it was extremely difficult to give him any input – he was so busy 'doing his own thing' that he could tune me out almost to perfection. It was paradoxical that although he had travelled several hundred miles to come to me, he gave every appearance of *not* wanting to hear what I had to say.

I found myself watching his work and racking my brains to figure out what was going on, and it was only after he left that I think I really understood. I suspect that it was very important to this rider to win. If he did not win then the horse would win; and if the horse won, then he would lose. Since he could not bear the thought that he might lose, he had to win ... and he had to keep going until he did (which of course gets harder and harder as both he and the horse become more and more fatigued). Underlying all this was a map in which riding was, in effect, a battle: in this contest, one party wins and one party loses. The subsequent pitting of wills meant that there was little potential for a win/win solution.

I have a horrible suspicion that my old pupil may in fact have learned his battling from me – or more likely, that I reinforced an attitude which was already present in the maps which guided other areas of his life. For back in the bad old days I had to win too. Now, when I am working a horse (especially one well entrenched in evasive patterns) I find it helpful to have the attitude, 'Come along, horse, I'm on your side. I'm doing all I can with my body up here to make it possible for you, and I know you can do it – even though you think you can't. I'm routing for you here with everything I've got.' That puts me on the horse's team, and it takes any possible conflict out of the situation. But it took me a long time to develop this attitude, and through this change I realised that one of the most important parts of learning is mindwork. For as we said in Chapter 1, the learning that ensues from *changing your map* is hugely greater than the learning that can possibly take place *within* your existing map.

One of my pupils, who has probably made more outstanding progress with her riding than anyone else, was giving me feedback during a lesson one day when she said, 'Well, we lost it just then because our seat bones went out behind us. Oh, I mean mine did, but I suppose his did too!' She had got to the point where she no longer thought of the horse as *separate* from herself. Winning was not on her agenda.

Another pupil found her appreciation of the horse's role in their work together changed enormously after she and her husband started taking ballroom dancing lessons. 'Whoa, whoa,' she found herself saying to him, 'You've got to half-halt, I'm not on the bit!' For the horse's role in the riding partnership is not unlike the woman's role in dancing; he gets to follow rather than lead. But he is not subservient, and is not doing battle.

Imagine, from the horse's perspective, what it must be like to change from working with a skilled rider to partnering one who is less skilled. Think of ballroom dancing, or perhaps of rock-'n'-roll, or jazz dance, and remember how fabulous it is to dance with a good partner. (I hope you have had this experience, which I consider one of life's great joys.) You do not even need to know the steps to feel confident, competent, and to enjoy having a ball; it is as if *you are danced*. But then with your new partner nothing works. You are pushing and he is pulling. Instead of experiencing that easy, unquestioned enjoyment, you find yourself thinking, 'But I can't do this, I don't know the steps.'

Few riders can lead their horse like a good male dancer leads his partner, and many of us have issues about power and about winning – just like my friend above. But inevitably, there are as many variations on the theme as there are people. Even the opposite can be true. Maddy came on her third course with me bringing her boyfriend's horse, for she had finally had one too many frightening experiences riding her own pony on the roads. He was a difficult, highly strung character, with one of the biggest push backs I have ever encountered (see Chapters 3–4). All we could do in the face of this was to build Maddy's skills and her confidence, and hope that she would one day be a match for him. But this other horse was a sweetheart, whose basic message was 'Please ride me right, I could look so beautiful if only you would ....'

As a result of Maddy's previous work with me, she was already very close to riding him right, and all she needed was to 'put a lid on the end of the toothpaste tube' – so that the bit functioned as a barrier which stopped all the 'toothpaste' (or 'stuffing') from leaking out. But she was so reluctant to do this that during her last lesson with me, I decided to walk along with the horse, placing my hands on the reins and acting as an intermediary between them both. Once she had taken up the correct contact with me, and I had taken up the correct contact with the horse, I was able to leave them be, and they were able to sustain some good work.

But Maddy was not impressed. 'I feel cruel,' she said, as her horse progressed around the school in a walk which would have earned them an 8 in a dressage test. 'I feel I have no right to do this to him,' she added, now trotting round on a 7, with her horse all but smirking. ('See how wonderful I am? I always knew I could look like this!') I do not think I could ever have persuaded her to ride in this way if her horse had showed any kind of reluctance – and even his obvious approval did not seem to boost her confidence. 'Hmmmm,' was about all she could say at the end of the lesson – and since I have not seen her since, I am not sure how she is riding now, or what she is thinking. The limitations on her riding obviously do *not* lie in her physical skills; quite clearly, they lie in her map.

To understand more about the maps which guide our expectations of our horses, we need to turn to psychology. Transactional Analysis, which was one of the first of the modern approaches, gave us tremendous insight into human communication. Thomas Harris's book *I'm OK, You're OK*, and Eric Berne's *Games People Play*, have both become classics. Many of us emerge from childhood still in the basic stance of 'I'm not OK, you're OK', running all of our adult-to-adult interactions as if we were a child suddenly faced with a parent or other adult in authority. At times, we find clever ways to turn the tables; so instead of feeling one-down we contrive to feel one-up — picking on someone weaker than ourselves so that we can be 'OK' whilst they are 'not OK'. Very few people relate from the stance of 'I'm OK, you're OK', which is often called *levelling*, since no punches are pulled and no one is perceived as inferior. The person who can do this needs no overt displays of power for people — and horses — to know that she is powerful. Indeed, she is more likely to indulge in overt displays of kindness. Within these, she is able to 'walk her talk'. She is *congruent* and *coherent*, meaning what she says and saying what she means.

Victims, rescuers and persecutors

However, the games that people play are based around *not* saying what you mean, and they revolve around the myriad triangles which are composed of victims, rescuers, and persecutors. People with tyrannical inner judges often feel victimised by them, and are playing these games internally. Sadly, they are likely to play the same games in the external world. But to really appreciate how these interactions can go round and round forever (in the external as well as the internal world), it helps to play a game where each person in a small group is handed a card stating one of the roles. Then, without disclosing your role, you all start to interact, choosing any subject matter whatsoever. Every now and again you all change cards, continuing the scenario in your new role. The encounters that ensue are often hilarious, yet tinged with realism — for each person discovers their favourite and their least inhabited roles, along with their particular *style* of persecuting, rescuing, or being victimised.

The critical point is the realisation that each of these roles is dependent on the others: victims need persecutors as much as persecutors need victims. Each role is meaningless without its counter-point, and inevitably, we all take our favourite stances with us as we relate to our horses. The most obvious rescuers are not found *on* horses, for they simply keep fields full of old-age pensioners who cannot possibly earn their keep. But as we shall see, the rescuers who ride expect payment — for they need to be *loved* — so the 'love' that they *give* comes at a price. Whilst their interactions with their horses may look warm and cosy, there are so many strings attached that they are far from game-free. Then, to complicate the issue, when a rescuer's payment is not forthcoming, she can very quickly turn into a persecutor.

Andrew was so determined not to be a victim (and to lose) that he too became a persecutor, determined to win at all costs. Maddy, who had been persecuted by her pony, was in fact able to level with her new horse; but to be anything other than a victim was so unfamiliar to her that she felt, subjectively, as if she was persecuting him. The desire to win in competition turns many riders into persecutors, although there is no inherent need for this to happen. Many of the world's riding instructors and trainers, who were persecuted during their days as young students, mature into persecutors who victimise the next generation ... and so it goes on, until someone finally stands up and levels with them, saying, 'I am not willing to take this anymore.'

....

Speaking the horse's language

The rider who levels with her horse, and the instructor who levels with her pupil, both foster a partnership which is based on mutual respect, and in which there is no game playing. Since the rider sees what *is*, she is a good learner, noticing feedback and 'milking' her experiences with the horse for all of the learnings that they offer. The obstacles which appear to stand in her way will have far less impact on her than they do on other riders, who will appear to struggle much, much more. From both levelling and learning she gains an appreciation of horse-nature, ensuring that she is a fair task-master (rather than a persecutor) but that she is not a walk-over (who falls into the role of the victim). She 'reads' her horse very well – and when she reaches the level of subtlety that she can 'say it in horse' (instead of insisting on the language 'human') she finally crosses the great divide between our species. When she meets the horse on his own home ground her language becomes *coherent* to him – and anything less than this will (from the horse's perspective) be a jumbled message that he has to decode. This hugely magnifies the game-playing possibilities of both species: but sadly, this is our norm.

The rider cannot possibly reach the subtlety required to 'say it in horse' when her vision is clouded by the insecurity of having to be perfect, having to win, having to prove to herself that she can do it, or even of having to be loved. Few of us are 'clean' in our interactions with our horses, and whilst some of our games are obviously abusive, the rescuers' games masquerade in the guise of love and kindness. The sweet-talking owner who insists that her horse should 'love his mummy' and want to please her is in fact basing her relationship on coercion and bribery. As Vicki Hearne points out in her book *Adam's Task* (which is an easy to read, highly philosophical book about animal training), the depth and the authenticity of the horse's knowledge about us make bribery and 'love' a language which is meaningless by comparison, for he is fathoming the human - whether she be on the ground or on his back - in ways we can barely imagine. This 'love' is, anyway, only the other side of the coin to dislike and abuse, for when the horse obeys – or fails to obey – the sweet-talking owner who is longing for her love to be rewarded, he is put in the terrible position of *bearing responsibility for the rider's emotional state.*

This is an awesome burden, often visited on spouses and children as well as horses. Every step the horse takes then becomes loaded with meaning, and could potentially unleash a tirade of either sweet-talk or abuse. Emotional appeals to the horse really muddy the waters of human/horse communication, and when riding becomes contaminated by questions about whether the horse loves his 'mummy' more than he loves simply being a horse, the rider is in big trouble.

As an antidote to this, the American Western trainer John Lyons suggests viewing the rider/horse interaction in the way that a policeman or traffic warden views giving tickets to errant motorists. They have no need for appeals like 'How could you do this to me?' or disparaging comments like 'I thought I could trust you.' Instead they just give you a ticket (and in a gesture of consummate goodwill they might even say 'Have a nice day' as they do so!). So instead of using emotional blackmail, you too can just 'give the horse a ticket' whenever you need to – as long as both of you know the rules of the particular game you are playing, and both of you know that actions have consequences.

It is interesting to realise that the frequency with which tickets are given does not depend on the amount of liberty that you (or the horse) are allowed; for motorists are equally likely to break the speed limit, whether it be set at 30, 40 or 70 miles an hour. Horses, like motorists, will probably go ten per cent over any limit that is set, and undoubtedly, good riders set very stringent limits which are not negotiable – for they know that the horse will never be anymore particular than they are. Giving the horse a ticket will re-establish any limit for a while; but horses, like people, can become immune to the presence of the policeman. Supposing one was sitting with you in the back seat of your car; you would be a very law-abiding driver for a while, but then your presence of mind would begin to slip, and the policeman would soon have to give you another ticket.

Yet despite the liberties the horse takes, he also has a capacity for caring about balance and symmetry – and the more he cares, the more we need to care; for the less he will tolerate our incoherence. The horses who care the most are the ones whom we call 'crazy', a diagnosis which seems to fit simply because we have not been able to match the precision of their demands. No one has ever talked 'horse' to them in a meaningful way, and 'human' is a language they have come to despise – for its inherent contradictions have gripped them in the stranglehold of rage or terror.

Then there are the horses who need an unusually high number of tickets: they are not merely forgetful, instead they repeatedly *test* how committed we are to the forms which we claim have importance. These types of horse refuse to be mediocre. Not for them the average horse's response – the dulling of the senses, and the withdrawal from intimate conversation about the precise nuances of the human/horse interaction.

In a similar vein, Vicki Hearne talks about 'hard dogs', 'who will give you a proper time of it in training, testing the coherence of your right to command at every turn.' When you say 'Sit,' they are extremely precise judges of whether you really *mean* 'sit', and of whether 'Fetch' is negotiable. Few people retain the congruence which these dogs demand, for so many of us have ourselves sold out to the inauthenticity which underpins so much human communication. The hard dog, like the hard or crazy horse, insists that how we talk is extremely important; he is much more discerning than the average person, he recognises our games and our incoherence and he 'don't take no bullshit'.

Sadly, the kinaesthetic language of riding and handling horses is a very difficult one to be congruent in, and to mean well is certainly not enough. For the horse's kinaesthetic sensitivity is so great that what we intend as a whisper is probably perceived as a yell, and what we think of as 'nothing' is probably perceived like the crackling on a badly tuned radio which so easily drives the listener to distraction. And how can the horse possibly know what these 'sounds' were intended to mean? However, the more far-reaching question asks, 'How can he possibly know which of these sounds are supposed to mean anything?'

Yet they do have meaning; they *cannot not* have meaning – probably (as I explained so carefully in my first book) a very different meaning to the one which the rider intended. So if the rider is to match her intended meaning to the meaning that the horse will make of her communication, she must say it in 'horse'. But to view this as a one-way communication is supremely arrogant, and for the rider/horse interaction to be meaningful, there must be a dialogue. Thus the masterful rider hears and responds to her horse's communication when he whispers, the average rider makes him shout, and many riders make him scream. Most riders are not listening anyway, for they so often tend to *infer* what will happen from what happened yesterday or the day before, and not from 'reading' their horse in each moment, and mirroring the way that the horse 'reads' them. To beings possessed of supposedly superior intelligence it can seem paradoxical that it is the *horse* who must teach us the subtlety of his language. If we are to earn the right to command in that language (in ways so respectful and appropriate that our idea will become the horse's idea), we have to be willing to listen.

The average rider might be well advised to team up with the average horse, who will forgive her for her blunt and clumsy communication, and will numb himself to her incoherence. But in settling for this both horse and rider have tuned their backs on the precision, the immediacy, the congruity and the beauty, that their contact could engender. So the horse never grows into the full expression of his 'horsonality', and the rider never learns all that there is to learn from riding. But at least this does less damage than the more ambitious rider – the persecutor, who instead of teaming up with her horse attempts to dominate and victimise him. She is so full of all that she can teach him (in the language 'human') that she lacks any sense of the humility that is required to level with him and become a fluent speaker of 'horse'.

....

In our adult lives, we all play a variety of roles, and within these, we may or may not initiate games, or agree to take part in other people's games. Our lives have become so much more complicated in the last few decades that our game-playing possibilities have become endless, and since none of us have yet reached enlightenment, none of us are completely game-free. But even children can learn how to level with others, and to interact in healthy ways. We desperately need these skills, bringing them into our new roles which – for women – can range from rider and horse owner, to wife and mother, business woman and bread winner. As we play the roles traditionally ascribed to men as well as those traditionally ascribed to women we have (in theory) twice the opportunity, and twice the freedom. Yet the 'you can have it all' theory really boils down to the fact that we now have the perfect means through which to get *twice as exhausted.*

The search for the self

All too often these roles are in competition with each other, each one vying for time and energy. It is as if each were a separate character, and these 'subpersonalities' have different competencies, and different needs. Often, their different value systems are in conflict with each other – which accounts for much of the stress we can experience in life. Also coming along for the ride are the parts of us that do not cope so well. You might prefer never to feel 'not OK', and the 'worm in the brain' is undoubtedly *not* (at present) your greatest ally. You can think of this whole bunch of 'subpersonalities' – young and old, weak and strong – like a gaggle of people who have been bundled onto a bus together, each bringing their own separate agendas onto the same journey. But the journey is your life, and the burning question is, 'Who is driving the bus?'

I hope that your 'bus' includes someone whose area of expertise is learning – it certainly did when you were two, but that character may well have gone to ground, and lost its insatiable appetite. If you imagine the learner in you as a person (animal or thing) in its own right, who or what would it look like? What age would it be? What would it wear? What kind of things would it say? What is its current attitude to life and learning? How would it describe itself? If this character is less-than-endearing, do not worry; it has undoubtedly suffered at the hands of teachers, and may even want retribution. But whatever guise it appears in, appreciate that it undoubtedly has a positive intention for you, whether this be to ensure that you have fun whilst learning all that you will ever want to know in life, or whether it be to protect you from a system which has delivered only unpleasant experiences. Diana Beaver's book *Lazy Learning* will give you a good introduction to him or her, and may well take your learning (of anything) to a new level.

The less-than-savoury parts of ourselves do not go away, whether they be inner judges or frightened children. But they do respond to tender loving care. The parent, adult and child positions of Transactional Analysis do not just give us a way of understanding our ways of relating in the external world; they also show us how we relate to ourselves. For we can parent our own inner child, either with the judgements which keep it 'not OK', or in supportive ways which help it to strengthen, grow and develop.

In this view of the psyche and emotional health, making reparation and negotiating between the needs of different subpersonalities is often a significant part of healing ourselves, and (however irrelevant it may appear), it can have a significant impact on our effectiveness whilst riding. But our biggest problems arise when we become so identified with one particular character that we think this *is* who we are. This character then runs our brain, and our life. However, 'I' am not just a working woman, or a rider, or a mother, or an impatient old crone, or one of life's misfits, or a brilliant teacher. 'I' am the observer who can recognise all of these positions, and whose essence is strengthened every time that I do so – as well as every time that I notice one of my games and decide either not to play it or to play it *consciously*: to have fun with it, to ham it up a bit, and to know that 'it's only a game'.

This 'I' is like the conductor of an orchestra, whose players may play in harmony, may cooperate or compete, and may even be playing different tunes. The 'I' is – hopefully – the one who 'drives the bus', and runs your brain. It is the one who experiences the silence of meditation, the 'oneness' of a magical ride, or the delight of any flow experience. It is the 'I' that we all hope to find by engaging in something as demanding as riding, which is potentially a *transcendent* activity. For when we cease to be aware of ourselves as separate from the action we are performing, we are able – for a while – to leave behind the petty concerns of our personalities. We then function from the 'I'. But this is a delight which we often lose again when we are in front of a dressage judge, and when we step off our horse into the hurly-burly of everyday life. All of Csikszentmihalyi's research suggests that the pursuit of the self or the 'I' is what gives meaning to life. It is not even so far-fetched to suggest that at least some of us ride to *find out* who we really are.

How sad it is that our culture does not recognise this, and that so many agencies in society are intent on convincing us that we will surely find happiness if only we earn, save, and spend enough money. Even the teachers of flow activities can rarely give their pupils the greatest gift that they actually have to offer. Riding teachers in particular rarely recognise that lessons learned on the horse can add tremendous richness to the rest of life. For we so often think that when we succeed in *doing* so-and-so, then we can *have* what we always wanted, and then we will *be* happy. On the contrary; when we generate our own happiness – by *being* in the moment, *being* aware of what is, and by living in flow – we can take it with us wherever we go. Then we can *have* peace of mind, and we can *do* whatever we want.

CHAPTER EIGHT
······················
Bodywork
······················

Postural patterns

ONE OF MY MORE ASTUTE PUPILS (who has a rather perverse sense of humour) once suggested that I should market myself as a teacher for the 'normally disabled'. But despite her obvious enthusiasm, she never managed to convince me that this label would indeed bring people rushing in their hoards for riding lessons. The term 'physically challenged', however, gives us a more accurate (and contemporary) way to describe how many of us perceive ourselves in relation to riding. If you do indeed feel physically challenged by it, I wholeheartedly recommend Oliver Sacks' poignant and humorous book *A Leg to Stand On* (and I also recommend it to the trainers who cannot understand why their pupils are experiencing such problems). It recounts his recovery from tearing his quadriceps tendon; but whilst his doctors and physiotherapists expected perfect functioning almost immediately after his operation, he could not feel or move the leg. He was suffering the strangest aberrations to his body image – feeling that his leg was 'utterly strange, not-mine, unfamiliar' – but when he could not move it they accused him of not trying. He writes with touching humour about the ramifications of his plight and his medics' failure to understand it. His story will hit a chord with many of us.

But whether 'physically challenged' or not, few riders see the link between their body's limitations and their horse's way of going. My contention is that whatever stage we have reached in our riding, the horses we ride will simply mirror our physical problems back to us. This leaves us either 'shouting louder at the natives', or realising that we ourselves are implicated – and that some learning or refinement needs to happen on our part before we cause yet another horse to take up the same evasive pattern as the last. The extent of this phenomenon is such that farrier David Nicholls AWCF has coined the phrase 'rider-induced lameness'. The converse of this syndrome (noted by the same farrier) is that riding-school horses seem to stay surprisingly sound for an unusually long time, which he attributes to the fact that they deal with a wide variety of riders, and are never forced to maintain a particular defensive position in response to the idiosyncratic body use of one.

In the nineteenth century, when Victorians were convinced of the God-given perfection of the human frame, they developed a concept which was later referred to as 'the wisdom of the body'. The suggestion was that certain balanced states of posture and organic functioning are natural and normal, and that the body will automatically return to them after stress and disturbance. Young children up to about four years old do indeed show beautiful posture, and very integrated movement which seems to come naturally to them: but they do not retain it into adulthood. 'The wisdom of the body' does not endure, and early in this century our postural problems were blamed on the world in which we live, with the realisation that both education and industrial work put people into 'monotonous and trying positions' for hours on end.

This is undoubtedly true, and the stress of going to school, sitting still, and learning the near-point skills of reading and writing seems to coincide with the loss of the child's innate body-wisdom. But our working conditions cannot be blamed for everything, and with the advent of orthopaedics it became increasingly clear that man is imperfectly adapted to his environment. For the upright posture, as Desmond Morris demonstrates so well in his book *The Naked Ape*, brings its tremendous freedom at the price of enormous instability and many mechanical problems. The vertical predicament of *Homo sapiens* has not even been solved by ergonomists who spend their lives designing chairs, car seats, desks and machines which will supposedly allow us to sit or work with less fatigue and strain. Their research has never produced the expected results; for their equipment has been made for the average person who misuses her body. This suggests that it is perfectly designed to perpetuate the postural habits of the masses!

The muscles in the body form four layers. In the innermost layer lie the postural muscles: these include the small muscles which join each of the vertebrae, as well as the small muscles lying deep inside the neck. Their primary role is to keep the body upright. The next three layers of larger muscles are used for movement. But if the postural muscles are not working well – or if the body is so far out of alignment that they can no longer hold it up – the movement muscles take over the job of supporting it. Even *the muscles that raise your shoulder blades* will attempt to hold you up if necessary – for the body believes that punishing collisions with the planet must be avoided at all costs! This can make it impossible for you to drop your shoulders, or to have free movement of them. When the large muscles of the neck take over the role of keeping your head up, you will find that your movement becomes much more restricted. You may find yourself turning your head, neck and ribcage all in one, when all you need to do (in theory) is to turn your head. But you may also suffer from tension headaches. So releasing your neck muscles – and dealing with the cause instead of the symptom – will help you far more than relying on drugs.

One of the times when the body is least able to return itself to a balanced state is after the stress of the startle reflex. This whole sequence of events is triggered by a burst of adrenalin from the adrenal glands, and if we really did follow through with 'fight or flight' we would put this adrenalin to good use, working our heart and muscles. Then the body would naturally return to calmness. But usually we do not do this: we are primed for action but we take no action. So our jaws remain just a little bit tight, and our shoulders slightly raised ... and the cumulative effect of many startles is to leave us in a permanent state of tension. A re-education process is then needed to help us become more poised and effective riders who do not just inflict these patterns of tension onto our horses.

It is unfortunately, but undoubtedly true that the more emotionally stressed we have been, especially as young children, the more our bodies bear witness to the fears of our past. It is fearful situations – in which fight or flight are not possible options – that cause the flexor muscles to dominate over the extensor muscles, protectively curling the body towards a foetal position. This, as we have seen, is a really damaging pattern for riders. But although many of us do indeed show a habitual startle pattern, there is much more to it than this.

If you spent much of your childhood grovelling, embarrassed to be alive, or feeling hard done by, these patterns too are written in your body (and also in your energy system) for all to see. We do not need to be trained bodyworkers to pick out the predominant patterns: we see them in each other without even realising that we do so. For often we know instantly whether or not we will like someone – even before they have opened their mouth – and we base our judgements on information given by their body.

As young children we also inherit family patterns, for we unconsciously imitate the postures of others – even to the extent that youngsters often reproduce the limp of a parent when they themselves have no need to limp at all! (I recently went for a walk with someone who limps, and found it incredibly difficult not to imitate his gait.) Siblings sometimes all show the posture of depression – copied, perhaps, from their mother, who copied it from her mother, who copied it from her mother ... thus passing a depressive state down through the generations. But beyond these familial patterns there is the effect of peer pressure (it's so good to look cool), and a need to conform to images of 'the body beautiful' that are presented in advertising and television. Hidden underneath these are more long-standing cultural patterns, which we all take in with our mother's milk. Their effects are inescapable, and they are all the more insidious because they take so little time to begin to feel 'right'.

During my training in Neuro-Linguistic Programming we did an extremely interesting exercise, where one person mirrored the standing posture of another, with a third acting as an observer and if necessary as a coach. When a very good match had been obtained – including a synchronisation with the first person's breathing pattern – the second person was asked, 'As you stand in this position, what simple statement comes to mind about yourself and the world?' The second person's offerings were always uncannily true for the first person, and could have been anything from 'I won't be beaten', to 'I'll never make it'.

It became abundantly clear that our bodies are indeed a print-out of our thoughts – and a skilled bodyworker can 'read' the layers, taking educated guesses at the attitudes and traumas which occurred at different ages. (It is never worth lying to a good bodyworker: they will always see through you!) The patterns which have been set up rarely help us in living wisely and riding well. Although they feel like 'home', the truth is that they have taken us so far out of sync with ourselves that it can take a lifetime for us to peel away the layers and discover who we really are in our own right.

Accidents also take their toll, often adding to our asymmetry. (Remember my pupil who had her arm in a sling for a year, and the one whose eyesight was damaged through a forceps birth – see Chapter 6.) If you break your leg and are forced to carry all your weight on the other one, you are likely to continue weighting the healthy leg more than the damaged one, even after healing has taken place. In fact, you might well do so for the rest of your life! As well as the *mechanical* necessity to compensate for the injury, the bodymind also has an *emotional* need to compensate, which is driven by its in-built self-preservation mechanism. So if you have fallen, say, to the left, you do not need to have sustained much more than bad bruising for the message, 'Never, ever, ever do that again' to register in your system.

I am sure this has happened to me, for at one stage, straightening my asymmetry – which makes me collapse to the right – would evoke a wave of fear in which I felt that my left leg would not support me. Other factors were telling me that I was straight; but knowing this did not make the fear go away. The knock-on effects of the accident are always more complex than they first appear, however, for as your movement incorporates the gait abnormalities it imposes, you must be stopped from falling over. So this initial pattern induces *yet more layers of compensation*; your ribs scrunch together and your head tilts over, as the layers are built up, one upon another. The system incorporates into your posture, your movement (and your riding) both the original errors and the errors inherent in the attempts to correct them.

The results of misuse

Within our society we expect that older people will be bent forward, with rounded backs and unsteady legs, as if these signs of aging were indeed inevitable. (Think, for instance, of the road signs that warn us that elderly people may be crossing the road.) But they are certainly *not* inevitable, for many native peoples age far more gracefully than we do, and even within our high-speed western world, some individuals retain the integrity of their body well into old age. Generally speaking, we have trained ourselves not to notice the normal postural peculiarities of the average man walking down the street – even though their cumulative effects show up so clearly after another twenty or forty years of living.

In his book *The Alexander Principle*, Wilfred Barlow tells an old joke which makes this point with wry humour: 'Amongst the bosoms and bottoms of seaside front picture postcards, there used to be one of a decrepit old man, standing unsteadily in a doctor's surgery, legs splayed out, holding on to the furniture and saying, "Well, doctor, how do I stand?" and receiving the inevitable answer, "Honestly, I can't imagine." When I look at the hunched backs, twisted spines, fixed pelvises and hopelessly inadequate legs and feet which trudge through my clinic, I also often find it hard to imagine just how they manage to stay upright at all!'

More than three-quarters of the population over forty-five complain of back ache, and an enormous number of working days are lost through it each year. Whilst *Homo sapiens* is not perfectly adapted for walking, standing, and sitting (or riding a horse) much of this pain is the result of *misuse*. I find that many hollow-backed riders have back pain which is easily eradicated when they take on the posture of 'neutral spine' (see page 246). The same can be true of round-backed riders. I felt particularly good about a rider who had had back operations, intensive physiotherapy, and who (according to her doctors) should really not have been riding. But after her first riding course with me she was able to throw away her walking stick. Someone, somewhere, had missed the obvious.

Hip replacements are also the result of misuse. People who walk with their upper body leaning forward (as the British tend to do, as they scuttle to work in the rain), are putting pressure on a part of the hip socket where the cartilage lining the joint is rather thin. If the body is then so compressed that the thigh bone becomes rammed into the hip socket, there is a strong likelihood of the cartilage being worn away. The person who walks upright, and who uses the joint in the way that nature designed it to work, is unlikely to have problems. How unfortunate it is for so many people that we only take action – indeed we only see that something is wrong – so far down the road that we are forced into drastic measures.

We are lulled into our false sense of security by 'sensory motor amnesia': we contract our muscles and contort ourselves into various positions, but do not know that we are doing so. Part of the brain beyond our conscious control is continually signalling muscles to contract – and we soon reach a point where we cannot relax these muscles, cannot even sense them, and often *cannot remember what it was like to live without that tension*. We may just know that our muscles are fatigued and sore (as we might expect them to be after any over-exertion). When we finally consult a doctor, he will probably diagnose us as having a pinched nerve, arthritis, tendonitis, bursitis, or a bone spur – and ultimately may perform surgery or inject drugs.

Doctors are trained to look at the small picture, assessing the structural damage in one part of the body, without considering the whole. When a *thing* is the cause of the problem it must be altered either chemically or surgically; if the damage results from function and not from structure, then a lost *ability* is the problem. This can be restored through re-education – restoring a sensory deficiency through unlearning what has been learned, and remembering what has been forgotten.

....

As we look at old, bent-over people, we commonly presume that the bones of the skeleton have somehow collapsed over the years, as if the burden of life has gradually compressed them. But this presupposes that the bones have the function of holding our tissues in place – as if they were rather like the steel frameworks and concrete pillars of modern office blocks, which hold them together and provide the structure that everything else is attached to. But if you see a skeleton in a school laboratory or a doctor's office, you will find that the bones are wired and bolted in place – they are not welded together like the beams of some great building. Our joints are fluid-filled gaps which prevent our bones from touching, and it is the *soft tissues* of the body which hold the bones in place. The bones themselves are best regarded as spacers, whose function is to keep a set distance between our joints.

The body as a tensegrity structure

The body is intended to be a 'tensegrity structure'. This concept was initially an architectural model, first advanced by Buckminster Fuller. The word 'tensegrity' is a contraction of 'tensional integrity'. But to understand his idea we need to appreciate that tension (as defined by an engineer) is the result of two things being pulled apart, thus the cables which hold up a suspension bridge are under tension. Compression is the result of two things being pushed together, so you compress an accordion. When we talk of tension in the body, we are commonly thinking of parts being pushed together, not pulled apart – and to an engineer, our commonplace map is extremely suspect. So if you collapse to the right when you ride, and your upper body leans that way, an engineer would

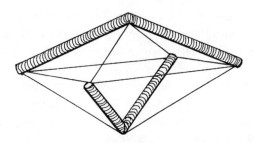

Fig. 8.1 The tensegrity cube. Its rigid parts (represented by the thicker lines) correspond to bones, and the cables (fine lines) correspond to muscle/tendon/ligament/fascia. In both the cube and the human (and equine) body, most of the stress is borne by the tensional cables, and remarkably, the cables of connective tissue within the body can support thousands of times their own weight without stretching or snapping.

say that your right side is compressed and your *left* side is tensed.

We commonly say that we are tense whether we feel emotionally pulled in different directions or feel as if we are carrying some enormous burden. But when we look and feel burdened, we would more rightfully call ourselves 'compressed'. If the body really was a compressional structure, with our head pressing on the vertebrae of the neck, which in turn press on the vertebrae of the spine, with the shoulders and clavicles adding to the compression of the ribcage etc., we would not be able to counteract gravity even enough to be able to run and jump for joy! So if your body feels like a lead weight and functions like a compressional structure, you have undoubtedly settled for a state of far less emotional and physical flexibility and freedom than you are capable of.

Buildings throughout time have been held together by compression, with all the hard pieces in contact with each other. Their integrity and continuity are based on this, whilst in a tensegrity structure they are based in its tensional elements. Figure 8.1 shows a simple tensegrity structure; its rigid parts correspond to the bones, and its cables correspond to the soft tissues – muscles, tendons, ligaments and fascia. By analogy, the body is like a system of poles and guy wires, whose stability relies on the proper angles of the poles, and a balanced tension in the wires. We used this analogy in Chapter 5, noting how ridiculous it then becomes to tell a rider whose body is collapsed to one side to 'sit straight'; for she cannot do this by obedience alone – she must make adjustments to her 'guy wires'. Figure 8.2 contrasts a spine which functions as a tensegrity mast with one that rests on an imbalanced pelvic base, and whose guy wires pull it out of alignment. It shows very clearly the plight of the asymmetrical rider.

The tensegrity structure has the advantage that it distributes stress throughout the structure without allowing it to become concentrated in a few points where it would eventually become damaged. It uses a minimum of rigid materials (much less than a compressional structure), and yet it has more strength, more stability and more flexibility. If the tensegrity cube is compressed its solid beams are prevented from spreading by the tensional cables, and their strength is much more important than the strength of the beams. So it is in the body; but as soon as the lengths and tensions of the cables are not balanced, the whole structure loses stability. Then, when the body becomes misaligned, it can collapse into a compressional structure.

If we are truly vertical, and correctly aligned within the gravitational field, standing up requires no specific effort. But as soon as one part of the body is out of place, it is pulled even further out of place by gravity. We then set up a compensatory system of tension and compression to keep ourselves standing somehow, and in some parts of the body our 'guy wires' come under great tension. The spaces between our joints become squeezed, and the whole body becomes subject to the accumulated stresses that are seen so clearly in aging. The challenges presented by riding compound the effects of any misalignments in the body (so you may see them well before you are collecting your pension!). The good news is that when viewed from this perspective, riding well and aging well become one and the same!

A balloon approximates to a tensegrity structure, for the skin is its tensional element (i.e. it is pulled apart) whilst the air inside is its compressional element. However, if you damage the balloon's tensional element by pricking it, the whole structure collapses, which would not happen in a true tensegrity structure. But as long as the balloon is made of a strong enough membrane to keep it intact, it too provides us with a

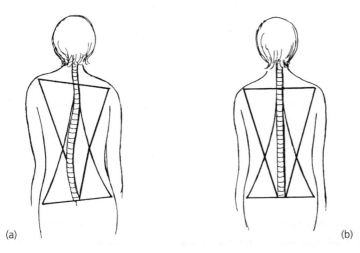

(a)   (b)

Fig. 8.2 The spine ideally functions as a tensegrity mast on a level pelvic base (b). The imbalanced base of (a) throws it out of alignment.

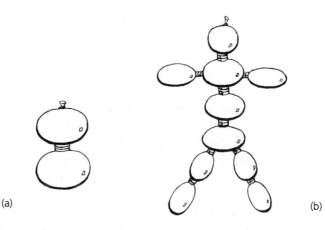

Fig. 8.3 The water-filled balloon stands upright when tied in the middle (a), and with more ties, as in (b), it can be made to resemble the human body.

good metaphor for the body – particularly if it were filled with water. Then, it could be made to stand upright by circling it with cords in the middle, as in Fig. 8.3a. Adding more cords could make it into a series of cylinders, and ultimately into the almost-human shape of Fig. 8.3b.

The shape is kept standing in the same way as a flower stem – by *hydrostatic pressure*. The cords which shape and bind the various compartments of our bodies are the connective tissues or fascia. (You know this as the thin white membrane which surrounds each muscle on a chicken leg.) Fascia forms a web of tissue which wraps the body as a whole and encases the large cavities within it. It also wraps groups of muscles, individual muscles, and their individual muscle fibres. It gathers the ends of the muscles into tendons, whose ends are continuous with the ligaments which bind the joints, and the fascia which covers the bones. Organs, nerves, and blood vessels are bound in the same way, giving compartments within compartments within compartments.

When connective tissue is properly adjusted, the hydrostatic pressure it creates is strong and balanced, which ensures that tensional forces within the fascia do much of the job of keeping us erect. Amazingly, you could suspend the bones of a skeleton within the appropriate segments of the human water-balloon, and they would be held in place by the pressurised walls of each bag. People who achieve this have a beautiful lightness to their movement; they ride and dance in enviable ways, and they really can feel as if their frame were suspended from the top of their head, giving them the sensation of being 'skyhooked'.

Whilst connective tissue plays an extremely important part in holding us upright, it is also implicated in any degeneration from the ideal of the tensegrity structure. It is semi-fluid and contains collagen, which is gelatinous, and it can change its state, just like a gelatin dessert. Held at the body's almost stable temperature it never becomes entirely liquid; but compression in any part of the body tends to make it more solid. This constricts the blood vessels which bring nutrients into the area, reducing fluid flow, which concurrently reduces the biological energy coming into the area. It also slows the removal of waste products, and when these are held within the tissues, they become less efficient. We may cramp, and/or feel stiff the next day. With smaller spaces between the compressed cells, large mineral molecules like calcium easily become trapped, increasing compression and reducing efficient functioning still further.

Under these conditions fascial collagen begins to set, changing it from an elastic membrane which allows reasonably free movement of the body parts it contains, to a harder, more rigid membrane that restricts movement rather than allowing it. It is through this process that we seize up and dry up as we age. Two parts of the body that were once free to glide across each other can literally become glued together. Much of the pain that we commonly associate with tense muscles results from the effects of rigid, constricting connective tissue, and not from the muscle fibres themselves.

Fortunately, like the gelatin dessert, the collagen within the fascia becomes more fluid if biological energy is returned to the area, and this can be done through the pressure and manipulation used in bodywork. As the gel becomes more elastic so do the tissues it contains, and the natural fluid flow is restored. With this extra fluidity the body becomes more adaptable, more elastic, and less rigid. As Joseph Heller and William A. Henkin point out in their book *Bodywise*, it has 'a wider latitude of movement available to it − more possibilities for more different kinds movement in more directions under more varied circumstances ....' A tensegrity system with much more fluidity serves us far better than a rigid, mechanical, compressional system. Since life is a process of continual change, the latter is bound to cramp our style.

....

When our connective tissue 'sets' it is not only the body which becomes permanently fixed in certain postures. Our emotional attitude becomes set too − or at least, it becomes more restricted, with familiar emotional states becoming a 'home' that we rarely leave. Conversely, the body can also become fixed in habit patterns based on what we are trying *not* to feel and do, whether it be not to cry, not to hit out, or not to run away. The ultimate irony is that in our attempts not to feel pain, our frozen postures place an equal limit on our ability to feel pleasure.

I can recognise some of these patterns in myself, although they are infinitely less than they used to be before I set out to unravel them. I was

Unravelling your patterns

a very timid, and often frightened child, and on many occasions I longed to disappear in a puff of smoke. One of my strategies for being not seen and not heard was to tip-toe everywhere. I was still tip-toeing in my late twenties, when I first became aware that I was doing it. I began, deliberately, and consciously, to put my heels down on the ground. (Just imagine the amount of contraction that is needed to constantly defy gravity, and keep them up off the floor!). I then went through a phase where I would wake up in the middle of the night with the soles of my feet screaming in agony: the structures on the underside of my feet, and especially the large tendon which covers most of the sole, had developed *shorter* than they would have done if I had been walking normally, and I was now beginning to stretch them.

Over a fairly short period of time they adapted, and now I have a much more full and secure contact with the ground. Needless to say, I also feel much more secure in my life as a whole, and more able to manifest my visions in the physical world: I have certainly possessed the character traits that bodyworkers have consistently noticed in tip-toers, who are often highly imaginative − the floaters and dreamers who have a rather tenuous link with our planet, and have a difficult time coping with the demands of the everyday world.

I also had (and very occasionally still have) a tendency to curl my toes under stress, as if clutching at the ground. But my toes never became permanently curled, as they do in some people. The only way I could 'hold my ground' when challenged was to hold onto it with my toes − toes that were instinctively preparing to run, but had received the order not to. So their thwarted attempt now served to hook me onto the spot. If I stand and curl my toes now, I can feel how much tension is generated not just in my feet, but also up the back of the calf and the back of the thigh. I used to live with this much of the time, and can see how 'clutching' − not just with my toes but also with the whole of my body − became a way of life for me, my major strategy for dealing with difficult and inescapable situations. Inevitably, this strategy has also manifested itself in my riding. It does not take a genius to realise how de-stabilising it was.

But this is not the whole of the story. As I began to unravel the asymmetry which tends to make me lean to the right and weight my right leg more than my left, I realised that the protective pad of fat under my left heel was far thinner than under my right. Since it had never been needed, it had not developed fully: so for some time, standing with my weight evenly distributed between my feet made me feel as if the bone of my left heel was digging rather painfully into the ground!

My knees, too, have been involved in the process of holding me up off the ground, and have been the seat of an enormous amount of constriction. I am sure that my knees were the major cause of my very unstable lower leg in riding, and of my chronically cold feet – without a hot-water bottle, I was doomed to stay awake at night. Lying in bed, my lower legs used to feel far less solid than the rest of me, almost as if they were withered stumps. But there was one night when I was able to change this quite dramatically, using the 'energy exercises' that we will come to in Chapter 9 (page 240). Since then, I have learned how to release the tension that holds me up off the floor when standing, and as I do so, I can literally feel my body drop down a little. My calves and feet have warmed up. They feel much more solid, and I have noticeably more control of them in my riding.

I could go on and on, looking back over a process that now spans a number of years, and that I am very grateful to have gone through. Over time I have become more 'grounded' (the term that bodyworkers use to describe someone who really has their feet on the ground), and also more centered – and the changes in my riding are only one manifestation of the pay-offs this has yielded. My descriptions may make me sound like an unusually non-functional human being, but I see many people who are dealing with patterns which are equally profound. Some are grappling with these in a very productive way, whilst others are stoically pretending they are not there, or wishing they would go away. They never will.

....

Many people can successfully deal with the body purely as a mechanical system. But – like the waves of fear which I experienced as I first began to sit straight – the emotional patterns carried in it sometimes make themselves known to you despite your wish not to be introduced. It is almost as if feelings and memories are stored in the tissues themselves, coming to light only as the body releases its holding: so it pays to take it slowly – which is, in most cases, the only way that you *can* take it, for bodies adapt slowly. But there is delight to be had in shedding excess baggage and becoming a more fluid, streamlined system. For as you become less fixed, you gain the huge advantage of becoming much more able to improvise – whether you are on or off a horse.

The best way to begin to appreciate just how much your own body deviates from an ideal stance is to do a 'body reading' whilst standing in front of a full-length mirror. But this has to be done in a non-judgmental way, simply observing, without trying to change anything and without criticising yourself for being the shape you are. It is best done with a friend whose role is to help you remain non-judgmental, so that you do not look with the distorted vision of the anorexic. Since it is difficult to do the exercise and refer to this book both at the same time, she can be your stage manager, and an external eye who can move to any vantage

Doing a 'body reading'

point. Ideally you should wear a close fitting T-shirt and a pair of leggings which will allow you to see the outline of your body.

Firstly notice, do the tips of your fingers hang down by your thighs at the same level, or is one hand lower?

Then look at your shoulders: is one lower than the other, and how does the length of your neck and the shape of the muscle differ on each side as it slopes down towards your shoulder?

Is your head on one side? If you dropped a plumb line from your nose, would it pass through your sternum and belly button, and then bisect your pubic bone as it drops to the ground, arriving midway between your feet? Or are all these bits of you not actually lined up? (Remember, do not change anything, just notice.)

Observe your elbow on each side: does one hang further away from the indentation of your waist than its partner on the other side?

Does the shape of your waist differ on each side?

If you drop another plumb line from the top outer point of each shoulder, does it pass through your thigh, or outside of it?

How do the two sides differ?

It is highly likely that your ribcage is displaced to one side, and also compressed on one side. As we saw in Chapter 5, it may also have a rotation: perhaps your friend can see if one shoulder is in fact further from the mirror than the other, and whether one shoulder blade lies flatter against your back than the other. If you are on your own, you can detect a rotation by standing with your heels about two inches away from a wall, and your feet about eighteen inches apart. Without moving your feet, rock your body back to the wall. Which part(s) of you touch it first? If you have a significant rotation, one side will touch before the other. Do your shoulders and your backside both touch the wall at the same time? If your shoulders touch before your pelvis, or your pelvis touches before your shoulders you are not standing in alignment.

When you have both your shoulders and buttocks touching the wall, there will be a hollow in your back. This will disappear if you let your body slide down the wall a little, so that your knees bend, and you are in an 'on-horse' position. You will then have a level pelvis (and a much less protruding stomach!). Have your knees come in towards each other, or are they still over your toes? Does the back of your head touch the wall? If so, you are pulling it up and back, for if your ear, shoulder, hip (i.e. greater trochanter) and heel are aligned, your head will not touch the wall.

When you are back at the mirror again, look at your feet. Is one rotated out more than the other? Do they carry the same amount of weight?

A variation of this exercise is to stand on two scales in front of the mirror, with your stage manager and two people who can read them for you. The difference in the weight they register can be a real shock, as it

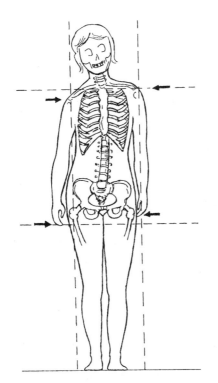

Fig. 8.4 The pattern you see as you do your body reading may well mirror the pattern you see here, suggesting that your spine is curved as shown.

was for Denise (whom you met in Chapter 6). But this difference can change significantly if you then repeat the exercise sitting with one seat bone on each scale. I have seen the asymmetry become both more and less exaggerated, showing that the overall pattern of compression and compensation within the body can be extremely complex.

You may or may not be able to piece together a pattern from this, depending on just how complicated your own particular body is, and how good you are at observing it. But it is highly likely that the image you see in the mirror will look something like the drawing in Fig. 8.4, suggesting that your spine could be curved, as shown.

Most people – like most horses – have a 'C' shaped curve to their spine, but some have an 'S' shape. These exercises can give you a tremendous amount of information, but it is hard to know exactly how and where to begin undoing the pattern. For if you stand on your scales and try to make them register exactly the same weight you may only succeed in putting yet another layer of compensations over the top of the layers you already have. There is no guarantee that you will indeed succeed in undoing your 'kinks' – in fact, since we do everything we do from within the limitations of the map which guides our present functioning, there is almost a guarantee that you will not!

....

Patient vs pupil

For most of us, the effect of these patterns is so profound that it is no mean achievement to sit well, and to stay glued onto the saddle with a level pelvis and two equally weighted seat bones. The next challenge is to motivate the horse, contain his energy, and lift his back. Circles add the extra dimension of working to both directions without collapsing left or right. Meanwhile, your horse's main aim in life is probably to ensure that *you* remain disorganised enough to allow *him* to maintain his own pathology. So in some of the movements (if not all the time) you are likely to feel as if you have your back up against the wall. Very few people have sufficient muscle tone, physical integrity, and pelvic dexterity to deal with the situation, and very few riding trainers really appreciate the problems inherent in it.

In my own learning, I had to start from scratch, with no one to help me, no clear map of riding, and a very out-of-sync body. As I started developing my work, it gradually began to dawn on me that bodyworkers could help me far more than most riding teachers: for even those teachers who understood the importance of correct alignment lacked good ways of explaining themselves. They expected instant obedience to their commands – not a process of unravelling patterns and rebalancing 'guy wires'. Essentially they gave me information about the problems I had to solve, but not about *how* to solve them (giving me declarative but not procedural knowledge). So they threw me back on my own resources and made me seek other avenues of help.

There are many different bodywork techniques to choose from, each of which approaches the problem in a slightly different way. But they all aim to help the body function as the tensegrity system it was designed to be, and to release its compressive tendencies. Most approaches manipulate soft tissue – the muscles and fascia which so easily harden and become restricted. Whilst the 'no gain without pain' philosophy holds true for some types of bodywork, others completely circumvent it, allowing you to have a dreamy, peaceful, time on the practitioner's table. But this does not imply that the techniques are less effective, and I have often experienced that when it comes to bodywork 'less is more'.

In all of these approaches you as the client are essentially passive. So although you can expect to feel much different after a treatment (a good massage, for instance, is one of the most relaxing experiences possible), your awareness of your body will not necessarily increase. So unless the bodyworker has really reached the core of the problem, you may retain a tendency to recreate the holding patterns that brought you into treatment in the first place.

As well as the many manipulative procedures, there are also the more subtle re-education approaches, the best known being the Alexander Technique and the Feldenkrais Method (with Feldenkrais work being better known than Alexander work in the USA and Australia, but less well known in the UK). They too are hands-on techniques, but they create change in a much more conscious way, demanding active participation from the pupil (no longer a patient) whose body awareness should increase hugely as her functioning becomes more streamlined. The lessons demand that you observe yourself, encouraging you to notice your body in a way which mirrors the commitment and awareness that is needed to ride well: indeed, they may even teach you what this means, and show you how to bring the same quality of attention into your riding.

Doing bodywork (of any form) does not teach you to ride. But the re-educational approaches which develop postural and movement awareness undoubtedly do make the body a far more fertile soil for learning any subtle physical skill. They increase the likelihood that you will appreciate the limitations of 'home', and will become more willing to leave it as you develop your riding technique. You are far more likely to be able to do what you are told to do, and what you know you ought to do – whether it be stabilising your lower leg, stilling your left hand, facing more to the left, or opening the angle at your hip joint. With increased sensory appreciation you will recognise when you are doing it right, and when you have over-killed on a particular correction, and when you need to back off. The bottom line is that your *image of what you are doing* is more likely to match your body *as it actually is*.

This makes you much less dependent on your teacher, and far more able to experiment with new feelings and to teach yourself. But you will always have your blind spots, for we are all so ingrained in our pattern of functioning that we cannot see beyond it. We become exactly like the goldfish who would never discover water: just as the talented rider cannot separate herself from the ways in which she does it right, we cannot separate ourselves from the ways in which we do it wrong.

F. M. Alexander, and Moshe Feldenkrais, the originators of the two systems, devised their approaches to working on others through keen self-observation. Both were tremendous innovators, who were driven to do this by their own problems. Alexander was an actor, who frequently lost his voice when reciting. Since this only happened in performance, and the doctors' answer of more and more rest did not alleviate the problem, he realised that he must be doing something to himself to make this happen. He began a painstaking search to find out what it was. Feldenkrais was a black belt in Judo (as well as a research physicist) who suffered a knee injury which incapacitated him. Both men went on to train teachers in their method, and have left legacies which can benefit everyone – although dancers, riders, musicians and athletes are the people most in need.

Feldenkrais teachers hold classes in 'Awareness Through Movement', and also give one-to-one sessions in 'Functional Integration'. They approach the body from the angle of the nervous system, working from the basis that a muscle can only do what it is told to do by the brain. Feldenkrais work aims to move you beyond your habitual and rather crude movement patterns by encouraging you to use other neurological pathways which lie dormant. This increases your 'active neural network density', affecting the way that the movement possibilities of your body are mapped within your brain (remember the homunculus on page 167?). In her book, *The Centered Skier*, Denise McCluggage talks of 'breaking up clods of habitual movement, like a gardener breaks up clods of earth with a hoe', and this is precisely what the Feldenkrais Method sets out to do. It reprogrammes the brain and nervous system, using fine differentiated movement to make it function in a more fine and differentiated way.

As an example of habitual movement, consider the way that we normally use our head, neck, and eyes. Turning to look at something implies that you move your head, neck and eyes all in one. Doing this over a lifetime reduces the movement of the eye in its socket, and limits the freedom of the neck and head. So if you try turning your head in one direction whilst moving your eyes in the other, and then continue moving slowly and easily within the range that is comfortable, you will soon recover some of the loss. If you were then to move your shoulders in one direction, your head in the other, and your eyes in the same direction as your shoulders, you would recover even more movement possibilities. You would also gain a graphic understanding of the meaning of the phrase 'non-habitual movement'!

If you try this now, you might be surprised to discover how strange it feels, and how hard it is to do. If your brain is struggling to make sense of the directions, set up your starting point (face to one direction; keep your eyes and shoulders in place, but turn your head the other way), and begin from there by reversing the position. Keep reversing it, until you can move easily within your limits without becoming confused. Whilst this exercise may seem trivial or irrelevant, it amply demonstrates the disorientation which often accompanies a change in your habitual patterns.

For another experience of disorientation try folding your arms, and then unfolding them and folding them the other way. Or clasp your hands together, and then unclasp them and clasp them the other way (so that the other thumb is closest to you). The same sense of disorientation often accompanies a change in the patterns you use when you are riding, and as we have seen, this constitutes a major part of the challenge of learning. If you refuse to feel strange, you remain trapped by your own habitual patterns, and your lost movement possibilities will continue to affect the ways in which you walk, talk, and ride.

....

In 'Awareness Through Movement' lessons the teacher takes you through small simple movements, usually done lying on the floor, which are gradually built up into a sequence. These are done very slowly, with awareness, and in a way which never pushes you against your body's limitations and into pain. Each part of the sequence is repeated a number of times before the next piece is introduced, and there are frequent rests. The time taken, the repetitions, and the absence of pain and stress create an optimal learning environment (and as one of my colleagues once said during a Feldenkrais class, 'If this is the ideal way to re-train the nervous system, look how heavily the odds are stacked against us when we work in the arena with riders and horses!').

The
Feldenkrais
Method

When Feldenkrais worked with someone who had an obvious neurological problem (perhaps after a stroke), one of the questions he always asked himself was, 'At what stage in development would the lost ability originally have shown itself?' He then started his work with the person using movements typically done by babies or children who have not yet reached that stage. This allowed him to build from a base where the person's functioning was still intact. Many 'Awareness Through Movement' lessons follow the sequences through which babies first begin to move and develop skills, but to us as adults the movements seem extremely strange. I have often found myself wondering how anybody ever managed to dream them up – yet within the deepest recesses of our brain many of the movements are familiar territory.

As we grow, our limbs become relatively much stronger in relation to our torso, and thus we begin to rely on them to generate movement. But when we are very young, their relative weakness means that we naturally organise our movement from the core muscles of the body. It is this organisation which we are attempting to regain as adults, and particularly as riders. One well-known lesson, 'The Pelvic Clock', is a wonderful one for riders, since it highlights differences in functioning of the two sides of the pelvis, and then helps to lessen the discrepancy. Often in a Feldenkrais lesson, a sequence is learned and performed on one side of the body, and then done on the other side only as a mental rehearsal. (Indeed, in my first book, I introduced the concept of mental rehearsal by using 'The Feldenkrais Arm Exercise'.) As you might expect, the ease with which the final movement is performed is the same as it would have been through actual practice.

During 'Functional Integration' lessons you lie fully clothed on a low table, and the teacher now uses her hands to address the same questions asked in an 'Awareness Through Movement' lesson. She touches and moves you gently, seeking to detect the places where movement does not 'go through', where the impulse might become blocked, dissipated, or diverted. Within this framework she locates the places that over-work, and the places that do not work enough. Then, having discovered what you know how to do, she leads you from this old familiar territory into new possibilities. A teacher will rarely work directly with an area that is painful, but will seek to alleviate pain, for this often occurs in an 'innocent spot' – for instance in a place where a part of the body which moves a lot meets a part that is stuck and allows little movement.

In *'Masterclass'* I wrote at some length about my own experience of 'Functional Integration', and the difference it made to my errant left leg. This had always seemed to have a life of its own, and the lessons moved me through some strange neurological aberrations which I do not think I could have shifted just through riding. I would leave a lesson walking differently – in a way which felt so good – only to find myself back in the old pattern a few minutes, hours, and eventually days later. I gradually learned how to put myself back into the new pattern, and as a result, I do not now wear the heel of my left shoe in the peculiar way that I used to. Over the ensuing years it has become clear to me that the pattern stems from the rotation of my ribcage, and further lessons have helped me to recognise the feeling that is truly 'straight'. The benefits for my riding have been immense, and I would wholeheartedly recommend both group and individual sessions, even to people who do not think they have any particular problems.

....

The Alexander Technique

Lessons in the Alexander Technique are usually given one-to-one, and through them you learn to prevent the habitual tensions which pull the skeleton out of alignment and restrict the freedom of the joints. The teacher begins by explaining some of the principles of the work, making it clear that you cannot be left to yourself to sort out your muscular problems. Her great concern is that you will try to straighten out your body by using such crude attempts that you add another layer of compensatory tension on top of the habit patterns which already exist. She also makes sure that you understand (intellectually at least) the strength of habit.

As every muscular action is a response to a stimulus received in the brain, changing the way you use your muscles means that you have to change the way you respond to these stimuli. Once you become aware of a stimulus – for example, the decision to sit on a chair – you can influence its outcome by refusing to respond. The act of not responding is known as 'inhibition' and its importance lies in the fact that for a moment it creates a *space* in which non-habitual response can take place. Until this space is created you are run by your habits.

According to Alexander, the key to coordination, which he called 'good use', is the relationship between the neck, head and back. The extent to which we observe this relationship – which requires a relaxed neck, a spine which is not contracted and a head poised on top of the spine – determines how well we use our bodies. Most teachers work with the pupil moving in and out of a chair, using this as a means of teaching coordination. Within this movement all the major joints and a great deal of the muscular system are involved. At the same time, the habits associated with the movement are very strong.

The teacher, while continually making gentle adjustments to the alignment of your body, asks you to think of sitting on the chair, and then asks you to refuse to respond to this stimulus by saying 'No' to yourself internally. She then asks you to repeat to yourself certain verbal messages ('directions') which are designed to prevent you from interfering with the neck-back-head relationship. Meanwhile, she reinforces this alignment through the contact of her hands. After working in this way for some time, habits such as pulling the head back, lifting the chin and shortening the muscles at the back of the neck (as if you were trying to pull yourself out of the chair by your neck and chest) give way to a movement of great economy in which the head leads the spine upwards while the thighs do the work of raising your backside. This work exercises the hip, knee and ankle joints without disturbing the relationship of the head, neck and back. It mirrors the mechanism of rising trot.

The shortened neck and lifted chin was precisely the posture that Alexander found to be the cause of his voice problems. Interestingly, it is also the posture of the hollow-backed rider, the rider who pokes her chin, and the horse who pokes his nose. The change that Alexander made in his own 'use' (and that of his pupils) was to free the neck, so that the back of the head lifted slightly, and the chin dropped. In effect, he brought them 'onto the bit'. Thus the Alexander directions encourage you to 'Let the neck be free, so the head can go forward and up, the back can lengthen and widen, and the limbs can fall off the back and away from each other.'

Interestingly, Alexander's understanding of the way in which the average person needs to change her 'use' mirrors my own understanding of the changes made by the developing rider. In his book *The Alexander Principle*, Wilfred Barlow (who was one of Alexander's pupils, and a great contributor to the field) says, 'the pupil will learn to release tension which was previously unconscious, but in all probability the pupil will be expected to replace unnecessary tensions by additional work in other muscle groups which previously had been undeveloped. Many people ... will find that they have to put more work into their lower back and thighs if they are to release excessive tension which they have been making in their neck and shoulders. The over-tension in their neck and shoulders will be replaced by more tone in the lower back and thighs ....' If this is true off a horse, simply in moving through the world and getting in and out of a chair, how much truer it must be in riding!

Much of the work in an Alexander lesson is done lying (fully clothed) on the teacher's table, and sometimes (for both riders and non-riders) a saddle is used, for sitting astride frees the hip joint like no other position. Very slowly and carefully the teacher makes adjustments to the pupil's body to encourage the key neck-head-back relationship. As this relationship develops, changes in the overall pattern of tensions take place of their own accord. Simultaneously verbal directions encourage the body's release by counteracting the habitual tendency to contact. Thus over time, the body learns to let go, changing from a compressive system to a tensegrity system. The subtlety of the process is such that all the time the teacher is working on the pupil, she must also be working on herself; for if her own body were in a state of contraction, her hands could not make sense to the pupil's body, and they could not unequivocally communicate the message, 'It's OK to let go.'

I had a number of Alexander lessons quite a few years ago, and then came back to the technique about three years ago. In those early lessons, I do not think I grasped the principle very well – this was, perhaps, because I worked with teachers who did not give verbal directions so I was less clear about their aims than I might otherwise have been. The technique tends to work slowly, however, and some teachers seem to revel in its mystique (for it is quite hard to explain). Their insistence that it is far too subtle and sophisticated for the average person to understand saddens me (and reminds me of the delight which good riders seem to take in preserving their own mystique). It does the technique no service.

Despite my sense of 'not getting it', the first response of my new teacher several years later was, 'Wow, you can give directions well!' I believe I had taught myself to do this, partly through my riding, and partly through learning how to regulate my energy, so that I could combat my tendency to feel physically unwell. The same teacher, Trisha Abrahamsen MSTAT (a rider herself) has also noticed that other riders, as their skill level improves, show a much more integrated body, with a strong mind-body connection that now works *for* them rather than against them. Riding well and releasing the body well are both examples of 'you think it and it happens'; the mind-body link-up becomes primed through practice, and much more consciously available.

Many Alexander teachers stress that when learning the technique you do not *do* anything, in the way that we normally think of 'doing'. Some describe the technique as a process of 'non-doing': its essence lies in *not* doing the old habit, but in taking the *mental* steps of inhibiting and directing. As in mental rehearsal, you *think* change rather than *do* change, and here lies some very important learning for riders. For – whilst riding also requires muscle power – learning how to *think* change is of great importance on horses.

Pupils are discouraged from practising after their early lessons; for faulty sensory appreciation is bound to affect the outcome. Once you have grasped the principles of the technique, you can continue to work on yourself between sessions. So I can now 'ask' my back to lengthen and widen, and feel it expanding as I do so. But on several notable occasions, when my life has become unusually stressful, I have completely lost this ability. It was as if someone had flipped the switch in my brain which links the thought and its manifestation, putting it into the 'off' position. Eventually the connection became re-established, and without the lessons, I might not have noticed how far out of sync I was! Anyone whose bodymind was in a permanent state of seize-up would find it hard to understand the technique, and it might take an exceptionally good teacher and quite a long time for her to benefit from it.

The Alexander Technique has a strong philosophical basis, and one of its primary aims is to encourage the pupil to take responsibility for her bodymind interaction, locating the instant between a stimulus and its response and using 'inhibition'. If you are about to scrunch up your neck as you rise (not very gracefully) from your chair, saying 'No' to the thought might well be enough to stop you from resorting to the old familiar pattern, giving you enough time to 'plug in' the new one. But in other situations more may be required.

If you are a nervous rider about to collapse into the foetal crouch (the frozen, curled-up posture of the body which cannot fight and cannot flee), 'No' may not be sufficient – and you may need much more information about what to do instead. Strong preventative measures are required, for once you are caught in the grip of the foetal crouch it is too late, and you no longer have the possibility of conscious thought.

Many riders find that the most difficult moment to drive a wedge in between stimulus and response arises when they are coming up to a fence and realise that they are about to arrive at it wrong. When you are in this situation, can you sit still, with quiet determination, and wait for your horse to sort his legs out? Or do you 'hook and look'? Perhaps you tip forward, collapse on his neck, and 'drop' him. Or make a massive kick – launching yourself forward in the hope that your horse will make a huge stand-off.

I made a tremendous step forward in inhibiting my own version of this scenario when I realised that the sequence of my panic began as I curled my toes up. If I can stop this from happening, the rest of the sequence is not invoked. (I was very proud of a pupil who realised that his began with the change to focused vision, and if he can maintain his peripheral vision the stack of dominoes does not fall.) Until I discovered this, however, I had not tracked down the instant in time when the wedge between stimulus and response could be driven home. This timing is crucial, for to be successful you have to catch yourself at the *merest inkling of the thought* which sets the whole process in motion.

Another facet of human behaviour which is addressed by the Alexander Technique is 'end-gaining'. This was Alexander's term for what happens when you pay attention only to the result you want to achieve, and not to the *means whereby* you achieve it. (And in the more insidious cases – as we said in Chapter 7 – you pay attention to the result you do *not* want to achieve, which has even more devastating effects!) When you have enough skill to evoke the pattern you want (e.g. shoulder-in) as a whole, then all is well; but as soon as you hit a problem (perhaps you find yourself pulling on the inside rein), you need to know what to do about it. This means that you need to return to the *means whereby* you create shoulder-in, making the adjustments which enable you to free your inside hand. In end-gaining, it is your refusal to re-enter the TOTE (see Fig. 6.7 on page 181), which stops you from discovering the operation which would streamline your functioning. Thus the choice to keep end-gaining is the choice to pull the horse about.

For some people, the Alexander Technique becomes a way of life. One man I know split up with his girlfriend who was training to be an Alexander Teacher, saying, 'Well, her idea of a good night out was lying on the floor with her knees pointing up towards the ceiling and three paperback books under her head ... and it certainly wasn't mine!' Wilfred Barlow himself tells a joke against the technique when he writes about a pupil who hated flying, and was suffering badly on a very rough flight. His pupil told the story of 'sitting nervously with a paper bag in front of his mouth, prepared for the worst, and of the man in the seat next to him saying 'I don't mind you being sick, but I do wish you would stop saying head-forward-and-up, back-lengthen-and-widen!'

I have seen riders put training in the Technique to extremely good use, and I have seen others who somehow do not put two and two together – usually, I think, because they have not given the Technique enough time to work its magic. Some (often with knowledge that is only secondhand) have just grasped the idea of 'thinking of growing taller, as if you were being pulled up by a string that is attached on the top of your head just above your ears'. So they 'grow taller' by pulling their ribcage up away from their hips, hollowing their back, and holding their breath. This is not what the Technique is about; in fact it is a travesty of a much more subtle expansiveness, and of the principles involved in its teachings.

Many Alexander teachers question my understanding of riding – and in turn, I question theirs. For sitting on a saddle on a saddle horse is not the same as sitting on a saddle which is being moved by a real horse as he bounces along at eight miles an hour. If indeed it were, then riding would require much less skill, and much lower muscle tone – for there would be no need to generate a push forward in the body which matches the thrust of the horse's hind legs. You would simply give your Alexander directions and all would be well – as it is on the still saddle.

It is obvious to everyone that the Alexander teacher cannot teach golf, and cannot teach the violin – even though she can transform the body into a more refined tool for learning these skills. But the confusion between the still saddle and the saddle on-the-move leaves some Alexander teachers convinced that they can teach riding. Since they misunderstand its demands, they accuse me of advocating an approach which involves far too much tension. But even without the need to stay 'with' the horse, it is this high muscle tone in the working muscles of the thigh, abdomen and pelvis which – as Wilfred Barlow stated – allows the muscles of the shoulders, neck and arms to release. Like the Alexander Technique itself, the learning involved in riding is primarily a 're-education' process, and not a 'relaxation' process.

....

The rider/horse mirror

One of the most profound implications of the Alexander Technique for riders lies in the realisation that when a horse is working well, his neck becomes free so that his head can go forward and up, and his back can lengthen and widen. When he is above the bit, he shortens his topline, raises his chin, and pulls himself along from his front legs. This mirrors the way that most people use their neck and shoulders to lift themselves out of a chair. There is a profound mirror relationship between the horse and rider: thus a hollow-backed rider will usually be seen riding a hollow-backed horse. Both of them have lengthened the muscles of the belly, the chest, and the front/underside of the neck. At the same time they are compressing the muscles which pass along the spine and neck and connect into the back of the head.

If the muscle groups of the shoulders, neck, and chest are the dominant ones for the rider (who is pulling rather than sitting), they will also be the dominant ones for the horse, who will not (indeed cannot) volunteer to change his way of going, and to push himself along from his hind legs instead of pulling himself along from the front ones. The moral of the story seems to be that good movement emanates from the head/neck/back relationship, and that when this is in sync, the limbs fall away from the back and take care of themselves. This idea is supported by zoologists studying animals in the wild, for a gazelle will always lead with its head, lengthen its spine, and obtain its power from its hindquarters. But so often we think of organising ourselves (and perhaps our horses) by thinking about the *limbs*, and not about the *centre*, so we do not pay attention to the head/neck/back alignment.

This philosophy supports my belief that the most important factor in straightening a horse is the rider's reorganisation of the bulge of his ribcage. For if this is off to one side, it will send his head and neck – as well as his limbs – in spurious directions! Any attempts to deal with these without thinking about his back tends only to compound the problem! To reorganise his head/neck/back alignment we have to pay attention to *our own* – for so often the horse's posture is again a mirror of the rider's, and she too has her ribcage displaced to one side.

I would go so far as to say that good riders are, through their way of sitting, doing bodywork on their horses. Instead of having their hands on their pupil's body they have their backside and thighs on it – and the proportions are not dissimilar to hands-on work with humans. But the only part of the horse they can touch in riding is his back and ribcage, and their aim is to lengthen it, and release the compression in it. They do this by staying out of the mantrap, creating a push forward which is bigger than the horse's push back, and turning their thighs into the girders over his suspension bridge. Through this they draw his back up, and encourage his belly muscles to shorten and support his abdomen. This leaves him able to lead the movement with a freely functioning neck and head.

....

Riding as a martial art

The approaches mentioned so far are examples of either the 'mechanical tradition' of bodywork, or 're-education' approaches, but there are also the 'energetic tradition' and the 'psychological tradition'. The energetic tradition (discussed in *For the Good of the Horse*) encompasses acupuncture, acupressure, Shiatsu, and healing techniques which detect blockages or imbalances within the chakra system and the body's energy field. The psychological tradition, known as Bioenergetics, focuses on the emotional patterns and assumptions which accompany the client's 'muscular armouring'. This enters the realm of psychotherapy rather than learning or healing.

There is one other tradition of bodywork, often referred to as the 'integrative tradition'. This encompasses yoga and the martial arts – and I believe that riding (or dressage riding at least) should be included here as well. These approaches are integrative in that they devote some attention to balancing the body as a mechanical system, some to the connections between physical misalignment and emotional patterns, and some to balancing the energy fields of the body. They also contain an element of meditation, for they seek to generate a calm, focused state of mind as well as a high degree of awareness. Their ultimate aim is the integration of body, mind, and spirit.

In yoga, the practice of meditation is combined with physical postures which are designed to affect particular organs and muscles of the body. Unlike Feldenkrais work, which encourages you to stay within your comfort zone, the yoga postures are designed to take you to your edge – the place where you feel how the tightness in your body limits your flexibility. So within the yoga postures you place yourself up against your body's limits, using focused awareness and particular breathing patterns to 'breathe your way through' them. In yoga philosophy, you will learn nothing new if you back away from your edge: in fact the bodymind will then gradually tighten up more, and constrict you further. But if you attempt to push through your limits you again do yourself no service, for the body fears the consequences and becomes even more self-protective. Instinctively the muscles tighten in order to stop their fibres from tearing, and this gives you a bigger resistance to work against. Even if you temporarily appear to become more expansive, you are likely to do yourself harm.

In his book *Bodymind*, Ken Dychtwald writes about yoga, saying, 'Physically when I approach my edge gently and consciously, my body responds by focusing energy and attention on this spot, encouraging the blood and energy to bathe the related muscles and organs with vitality and life, thus allowing me the experience of true growth and nourishment. But if I do not try to reach my edge, my body, having no point of focus, will find it difficult to isolate the place and nourish it, and little growth and improvement will follow.' However, the practice of yoga soon begins to affect not only your body, but also your thoughts, attitudes, and feelings. Its calming, centring, integrating effects soon permeate the lives of those who practise it, and in this ancient tradition, the yogis transcended many of the limitations that we regard as inviolable. They altered their brain-waves, lowered their heart rate, stopped their breathing, and lay on beds of nails. Whilst this is not necessary for riders (although I wonder sometimes when I sit on the saddles that some people seem to love!), the practice of such a discipline has a lot to offer. It builds the state of mind which facilitates peak performance.

The martial arts, as practised in western countries, range from the quiet slow movements of T'ai Chi to more vigorous forms like Tai Kwan Do. They too provide a medium through which to observe your own body, unravel its patterns, and build the state of 'flow'. The skilled martial artist becomes so centered that little disturbs her: through progressive training in gradually more challenging situations, she learns how to become causal rather than reactive, even in the face of an attacker. This happens over years of practice, and there is no quick fix in ten sessions!

Part of the learning process is the way that you come face to face with your emotions: for your enthusiasm, frustration, and boredom, (whatever your favourite patterns might be) will each come round in turn, demanding that you find a way to move through them and re-find your centre. Both your struggles and your successes will throw you off balance, requiring you to refocus yourself, and redefine your commitment to yourself and the learning process.

In their book *Bodywise*, Joseph Heller and William A. Henkin discuss the martial arts, saying, 'All of them devote considerable attention to balancing the practitioner's psychological, physical, and energetic elements, because until the body is balanced both at rest and in motion, a person cannot truly recognise how her outer and inner environments reflect one another, and how she is the embodiment of both, as well as the fulcrum around which they hover. By maintaining balance and poise we learn how the energy around us affects our own balance, and in so doing learn to direct our energy so that it can influence our surroundings.'

What better medium could there be for learning this than riding! I found it no surprise to learn that Chogyam Trumpa, who left his life as a Tibetan monk to live in America and marry, once described dressage as 'the ultimate martial art'. We, as riders, would benefit enormously from a martial arts understanding of energy, which translates into the ability to focus the mind, to use the minimum number of muscles to the maximum advantage, and to perform in a state of 'effortless effort'. The talented riders who can do this have no appreciation of what it is that they really need to teach, and until they do, a good teacher of the martial arts can offer riders a tremendous amount. She teaches a way of being, thinking, feeling and perceiving, which can then be translated from one learning medium to another. (The Ki Aikido exercises in Chapter 9 should give you a good idea of the benefits.)

To perform in a centered way, and to direct your energy so that your horse becomes an extension of yourself, is to be in a state of grace. To call this 'heaven on earth' might seem rather far-fetched, yet most riders would describe this state of 'flow' as one of the most blissful experiences they have known. But what is a very occasional experience for most people (a hit-and-miss affair, with many more misses than hits) can become something that you know how to do – a way of being, which permeates life as well as riding. Sadly, I see very few top-class riders who have taken the state of being that they ride from, and then applied it to the rest of their lives. Perhaps it is inevitable that those who have worked the hardest to get it are the most appreciative of its benefits.

CHAPTER NINE

....

Fit and Able

....

HOW LUCKY WE ARE that riding is a skill in which one can peak rather late in life. For to be over the hill at eighteen – the lot of the gymnast or the swimmer – would be my idea of hell. Fortunately the accumulated knowledge gleaned from many years and many horses (along with the maturity which this gives), is such an important facet of our skill that it easily compensates for any loss of our physical prowess. As we age, we have an unusual luxury, for we can choose to make riding as sedate or as challenging as we wish. We can confine ourselves to the dressage arena, or become a 'galloping granny' (and I am told that there is a group of older riders in California who call themselves 'Fossils over Fences'). We can even follow in the footsteps of Lorna Johnstone, who proved that it was possible to compete creditably in the Olympics at the age of seventy. People of all ages, sizes, shapes and fitness levels can enjoy riding, and make of it what they will; for on the bottom line, we all have the option to treat the horse like a mobile armchair.

The athletic demands of riding

Perhaps it is because of this that few riders appreciate how taxing it is to ride well. We in Britain have a great tradition of getting our horses fit and ready to perform in their appointed discipline. We map out their fitness programmes to the Nth degree, but gaily assume that we ourselves will inevitably get fit enough simply by riding. In fact, we may not even do this, preferring to sit at our desks and do our high-powered jobs whilst someone else does the fittening work for us. Back in 1968 Jane Bullen (now Jane Holderness-Roddam), who was preparing to ride Our Nobby in the Mexico Olympics, became famous for skipping on the roof of the hospital where she was training as a nurse. But I know a few people who have not taken their fitness so seriously, and the broken bones they sustained during competition were probably directly related to that choice.

When we think of rider fitness our thoughts turn to jockeys, and to those who compete in the highest levels of eventing and endurance riding. We think of cardiovascular fitness, and of the punishment taken by the thigh and back muscles when the rider must remain in a galloping position. We think of the stresses and strains of endless hours of riding – the rubs and the sores, and the cold or the sweat, which make life in the saddle uncomfortable. But we rarely think of the punishment taken by the horse when a fatigued, low-toned, disorganised rider becomes (even more of) a burden. Neither do we acknowledge the physical demands of pure good riding - the high muscle tone which maximises our abilities, and enables us to work the horse so correctly that he too can maximise his.

We riders do not think of ourselves as athletes. For we have traditionally believed that the *horse* is the athlete and that we 'push the buttons'. But this is an attitude which does not hold water – and Formula One racing-car drivers are amongst the fittest athletes in the world! Some research done in Spain showed that a show-jumping round was a greater cardiovascular stress for the riders concerned than it was for the horses (given the resting and maximum heart rates of both species), which certainly goes to prove that we are not sitting up there doing nothing!

But we riders are not alone in thinking of riding as a sedentary activity; a colleague of mine recently showed me a magazine article which listed various activities in order of the fitness levels they required. Riding and housework were last on the list – and whilst the 'researchers' might be forgiven for not realising how out of breath you can become whilst riding, and how much of a sweat you can work up, to not know this about housework is beyond the pale!

Whilst the approach to rider fitness outlined in this chapter is more rigorous than most, its idiosyncracies have become abundantly clear to me through being one of a group of twelve elite coaches from various sporting disciplines who are undertaking an academic study in coaching. The others talk endlessly about the fitness programmes they set for their athletes, and at the end of the day they race to the gym, desperate to work out – and I am left standing! Athletes of every discipline (other than riding) increase their fitness through exercise regimes which go beyond the practice of their primary skill, and it is well known that once football players have embarked on their season (giving them little time for circuit or weight training, etc.) their fitness level *drops.*

Thus the specialists who teach on this course are convinced that serious riders ought to be doing fitness training over and above riding and its associated chores. But this is not part of our established culture, and the idea would not go down well with most of the more leisured riders I know! At the other end of the spectrum, I would hardly dare suggest it to the overworked grooms and horse owners who are already chasing their tails from dawn until dusk.

If you decide to embark on a fitness programme which goes further than the suggestions given here, you will find that very few texts are neither too simplistic nor too complex for your needs. I particularly like

The Stretching Handbook by Francine St George, which gives a good overview of fitness. The professionals at your local gym will also help you, but will not understand the specific demands of riding. Bear in mind that fitness is a complex field, and that if you skew your programme too much in one particular direction (for instance by focusing on strength whilst ignoring flexibility) you can do yourself damage.

Some event riders do indeed run, skip or swim, which gives them a good aerobic workout. Riding a bicycle without sitting on the seat is another option, which particularly stresses the thigh and back muscles. Aerobic exercise takes place at an intensity low enough that sufficient oxygen (attached to the haemoglobin in the blood) can reach the muscles to fuel their performance. Once the heart rate is elevated to a certain level there is not enough time for the exercising muscles to utilise the oxygen taken in with each breath. Metabolism then takes place *anaerobically* (i.e. without oxygen) and the cells draw on their reserves of stored fuel. This is much less efficient, and we cannot sustain it for extended periods of time. It creates waste products which cause both cramp and the delayed onset of stiffness.

In your aerobic range your heart rate lies between 60% and 80% of 220 minus your age (i.e. between 120 and 160 beats/minute if you are twenty years old; 114 and 152 beats/minute if you are thirty; and 108 and 144 beats/minute if you are forty years old). If you cannot whistle or talk while you are riding, you have probably exceeded this range, and are working anaerobically.

For my own interest I have a heart rate monitor which I encourage pupils to wear. In walk, most people's heart rate lies between 100 and 110, i.e. beneath the aerobic range. Thus the cardiovascular system is not stressed enough for there to be a training effect (unless you are older and extremely unfit). Most riders work out in trot and canter at between 150 and 160 beats/minute, within or above their aerobic range. The heart rates at the higher end of the scale are more commonly brought about by stress and anxiety than unfitness (and one of my colleagues once clocked a rider at 187 beats/minute in walk, and deemed it too risky to let her trot!). I have done little research with riders who are galloping and jumping, but believe that they must be working anaerobically. The best way to make this more efficient is to couple short bursts of anaerobic work with a good base of aerobic training, since this determines the overall efficiency of the heart and lungs. However, to have a training effect aerobic exercise needs to be continuous for fifteen to twenty minutes, and in our schooling we rarely maintain this heart rate for that length of time.

A small proportion of riders pull weights. Although this can be helpful, it does not actually replicate the demands of our sport, and exercise physiologists appreciate more and more how fitness is specific to a particular task or coordination. So trotting, for instance, gets your horse fit for trotting, whilst cantering gets him fit for cantering. If you work him with a hollow back, you strengthen the muscles and the neurology which sustains this carriage. It is the same for the rider.

Since we move so little, our primary need is to stabilise our bodies at high tone – and thus it is exercises based on *isometric muscle contraction* which provide the most benefit. On a recent course, the two lowest-toned riders (who were positively 'flopsy') had actively worked on their fitness: one ran five miles a day, and the other worked out at a gym three times a week. But this had not built their isometric strength – presumably because holding the muscles at high tone involves such a different motor programme to running or pulling weights. Conversely, isometric exercises, which were much more popular in the 1960s than they are now, were abandoned because they did not replicate the muscular demands of running etc. However, they do fit *our* sport; we just need to understand its biomechanics, and to fully acknowledge the fact that *we* – as well as our horses – are athletes.

....

Exercising with awareness

The subtlety of the coordination required in riding means that there is far more to it than simply having an efficient heart and strong muscles – and being Arnold Schwarzenegger does not give you any guarantee that you will ride well (although I am told that he does). Anyone who embarks on changing the biomechanics of her riding is placing a tremendous demand on a body which is more or less unprepared. So inevitably, a small proportion of the people who come on my courses decide that riding in the way I advocate is such hard work (compared with what they are used to) that they would rather not bother! Whether their mind or their body gives out first is open to question; but beginning with a highly toned body reduces the strain on both – for in a body with the appropriate *texture* there is far less need to struggle.

There are a number of exercise systems, from aerobics to weight training, Pilates (see page 266) and Callanetics (page 267), which are tremendously helpful in preparing your body to ride well, making it physically able to meet the demands placed on it and a much more fertile ground for learning. But many of the exercises that I have devised are more subtle than this, helping you to discover the most effective coordination for riding, and to understand the challenges it poses. To my mind the most helpful exercises are not simply done by rote; they increase your *awareness* both of your own particular 'kinks', and of how you feel when your body functions well. As you do them you practise 'pressing the button in your brain' which activates a particular muscle – clocking up a few of the ten thousand repetitions which are needed before this neurological connection works automatically. As you move from being unconscious of your incompetence through conscious competence, so you develop both the precision and the strength and endurance of that desired coordination.

The exercises in this book are an adjunct to those in *Ride With Your Mind/The Natural Rider,* which I still recommend wholeheartedly. (The 'Masterclass' book does not contain any exercises.) The floor exercises in *Ride With Your Mind/The Natural Rider* are a very good beginning point, and the 'Aikido arm exercise' and the 'push-pull exercise' are invaluable for understanding the dynamics of riding. Whilst all the exercises in that book and this are designed to enhance the rider's technique, the stretching exercises included here are helpful to prevent injury, and to stop the pursuit of riding from deforming the rider's body so much that she becomes muscle-bound and permanently horse-shaped! Despite my insistence that riding is good for you on every level – from your body and your mind, to your soul and your spirit – it does have its drawbacks and, like any repetitive activity, it will take its toll on the body.

I believe that many people who swear by exercise do not look at the body's functioning through a fine enough microscope (and I am still attempting to convince tutors on my degree course that working out in the gym is not the answer to everything). For if your body is out of true – as it almost inevitably is – what do you do to it by pushing it further and faster? To put it another way: if you noticed that the wheel balance on your car was not adjusted correctly, would you take it to the garage, or drive it another two hundred miles? Most athletes and exercise fanatics drive their body 'another two hundred miles' without even considering that it might be much more appropriate to find a bodyworker, and to get themselves a 'wheel balance'. Virtually all of the riders who come on my courses have made the eminently sensible choice to have a 'wheel balance' instead of riding another two hundred miles. To train a misaligned body can be both dangerous and futile, so I believe that any holistic approach to exercise must begin with awareness.

....

Energy exercises

I will begin with some of my favourite exercises, the energy exercises I have referred to earlier. I have a particular fondness for these because many of them are best done lying in bed (and I hate going to the gym). These are, essentially, exercises in perception. Yet how you perceive your body is also how you organise it, affecting all the layers which lie between your subtle energy and your gross muscle use. 'Pushing down the plunger', for instance (see page 52), is a perceptual and energetic change which in turn changes your muscle tone, power, posture, and use.

The way that our energy field organises our physical body was brought home to me recently when an unusually novice rider appeared on one of my courses. She was short and round, and was sitting in the armchair seat, riding a hollow-backed, downhill Quarter Horse who slouched along with no impulsion. It was not an inspiring beginning! My course organiser was mouthing words of apology (for she had expected a much more experienced pair) as I set to work thinking, 'This is not going to be easy.' Yet my pupil and I had a wonderful time together, and I achieved more change with this woman than I ever have with any rider at this level. In the process I said less than I have ever said before.

At the end of the first lesson her alignment was good, her rising-trot mechanism was good, and her horse was on the bit – ears out sideways, paying attention and moving with impulsion. I found myself thinking 'I wonder if we can do this again tomorrow?'; but we did – and we improved on this baseline each day. The key was this rider's energy system, which was so healthy that I never had to teach her to 'push down the plunger', never had to teach her to 'close the leaks', and never had to teach her how to aim her bear down. Her focus of attention was also extremely good, and I would say that in energetic terms, she is one of the healthiest individuals I have ever met. It was this which made riding so easy for her – even though a casual glance at her body would not have made one define her as talented.

The aim of the following exercises is to help you attain the energetic functioning which was, for her (and other more obviously talented riders) a given gift. If you yourself are talented, or if you are happy to treat your horse like an armchair, you may well not see the point in these exercises. If you are *not* talented and you want to ride well, perceiving at this level of subtlety will open the door to enormous change. You ignore it at your peril. (But if you cannot come to terms with my approach, move on to the next section!)

This first exercise comes from Ki Aikido*, and can be done standing, sitting, or lying, at any time and in any place. One of its basic principles is that you 'keep one point': this is the point of the 'low down bear down', the body's centre of gravity and its second chakra, deep within the body at bikini-line level. Become aware of that point, and think of focusing your energy there. You might point to it with your finger, saying to yourself 'keep one point'. You might think of your body like one of those cafétière coffee makers, where you push down a plunger once the coffee has brewed, keeping the coffee grounds at the bottom of the jug.

---

* I am grateful to Alan Mars, a Ki Aikido black belt, instructor and Alexander Teacher who introduced me to these exercises.

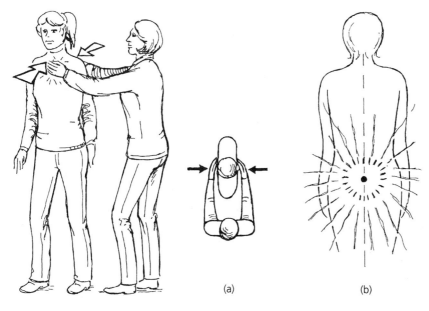

Fig. 9.1 Keeping one point: (a) the position of the tester; and (b) your energy sphere.

So, you can now go about your daily business, keeping one point. And if you should choose to share what you are doing with anyone, you can play an interesting game with each other. When you do not have your one point, ask your partner to stand by your side (not in front of you), and put her hand between your shoulder blades. She then exerts a smoothly increasing pressure which lasts for about three seconds, pushing directly forwards. (See Fig. 9.1a.) If you withstand that push, have her put her hand on your upper chest, and exert a similar push directly backwards. Many people find that they are only strong in one direction: so if your partner changes the direction of her push without warning, she may well catch you off guard.

When you have your one point, she can offer both challenges again. The chances are that you will stay put, feeling that you expend very little effort. Once you have clearly established the feeling of keeping one point, deliberately *lose that point*, feeling what happens to your body and your energy system. (I feel as if something – my energy – flies from my one point upwards and outwards to the edges of my body.) You could also repeat her challenges whilst you thought of the centre of your forehead, or thought about trying to be strong by bringing many muscles into play. In both cases, you are likely to be so top-heavy that you test weak. Since you do not want to be left in such a disintegrated state (albeit such a common one for us Westerners) come back to your awareness of the one point.

One of the other principles of Ki Aikido is 'extending Ki'. (The syllables 'Ai', 'Ki', and 'Do', each have a specific meaning: 'Ai' is 'harmony', 'Ki' is 'energy', and 'Do' is 'the way'. So the phrase translates as 'the way of harmony with energy' – an apt philosophy and training for riders.) So now extend your energy, as if your one point were the centre of a sphere – see Fig. 9.1b. When you think of a person or a situation that you like, you naturally radiate a good positive feeling, extending Ki. So think of someone you like whilst your partner tests you again. You should test strong. Next, think of a person or situation that you *dislike*. As you recoil, so does your energy sphere. You will probably test weak. Since you do not want to remain in this state, return once more to your one point and to extending Ki.

You can even go one stage further and do 'energy gymnastics', seeing if you can radiate *so much Ki* in the face of the situation you dislike that you still test strong! (Believe it or not, this simple exercise is the basis of many techniques for stress reduction and energetic healing.) An interesting variation on the theme is to do the exercise whilst thinking of riding, or of a training session, of a competition, of jumping three foot, three foot six etc., and to see how far up the scale you can go before you need energy gymnastics to help you!

The next exercise is best done lying in bed on your side, and if you have difficulty sleeping, this (and your one point) could be just the antidote you need. In your mind, sense the edges of your body, and notice how well defined they seem. (Linda Tellington-Jones believes that horses who do not like to go into trailers cannot tell where their edges are: thus they do not know if they will fit in. To aid their perception she advocates stroking their body with a stiff four-foot dressage whip, which she calls a 'wand'. My premise right now is that people have the same difficulty in sensing their edges – although I have never advocated using a 'wand' as part of their education!) So how clearly can you tell where your body ends and where the air around you begins? If your skin were a bag, would it be intact? What would this bag contain? Can you make its contents feel more solid, more like sand or putty? If this is easy for you, work through your body, increasing your sense of solidity. If it is difficult, just notice the areas of your body which seem more firm, and those which are more 'airy'.

As you continue with this, think about your face, and the shape it would make if seen from inside the back of your head. Does thinking about this make it seem like a more distinct boundary? Feel your back, and think of the shape of a low-cut swimming costume. Does your skin form a clear boundary all the way down to this line? What about below the line? Many people do not have a clear sense of their edges all the way down to their backside and seat bones, for we are typically much more aware of our *fronts* (which we can see) than we are of our *backs*. Thinking of your one point will help, and you can even imagine pulling your energy back into your body. (Think of a fisherman hauling nets back into his boat.) When you can do this, you will close your 'leaks'. You will probably feel your muscle tone increase, and you will instinctively know when the boundary of your back is complete.

Working with the Rider's Belt helps people to become more aware of their back, and to make their skin into a more solid boundary, with their 'plunger down' and their 'leaks' closed. In addition, an extremely useful exercise which you can do every day is to stand in an 'on-horse' position, and to wrap a large bath towel around your back. Begin with it up by your armpits, and then gradually move it down. In each position, push back into the bath towel whilst also pulling forward on its ends (and maintaining your vertical alignment without hollowing or rounding your back). Then see if you can recreate that same feeling when the bath towel is no longer there. (You are then helping yourself to establish the dynamic of Fig. 2.9 on page 62.)

To gain a sense of strength and solidity within the pelvis, a strong energetic boundary in the lower back is tremendously important. For if you 'leak' here – or anywhere else – as you ride, your energy system will thwart all your best efforts to gain the high tone and the push forward that are needed to ride well. So now, turn your attention to your thighs. If you consider the whole length from the greater trochanter to the knee, which parts of it can you feel most clearly? Where do you 'leak' the most? Very few people have a clear perception of the upper part of the thigh, especially on the outside and/or the back of it. Can you get a more distinct sense of both your thigh bone, and of your skin as your body boundary? As you do this, think of extending your thigh bone out of your hip socket. If your thigh is to function like a girder over the horse's suspension bridge (see page 99, and Fig. 4.2 on page 100) you need to be able to feel this clearly, for an energetic 'leak' will make it compressible, destroying the integrity of the framework by which the rider shapes and contains her horse.

Still lying in bed, how clearly can you feel your lower legs and feet? Does your ability to perceive your body end at your knees? It does for a significant proportion of the population (who usually have chronically cold feet): if their skin were a bag, it is as if the bag disintegrates here, and its contents pour out unchecked. Can you somehow keep the bag intact, down to and including your feet? Again, think of drawing your energy back into it. For many people this change is the most difficult of all, but if you want your lower legs to function well when you ride – to look and feel as if they are full of putty and not air – then your energetic connection with them must change. Otherwise, nothing you attempt to do will work.

It is the ethereal, low-toned riders (usually women) who benefit the most from these exercises, and if your skin feels like a solid boundary all over your body, then you are probably a natural rider. You can probably very easily do the last variation on the theme, which is to imagine that your body is full of ice-cream, and that you could somehow scoop it out, pressing the scoop against your skin to remove every last piece, and thus sensing your edges from the *inside*.

Many people do not find these exercises easy, especially on the first attempt; but they are worth taking time over and doing every night. Then, as you understand them, you can take the energetic integrity which they create with you into your riding.

I, for one, wish it had not taken me so long to understand about energy – my riding and my health would have benefited enormously if I could have made sense out of the odd comment thrown my way by healers and therapists. (One even said 'You must learn to control your energy,' leaving me with no idea of how I was supposed to do it!) My body was rather like an energetic sieve, and I could not contain enough Ki to recharge my batteries and then extend energy outwards. Strange though these exercises are, I am quite convinced that once you can make sense of them, you can make sense of riding, gaining the ability shown by the novice pupil I described earlier. They will not make you lose pounds of fat; but their effects can be far greater than endless hours of sweat in the gym, or of struggle in the saddle!

....

Diaphragmatic breathing If you have actually done these exercises, you will probably have noticed that your breathing pattern changed in the process. Breathing is a big stumbling block for many riders, especially when coupled with bearing down. So begin by lying on the floor, with your head on a couple of paperback books, your knees bent, and your feet flat on the floor. Take some time to relax and feel your body, and then notice which parts of you move as you breathe. Does your chest rise? Does your stomach move up or down as you inhale? Put a large book on your stomach, and make sure it then *lifts* as you breathe in. Is this very different to normal?

Many people pull their stomachs in as they inhale, breathing only into their upper chests – but this hugely decreases their lung capacity, and it also makes it almost impossible to 'keep one point' and to 'keep your plunger down'. In diaphragmatic breathing, the diaphragm is pulled down with the in-breath, filling out the stomach and creating a vacuum in the lungs that fills with air.

Now clear your throat. As you do this, you will automatically bear down, and the book will lift. Do it again, but afterwards, keep bearing down. Now, the book should stay lifted, both on the in-breath, and on the out-breath. To help you, make the sound 'pssst' as you breathe out, and think of generating enough force to blow a blockage out of a drinking straw. The more you practise this, the less effortful it will seem (remember Sarah from Chapter 2, who got it really well after practising for the whole of a three-hour car journey!). You do not have to bear down very strongly, for it is the basic *pattern* and not its strength which is important right now. For this is the blueprint for how you breathe and use your abdominal muscles as you ride.

It is also helpful to realise that breathing is an activity involving your *back*. As you sit or stand, put your hands on the lower back part of your ribcage, and feel it expand as you breathe in. You could imagine that you have gills there, like a fish, and that the air is drawn in through these. This should help you become more aware of your back as a whole, perceiving your edges more clearly, and perceiving the thickness of you that lies *in front of* your back.

When both your breathing and your awareness of your body includes your back, and not just your front, you become what Alexander Teachers term 'in your back'. Perceiving your back clearly, and breathing from your back are prerequisites to 'using your back': if you are only aware of your *front* you will always be a weak rider. By 'coming from your back' you become much more effective, able to 'keep one point', and 'keep your plunger down' much more easily. Then, you can push from the back of you towards the front of you as if you had no thickness, and generate a very strong push forward. The horse immediately knows the difference between you and a rider who is 'airy-fairy'.

....

Neutral spine

This next set of exercises is far less unusual, and is intended to help you find the correct position for your spine and backside when riding.

Sit on a hard chair and place your hands beneath your seat bones. (Palm down is usually most comfortable, but this learning experience needs to be taken in small doses to ensure that you do not squash your hands!) Just sit normally, and notice where your seat bones point. How do you have to adjust your alignment to make them point straight down? Move between the extremes of pointing them backwards and forwards, noticing if you have an approximately equal range in both directions, or if you have more movement in one. (You are positioning your body as shown in Figs. 9.2b and c, overleaf.) This is very telling, for it shows your innate tendency, which will usually determine the way that you walk and sit as well as how you ride.

To get an even better read-out on the correct position for your body,

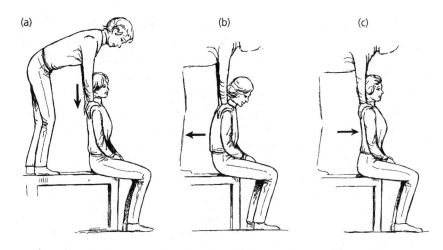

Fig. 9.2 Neutral spine: (a) a strong test resulting from a neutral spine; (b) the chest collapses and the middle of the back rounds outwards when the seat bones point forward; (c) the back hollows and the front of the body lengthens when the seat bones point back.

we can consider the physiotherapy concept of 'neutral spine'.* The spine is a series of curves: the small of the back (which is the lumbar spine) curves forwards, the ribcage (or thoracic spine) curves back, and the neck (or cervical spine) curves forward. These curves vary in size from person to person; but the overriding factor is that however big they are, they must be in balance with each other. Testing this is a two–man exercise not without its dangers: for you need to sit towards the front of a hard chair (a sturdy tack box may work better), with a willing partner who will climb onto the chair and stand behind you on its seat. Thus she needs to be aware of her safety; but so do you, and if you have or have had back pain, either do not do the exercise or make sure that her pressure is very light to begin with. You *must* back off before you start to feel pain.

Your partner presses down onto your shoulders, lightly at first, but then progressively harder, using slow, rhythmic movements which gradually build up to about fifty per cent of her weight. Her arms remain vertical, with her upper body right above you, and her hands as close to your neck as possible. (See Fig. 9.2.) When she presses, where does your body give? Does your chest collapse (implying that you are round-backed) or does the small of your back compress forwards (implying that you are hollow-backed)? Your partner needs to feel that her pressure does not deform your posture, but that it compresses you into a solid structure, passing straight down through you to your seat bones.

---

* I am indebted to my colleague, Anne Howard, an American physical therapist, rider and teacher, who to my knowledge was the first to apply this idea to riders. I am also grateful to her for introducing me to 'Gymnasticballs' and the spinal stabilisation exercises included here.

From her vantage point, it may be clear that your body has a twist in it (remember our discussion of the effects of unequal development in the psoas muscles on page 134, and the body-reading exercise on page 219), and that as a result, one side of your body gives in response to her pressure. When you have your body lined up in 'neutral spine', neither side will be 'squidgy', and your partner can press hard without causing you pain. (But do be careful as you search for this alignment. If you are having trouble finding it, you might consider seeing a physical therapist.)

In the correct balance your seat bones will usually point straight down, but there will be some individual variations on the theme. Your partner's perception of your 'neutral spine' will be more reliable than yours, for as always, your habitual way of sitting will make it hard for you to give an objective analysis of what is actually happening.

....

'Popping up'

Next, we will do an exercise which addresses the issue of 'popping up' off your seat bones, which we have mentioned several times. Like most of the exercises in this chapter, this is also demonstrated on the videotape, 'A Rider's Guide to Body Awareness', and it shows how many possible interpretations there are for the apparently simple word 'sitting'! Once you have found the correct basic position for your seat bones, sit on your hands again and tighten up the muscles between them and your seat bones. This will lift them up off your fingers. Some folks will be able to create a very thick layer of flesh beneath them, others a much thinner one. There are also some people who have a tendon (rather than a muscle) directly beneath one or both seat bones. Since it is so painful to sit directly on this, every time they sit down they have to choose whether to position it to the inside or the outside of the seat bone. (If you are marvelling at this information, be happy that it does not apply to you! This is a very unfortunate conformation for a rider, and I can only assume that it stems from an extra long tendon which attaches the hamstring muscle into the back of the seat bone.) The best remedy can be to deliberately 'pop up' slightly, since this leaves you sitting on muscle bulk, not on the tendon.

If you slowly 'pop up' a number of times, you will discover that there are two muscle groups involved. The first one that tightens lies to the outside and back of each seat bone, going round it in a quadrant of a circle. If the seat bone were at the centre of a circle and 12 o'clock were straight ahead, this would be from 3 o'clock to 6 o'clock on the right seat bone, and from 6 o'clock to 9 o'clock on the left. The second muscle pulls in under the seat bone and lifts it up. It is the top of the hamstring muscle, which runs down the underside of the thigh, and usually it is by far the stronger of the two. (See Fig. 9.3 overleaf.) It leaps into action with great

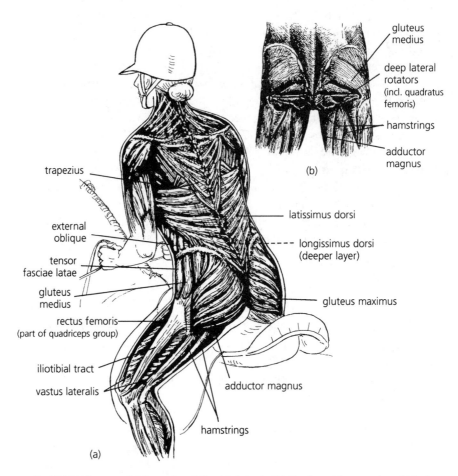

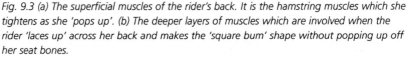

Fig. 9.3 (a) The superficial muscles of the rider's back. It is the hamstring muscles which she tightens as she 'pops up'. (b) The deeper layers of muscles which are involved when the rider 'laces up' across her back and makes the 'square bum' shape without popping up off her seat bones.

gusto: in fact, most people find that after the hand, arm, and shoulder girdle, the hamstring is the muscle in the body which most wants to join in the action when they are riding. You will almost certainly find the first muscle (quadratus femoris and the other deep lateral rotators of the hip joint) much weaker and more difficult to isolate. Go very slowly and do lots of repetitions as you seek to differentiate the two.

Being able to contract these muscles separately enables us to look again at how the rider can make herself narrower from side to side, thus enabling her pelvis to fit across the horse's long back muscles as shown in Fig. 5.11, page 139. She has to narrow in without 'popping up': it is as if the 'goo' of her insides is pushed forward (through bearing down) rather than up (thus lifting her seat bones off the saddle). When I first discovered and taught the pinch, I suggested making yourself feel narrower in between the greater trochanters of the femur (shown on Fig. 9.7, page 252), as if there was a bolt between them and someone was tightening a nut which pulled the two sides closer in together. The descriptions on pages 66–67 (including the exercise in which you aim each seat bone towards the opposite ankle bone) are updates on this. I developed these because in response to my original description, many people involved both of the muscle groups already described and 'popped themselves up'.

To avoid this, the rider must tighten the first muscle group but not the second. The exception to the rule is offered by people with the extra long tendon, and people who are so thin that they need some additional padding between their seat bones and the saddle. You might wish you were thinner – but you and your horse both suffer horribly when you have two stiletto heels poking down through your flesh and into his back! Doing the pinch in its original form has saved a number of very thin riders from having to stuff shoulder pads down their underwear to stop themselves from drawing blood!

However, the amount of flesh in your backside is one of the most important conformational differences between riders, and if, in contrast, you have so much flesh that you cannot find your seat bones, practise sitting on chairs on your hands until you finally work out where they are. (If this is the case, you might also consider doing the Callanetics exercises which I will talk about later – see page 267.)

But before we go further, you need to be able to locate the greater trochanters more clearly, and to discover the part they play in riding. To do this, sit on the floor, with your legs out in front of you, your knees bent and your feet flat on the floor. Put the palms of your hands slightly behind you and to the side and lean back on them. (See Fig. 9.4a.) To begin with,

Fig. 9.4 Rolling between the seat bones and the greater trochanters: (a) the starting position; (b) rolling onto the left trochanter; (c) balancing on it!

make sure you can find your seat bones, which will point slightly forward in this position. You may need to lean back slightly as you search for the bony knobble of the trochanter, which will stop you from falling over. It is even possible to balance solely on it, with very little of the rest of you in contact with the floor! (See Figs. 9.4b–c.)

Now roll towards your mid-line, so that you sit on the seat bone on that side. Roll to your other seat bone, and finally to the greater trochanter on the opposite side. Reverse the sequence, and keep rocking from side to side via each bony knobble in turn. A variation on the theme is to take the starting position shown in Fig. 9.5a and move your shoulders to the side, leaning on your hand, until you find the knobble of the trochanter. In this position rock towards and away from your mid-line a few times, rolling between the seat bone and the trochanter. In theory, you should be able to find both of them clearly, and to feel a distinct 'glunk, glunk' as you roll over the two muscles which lie in between them. (These again are the top of the hamstring muscle, and the quadratus femoris.) Then mirror-image your position and repeat the movement. You may find one side much easier than the other – in fact, on the difficult side you may have trouble locating both knobbles (and the 'glunk, glunk'), and you may need to experiment to find them, perhaps changing the position of your legs to that of Fig. 9.5b. This exercise really shows up your asymmetry; doing it regularly will help you begin to counteract it.

Now, come back to your chair again, and put your fingers on the greater trochanters. They will probably be about two inches off the chair. With your knees apart and your thighs making a 'V' shape, see if you can rearrange your flesh, tucking it in under your backside so that the knobbles – and your fingers – are much closer to the chair. (See Fig. 9.6 a–b.) You are now sitting primarily on the quadratus femoris muscle,

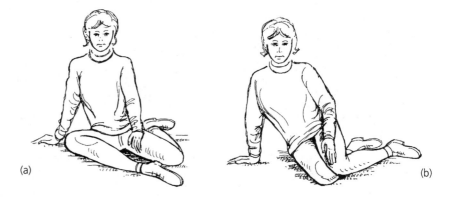

(a)   (b)

Fig. 9.5 From the starting position of (a) rock your shoulders towards the hand on the floor, supporting more weight on it as you locate the trochanter. Then rock between the seat bone and the trochanter. If you have difficulty, move your legs to the position shown in (b).

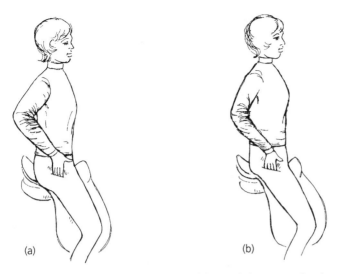

Fig. 9.6 When sitting either on a saddle or (more easily) on a chair, put your hands on your greater trochanters, as in (a). Then tuck your flesh in underneath your backside, bringing the trochanters closer down to the saddle or chair, as shown in (b). Notice the difference between the shape of the rider's backside in (a) and (b).

which lies between the seat bone and the trochanter, covering the neck of the femur. (It may help to look at Fig. 5.10. on page 138, which compares the structure of the pelvis to a child's bicycle with stabiliser wheels. Thus I often call the trochanters the stabilisers.) As you sit like this, be careful that you keep your seat bones pointing straight down, and do not round your back. We have now arrived, I believe, at the feeling which good riders have attempted to describe with the words 'spread your seat out'.

This phrase was in vogue in my youth, although one rarely hears it now. What I used to do when I heard those words was practically the exact opposite, for I would pull my flesh right out to the side, lifting the trochanters in the process, and sitting only on my seat bones. I have met very few people who had not made the same interpretation, and the vast majority of women sit on horses (as well as chairs) by resting on their seat bones rather than their trochanters. A woman who rides with her stabilisers down looks and sits much more like a man, for her backside becomes square and firm rather than round and spongy, mirroring the natural shape of the male backside. (See Fig. 9.7 overleaf.)

Both sexes sit primarily on the bony rami, which join the seat bones to the pubic bone, and function like the rockers on a rocking chair, or the runners on a sledge. But since the pubic bone is shorter than the distance between the seat bones, they narrow in towards each other at the front. They are more parallel in men, whose seat bones are closer together than most women's, and this creates a significant difference in the saddle shape

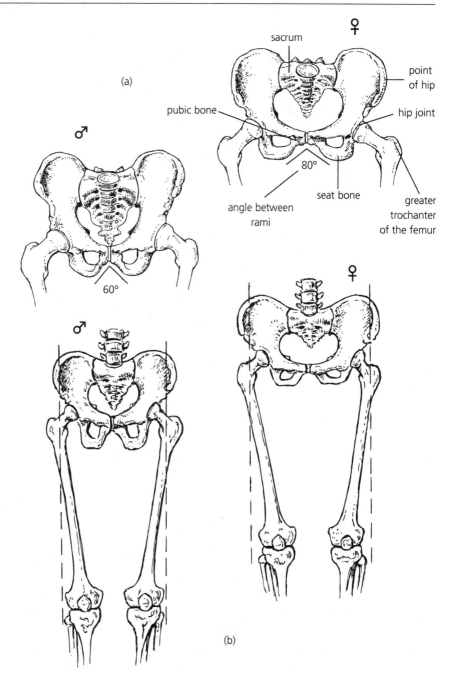

Fig. 9.7 (a) The difference in shape of the female and male pelvis. (b) How the thigh bones are angled differently in each sex. (c) (on facing page) The surfaces of the female and male pelvises as presented to the saddle. Women need a saddle wide enough to accommodate the width between their seat bones. The line of the pelvic axis is much more towards the pubic bone in a woman; in a man the hip sockets lie further back on the line of the rami. This makes it easier for a man to sit in a way which makes his backside look square.

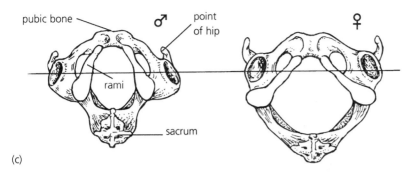

(c)

which suits each sex. (This is discussed in more length in the saddlery chapter in *For the Good of the Horse*.) More novice riders need to think of the rami being the *outside edges* of their sitting, and of getting the gusset of their underpants down onto the saddle. More advanced riders need to get their stabilisers down so that the rami become the *inside edges* of their sitting, and they sit predominately on the flesh which covers the neck of the femur.

The male pelvis has the hip joints and stabilisers relatively further back than they are in a woman's pelvis, and this makes it much easier for him to get his stabilisers down. This gives that diagnostic square shape to his backside, creating a crease in his breeches in the line where the leg meets the body.

Interestingly, only one woman I know has done the above exercise, got into the true 'spread your seat out' position and said, 'Ah yes, now this feels like riding!' – and she had already proved her supremacy by becoming an Olympic competitor! This way of sitting is *extremely unnatural* to most women, and I originally discovered it after I noticed a change in the way I was sitting in my car. I had ridden unusually well, put my horse away, and rushed off to run an errand. I noticed that I was sitting strangely, but then thought no more about it. On about the third time that this happened, I realised that I had found an important piece in the puzzle and needed to pay more attention. Thus the notion of sitting on your stabilisers was born, and it subsequently developed into an understanding which encompassed this exercise.

Notice also that when you sit on the necks of the femur, your thighs form a 'V' shape. So if your thigh bones could continue, by magic, on beyond your hip joints, they would meet at point just behind your backside (see page 66 and Fig. 3.1 on page 67). This should remind you of the 'pain exercise' which we did on pages 67-68, and it is the feeling that I originally cottoned on to when I discovered the pinch. It is extremely important, for when you pull the flesh out to the side and sit only on your seat bones, your thighs become *parallel*. In this position they will never form an effective framework around the horse. Again, move between the two positions until this is clear to you. Realise that the idea of the pinch contains a paradox: for by pulling down the flesh and the greater trochanter you have actually created a *wider* base of support, but concurrently you have made yourself feel *narrower*.

Keep moving between both positions, sitting on your seat bones (with your thighs parallel) and then on your stabilisers (with your thighs making a 'V' shape). With the flesh pulled down tighten the quadratus femoris muscle between the seat bone and the trochanter. With any luck, you should now find that it is very much easier to isolate – for in the true 'spread your seat out' position it is almost impossible to tighten your hamstrings and 'pop' your seat bones out of the saddle. It gives you a very stable base – far more secure and effective than sitting on two tiny 'stiletto heel' seat bones, or on the thick layer of flesh which you create if you 'pop up'.

As well as making a woman's backside look more square, this pelvic arrangement also makes her sitting more solid, for she loses the 'sponginess' in the hamstring muscles which otherwise gives her seat bones much more up-and-down movement than the saddle. (See Fig. 3.4, page 83.) You can become one stage more solid by imagining that your feet are stapled to the floor, and by pulling your feet towards your backside, and your backside towards your feet (without moving either). If you were actually riding this would give you tremendous stability in your lower leg and a very deep seat. If you return to the position of sitting solely on your seat bones, you will discover that you cannot do this half as effectively.

The position you are sitting in now should be reminiscent of the position you found after doing the boards exercise on page 136 and getting 'both sides on'. That exercise also leaves the rider sitting on the necks of the femur and the quadratus femoris muscle. As shown in Fig. 5.11 (page 139), these should lie *across* the horse's long back muscle on each side – and whenever I (or anyone else) has talked about having the *seat bone* on top of the horse's long back muscle, we would have been much more accurate if we had talked about having the seat bone on the inside edge of it, and the *neck of the femur* lying across it. As we have seen, it takes some doing to get 'both sides on' as opposed to 'one side on and one side off'; but the ability to organise both of the horse's long back muscles yields tremendous pay-offs.

I have met a small number of riders – always unusually talented – who thought that the underside of the trochanter was indeed the seat bone, and I suspect that the great Masters who formulated our traditional map of riding never realised that their backside contained four bony knobbles, not two! The fact that it has taken me fifteen years to research and understand this, leads me to mistrust other people's more blasé interpretations of what we sit on. The notion of a 'three-point contact' is made obsolete by this understanding, and whilst there are many, many ways to sit, this is the only one which really yields results.

My backside has actually changed its shape through doing this exercise and riding with my stabilisers down, and the relative strength of the two muscle groups has altered. The first one now leaps into action at my command, and the second is much weaker than it used to be, so that even if I engage it to its maximum my seat bones do not 'pop up' as much as they once did. Many of my colleagues report the same changes. But I still often find myself driving my car and sitting on the neck of my right femur and on my left seat bone – mirroring the tendency I have when I ride. But virtually everyone I meet on my travels has not yet got this far; the hamstring is their dominant muscle and they 'pop themselves up'. The women who formed the exception to this either showed exceptional ability, or were so thin that riding was a painful experience!

....

This next set of exercises, designed to increase the muscle tone of both the thigh and the calf, is much more straightforward. One of the easiest ways to gain the necessary control and strength in the riding muscles is by learning to stick out the tendons which insert the major muscles into bone. One of the most important is the quadriceps muscle at the front of the thigh, so, sitting in a chair (or in the saddle) press down on one knee with your hand, whilst simultaneously trying to lift it. (You did this same exercise with a partner in Chapter 3 (page 75), and this whole sequence is similar in its effects to the exercises you did there.) Put the tips of your fingers of your free hand in the angle between your leg and your body, and feel for the tendons – you may only feel one, but actually there are two which are very close together, and which insert the front thigh muscles into the bone just beneath the point of your hip. As you try to lift your knee these should stick out, for you are contracting them isometrically. Your aim is to learn to stick these tendons out at will, without needing to press on your knee. (See Fig. 9.8a overleaf.)

The tendon exercises

The other end of the quadriceps muscle lies just above your knee, and its tendon actually *contains* the knee cap, passing over the front of the knee joint and inserting into the tibia, which is the large bone of the calf. Whilst sitting or standing, reach down to your knee with your hand, resting the leg you are testing on the ball of your foot. Put your thumb and your first finger above and below your knee cap, and think of pushing your foot forward against a resistance. You should feel the tendon stick out, above and below the knee cap. You can also do this exercise when

Fig. 9.8 Sticking out the tendons.

(a) Finding the quadriceps tendon by pushing down on the knee whilst simultaneously trying to lift it up.

(b) The tendon surrounding the knee cap is easily found when sitting on a balance stool, or standing with the leg bent, and pushing the foot forward as if against a resistance.

Think of pushing foot forwards

(c) Pushing the foot back against a resistance activates the tendons of the hamstring muscles, behind the angle of the knee.

Push back, or think of pushing back

(d) By putting something between your legs and then squashing it, you can stick out the adductor tendons at the top inside of the thigh. Although your lower arm is very convenient, using it has the disadvantage that you must lean forward as shown.

(e) If you stand on one leg and cock the other, as if pushing your heel out against a resistance, you activate tensor fasciae latae, located in the indentation below and behind the point of your hip. This muscle can be strengthened by standing or walking in an 'on-horse' position with a loop of Theraband just above the ankles. Turning the toes out whilst walking like this strengthens the muscles of the lower back.

Think of pushing heel out

(f) Bending down to put your hands around your ankle, feel for both the Achilles tendon at the back, and the tendons at the front which lift your toes.

sitting on a balance stool. (See Fig. 9.8b.)

The opposing muscles to the quadriceps are the hamstring group. At the top end of these, where they insert into the seat bone, you do not want to contract them, for this (as we have seen) lifts you out of the saddle. But further down, the muscle group also needs to be in an isometric contraction, opposing the quadriceps. The best way to activate them is to stand by a wall and place the fingers of both hands behind your knee on the underside of your thigh, searching for the tendons which insert these muscles into the bones of the calf. Towards the inside are two tendons, which are so close together that they may be hard to separate. On the outside there is one tendon, which most people find harder to activate. Stick out the tendons against your fingers by thinking of pushing your foot back against a resistance (as in Fig. 9.8c). If you are having difficulty with the tendons on the inside turn your toe in, and if the difficulty is with the tendons on the outside, turn it out. Ideally, though, you need to be able to stick out both sets of tendons without needing to touch them, and with the toes staying forwards.

The adductor muscles on the inside of the thigh come next. To activate them, put something between your knees (your lower arm will do, but something larger like a mailing tube would be better), and push your knees towards each other. (See Fig. 9.8d.) The tendon you are sticking out is right up in the corner where your thigh meets your pubic bone.

To find tensor fasciae latae, one of the abductor muscles which opposes these, stand up and place the fingers of one hand in the indentation just below and behind the point of your hip. Then cock your leg, rotating your heel out and your knee in, and feel for the muscle bulging out against your fingers. (See Fig. 9.8e.) To work this muscle, stand in an 'on-horse' position, rotating your toes in, and pushing your thighs out as if against a resistance.

Better still, put a belt or a loop of Theraband (thick rubber like a giant, wide elastic band) just above your ankles, and counteract its pull by holding your legs apart. If you feel really keen, start walking like this; you will look so ridiculous that anyone watching will be greatly amused (you may even rival Monty Python's 'Ministry of Funny Walks') – and if your abductor muscles are not very strong, you may find that you cannot even hold your legs apart! You will not be able to walk like this for long; but if you continue walking and turn your toes *out,* the stress will move from your outer thighs to the muscles across your lower back. People who have found it hard to activate these (and to 'lace up across their back') have used this exercise to finally understand what they should do, and to build their strength.

Next, sit down again, and place both hands around one of your ankle joints, with the fingers in front and the thumbs at the back. The fingers rest over the tendons which go to your toes, and your thumbs cover the big Achilles tendon. (See Fig. 9.8f.) Stick out all of the tendons. What happens to your toes as you do this? You should find that they spread out and lift, bringing your toenails towards the top of your boots. Practise until you can activate these tendons easily. Many people have stories about the instructor who suddenly said 'toes up', and who helped them much more than years of being told 'heels down'. I have a suspicion that this really worked because it made them stick out the tendons.

To fully appreciate the implications of all this you need to stand in an 'on-horse' position, and do a variation on the theme of the 'pain exercise' (see page 67). Stick out the tendons around your ankles, bringing your toes up. As you do so, think of a gap in your ankle joint, as if your calf bones could lift away from the bones of your ankle. Stick out the tendons behind your knee, and think of a gap in your knee joint. Do the same with the tendons at the top of the thigh, thinking of a gap in your hip socket. (I discussed the importance of gaps in the joints in 'Masterclass', comparing the rider to a wooden puppet whose limbs are joined by a little metal ring. It is the gaps which keep your body functioning as a tensegrity system (see page 213 and Fig. 8.1 on page 214), and I regard them as extremely important shock-absorbers.)

Concurrently, aim your right seat bone towards your left ankle bone, and your left seat bone towards you right ankle bone, as you did in the exercise on page 67. Also think of pushing your thighs out as if against a resistance, and of turning your heels out to activate tensor fasciae latae. Hold this position until you can really feel all your muscles working, and remember that if it does not start to hurt you are not doing it right! When you are ready, let everything go. You should feel that your body drops *down:* for sticking out the tendons and thinking of gaps in the joints, makes you look taller, and helps you to lift the horse's back instead of squashing him.

An even better 'hard sell' for the benefits of muscle tone is to stand on one leg, holding onto something for support, and to swing your free leg, firstly from the knee, and then from the hip. Next, stick out the tendons at the knee and ankle on this leg, and swing it again. This time you will only be able to swing it from the hip. (See Fig. 9.9.) After a while, let go of the tendons; the difference in its texture should be immediately obvious, and perhaps now you can understand more clearly the difference between a 'noodley' body, and a highly toned leg which creates a framework around the horse. (This has been christened the 'dead leg' exercise by people who know it well.)

If you do this with each leg in turn, you will probably find that one is significantly stronger than the other. To strengthen the weak leg, stand on your strong leg just in front of a wall; slightly bend the knee and ankle on

Fig. 9.9 The 'dead leg' exercise in which you stick out the tendons at the knee and ankle whilst swinging your leg from the hip.

your weak leg, and push your heel back into the wall. (This is similar to Fig. 9.8c page 256 and you are now pushing against a resistance, as you did in the mounted exercises on page 75 in Chapter 3.) Once you have done this, you will find that the leg is more highly toned when you swing it again.

You should now know enough to be able to train virtually all of your riding muscles to contract isometrically. Sticking out the tendons is the best way to activate the muscles of the thigh and calf, and to activate the muscles in the torso (which do not have these rope-like tendons) you need to practise bearing down, 'lacing up across your back', 'engaging your boards' and sitting on *with your stabilisers down*. Exercise physiologists recommend contracting your muscles at two-thirds of their total strength, sustaining this for six seconds, and performing ten repetitions. Do this three times a day and you will become stronger within a few weeks. You can do much of this sitting at your desk, and talking on the telephone.

....

Exercises in which you push against a resistance demonstrate very clearly the muscle use of riding. Interestingly, the complementary health care systems Touch for Health and Applied Kinesiology employ tests like this to diagnose strengths and weaknesses in the body. The classic test, often used in the diagnosis of food allergies, is to have the client hold her arm out in front of her whilst the tester pushes down on her wrist. (Meanwhile, the client has a sample of the food either on her navel or possibly in her mouth.) A gradually increasing pressure is applied for about three seconds. If the arm stays strong all is well; but if the client cannot resist, or if her arm shows the slightest 'mushiness', there is some

Muscle testing

cut-off or reduction in the energy flow within all the systems in the body which affect that muscle. Thus it becomes unable to respond to the neurological message which tells it to contract.

Remarkable as it may seem you can even test the integrity of the whole bodymind system by saying 'My name is ...' as somebody applies the test. Then repeat the test, but lie about your name. As you do so, your arm will test weak. More complex tests are done with the body in a position which isolates a specific muscle from the group it usually works with. The test for the psoas muscle, for instance, (which I am giving you because it is so notoriously difficult to feel) is done with the client lying face up with one leg raised to about 45°, and slightly to the side, with the foot pointing out. The tester's hand stabilises the opposite hip whilst she presses against the ankle, pushing the leg out and down whilst her client attempts to resist. (See Fig. 9.10.)

In Chinese medicine the psoas muscle is associated with the kidney meridian, and the kidney itself. Although practitioners would not claim that a weak test means a weak organ, it does imply a blockage or constriction in a portion of the kidney meridian energy flow. The practitioner would then use acupressure points, as well as other techniques, to strengthen the weakness. A re-test confirms whether this has been successful.

So strength or weakness in riding terms may well refer to far more than just muscles, for each one relates to a different meridian and a different organ. The implications of this are so huge that my brain can barely handle them! So anyone who finds that their body is no match for the demands of riding may find that a visit to an Applied Kinesiology or Touch For Health practitioner pays dividends. For they insist that muscle *weakness* (rather than spasm or tension) is one of the most important

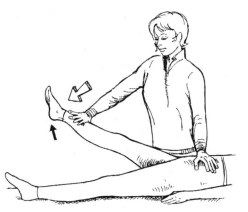

Fig. 9.10 The test used for the psoas muscle in Applied Kinesiology. The client should be able to resist a three-second pressure given as shown.

diagnostic signs of a problem within the body. Wherever a tight muscle holds the body in flexion, they look for the weak muscle that opposes it, and they test and treat this muscle. Only if this fails do they employ techniques which weaken the strong muscle. This means that they are following exactly the opposite philosophy to a massage therapist.

This has profound implications for the ways in which we think about muscle imbalance, and it has significantly influenced my thinking. As I said on page 84, many riders suffer from the fact that the flexors at the front of the body dominate over the extensors at the back of the body, creating a tendency for the knees and shoulders to come closer together. By comparing opposing muscle groups to the springs on a restaurant swing door (see Fig. 3.6, page 85) we determined that lengthening the shorter muscles will have limited effect, since as the counterpart of the long springs, they must immediately tighten again to take up the slack. This means that increasing the tone in the muscles at the back of the pelvis – as well as the back of the thigh – will be the most effective way of keeping the angle at the hip joint open. 'Pushing down the springs at the back' (see Fig. 3.5, page 84) is a helpful way to do this, but it may be surprising to realise that something as non-strenuous as the energy exercises we did earlier are also a good start. For the riders with long, low-toned muscles are the riders who 'leak'. By closing the 'leaks', they firm up their muscles.

....

I often think that riders who talk about the importance of good balance are really talking about the importance of *muscle balance*. It is muscle *imbalance* which causes the body to fold forward at the hip joint, and which pulls it out of the alignment of 'neutral spine'. A rider with good balance remains stable – suggesting that it also relates to the body's texture, and to the rider's ability to 'keep one point'. So it is not surprising that a very useful group of exercises for riders are actually used by physical therapists who need to increase the 'spinal stabilisation' of people who are prone to back pain.

The following exercise must be done with a partner. Lie on the floor on your back, with your knees bent and slightly apart, and your feet flat on the floor about pelvis width apart. To approximate the 'neutral spine' position put a hand under the small of your back; then remove your hand, but keep this small arch throughout. (The floor exercises in *Ride With Your Mind/The Natural Rider* were done with the small of your back on the floor. But for these exercises, keep a slight hollow.) Your partner kneels to the side of you and takes hold of your knees, exerting a gradually increasing pull which, if you were not resisting, would draw them towards

Spinal stabilisation exercises

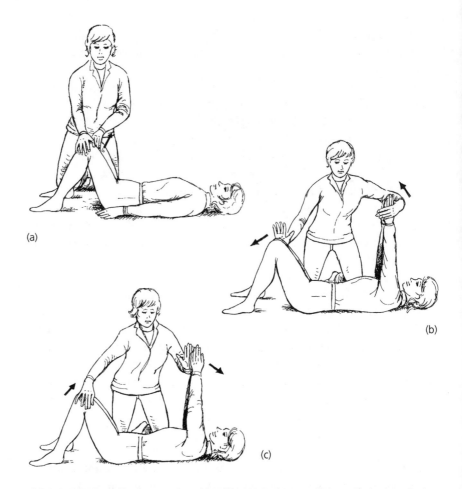

Fig. 9.11 Spinal stabilisation exercises. (a) Pulling on the knees, which can be both pushed and pulled from both sides of the body. (b) and (c) Pushing on the knees (which are now together) and pulling on the hands as the arms make a steeple, and vice versa. These should be repeated on both sides of the body, noticing differences between the two sides.

her and the floor. As she does this, endeavour to keep your knees pointing towards the ceiling. (See Fig. 9.11a.) When positioned first on one side of you and then the other, she can pull your knees towards and away from her whilst you resist.

Next, put your knees together, and raise your arms to make a steeple, so that your palms are touching and your fingertips point upwards. Now your partner can place one hand on your hands, and one on your knees, pulling them in opposite directions. (Again, she should do each push and pull from each side of you. See Figs. 9.11b–c.) Ideally, the four corners of your shoulders and buttocks should stay down on the floor; but your asymmetry will in all probability be abundantly clear, for you will stabilise your body much more easily against some of the pulls than others.

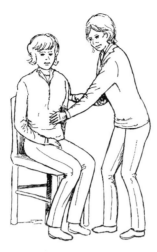

Fig. 9.12 Testing for stability in the side/side plane, by pushing on the body. One hand is on the shoulder, and the other on the waist. This subject is unmoved by the push.

Figure 9.12 shows another helpful variation on the theme. As you sit in a chair with your legs slightly apart, your partner places one hand on your shoulder and the other on your waist, and pushes directly sideways. Ideally, you should easily be able to resist her push, staying upright with both seat bones on the chair and no displacement of your ribcage; but again, you are likely to give way on one side. Repeat the same exercise with one 'board' in place (asking your partner to push from both sides) and then with both boards in place. You will find that as a minimum requirement to withstand her push, you need to activate the board on the side furthest away from her push.

As with all of these exercises, the key lies in working out exactly how you need to organise your body to become stable. Transferring this learning to your riding can yield tremendous benefits.

Other spinal stabilisation exercises use a 'Gymnasticball', also known as a 'Swissball'. These big blow-up balls are not so different to the 'Spacehoppers' or 'Hippity-hops' which partnered a whole generation of pony-starved children. Physical therapists find that persuading people to go home and do exercises with the ball is much easier than convincing them to do any other kind of homework, for the balls are tremendous fun. Feedback is instantaneous, and one sees improvements very quickly. They come with an exercise handbook, and it is easy to see which exercises are useful for riders. Initially, just sitting on the ball with your feet off the floor challenges your ability to balance, and the way you tend to roll off the ball yields a tremendous amount of information about your asymmetry. (See Fig. 9.13a, overleaf.)

The exercise shown in Fig. 9.13b does not look as if it should be

(a)   (b)

Fig. 9.13 The 'Gymnasticball'. (a) Sitting on the ball with feet off the floor. Larger balls make this harder, and with the 95cm diameter ball (or on any ball on which you cannot easily touch your feet to the floor), you should have a spotter who will catch you if you fall back. (b) Marching, which is very much harder than it looks. The aim is to keep the upper body upright as you lift each leg in turn.

taxing; but you are being deceived. It is remarkably hard to sit on the ball with your feet on the floor, and then to lift each one in turn. For in this exercise, which is known as 'marching', you have to keep your trunk aligned evenly over your pelvis (in neutral spine) whilst changing your base of support. If you do this in front of a mirror you can immediately see how you lean or contort your body whenever you lift one leg (if not both). For being stabilised only by the side of your weaker iliopsoas muscle leaves you very wobbly. One of my more fastidious pupils puts a marker on her mirror, lines her nose up with it, and uses this a very precise way to test herself!

The ball provides an exceptionally good medium through which to develop muscle control and stability, for as you learn to stabilise yourself on the ball you discover corrections which are also needed in your riding. Other exercises include the 'prone bridge' and the 'supine bridge': just maintaining these positions is surprisingly stressful, and moving your legs within them is unbelievably difficult! (See Figs. 9.14 and 9.15.)

You can also use the ball to practise your sitting trot (and the 'Rider's Guide to Body Awareness' videotape gives a clear visual picture of mechanisms which are right and wrong). Bounce up and down on the ball, and notice if you hollow or round your back. Some riders hollow on the way up, which has the potential to damage the intervertebral discs, and others round their back on the way down, which has the potential to damage the facet joints between the vertebrae. Some alternate the two, which has the potential to damage both! The lumbar spine was not designed to be used as a joint, and in effect, each of these mechanisms sends a whiplash up your spine with each step the horse takes.

Fig. 9.14 (a) The beginning position to get into the prone bridge, and (b) rolling out into this position, (c) holding it, and (d) marching in it. To maintain neutral spine, think of keeping your hips up and your pelvis level.

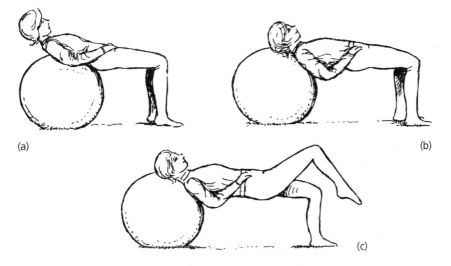

Fig. 9.15 From sitting on the ball, roll like this (a) into the supine bridge; (b) holding the supine bridge; and (c) marching in this position. To maintain neutral spine, think of keeping your hips and your 'withers' (i.e. thoracic curve of your spine) up.

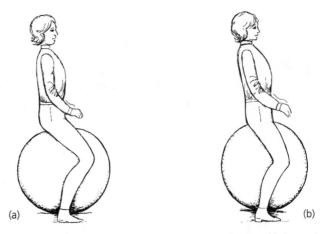

(a)   (b)

Fig. 9.16 Using the Gymnastic ball to mimic sitting-trot mechanism: (a) shows the 'down' in which the rider's feet are at six o'clock and her pelvis at 11 o'clock. In (b) on the 'up' her pelvis moves forward and up to twelve o'clock, and is over her feet, with her torso slightly behind vertical.

When the 'give' lies instead in the hip joints, the rider's sitting mechanism maintains the stability of the spine. In the 'down' her 'Z' angles are closed (See Fig. 3.8, page 86), and her backside is actually slightly behind her feet. In the 'up' – which also takes her pelvis *forward* and over her feet – the 'Z' angles open, and her torso is slightly behind vertical. (See Figs. 9.16a–b.) If the rider's feet are placed at 6 o'clock, her pelvis begins at 11 o'clock, and the 'up' beat moves it to 12 o'clock (i.e. over her feet). It is important that the rider does not go 'over the top of the clock', for this will put her into extension pattern; but if she does not 'get to the top of the clock' the horse cannot move so freely underneath her. Every rider should have a Gymnasticball, for we can all benefit from the strength and skill it promotes. Also, you need far more practice in the basic skills of riding than your horse ever did or ever will, and by using the ball you can transform some of the mundane chores of life into useful exercises. I am balancing on mine right now as I type this page!

....

The Pilates Method and Callanetics

A number of patented exercise systems have also proved useful for riders, and the Pilates Method is one. It was developed by Joseph Pilates, who grew up in Germany but spent the First World War in England, where he became a nurse. He experimented with ways to strengthen his immobilised patients, and had them pull on springs attached to their hospital beds. His discoveries led him to design mat exercises and other exercises which utilised the resistance provided by various pieces of specialised equipment. The Pilates Method evolved on five main pieces of equipment, and until very recently this method has been used predominantly by dancers. It is more widely known in America than in the UK, since Pilates emigrated there in 1926.

The Pilates Method is now taught both by physical therapists and certified instructors, usually in one-on-one sessions, and sometimes in closely supervised small groups. It has freed several people I know from long-term back pain, and it aims primarily to strengthen the muscles of the abdomen, lower back and backside. Instructors pay great attention to controlled breathing, to the alignment of the body, and to releasing the shoulder girdle. Furthermore, the method encourages precise movements rather than mindless repetitions, so it increases body awareness, and facilitates harmony and balance. Since these are all issues for riders, the method is a huge, untapped resource, which I hope will become more widely available in the near future.

Callanetics is another exercise system which has benefited many riders, especially those who want (and need) to slim down and increase their muscle tone. I regularly suggest these exercises to people who cannot find their seat bones, and whose inner thigh muscles are not strong enough to enable them to balance out of the saddle (as if at the top of their rise in rising trot) without pressing hard in their stirrups. Callan Pinckney's first book, *Callanetics*, was published in 1984, and many other books and videos have followed.

Callan left the American south in 1961, as a rebellious college drop out, and she travelled Europe, Africa, India and Japan for the next ten years. She was born with spinal curvatures, and wore leg braces for seven years of her childhood – but amazingly, once she was free of these, she studied classical ballet. However, the years spent travelling took their toll; she carried a heavy rucksack, did menial work, and suffered the huge gains and losses in weight which accompany illness and bad nutrition. By the time she woke up to the fact that she needed to look after her body, she was in constant pain.

Returning home via London she began her rehabilitation programme, and her first job back in America was in an exercise salon. But she did not approve of the way that clients' bodies were being treated, and this led to experimental work on herself which gradually evolved into her system.

Callan's physical problems led her to devise exercises which are safe for people with weak or damaged backs. They are also tremendously effective, and she believes that 'an hour of these exercises equals approximately seven hours of conventional exercise and twenty hours of aerobic dancing, as far as firming the body and pulling it up are concerned'. Her books and videos show photographs of her students after their first, third, and fifth sessions, etc., and you literally see stomachs, backsides and thighs disappearing before your very eyes! I have seen this too in myself, and in the friends and pupils who have done her programme. However, in these early stages people often 'gain weight' whilst dropping several dress sizes, for muscle weighs heavier than fat. The only snag in the whole system (and there had to be one) is that the exercises are physically very taxing, and I would be hard pushed to describe them as fun.

Each exercises session begins with a gentle warm-up, moving on to sets of exercises which are designed to work on specific body parts. In each one the starting position puts the muscles concerned under contraction, and then small delicate movements – like raising and lowering your leg half an inch – require further contraction of the deep muscles in that area. Soon, you begin to feel these muscles working, and as you learn to isolate them you can do the movements in an even more controlled way. Callan claims that when one layer of muscle has been completely worked, the layer beneath it will take over, and that 'even people who consider themselves Super Klutzes – they can't walk and talk at the same time – gain control of their bodies [by doing these exercises].'

After you have worked your stomach muscles, legs, backside and hips, Callan prescribes some stretches before using more exercises for the pelvis and thighs. Her 'pelvic rotations' and 'pelvic scoop' have become part of the daily routine of many riders I know, and I often use her 'inner thigh squeeze' in workshops. She believes that many thigh exercises are incomplete, for 'most are stretches, without the all-important balancing action of a contraction. Unless your muscles are contracted, you will have well-stretched legs with mushy, dangling inner thighs.' Without contraction, you will not firm up your muscles. Stories like those I told on page 238, about the low-toned women who regularly ran and worked out, lead me to believe that she is right.

....

Strength, flexibility, endurance and balance

The three elements of muscular fitness are generally considered to be strength, flexibility and endurance. To this, I like to add balance (i.e. muscle balance), thus ensuring that we maintain an overview which considers the body as a whole. Stretching a muscle after it has been contracted keeps it flexible, and fortunately, stretching does not lead to any reduction in muscular strength. When you train with weights, adding more resistance develops your strength, whilst adding more repetitions trains your endurance. Given that we women compete on equal terms with men, weight training is particularly beneficial for us. For without strength training, women's strength is usually found to be 25-28% lower than a man's when measured in proportion to body weight. However, when women undertake weight training this difference all but disappears.

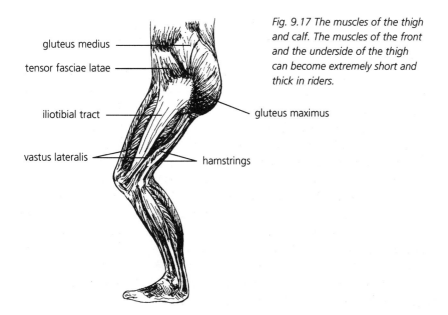

gluteus medius

tensor fasciae latae

iliotibial tract

vastus lateralis

gluteus maximus

hamstrings

Fig. 9.17 The muscles of the thigh and calf. The muscles of the front and the underside of the thigh can become extremely short and thick in riders.

Training with weights will only decrease flexibility if weight training exercises are not done through the whole range of motion of a joint. So repeatedly exercising a muscle or muscle group in a fixed position causes the connective tissue within and around the muscles to adapt to this position, and become shortened. This type of static exercise is, I fear, exactly what we do when we ride.

On good male riders in particular, the riding muscles have often become so short and thick that one sees tremendous bulk in the hamstring muscles at the back of the thigh. The iliotibial tract at the side of the thigh (which is a band of fibrous tissue) is then clearly defined, and the quadriceps muscle at the front of the thigh bulges as well. (See Fig. 9.17.) A number of physical therapists have suggested that riders should stretch before and after riding: yet despite the fact that all other athletes stretch, few riders bother – even when told of the benefits. Warming up (a gentle jog on the spot) and then stretching before you get on protects you from injury; but by stretching when you get off (in a way I will describe later – see Fig. 9.18) you can prevent your muscles from becoming short and thick, restricting your flexibility. To add to the case for stretching, these bulky muscles are not exactly attractive.

The warm-up before stretching literally *warms up* the muscles, increasing body temperature and cardiovascular activity. Thus more oxygenated blood is sent to them before they are stretched and then finally put to work. Joints, like muscles, have a greater range of motion at higher temperatures, for tendons and other connective tissues become more extensible. Horses move their joints very much more than riders, increasing their need for a progressive warm-up. But the fibres of a cold muscle – whether human or equine – are easily torn, and commonly, we take few protective measures.

Riders who rush into their work may not understand the body's need for a gentle warm-up, but often, they knowingly skimp on warming down, racing on – as we all do – to the next of life's demands. The protective effect of gradually warming down lies in letting the body cool more slowly than it would if suddenly left to stand. Gentle exercise at the end of a workout assists in the removal of the waste products of exercise, for the heart alone is not efficient enough to pump them through the veins, and the lymph vessels also work most efficiently when massaged by the squeezing action of muscle contraction. To leave a build-up of waste products in a hard-working muscle is easily done, for muscle soreness is delayed in its onset.

Traditionally, we have taken much better care of our horses than we have of ourselves – and if you follow the age-old advice of walking your horse the last mile home, he is much less likely to break out into a sweat. But if you get carried away as you ride, you will probably consign your horse as well as yourself to the uncomfortable and demotivational effects of soreness the next day.

....

Rider injuries

Only one pupil of mine has ever injured herself since she began working with me: this is Denise, whom you met in Chapter 6. Because she was so asymmetrical, the left inner thigh was overworking and the tendons of her adductor muscles on the left side (inserting into the corner of her pubic bone) were, quite literally, stopping her from falling off to the right! After her first course, when we were not yet ready to bite off this problem, she went home full of enthusiasm, and rode every horse she could get her backside on. When one of those adductor tendons began to hurt, she ignored the pain – even though she instinctively knew that it was not the run-of-the-mill discomfort of riding, and ought to be classified as 'bad' pain.

Over the following months, she kept ignoring it, until she finally realised that she had to admit her folly and seek medical help. She was referred to a specialist who feared that she had 'rider's bone', an apparently quite common injury sustained mostly by dressage riders and a few event riders (who are actually more likely to tear the gracilis muscle, which runs down the inside of the thigh). Denise had adhesions between one of the adductor tendons and its sheath, but fortunately, this had not reached the stage when bone is deposited between them. Once this happens little can be done.

Her thigh was stretched under anaesthetic, and she had to stop riding for a while. When she began again her orders were that she had to stretch the area more than she contracted it: this meant that five minutes of stretching earned her five minutes of riding, and she had to do additional stretches once an hour. By now, she had been frightened enough to stick rigorously to her programme – and she was also highly motivated to find ways of making her right side share in the action! She was perhaps more fortunate than German rider Uwe Sauer, who in the Grand Prix test of the 1985 European Championships, tore the tendon of the quadriceps muscle (at the front of the thigh) where it inserts into bone just below the point of the hip. When I discussed this with Wayne Rasmussen, who practises sports medicine in Seattle, Washington, his response was, 'Well, I hope he actually broke a piece of bone off with the tendon, because this would be much easier to heal than if the tendon alone had torn away from the bone.'

It is worth noting, however, that Wayne, who works with many riders, finds that the vast majority of riders' injuries do not occur in the saddle, but as the result of lifting badly whilst doing stable work. Again, keeping neutral spine throughout any activity protects your back, and if you bear down and bend your knees as you lift, you will last much longer. Bending over and twisting does most of the damage: one pupil of mine with permanent low-back pain virtually eradicated it by kneeling on one knee rather than bending over whenever she picked out horses' feet. (But if you decide to follow this potentially dangerous practice, please choose your horses carefully!) The stable hand's bad back is commonplace, but how interesting it is that we never hear of injuries like 'rider's bone', for it must be common enough to deserve its name!

Uwe Sauer's experience supports my premise that riders are *weight lifters,* who barely move, and who utilise the muscles of the thigh, calf, pelvis and abdomen. (I often wonder if he spent his spare time teaching riders to relax, for if he did, he certainly did not practise what he preached!) There, in that high-stress situation, he must have held his quadriceps muscle in the ultimate of isometric contraction, using it to counter-balance his body weight and to lift the horse's back. Obviously this is effort – and unless you are exceptionally fit you should expect to feel it, probably in the inner and front thigh muscles, and sometimes in the outer thigh and the abdominal muscles. Anyone who listens to their body (which Denise did not) can differentiate between 'good pain' – the feeling of a slight stretch – and 'bad pain' which indicates the danger of injury. But few people have Denise's masochistic tendencies, and most riders seem to think that because they have been riding for years they should not feel anything!

However, this is a justification for being a passive rider, who uses the horse like a mobile armchair and lets her body weight fall down the mantrap. If you were a dancer or a gymnast, you would take your daily workout much more seriously, taking each stretch to the edge of pain – and this would gradually increase your range. If you trained with weights, you would keep pushing yourself that little bit extra, adding more weight if you were seeking strength, and more repetitions if you were seeking endurance. Only by doing this do you increase your body's limits, enabling you to do more for longer. So it is with riding.

One review of my videotape series made me sound like the ultimate sadist, demanding that riders should be screaming in agony. This is not true. The 'edge' of pain is a very particular place, which needs to be honoured. This was really brought home to me by one man I teach who had cycled competitively in gruelling long-distance races: his version of the 'edge' of pain was clearly not the same as mine! I was also rather slow to realise that as a particularly highly toned man he needed encouragement to back off, to *relax* his muscles, and to think of being softer and more fluid. (Perhaps this is why our traditional, male-dominated theories of riding speak as they do.) But rarely do I say this to women. One notable exception was a rider who was slightly built and under five foot. She rode large warmblood horses, and had tried to make up for her lack of size by contracting her muscles to the point where she was practically in seize-up. Again, she had to do less and become more fluid; but most women need to work extremely hard before they can firm up their bodies to the right texture.

This is where the Callanetics exercises, the Pilates exercises, the various isometric exercises, the Gymnasticball exercises, and training with weights all come into their own. One rider who was extremely weak when I first met her signed on at the gym, and trained herself from the point of being able to lift only ten pounds on each leg to lifting forty – and her riding changed immensely. Another rider, when she went to the gym and began pulling weights, discovered that she could lift forty pounds on one leg and only twenty on the other! By the time she had evened this up she was in a state of complete confusion, for the asymmetry corrections which she had come to depend on in her riding were no longer appropriate!

One desperate pupil who was consistently thwarted by the strength of her horse's push back, put herself on a rigorous training programme which included running, working out at the gym, and watching television whilst performing isometrics, and in particular whilst using the Theraband (see Fig. 9.8e, page 256). This made a tremendous difference. Her rigorous approach stemmed in part from the realisation that during the weight-training exercise which strengthens the inner thigh (pushing both thighs inwards against a resistance), her left leg lagged behind her right, doing much less of the work – just as it did when she was riding.

So she woke up to the fact that the more subtle aspects of her 'use' on each side needed to be addressed both on and off the horse. Fortunately, she did not mindlessly repeat the exercise and 'drive herself another two hundred miles', strengthening her strong side at the expense of her weakness. But one pupil who did this met her Waterloo not through riding, but by becoming a fanatical weight-lifter who never stretched: when her back finally gave out, her chiropractor blamed the injury on the exceptional tightness of her muscles.

....

Stretching is universally considered as the antidote to repeated or prolonged muscle contraction. When I began investigating the field of exercise physiology, I had the naive expectation that each practitioner I talked to would offer the same prescription. I soon realised how wrong I was, and within different schools of stretching there is tremendous variation in the specific stretches that are deemed good or bad for you. The primary arguments *against* a particular stretch centre around the stress that it places on the lower back and/or knees. The other bone of contention is whether it allows cheating, through which you unknowingly move your body out of position, stretching different muscles to the ones you think you are stretching. There is also disagreement about the length of time each stretch should be held for. Most people agree on somewhere between six and thirty seconds; but despite the differing theories and philosophies of stretching, there is unanimous agreement that whatever else you do, you should never bounce within a stretch.

Stretching

The bodyworkers who have devised and taught stretches for riders have taken a number of different approaches. Gloria Moore, an American massage therapist who now works exclusively with riders (she likes our dedication, and finds us a pleasant change from people who did not care enough about their bodies to actually do her exercises), teaches them in half-day workshops. This enables her to monitor each person very carefully. Some of her stretches involve sitting or lying down, and she uses a seven-foot rope, put around the sole of foot, as an aid in stretching the calves and hamstrings. She also gives individual sessions which utilise active assisted stretches. Here, she moves your body into position and applies light pressure to effect the stretch, and she likes to use many repetitions of a three-second stretch. Active assisted stretches are deemed by many exercise physiologists to provide the most effective stretches of all, and doing them with a skilled clinician gives you a detailed perspective on the asymmetries within your muscle system.

Joan Collins, a British physical therapist who has worked with the

British Endurance Riding Team, recommends simpler stretches that do not need to be done on the floor, and can be done when you are on the telephone, waiting for the kettle to boil, or even in a muddy field whilst preparing to ride. For she feels that there is much more chance of riders actually doing them if they can be integrated easily into their daily (riding) routine. If you do them after you have ridden, however, you have the advantage that your muscles will already be warm. Otherwise you should warm up for three minutes by marching on the spot, then jogging, then running, then running with your knees coming up in front of you, and then by kicking your feet high up behind you.

Joan believes that anyone who has a cumulative total of one thousand hours of riding will show some muscle tightness, and that stretching the psoas muscle should be the priority. Gloria Moore believes that the quadriceps is the most important muscle to pay attention to, and that most riders have about *half* the range of motion in it that they should have. Tightness in both of these muscles pulls the front of the pelvis forward and hollows the back, and a shorter muscle on one side causes the body to rotate; so their condition is highly significant. However, the hamstrings and adductors are also commonly tight, as are the buttock muscles and tensor fasciae latae (see Fig. 9.17). Nevertheless, the good news is that stretching for only six minutes once a day can mitigate the effect of years of riding within only about twelve weeks! If you then stretch three times a week you can keep your muscles from shortening again; so very little effort yields a huge pay-off.

Do not stretch if you have had a recent fracture, sprain or strain to any part of the back or leg; if there has been recent inflammation or infection in a joint; if you have osteoporosis, or if stretching causes acute pain, as opposed to a stretching feeling. Position yourself carefully for each stretch, and then push into it slowly, until you feel the appropriate muscle gently stretching. Think of easing yourself through your body's limits, and begin by holding a stretch for ten seconds, working up to at least thirty seconds, with three or four repeats of each one.

Figure 9.18(a–h) (see pages 276–277) shows two sets of stretches. The first set test your mobility in the most important muscle groups, the quadriceps, psoas, hamstrings, and adductors. If you cannot reach the positions shown, this confirms that you already have shortened muscles. The second set of stretches which have been chosen primarily for their simplicity, and the ease with which you can integrate them into your everyday life. Figure 9.19 (page 278) adds stretches for the back of the calf, the lower back, and the shoulders and upper chest. It also shows an exercise for strengthening the upper back, since long, weak muscles here contribute to rounded shoulders and a collapsed chest. Six to eight repetitions of this every day can significantly improve your posture.

Gymnasticballs can also be used for stretching, and the instructions included with them show many different options. I personally am a great believer in back stretches, and like to hang by holding onto a beam after riding (there may even be one handy in your stable!). But ideally, any exercise programme should be tailor-made for you. After all, your *occupational posture* – derived, perhaps, from driving or from working at a computer – may have influenced your muscle development far more than your riding, causing some muscles to shorten whilst their antagonists lengthen and weaken. But even this is built upon the posture you developed or mimicked in childhood, and which could have been influenced by virtue of being unusually tall or short. It almost certainly predates any damage which may have been done to your body by riding.

As soon as you exercise in a way which addresses your *muscle imbalance*, you do yourself far more good than simply performing exercises by rote. If your flexor muscles dominate over your extensor muscles (see Chapter 3) you may need to stretch your quadriceps, and strengthen your hamstrings, and to stretch and open your upper chest whilst strengthening your back. So to devise a tailor-made programme, you may need more help than you can get from this book. Also, most of us have one leg which is concurrently stronger and also less flexible than the other, and we can exercise specifically to even this up.

Each time you exercise, notice whether you feel any aches or pains. Are they old familiar friends, or new injuries? Do you need to modify your workout so as not to cause more damage, or is it facilitating healing? You may need to consult a professional physical therapist or trainer to help you make this decision, but your instincts (if you listen to them) are highly likely to be right.

To have a training effect any activity needs to be done at least three times a week. This is true whether it be riding, exercises which reinforce the muscle use of riding, or exercises which provide the antidotes to it. But when all else fails, mental rehearsal is a good substitute for actual physical practice (see *Ride With Your Mind/The Natural Rider* and Chapter 10), for it primes your neurology just like the real thing. Even though you may feel nothing happening, your muscles show measurable contractions in response to the feelings and pictures you make in your brain. It is helpful to remember that your neurology is the master system – for your muscles can only do what they are told to do by the brain.

In any exercise you do, pay attention to your body, and to the fullness of your breathing. Flood your body with oxygen and awareness, do not starve it. This added ingredient hugely enriches your experience, and makes you much less likely to 'drive another two hundred miles' and embark on an exercise programme which strengthens only your strong muscles whilst reinforcing any existing patterns of misuse. I firmly believe

Fig. 9.18 Stretches to test and improve mobility.

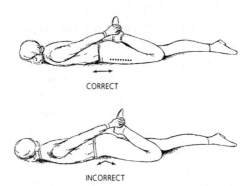

CORRECT

INCORRECT

(a) The test for normal range of movement in the quadriceps muscle. Your foot should reach your backside. Be careful that you do not raise your pelvis.

(b) The quadriceps stretch. As you hold your foot close to your backside keep your backside tucked underneath you. Do not let your body tip forward and your back hollow. You should feel the stretch in the front of your thigh. Alternatively, do the stretch on the floor as shown in (a).

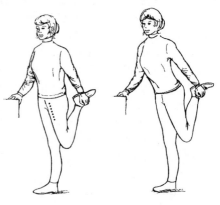

CORRECT   INCORRECT

(c) The psoas stretch. Begin by standing with feet about three feet apart. Rotate one foot through 90°, and then turn your body to face in the same direction. Now lunge forward over that foot, keeping your hips level and your back leg straight. You should feel the stretch in the groin area of your back leg.

(d) The test for normal range of movement in the psoas muscle. Your partner presses firmly on your backside to make sure that your pelvis stays down on the floor. She should be able to lift your thigh to 45°.

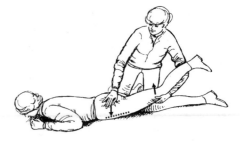

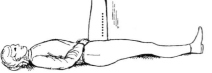

(e) The test for normal range of movement in the hamstring muscles. When lying on your back on the floor in a doorway, you should be able to get a 90° angle between your legs, bringing the whole of your calf and underside thigh against the door post.

(f) Hamstring stretch. Resting one foot on a chair or tack chest, lock that knee, and then bend the other, leaning forward slightly so that you feel the stretch in the underside of the thigh on the straight leg.

(g) Hamstring stretch. Stand with your feet about three feet apart, and angled slightly outwards. Then bring your chest down over one thigh, and grasp it. As you press your backside backwards, and attempt to straighten that leg, you should feel the stretch on the underside of that thigh. With a little practice (and with a safe horse) you can use this stretch as you pick out horses' feet.

(g) The test for normal range of movement in the adductor muscles. Sitting on the floor with your back vertical and your seat bones pointing down, you should be able to open your legs to 90°.

(i) The adductor stretch. Left, stand with your feet about three feet apart and face forward, keep your backside tucked underneath you and your legs straight, and move your pelvis to one side. You should feel the stretch on the inside of the opposite thigh. Right, lunge sideways, actually bending that knee, and feel the stretch on the inside of the opposite thigh.

Fig 9.19 More simple stretches that can be incorporated into everyday life.

(a) Stretching the calf muscles. With one foot about three feet in front of the other, and both feet facing forward, lunge over the front leg. Left, with the back leg straight you should feel the stretch just below the knee. Right, bending the back leg stretches the bottom of the calf muscles towards the ankle.

(b) Lower back stretch.

(c) Stretch for upper chest and the front of the shoulder. Standing at 90° to the wall, and with the palm of your hand flat against it, turn away from the wall slightly so that you feel a stretch over the front of your shoulder. Do this with your hand at various heights. This may need to be combined with exercise (d).

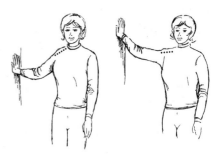

(d) A strengthening exercise for the upper back, excellent for correcting poor posture. Stand against a wall with your heels 7–15cm (3 – 6ins) away from it. Your sacrum, shoulder blades and head should be resting against the wall, with little or no gap behind your waist. If this is difficult for you, have it as your goal. Rest the backs of your hands on the wall at shoulder height, take a breath in, and exhale as you raise your arms above your head. Keep your stomach muscles tight – your aim is to keep your hands and elbows on the wall, whilst keeping your back as close to the wall as you can. Slide your hands back down the wall to shoulder height and begin again. Repeat the exercise 6 to 8 times, and if you are finding this easy, rotate your palms to face outwards.

that the ultimate limitation on your skill as a rider almost always lies in your 'use', and this brings us back full circle to the 'wheel balance' offered by bodywork systems like the Alexander Technique, or the Feldenkrais Method (see Chapter 8). To these we have now added some exercises in perception, and in directing energy; some alignment exercises, coordination building exercises, isometric strengthening exercises, and stretching exercises. Together with riding, these can form a practice which brings your whole bodymind system into balance. Or, they can be used to throw it even more out of true – for 'it's not what you do, but the way that you do it'. You may well benefit from strengthening or lengthening your muscles, especially if you are either out of shape, or are an extremely avid rider; but I still maintain that the most far-reaching improvements will almost certainly come from changes in your *perception*.

Stress, worry and anxiety

NATURAL COMPETITORS have a very positive response to stress. For them it becomes 'eustress', the extra challenge needed to bring out the best in them. It makes them find that extra bit of commitment and effort, focusing their attention better than they do in the everyday situation of training. Instead of being too laid back to perform well, they become what sports psychologists call 'psychologically activated', showing an activation pattern which is ideally suited to the task in hand. It is as if the rigour of the competitive situation hones the chemistry and the output of their bodymind system, creating an optimum state for good performance. But for most of us, the challenge of competing lies in stopping ourselves from falling apart; in contrast, we need to gain mastery over our bodymind chemistry and the focus of our attention.

Think back to the Aikido energy exercise of the last chapter, in which you 'keep one point': typically, you lose your stability when you think about someone you do not like, and when you think about a hierarchy of increasingly demanding competitions. One rider who has competed internationally in dressage remained strong through the thought of her national championships, was unperturbed by the European Championships and the World Championships, and then completely fell apart at the thought of the Olympics in Sydney in the year 2000! As soon as this happens (and especially if the thought of the local riding club show is enough to send you haywire) your task is to learn to control your 'energy body', and to stay grounded. You can put your faith in rituals – as so many competitors do – but relying on your pink socks or your lucky teddy to keep you out of harm is not half so effective as relying on your own ability to 'tune' your system. Adjusting this requires a very subtle kind of learning, and virtually everyone who needs it wishes they did not; but it means that if you win at the end of the day, you have actually won far more.

To understand how sports psychologists think about this, we need to define our terms very clearly. They define stress as 'a perceived phenomenon arising from a comparison between the demands on the person and his/her ability to cope'. Note the use of the word 'perceived': this implies that whether the person *thinks* she can cope is much more important than whether she *actually* can cope. Anxiety is then defined as 'feelings of worry and insecurity arising as a direct result of the perceived inability to cope with the situation'. So the eustress which can promote an ideal activation pattern for one person becomes threatening for another, turning feelings of stimulation and confidence into anxiety.

The concept of anxiety can be further broken down: one's underlying predisposition to be anxious is known as 'trait anxiety', i.e. it is a character trait, which is stable and consistent, enduring over time (although, as a psychotherapist, I do believe this can be changed to a significant degree). When anxiety is a short-term mood of an individual and specifically related to a certain event it is known as 'state anxiety'. So people with high trait anxiety are also likely to have high state anxiety in a competitive situation, for they are more likely to doubt their ability. However, the competition might trigger very little state anxiety for someone whose trait anxiety was low; so she would have a lower and more consistent anxiety level throughout training sessions, competition, and quiet work at home. This is shown graphically in Fig. 10.1, which plots state anxiety against the increasing challenges of practice and competition, also showing how this is influenced by high and low trait anxiety.

To give you an example of this in practice, let me tell you the story of one of my student teachers who was unceremoniously bucked off her very stroppy horse during a teacher training course. He had done this to her a number of times, and bucking was only part of his repertoire of naughty tricks (which might, of course, have been pain-induced, although in this case I suspected not). He had really undermined her confidence; she had become tentative in her riding, and wary of him. So there was

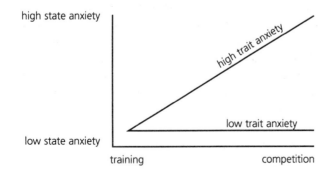

Fig. 10.1 Trait and state anxiety: the person with low trait anxiety will usually have low state anxiety in competition. But when trait anxiety is high, state anxiety is likely to be high as well.

indeed a discrepancy between the demand placed on her and her perceived ability to cope, and this stress was causing anxiety. She is, in fact, someone with quite high trait anxiety, and she had become worried about riding him before she ever got into the saddle. This particular buck was, however, the last straw, for as she emerged from the sand shocked and bruised, she pulled herself together enough to say, 'That's it! I've had it with him. Anyone want to buy this horrible bay gelding?'

Another student teacher was dying to get on. 'I can't say I want him,' he said, 'but would you like me to ride him for you?' If we had given him the Aikido stability test just before he mounted I bet he would have passed it (whilst the horse's owner would almost certainly have keeled over). As soon as he landed in the saddle, he began a phenomenal display of riding – infinitely better than he had shown throughout the rest of the course. For the challenge he was facing was worthy of his talents, and the added stress of riding this difficult horse stimulated, for him, an ideal activation pattern, creating eustress. To not really concentrate and not really 'go for it' was tempting on the other horses: but not on this one.

Worry is the mental or cognitive aspect of anxiety, and it operates on a very different timescale from its somatic aspect. Athletes often begin to worry about a competition some time before it happens, and for up to two or three weeks beforehand they can be thinking about the possibility of doing badly and of failing (in whatever way they define that term). Whilst the mental side of anxiety begins early, and often remains fairly

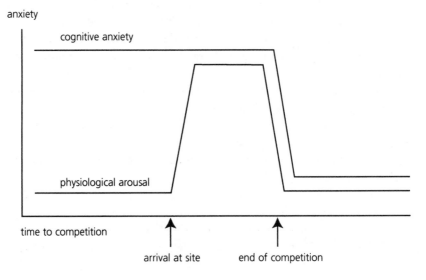

Fig. 10.2 The relationship between cognitive anxiety and physiological arousal in the build-up to and throughout a competition. Physiological symptoms usually peak on arrival and throughout preparation, stabilise as the competition begins, and drop right off as it ends.

constant throughout the lead-up to the competition, the obvious symptoms of *physiological* arousal usually begin when one comes face to face with the 'enemy'. Triggered by changes in brain chemistry, and particular by the hormone adrenalin, the 'fight or flight' reflex kicks in, and the body changes gear very fast. The physical symptoms of this are increased heart rate, sweating, and the need for the toilet. Disturbing as these symptoms are, they do have their uses: the thumping heart is directing more oxygen to the muscles, preparing them for action. Increased sweat reduces the probability of the skin tearing, and an empty bladder reduces body weight, enabling you to run faster (assuming, of course, that you do not get caught with your trousers down!).

In most people, worry before a competition catalyses a desire to try and train harder, in a desperate bid to make up for their perceived inadequacies. But for riders in particular, this attempt to solve the problem very often *becomes* the problem; for the last thing the horse needs is to become jaded, or even soured by his work just when you want him to be inspired and at his peak. I know a number of top-class riders who have surprised themselves by performing exceptionally well in a big competition which was held just after they had been away teaching clinics. Their absence protected them from the trap of over-training; but it did more than that, for their break left them more interested and more curious, stimulating the pure perception of a 'beginner's mind'. They came to their work afresh, knowing that they could not expect themselves to be at their best. What they failed to realise was that with their expectations lower and their awareness higher, they had a winner's mind-set.

Kyra Kyrklund tells the story of riding her horse Matador in the weeks leading up to the 1990 World Equestrian Games in Stockholm. She was living in Helsinki, working with a friend who was also competing, and sharing jokes about 'that riding club show in Stockholm'. Matador had been a highly respected dressage competitor, but following the Seoul Olympics in which he was fifth, he had suffered a serious colic. Following his surgery many people had written him off, so she knew that the expectations of the world in general were low. When her horse finally regained his strength and agility, she felt that she had been given the gift of more time with him. She was feeling at peace with herself and the world, and each day's riding was a celebration of this; she worked him in a large sand area, and did not even bother to mark out an arena.

When she arrived at the games, she kept herself to herself, and did not watch any of the other riders working – so she did not let anything undermine her state. She had the ride of her life to take the silver medal, and she looks back on that time with nostalgia; for it is all but impossible to repeat the special blend of circumstances which could generate such a centred, easy-going attitude.

Anxiety — although you feel it in the present — is actually about the *future:* about what might happen, what could happen, and what probably will happen if you persist in imagining it fervently enough! But as soon as you start your cross-country round the present moment becomes so demanding that you have no time to pontificate about the future: this means that it is often mothers and owners who suffer the worst nerves on the day of a competition, for they do not face the here-and-now ultimatum which enables them to trade anxiety for action.

This state of physiological arousal is also accompanied by psychological arousal, often defined by psychologists as 'the readiness of an organism to respond': it is the activation pattern we talked about earlier, which hones performance as long as it does not go over the threshold where you consider yourself unequal to the demands of the situation. Then, appropriate activation gives way to anxiety. Arousal is very much an umbrella term, with its implication that all the systems of the body are stimulated. But this is not always the case, for people who are extremely anxious can become listless and without energy, and each individual's response is idiosyncratic.

Muscle tone, for instance, should, in theory, increase with increasing anxiety, but mine decreases — and where others turn to wood I turn to jelly. We are all unique in our patterns of response, and it is much more helpful to recognise that each individual has her own optimum pattern for peak performance, and her own idiosyncratic way of losing it under stress. Dr Lew Hardy and Dr John Fazey, two of the foremost sport psychologists in the UK, draw an analogy between the human body and the amplifier on your stereo system. If the bodymind were a one-dimensional system, it would be like a simple amplifier with just one knob to control the volume, so an increase in stress would increase output as a whole, without there being variations, say, in the base or the treble. But the relationship between physiological arousal, pattern activation, and anxiety is multi-dimensional, and extremely complex. The bodymind system is more like an amplifier with many knobs, allowing you to fine-tune the system so that you can get the perfect adjustment for playing your favourite piece of music. It is a sophisticated (and in our analogy an expensive) piece of equipment.

....

Drive theory, the inverted U and catastrophe theory

In the 1940s and 50s 'drive theory' became one of the most influential theories of motivation in psychology, and it predicted that performance should increase as arousal, or drive, increased. (See Fig. 10.3.) But in practice, there is not a simple linear relationship between them, especially in sports. Instead, the performance of each individual's *most dominant*

performance

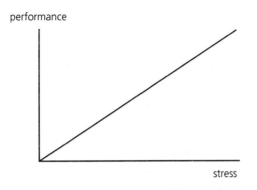

stress

Fig. 10.3 Drive theory suggests that as stress increases so does performance.

response increases with increased arousal – so only if this is the correct response will performance be improved. So in the stress of competition your old habits come back to haunt you, and your riding could regress three months. Perhaps you revert to fiddling the horse's head down, or pulling on the inside rein; for the 'new, improved you' has not yet performed the ten thousand repetitions needed for the new patterns to become automatic, and the dominant response. But your reaction to competition stress could be even more extreme, and I have heard a number of top-class riders say that the stress of their first international competition caused them to lose access to about *fifty per cent* of their ability.

After drive theory, with its obvious limitations, came 'the inverted-U theory' (see Fig. 10.4). This predicted that a certain degree of arousal would promote peak performance, with a decline in the individual's performance when arousal was either increased or decreased from this level. So too little arousal leaves the performer too apathetic to give her best: too much makes her anxious and tense. Our individual brain

performance

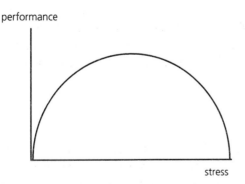

stress

Fig. 10.4 The inverted 'U' relationship between stress and performance suggests that increasing stress beyond a certain point can be detrimental to performance.

chemistry is so different that each person's optimum can occur in different situations – like my two students above. One needed to know she was safe before she could produce her best, whilst the other needed the challenge of a bucking bronco.

People with high arousal thresholds seek dangerous, exciting sports, and prefer gross body movements to fine motor skills. They become bored more quickly with repetitive tasks, and feel that they are being deprived of sensation. In contrast, having a low arousal threshold means that you can easily become chronically over-aroused, and are instinctively likely to avoid situations which might become too stimulating. But you are better at fine motor skills, and find challenge in the constant, repetitive practice which is needed to ingrain them. Your attentiveness means that you are likely to react more quickly and consistently, but you are also likely to be far more aware of risk.

This difference accounts, at least in part, for the difference between riders who are attracted to eventing, and those who ride dressage. This difference between people is often classified by sports psychologists according to the terms *extroversion* and *introversion*. If your place on the extrovert/introvert continuum is not obvious to you, ask yourself the question, 'When you want to recharge your batteries, would you rather be alone or with people?' Since I would choose to be alone, this puts me firmly in the class of the introvert, despite the fact that I love to give lecture-demonstrations, presenting my work to large audiences. But this would terrify many others, who think nothing of jumping the huge cross-country fences which terrify me! The ideal setting of our 'amplifier' does not remain constant in the face of different challenges.

The extrovert/introvert difference relates as well to the preference for an internal or an external focus of attention: faced with a large audience, I keep my attention focused *externally*, monitoring their reaction to my words – which I trust to come out of my mouth on automatic pilot. But in front of a big fence, I find it hard to trust my body's reactions, and to maintain that external focus of attention.

Kate, the Australian event rider who exclaimed that I had 'just spoilt riding for her' (see page 183), had a great reluctance to focus her attention internally, even though her flatwork improved very quickly by doing so. She wanted to ride instinctively, with an external focus of attention, as she had done with such great success across country, and she wanted to pay attention to *wholes*, rather than to *parts*. She wanted to be out of the TOTE, not in it – a performer and not a learner. But since the secrets of dressage riding had not revealed themselves to her as a whole, she had no choice (if she wanted to improve) but to deal with the nitty-gritty, focusing her attention internally, practising the small pieces. She had to suffer through the extrovert's nightmare (and the introvert's forte) – the ten thousand repetitions needed before each new pattern could become instinctive to her.

The performer who thrives in challenging situations has developed her resilience by matching skills with challenges as the stakes have become progressively higher. I can remember being horribly nervous before my first public speaking engagement – a talk to about twenty people gathered in a village hall. Now it takes at least two hundred to get my engine purring nicely! I often wonder if Mark Todd, who must have one of the highest arousal thresholds of anyone, *needs* to be approaching the Vicarage Vee (one of the most terrifying fences on the Badminton three-day event course) in order to reach an arousal level which makes him function optimally. But even this is not enough; for he achieves an even more impressive performance when he is facing the challenge on a horse he has never ridden before!

The inverted-U hypothesis also has its limitations. For when somebody goes 'over the top' their performance decreases very rapidly, and the curve should not be symmetrical. But in actual fact, it should not be a curve at all, for this implies that you could travel *backwards* on it, and that lowering the performer's stress level would enable her to return to peak performance. In real life this does not happen, and the latest update on the inverted U is 'catastrophe theory', which takes account of the huge amount of backtracking that is needed before you can return to your original level of performance.

The idea, proposed by Dr Lew Hardy and Dr John Fazey, is borrowed from the French mathematician René Thom, whose theory shows the way that changing forces interact to produce sudden, drastic changes. The two opposing forces in our case are *the desire to compete and succeed*, and *the fear of losing*. Each individual has these to different degrees – and within each of us they will be intensified in the competitive situations which are perceived as most stressful. So whilst each person has their likely profile, no two performance curves will ever be exactly the same. The equivalent dynamic is present in the frightened rider, whose *desire to ride* and whose *fear of falling* are also two changing forces.

Bold riders can rarely understand how the nervous rider is caught between these two cohabiting forces – they expect her to ride and be brave, or not to ride at all. We make the same mistake of expecting one dimensionality when we assume that the self-confidence of the best performers should banish all worry. This is not necessarily true; for a rider can believe that she has the ability to do well, that she and her horse are well prepared, and that her activation system will function well in the competition situation. Her desire to compete and succeed may be increased by this (strengthening one of the forces), but the consequences of the upcoming event may still worry her. They might perhaps worry her *even more* because she knows she is in with a chance, because she has a reputation to live up to, or because she is a team member determined to do her best for her club or her country. This increases her fear of losing, making her simultaneously anxious and self-confident, so that the two conflicting forces are even more intense.

The catastrophe curve (see Fig. 10.5a) shows that at lower levels of stress performance increases up to a certain threshold, where the performer perceives a mismatch between the demands of the situation and her ability to match them. This is 'the straw which broke the camel's back', and with the onset of anxiety, performance suddenly drops. Mathematically, there is a discontinuity in the curve: it is as if the performer falls off the end of it, landing at a much lower performance level. If her stress level is then significantly lowered, her performance improves slightly, and this may enable her to jump back up onto the original curve, for the two are now much closer together. Regaining the original performance level is indeed much more difficult in real life than was implied by the theory of the inverted U, and catastrophe theory gives us a much more realistic explanation of the vagaries of human experience. It also allows for the differences between people (see Fig. 10.5b).

Person A is capable of a higher performance than person B, but when she 'falls off the edge' she falls further. Although more talented, she is more prone to anxiety, and more inconsistent: she comes closer, perhaps, to being one of those creative geniuses who live on the edge of 'normality'. Person B is much more stable, but she lacks the flair of person A.

It is their tendency to worry about what *might* happen which accounts for much of the difference between them when they are both in the same state of physiological arousal. If worry were not a factor we could draw a shape much closer to the inverted U, and an increase in physiological arousal then has much less effect on performance. But as anxiety increases, it creates that devastating discontinuity: the sudden drop to a much lower level of performance.

....

Nerves and mental rehearsal

The distortion produced by excessive physiological arousal is most apparent in skills requiring fine control and balance – so riders, and especially dressage riders, are particularly vulnerable. But if the performer realises that she is 'off', and she attempts to make random adjustments to her 'amplifier', she may distort her performance even more! This is where you need to know yourself well, and to know how both you and your horse respond to the competitive situation. Just to sit down and relax, for instance, may not be the answer, for in many people this either does not

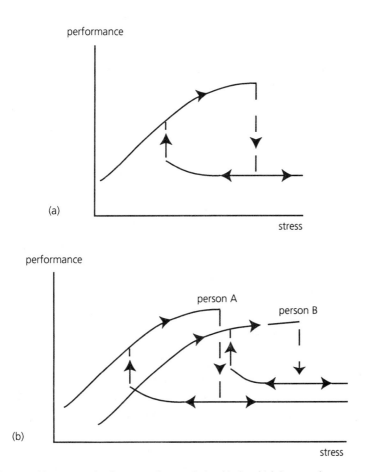

Fig. 10.5 (a) Catastrophe theory predicts a relationship in which increased stress can suddenly reduce performance, requiring a large reduction in stress before the original skills can be refound. (b) Shows two different performers: person A performs better than person B, but is mentally less stable. A lower level of stress causes her performance to drop, and it drops to a lower level than person B's.

work (essentially because they do not know how to do it), or it works so well that it quietens down all systems, when only some need to be deactivated. If you then try to perform from this state, you may give much less than your best.

Sports psychologists used to be intent on finding relaxation techniques which made the performer's nerves go away: they were considered a bad thing, which interfered with performance. But now, they are understood as a necessary part of the 'tuning' needed during an exceptional event, and the most important point is not how nervous a competitor becomes, but the *meaning* which she attaches to these changes in her body. If they undermine her confidence and make her anxious, their effects can become negative. If she simply acknowledges them, knowing, 'This is my body getting ready to give of its best,' then they can make her feel even more secure. For the paradox is that if she does not feel nervous, she is probably not finely enough tuned to produce her best performance.

The British Olympic hurdler David Hemery tells the story of the Munich Olympics, which followed the Mexico Olympics in which he had won the gold medal in the four hundred metres hurdle. Four years on, he knew that he was older than his best rivals, and possibly past his peak. He kept telling himself in preparation that he might not make it this time, and that he should be prepared for this. He thought he was being realistic and mature, and only on the day of the competition did he realise that he had actually been priming himself to fail.

As he prepared for the race he found himself in 'a bad dream of no nerves', and he dug his fingernails into the palms of his hands to try to wake himself up and make himself feel *something*. In the event, he took the bronze medal; but he felt that he could have won the silver if he had done more positive mental rehearsals, and had been psychologically activated and ready to run.

Some people suggest that your mental rehearsal should simply consist of seeing yourself collecting the first rosette. This undoubtedly has its value – and it might have saved David Hemery from his self-imposed plight; but a more detailed mental rehearsal of actual performance is an even more useful way to allay your fears. (I have written more extensively about this in *Ride With Your Mind/The Natural Rider*, and if you are not familiar with mental rehearsal, it would be worth looking at this.) Mental rehearsal can stop you from 'over-cooking' your horse in the build-up to a big competition, for it gives you the practice which you need and he does not (and it also gives you the security which that extra practice brings). It is an extremely valuable tool in learning, for you can clock up some of your ten thousand repetitions by doing them mentally, and can cut down the hours in the saddle which are needed to ingrain a new skill. Since the brain cannot tell the difference between real and imagined performance, it still sends nerve impulses to your muscles which result in a measurable (if invisible) contraction. You can even imagine making the corrections you are currently working on during your upcoming ride, for the more specific you can be, the more you will benefit from the practice.

When you arrive at a competition, check how the dressage arena is positioned, so that you can place it in context and not practice going the wrong way up the centre line! Once you have walked a jumping course, you know exactly what challenges the course builder has set, and you know exactly what you need to rehearse; but in your build-up to the competition at home, you can practise your best performance to date over spreads, uprights, corners, and those tricky combinations. Fill in as many details as you can – and realise that the amount of detail you can produce within your rehearsal tells you how much information your brain actually has about how to ride.

You cannot lose by doing mental rehearsal, and on the day of the competition, it is one of the best possible ways to help you find the ideal activation pattern. It can calm you down or rev you up according to how you do it – and if you need to, you can run around on your feet, simulating walk, trot, and canter in an area you have defined as your riding arena. (People may laugh, but you will not be the first to make such a fool of yourself. At least one top-level international dressage competitor does this regularly!)

If, in contrast, you allow your imagined ride to become some idealised fantasy, or some kind of short-cut which erases parts of your experience, you will not do yourself justice. A quick run through the test to check that you know where you are going is not a mental rehearsal: if you want to hone your physiology so that you can reproduce your own personal best, you must be realistic in the way you practise it.

Time your rehearsal, making it last as long as your test or your jumping round will actually take. How will you react when your horse tries to accelerate on the long side, when he falls out on the right rein circles, or when you have to prepare for the canter/trot transition? How will you line him up for that big spread on the top of the hill? At what point will you begin to set up the canter? Experiment with different options, and leave nothing to chance. When you enter the arena, you should feel that you have been there many times before.

....

Increasing your symptoms

A few butterflies on the day of the competition (probably the ideal symptom) present a different problem to feeling that your body is completely out of control. If you have such a low arousal threshold (and/or so little experience at this particular level of competition) that your knees are shaking, your palms are sweating, and there seems no end to your dashes to the toilet, then you could use some more first aid. Strange as it may seem, an attempt to *increase* your symptoms can be much more effective than trying to ignore them, or trying to make them go away through relaxation. For example, if you can make your knees knock even more, you have at least proved to yourself that you are *not* out of control – and if your knees will *not* knock more on command then the worst has already happened. But if, as so often happens, the attempt to increase the symptom actually makes them knock *less,* then you are already ahead of the game.

We all know that trying to go to sleep is almost guaranteed to keep you awake; but fewer people have discovered that trying to stay awake is a remarkably effective way of sending yourself to sleep! This is often called *paradoxical intention*, and it is equally paradoxical that trying to stay calm is highly likely to make you anxious; but trying to exaggerate the symptoms of anxiety is just as likely to have a calming effect. Simply noticing, out of ten, how intense your symptoms are will often reduce them. For in doing so you face your demon. You name it, and no gremlin likes to be named.

There is a very well-known story, retold again and again to psychotherapists in training, of the famous hypnotherapist Milton Erickson, whose skill and innovation made him a legend in his own lifetime. One of his clients was a concert pianist, who had fainted at the beginning of a large performance and was terrified of going on stage again. But he agreed to Milton's suggestion that he should set up a small performance in front of friends, placing a number of folded towels along the front of the stage. Then, when he came out to take his bow, he had to decide which one he was going to faint on.

Contemplating this choice brought some control into a previously unconscious chain of events, and it altered his relationship to his symptoms: for his concern became not *whether* he would faint, but *where* he should faint! This changed his perspective enough that the tactic actually worked, and he was able to resume his prestigious career. So you might change your relationship to your nerves by wondering when to get nervous, as if you were asking yourself, 'Shall I clean my tack now, or shall I leave it 'til later?' You could also wonder where to get nervous ('Shall I wait until I get into the start box?') or how to get nervous ('Would it be better to get really sweaty, or shall I just have butterflies?').

There is value in any approach which stops you from feeling victimised by your symptoms, and which gives you a more positive relationship to them. But the ultimate realisation is that to be nerve-less is the kiss of death.

....

Bad memories and good breathing patterns

The way you breathe has a profound effect on your physiology and your activation pattern, and thus it provides another tool which you can use to enhance your performance. To demonstrate this to yourself you might like to do the following exercise, which I learned from the American teacher and psychotherapist John Grinder. You need a partner, and the memory of two experiences, one in which you performed at your optimum, and another which did not go as well as you would have liked. Sit in a chair, close your eyes, and remember the bad experience. Replay it in your head as if it were happening now. What are you seeing, feeling, and hearing? Who is there, and what are the conditions like? Are you talking to yourself, or listening to the sounds of the outside world? Are you using

*Fig. 10.6 Breathing exercise.
Your partner stands behind and
to the side of you, with her
hands on your shoulders so
that she can easily mirror your
breathing pattern.*

your focused or peripheral vision? What is happening between you and your horse? As you recall this experience, your partner is to place her hands on your shoulders, standing behind and to the side of you so that she can both see and feel how your shoulders, chest, and stomach move as you breathe. (See Fig. 10.6.) She is to learn your breathing pattern, and the easiest way for her to do this is to mirror it herself.

Once you have a full, clear internal experience, and your partner has learned the pattern of your breathing, open your eyes, and shake yourself so that you come fully out of that memory. Then begin again, this time with your optimal experience. In your mind, be there totally, and involve all of your senses. Again, your partner is to learn (and mirror) your breathing pattern, and once both of you have achieved this she is to ask you to *keep your breathing pattern the same* as you return to the first memory. Since she is mirroring your breathing and has her hands on your shoulders, she will notice the instant your breathing begins to change, and she can quietly remind you to maintain the pattern. Meanwhile, you are to discover what happens inside your brain when you are faced with the demand of producing the *bad* memory alongside the *good* breathing pattern.

It is really worth taking the time to do this, for only when you experience the impossibility of combining the two do you truly understand how breathing underpins your state. For you will discover that you cannot get back to the first memory unless you change your breathing pattern.

This exercise has provided a powerful lesson for many of the people who have done it in my workshops, and it demonstrates how dependent our 'tuning' is on apparently minute adjustments – regardless of whether we are in real-life situations or performing in mental rehearsal. If changing our breathing pattern has the power to completely change the state we are in, it is a tremendously important tool which we can use to our advantage – whether our nerves relate specifically to competition (i.e. they accompany state anxiety), or more generally to riding (i.e. they accompany trait anxiety).

Think of it this way: it is as if the horse and rider have between them one television screen. The picture on the screen is determined by which of them projects their mental rehearsals (or their 'what ifs') more strongly. Let us suppose that the horse is running a horror movie about phantoms which lurk in the shadows. You are running your own movie about riding him forward and keeping him straight. If he can subvert your experience so effectively that you join him in his horror movie, it is as if he has control of the channel changer. Your aim is to keep the channel changer yourself – to produce positive mental rehearsals instead of negative 'what ifs', and to get him to join you. Should the horse succeed in getting you to join him, the ultimate irony is that he does not know that you are actually frightened of him (or in the competitive situation that you are frightened of doing badly). He thinks that you genuinely *are* frightened of phantoms, and so this is all the more reason for him to be frightened too!

When riders start to 'wobble' inside I often suggest that they think of bearing down like a fog horn – as if they would emit a low continuous sound, instead of a higher, more tremulous one. Some people feel as if the 'wobble' makes their energy system flicker like one of those dying fluorescent lights – so they need to bear down like a search light, and take time with the Aikido energy exercises of page 240.

Another important calming technique comes from John Douillard's book *Body Mind Sport*. Instead of increasing the power of your bear down by using the sounds 'grrrr' or pssst' (as I have always done) he suggests another method in which you breathe out through your nose whilst constricting your throat as if you were snoring lightly. This produces a low growl in the upper throat, and you feel a constriction there. Contrast it to normal breathing, in which you feel the air come out through your nostrils; when you constrict your throat you no longer feel this happening (although in reality it is). By analogy to the sound made by the Star Wars character Darth Vader, Douillard calls the technique 'Darth Vader breathing'. It makes you bear down particularly strongly just at the level where you get butterflies. Since it is impossible to bear down and have butterflies both at the same time, it banishes them.

In the ultimate 'wobble', the rider falls prey to the 'foetal crouch' (the frozen, curled-up posture of the body which cannot fight and cannot flee). Instead of bearing down, she sucks her stomach in and her energy sphere recoils completely. The rider who is caught in the foetal crouch cannot conceive of life-after-the-trauma – it has threatened her continuing sense of 'me'. She is responding like an amoeba, which recoils if you prick it with a pin, and has no sense of itself as causal rather than reactive. In contrast, my student teacher who was so keen to ride the bucking horse perceived each buck as a temporary blip and not as the end of the world. They did not threaten his sense of 'me', and it is this continuing sense of self and of time which enabled him to ride so effectively.

This is perhaps the most pertinent difference between riders who are bold and those who are nervous; for once the horse threatens your continuing sense of 'me' you are in trouble. The nervous rider might be running mental rehearsals of dire outcomes – especially if she has experienced a bad fall, or been run away with. But more often her 'what if' mental rehearsals actually end with her mental screen blacking out; so effectively, *they herald the end of time.* This makes it perfectly reasonable for her to be scared, and it explains why nervous riders often ride with more confidence after they have fallen off. For they then discover that they actually hit the ground instead of falling into a never-ending black hole. (Psychoanalysts call this the 'existential abyss', and would suggest that the rider with high trait anxiety fell into it often as a baby, perhaps when her cries for help went unheeded.)

The rider who has fallen off discovers that her sense of 'me' is still intact (despite her bruises), and this is a 'reality check' which reminds her how the world actually works. It keeps her mind in the here-and-now, and it helps her to ride more boldly, for she is then not hampered by the 'wobble'. This is often fostered by fears which *do not even belong in this situation.* Many of them have their roots in history (in previous visits to the 'existential abyss') and one could even say that riding can be like a 'coat hanger' on which those fears like to hang themselves.

Interestingly, one of the ways not to invoke those fears is to do something *so* dangerous that you do not have enough leeway to indulge in flights of fantasy. Thus some riders are more bold over bigger fences than small ones, and ride better over solid obstacles than show jumps. Event riders are much more likely to have this characteristic than show jumpers, who rightfully feel safer when the fences fall down! Since those unfinished mental rehearsals are a large part of the problem, one of the rider's most helpful tactics (both on and off horse) is to make sure that she completes them, taking them through to a positive outcome (her horse shies but she stays on; he bucks and she rides him forward). This may seem optimistic, but it actually has more realism than rehearsals which leave you dangling in that eternal black hole.

One of my pupils is an event rider who trains many young and difficult horses, and she finds it useful to ride potentially dangerous horses with an attitude of 'OK, horse, what's the worst you can do? Come on, show me your worst trick. Is that it? Is that?' This keeps her one step ahead of the game; her mind processes well, and she never falls prey to the trap of passively waiting for the worst. For when all systems go into 'shut down' the rider can at best just cling on. Here, as in any lesser manifestation of fear, the fear is maintained by those unfinished (or negative) mental rehearsals, and by the posture, the breathing pattern, and the energy pattern of withdrawing instead of 'going for it'. Change that, and you are no longer frightened, so if you can somehow persuade yourself to 'bite the bullet' you exchange anxiety for action, and you banish it.

I had a fascinating experience recently, riding a stallion who − when I first got on − was far more interested in the local talent than he was in me. As I found myself feeling rather nervous it occurred to me that I did not want the people watching to perceive me as tentative and insecure. Through my mind passed the words, 'It's as if I think I'm a china doll, and I'm worried I might break.' In that instant, I felt a release of tension in my diaphragm, and my nervousness vanished. I went on to ride the horse quite well, and I certainly got his attention. On the few times that my nerves returned, I reminded myself of the china doll. It has proved a useful tactic on several occasions since, adding credence to my belief that the body very often holds its fear in the diaphragm; thus you see the *effects* of this tension, but you do cannot see it directly. Those words that popped into my mind were a gift, and were (as we said in Chapter 6) just the right trigger for me, prompting the release of a tension which I must have been carrying for years.

Kate tells a story which demonstrates how unshakable she was from her mental rehearsals of riding well, and how her performance was improved by them − despite the fact that they were stimulated by the kind of 'psyche out' which might have been the downfall of a less steely-nerved rider. (Kate was the type of event rider with such a high arousal threshold that she could happily eat a steak sandwich far too close for her own good to the start of her cross-country ride!) Gawler three-day event was the setting for the final team trial before the Mexico Olympics, and she was the only woman in contention for a place on the team − at a time when it had previously been an all male affair. One of her arch rivals had asked her how she planned to tackle the most difficult combination: her answer was 'Straight through the middle.' Again and again he warned her against it, pointing out the difficulties of the striding, and the dangers involved. She knew exactly how he was trying to undermine her confidence, and this made her all the more determined. Each time as she responded, 'You're not going to put me off, you know, I'm going straight down the middle,' she became more and more angry, and more and more determined.

The human brain is designed in a way which made it virtually impossible for Kate to say those words without doing a mental rehearsal of them (whether or not she was aware that she was doing so). His descriptions never tempted her to run mental rehearsals of his 'worst case' scenario – although this would inevitably have accompanied his own rendering of the scene. In effect, Kate kept the channel changer, and in the event, she rode the fastest clear round of the day and was one of two riders who went faultlessly through the middle of the combination. The extra rehearsal and the absolute determination to prove him wrong gave her the ride of her life (but although she was second overall she was not selected for the team). Her rival did not attempt the combination – an extremely wise decision – for the chances of him living out his own prophecy would have been extremely high!

....

Spook-proof, bomb-proof and nerve-proof

The practical aspects of competition riding only add to its rigour, for if you arrive late, or if the weather turns against you, these obstacles to good performance can be far more significant than the obstacles you find in the riding arena. You are both flustered and soaking wet, and you have misjudged your warm-up time. The warm-up arena is horribly crowded, and your horse is intimidated when others come too close. The last time you came here he saw an imagined phantom behind the judge's box, and although you have prepared for that, you were not expecting the plastic flowers around the arena, which you know are going to blow his mind. The stakes are getting higher all the time; can you stay in the flow channel and respond to greater challenges with greater skills? Or will you fall off the edge of the catastrophe curve?

If you are late, of course, you only have yourself to blame (although blaming yourself at this point in time can only detract from the more helpful ways in which you could use your energy). At the lower levels, competitions are often held in less-than-ideal venues; but even at the top of the tree there will very often be something to distract you – and even with the best of preparation you can never control everything. One international competitor was telling me recently how common it is in Continental Europe to have about fifteen stallions all warming up together in a twenty by forty metre indoor school – and some of those are jumping!

One pupil of mine reached the height of her career by riding in the final team selection trials for the 1995 Pan Am Games; of her four tests, one was held in a hurricane with the arena literally blowing down around her, and another in the beginnings of a tornado. Some competitors at the World Equestrian Games in the Hague were held up on their way from the stables to the warm-up arena – and when they finally arrived there they found a bulldozer at one end, still moving and levelling the surface.

These are 'kill or cure' conditions, in which you either buckle under the strain, or find extra reserves of strength and skill which you did not know you had. But there will of course be times when circumstances conspire for you rather than against you, and fate chooses *you* to be the recipient of her helping hand. The rain clears up just before you mount, and the dressage is running late, giving you just the time you need. The rail you hit does not fall down, and the going suits your horse perfectly.

But instead of wishing and hoping for the improbable, you can mitigate the effects of the usual competition traumas by simulating them at home. Those who have the wherewithal to choose are often tempted to do their training in ideal circumstances; no one is allowed in the riding arena, there is a hushed silence, and all possible spooks are eliminated. But this insistence on perfection is very short-sighted: it may solve a short-term problem but it creates a long-term one – and it suggests that the rider has her self-image bound up with how well she performs. She is running away from the demons which might blight her performance: but when would she rather meet them – at home in the peace and solitude of her own environment, or out in the public gaze?

One friend of mine tells the story of a big international competition, where a well-known photographer clicked his shutter at just the wrong moment and spooked her horse during a test. She knew that compassion was not his strong point, and that he was unlikely to spare her the following day; so she asked a friend to take the film out of his (the friend's) camera, and to run around the edge of the warm-up arena, clicking as he went. Risking the quality of her warm-up was a brave thing to do before such an important test – but this was her insurance policy. Each of us decides how 'precious' we will be within our own home environment, and how wrong things have to go in the big wide world before we 'take out an insurance policy' instead of hoping for the best.

Cameras, spectators, and difficult conditions are easily blamed for our misfortunes – especially if we indulge in the illusion that everyone else is spook-proof, bomb-proof, and nerve-proof. But we never are the only nervous competitor, riding the only excitable horse; and if we are less experienced than other competitors, then we are only less experienced, not worse.

Despite our conviction that our every move is being watched, the spectators and the other competitors did not come specifically to scrutinise us (unless, of course, our family and friends have turned out in force – in which case they are on our side). The judge, demonic though she may appear, is longing to see a horse ridden really well, and to give some high marks – and if you do mess up, she will not throw rotten tomatoes. Our fears are hugely exaggerated, and based on the need to defend our ego. But even if you got bucked off in the dressage arena, your horse stopped for a pee during the test, or you had the most miserable ride of your life, you would not make history.

Many riders blame their bad rides on the sudden character change which overcame their horse on the day. But if you are well prepared this is unlikely to happen; and if it does, the trick lies in changing your tactics so that you *ride the horse you are sitting on today, not the one you sat on yesterday.* As we said on page 69, the horses who do this are usually extremely adept at 'doing their thing whilst pretending to do your thing', and in their work at home, they may well have you conned. The moral of the story is that the horse needs to be doing your thing at home. If he chooses his speed, chooses his track, and chooses his frame, and he does this with his ears pricked, looking at the view, then he is most definitely doing 'his thing' (however sweetly he does it) – and 'sight-seeing' will have an even greater attraction in the competition environment. He may not, however, do it so benignly when he really is a tourist.

With all the best will in the world, you can never perform better than your worst detail, and if your basic trot work can only be marked as a six, you cannot hope or expect to score any higher than six in any of the trot movements. If you practise only the work you are good at when you ride at home, and you show off to your friends, your worst detail will never improve. But if you use the opposite tactic and focus completely on the work which most stresses your horse, you could easily force the issue so much that you make him hate it. A balance has to be found, and it is your *attention to detail* in the basic work at home (the stringency of the tests which you set yourself within the TOTE model – see page 181) which determines the upper limit on your performance in competition.

....

Finding flow

Even if you easily keep your mind on the job, your butterflies do not diminish your skill level, and your horse has not undergone a major character transformation, you may still not be competition-proof. For many riders feel undermined by the sight of the other competitors who (as we look through our particular pair of not-so-rose-coloured glasses) can all appear to have more expensive, better trained horses. If this prompts you to change your riding, making a last-minute bid to match their standards, you are – at best – likely to leave your horse doing the equine equivalent of thinking 'What's all this? What's going on here? This isn't what we usually do.'

If your right shoulder-in is only worthy of a six at home, it is not suddenly going to become an eight just because you ride it harder during your warm-up. In fact, you are more likely to take your score *down,* by overworking the horse and compounding evasions. When you can work-in at a competition just as you would ride at home, with at least the same degree of focus, and *read your horse in each moment instead of simply going through a routine* – then you are up and running.

Before you get on, the tactic of increasing your symptoms can work wonders; but once you are riding, salvation lies in becoming so completely absorbed in your work that you *forget* to be nervous. Miraculous as it seems, the activation pattern which accompanies 'flow' banishes symptoms along with the other contents of consciousness. (This is the equivalent of the runny nose which miraculously dries up when you become absorbed in your work ... only to start dripping again when you 'come to' and realise what has happened!) The kill-or-cure ultimatum of real danger is much more conducive to flow than a threat to the ego; so in competition, jumping riders are more likely to find it than dressage riders. For merely looking stupid when you mess up can be far more paralysing than the threat to life and limb!

One of the teachers who has trained with me works with a particularly competitive group of pupils, and she often accompanies them to shows. Their performance has gone up immensely, partly because of their increased skill as riders, and partly because they now have so much more to focus their attention on. When they are in the warm-up arena or actually riding the test, they may or may not create a flow experience; but they do not fritter away their energy wondering who is watching and what they are thinking. Now that they have a more clearly defined task (for they know what to do and they know how to do it) they are much more able to keep their mind on the job. In this regard it is helpful to go to the competition armed with several *triggers* which have worked well for you in training, and to see if you can keep working with them in this more daunting situation. But if you want to be really brave in your warm-up, search for a new trigger, for there is nothing so captivating as the first experience of a new feel, which you perceive with all the freshness of walking into somewhere with a new and invigorating smell.

....

The self-serving bias

In the face of all the wild imagining that we do in competition, we are rarely as objective about our performance as we might like to believe. Within the framework of competition, sports psychologists talk about the 'self-serving bias' – the tendency to attribute our strong performances to our own skill level, and our weak ones to external mitigating factors. This enables us to maximise feelings of pride in our achievements, and to keep our self-image intact by minimising the shame of our disasters. This means that winners and losers in the same competition may attribute the outcome differently – to their ability and training (if they win) and to bad luck or difficult conditions (if they lose).

Riders may be more honest competitors than most, for it can be abundantly clear that they were lucky not to have a rail down, or unlucky to fall at a cross-country fence. Event riders interviewed on television after a successful cross-country round, usually make very modest attributions: 'My horse was so brilliant, and I was really lucky at the nineteenth fence.' These reflect very well both on them and on the sport – and probably do match what they feel in private. Most people are very generous towards their horse when they win (in a way which is probably rather self-effacing), but they are often distinctly less generous when they lose. Others try to minimise the damage by calculating that they would have been placed if only X, Y, or Z had not happened; although on winning, they rarely make the calculation that they would not have been placed if A, B, and C had not happened.

Dressage gives more scope than jumping for the 'self-serving bias' and we are more likely to say 'That judge doesn't like my horse,' when we score badly than we are to say 'That judge just happens to like my horse,' when we score well. We can attribute our result to luck – the factors that are external and unstable ('The going was really bad and the wind was so strong'), or to factors which are external and stable ('It was a more difficult test than I've done before'). The other possibilities are internal and unstable ('I rode really well on the day'), or internal and stable ('I know I am capable of doing this'). The learning you take away from either success of failure is determined by the attributions you make: so to consistently blame the conditions, or your horse, leaves you far less scope for improvement than if you perceive what you could have done to mitigate the effects of the unforeseen.

Seasoned competitors leave much less to luck than those who are less experienced. They may be riding their horse in a novice test; but at home he works at medium – which gives them far more leeway for error. I know hardly anyone who has decided not to take a British Horse Society riding examination until they were well above the standard required – most people sit them relying not on internal and stable factors (their skill level) but on external unstable ones: good-natured examiners, an easy horse for the lateral work, and one which is guaranteed to jump. I once heard luck defined as 'what happens when preparedness and opportunity meet': another very apt definition is 'Labour Under Correct Knowledge' (which I prefer to think of as 'labour using an unusually accurate map'). Kyra Kyrklund suggests that you maximise your chances of being 'lucky' in a test by riding the critical movements ten times during a schooling session at home, and counting how many times out of ten you can perform them well. Then (all things being equal, which they are unlikely to be) you can assess how well prepared you are, knowing your percentage chance of performing the movement well in the test.

Very few people segment their goals like this, and when I meet someone whose competitive goals seem rather far-fetched I like to break them down into their component parts. This injects a hearty dose of reality. It also provides a series of tests which you either pass or fail in your everyday work at home; for you might decide that only when you ride the movement well eighty per cent of the time at home will you have the green light to go out and do it in competition. For in dressage at least, your work in the competition arena is unlikely to be better than the work you can produce at home; your everyday work-out is the bed-rock of your performance.

....

Mastery vs winning   A rider's orientation towards competition is influenced tremendously by whether her goal is primarily that of *mastery,* or of winning. For the person who values mastery can be happy with her performance when she and her horse produce a personal best – or even a creditable performance – regardless of whether they win. But if winning and gaining approval from others are the rider's primary aim, she will not be satisfied with anything other than a first rosette. Tonya Harding, the ice skater who became famous for her alleged involvement in 'the Nancy Kerrigan affair' (in which Nancy, her greatest rival, was deliberately injured before the 1994 Winter Olympic Games) was apparently consistently told when she competed as a young girl that 'Second is the first to lose.' This is a philosophy that would put tremendous strain on anyone. For whilst only one person can win in the external world, everyone can win the 'inner game' – especially when they realise that mastery includes far more than (simple!) mastery of the skills of riding. There is mastery of the planning and logistics of competing, of your horse's long-term development, and of your 'tuning' on the day – including the mastery which survives in the face of adversity.

The American event rider Karen Lende O'Connor talked in a very interesting way (in *Practical Horseman,* December, 1993) about how her competitive goals changed as a result of a devastating blow she suffered in 1992. Her best horse, Mr Maxwell, was put down at Badminton, after a fall at the Vicarage Vee cross-country fence, which she considered to be the result of rider error. She kept eventing her other horses, but found that she was not riding with her previous zest: she was 'hooking and looking' for a stride in front of cross-country fences 'trying to control everything all the time – because some part of me felt that by having absolute control I could prevent what happened at Badminton from happening again'.

She knew that this instinctive survival mechanism was dangerous, and that it required a return to the drawing board. So at the suggestion of a friend she galloped racehorses in her winter break, and 'day by day on horse after horse, I regained my confidence in galloping in such a way that I had control but recognised its limits (the way that, driving a car at eighty miles per hour, I know I can stop but know I can't stop within five feet). A racehorse needs some feeling of independence even when you're on his back – and learning to allow that independence restored my faith that the less I dictated to a horse going across country, the better he'd go.'

She also rode one of her horses in a loose-jumping pen, without using reins, so that she could not dominate the horse's every move. When she returned to competition she was able to ride the horse forward into the base of show jumps without taking hold of his mouth, and she began to ride clear rounds. She also realised that the American Olympic show jumper Anne Kursinski had previously tried to teach her this – but at that time she had been able to win by riding in her old way, so she had not been receptive to the idea. But now that she was looking for new resources, it 'clicked'.

Another of her horses taught her to trust her experience with the racehorses: 'Galloping him involved giving up enough control so that he wasn't always fighting me for "total" control. If I was very quiet and used my half-halts in a finer way, anticipating when he might get strong instead of reacting when he made a bid, I could keep our rides from turning into a contest of wills.'

Karen's need to rebuild her skills led to changes in her short-term goals, and a need to focus on mastery. But her approach to her long-term goals also changed. International competition remained her focus, although she began to plan less than she used to: 'I used to think "I need to do well here so that I can go on and do well there", but no more. That kind of thinking takes my attention off the true focus of my work: the horses. I've decided that I won't "save" them for some big event by holding back from earlier competitions that I think they need for their development – or, just to meet selection criteria, run them at competitions I don't think they need.

'In the States I went to every competition with the sole object of winning; if my horse made a mistake we might lower our chances of USET selection. Here, though (in England), the focus is on producing a horse, not making a team. If your horse messes up one weekend you go home and work, come out and try again the next weekend ... and no one thinks the worse of him or you.'

This was a tremendous change in her philosophy of competing. In the intervening years she has concentrated far more on simply riding her horses as well as she can each day and in each competition, believing that by doing so, she is far more likely to produce a horse who is really ready for the big challenge. Her approach paid off, and she was indeed a member of the silver-medal-winning American team in the three-day event at the Atlanta Olympic Games. She also discovered that this attitude freed her to enjoy every step along the way *for its own sake*, for she was no longer perceiving it merely as a stepping-stone to greater glory. Whereas she used to do well and think, 'OK, I've got it. My programme's right on track for the World Championships or the Olympics', she now comes out of a successful ride thinking, 'I seem to be on the right lines – but can I do it again?'

As Julia discovered in Chapter 7, this attitude tones down the euphoria of 'getting it', and protects the rider from the sense of despair which ensues when she discovers that she has in fact not 'got it' (and that she actually needs another nine thousand nine hundred and ninety-nine repetitions!). It helps her to perceive each moment afresh instead of trying to reproduce yesterday, or trying to jump ahead to tomorrow. So on each ride she is far more absorbed in her here-and-now experience. This is far more likely to keep her in the flow channel, and the inherent rewards of this are so great that competitors who achieve it are unlikely to feel they have 'lost'.

A friend of mine was a journalist at a major international dressage competition, and as the medal ceremony was about to begin she watched the three highest placed competitors. The one who won was sitting on her horse with a look which suggested she was thinking, 'Well, of course I won.' The competitor who came third was scowling, and the one who came second was talking to her parents on a mobile telephone, grinning from ear to ear and bouncing around in her saddle. 'There's only one really happy person here,' was my friend's immediate thought. Perhaps the thrills of the outer game had palled for two of them, and only one of them had won the 'inner game'.

....

Toughness vs talent

Enjoying winning is easy – although, as the above story shows, even that is a thrill which can wear off. But it is not so easy to enjoy everything that goes into it – staying in the flow channel whilst you ride a cross-country round on slippery going in the pouring rain, or whilst you work in for your dressage in a crowded arena. Then there are the joys of climbing out of bed to load you horse at four in the morning, and riding him day in, day out whatever the weather, and regardless of how you feel. Many people add to this the demands of shovelling tons of horse manure, and/or juggling riding with work or study, and the demands of family or a business. Then, there is the ultimate torture of nursing a sick horse (or grieving a dead one) and watching your competitive hopes become unfulfillable dreams. In the face of this, we are each like the proverbial chain which will break at its weakest link — either within or beyond the competitive arena. In the face of these challenges, it is not surprising that sports psychologists are unanimous in their belief that *toughness* wins out over *talent*.

James E. Loehr, in his book *The New Toughness Training for Sport,* defines toughness as 'the ability to consistently perform towards the upper levels of your talent and skill, regardless of competitive circumstances'. Other athletes might think we have it easy: for although we lay our safety and our egos on the line, we do not face head-on combat, and a crowd who may be against us. Neither do we push our bodies to their ultimate limits for hours on end. But we know all about competition nerves, and the difficult conditions of wind, weather, and warming up — and we have the added dimension of sharing these with our non-human partner. Whatever the relative merits of our position, if we expand Loehr's definition beyond the competition arena to include the toughness needed in everyday life 'regardless of circumstance', I for one become awed at the enormity of the task which many competitive riders have set themselves.

Seasoned competitors like Karen Lende O'Connor have all recovered from difficulties and disappointment, demonstrating their toughness as well as their talent. But as well as surviving those times when the going gets really tough, they also survive the more mundane losses of form which affect us all from time to time. If you lose confidence, or enthusiasm, the important thing to remember is that you *have had* them; for that experience is stored in your memory, and you do not have to build it again from scratch. All you have to do is re-access it. So remember it and muse on it; day dream it, so that you mentally rehearse it without the stress of forcing yourself to do so. Think of someone you know who has it, and act 'as if' you are her. Or 'borrow' feelings of confidence and competence from other areas of your life. How would you ride if you were as decisive in front of a fence as you are in your business dealings? How would you ride if you paid attention to your horse's back just like you do when you watch a good movie? How would you ride if you were as confident of performing well as you are when you give a sales presentation?

The most successful competitors have experienced times which took them beyond confidence, to the feeling that they could do no wrong.

They were in a 'state of grace', which endured despite the challenges and the bustle of the competition environment. Whilst others may perceive them as aloof, competitors in this state often keep their own counsel to stop themselves being drawn into an everyday way of perceiving. Their state may or may not include the premonition that they are going to win, but it always includes a sense of inner peace, and the security of knowing that they and their horse are 'in tune'. Like Kyra Kyrklund's build-up to the Stockholm Equestrian Games, it is a magical experience.

Virtually everyone who has experienced this state will tell you that reaching it at will is extremely difficult. As soon as you fall into the trap of trying to reproduce it you are doomed; for by definition, you are not in the same state. So you have to a be a little more creative in how you use your brain. There is an elusive naivety to the winner's mind, which is why less-experienced competitors (like Lucinda Prior-Palmer – now Green – when she won her second Badminton at the age of nineteen) can sometimes capture it. 'Beginner's luck' is the same naive state, bereft of the high expectations, and the 'shoulds' and 'oughts' which create *interference* for the more knowledgeable performer who is trying to recreate her successes. But some people are exceptional; if they fall into this trap they dig themselves out of it, not by trying but by musing – like one friend of mine who mitigates the effects of her (occasional) bad days by sitting by the fire with a glass of wine and reliving some of her favourite rides. She never even realised how effectively she was reprogramming her brain. But she was unknowingly fulfilling the key prophesy of sports psychologists: that in the top levels of competition, there is often so little to choose between the fitness, technique, and speed of different competitors, that the winner is most likely to be determined by *how she organises her mind.*

....

The 'fifth state' Sports psychologists inevitably cannot define the complex set of adjustments which each individual must make to her 'tuning' in order to reach her optimal activation pattern. So the most practical way to study peak performance is to consider the *similarities* which hold for everyone who is indeed experiencing it. The centred competitor will easily pass the Aikido stability test in which you 'keep one point' (and this, coupled with mental rehearsal, would be a good way to help her get there). But the most far-reaching similarity lies in brain-wave activity; for if we could measure the brain waves of peak performers on a 'mind mirror' biofeedback machine, I believe we would see a 'fifth-state' pattern.

Biofeedback devices can teach you how to control virtually every bodily function, from the electrical resistance of your skin to the acidity in your stomach. Maxwell Cade, a researcher in radiation physics with tremendously impressive scientific credentials, was the first to use biofeedback to monitor the brain waves of people who meditated, and of a number of well-known yogis and healers. He studied them for many years, and taught biofeedback classes (which I was privileged to attend) until his death in 1985. His associates have continued his work, extending it to the study of successful businessmen, and outstanding performers in many different fields.

When you are wired to a mind mirror, a headband containing electrodes (each laced with a healthy dollop of conducting gel) is placed around your head. These detect electrical activity deep within your brain, which at levels of about 0.00005 volts is minute in comparison with domestic electricity – 240 volts in the UK and 110 volts in the USA. The wires from these electrodes eventually lead to a computer display which simulates rows of tiny red light bulbs. The right-hand half of the screen shows output from the right brain hemisphere, and the left-hand half shows output from the left brain hemisphere. Each row depicts the output lying within a certain frequency range: thus the bulbs which light up create a pattern, showing that within each frequency range, there may be more or less activity in each hemisphere. (See Fig. 10.7.)

Brain waves vary between 0.5 and 35 cycles per second. According to Maxwell Cade and other researchers, the delta rhythm, from 0.5 to 4 cycles per second (or Hertz) is associated with deep sleep. Theta, lying in the range from 4 to 7 Hertz, appears in dreaming, or in the semi-awake hypnagogic state which is characterised by rich, dreamlike imagery. Alpha, lying between 8 and 13 Hertz in adults (and between 4 and 7 Hertz in children), is the most prominent rhythm, which, on its own, usually denotes an empty, mindless state. Most people produce some alpha when their eyes are closed, but not when they are open. Alpha has recently been associated with inwardly directed attention, relaxed awareness, and feelings of well-being; but Maxwell Cade discovered that it requires the

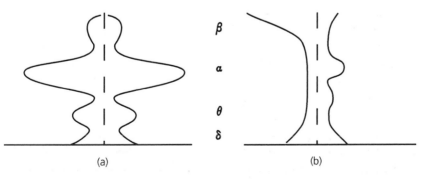

(a)   β   α   θ   δ   (b)

Fig. 10.7 The 'mind mirror' computer display, showing a fifth-state pattern in (a), and in (b) a typical everyday pattern which is not symmetrical between the two hemispheres.

simultaneous presence of beta (and theta to move beyond this 'empty mind' to one which can perform exceptionally well.

Beta rhythms, from 13 to 30 Hertz, are (when produced on their own) associated with normal waking consciousness – with an external awareness, with thinking, active attention, and problem-solving. With increasing anxiety, more beta waves are produced.

Maxwell Cade termed this beta activity the 'third state' (with dreaming sleep and the hypnagogic state being the first and second states, as shown in Fig. 10.8). But some philosophers have gone so far as to call this everyday state a 'waking sleep', suggesting that we live our lives in a twilight of consciousness. 'Compared to what we are capable of,' said the philosopher Ouspensky, 'our normal waking state is more like sleep-walking.' Huxley's 'measly trickle of consciousness' (see page 13) carries the same connotation; and although our senses *must* filter out some

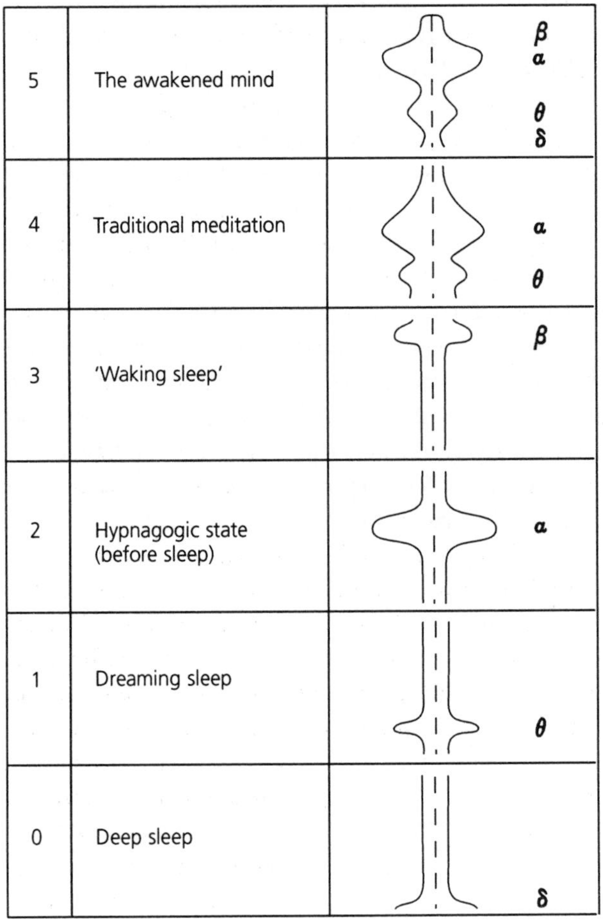

5	The awakened mind		β α θ δ
4	Traditional meditation		α θ
3	'Waking sleep'		β
2	Hypnagogic state (before sleep)		α
1	Dreaming sleep		θ
0	Deep sleep		δ

Fig. 10.8. The 'mind mirror' patterns of various states.

information in order to ensure that we are not continually overwhelmed, many of us filter out so much that yogis and mystics might consider us all but brain-dead.

If you have to live in the flight path of an airport it must be a blessed relief when you cease to hear the aircraft; but how sad it is if you also cease to notice the song of the birds, the rustle of leaves, or the sound of your own footfall. As a rather jaded adult, it is unlikely that you see as a child sees – with the richness of colour and shape which accompanies the wonder of seeing *as if for the first time*. As children develop, their brain-wave profiles change, and predominantly delta waves are shown by the baby during her first three or four months of life. But then theta waves become the dominant activity, with alpha appearing at age five. As the child becomes a teenager theta declines, alpha increases, and beta appears. This marks the loss of the relaxed alertness which gives children their spontaneity. In contrast, adult experience – with its predominance of beta waves – usually brings with it the need to immediately label everything, or to rationalise our experience away.

This everyday consciousness, with its reduced sensory experience, is also characterised by the continual chatter and business of the 'butterfly mind' which hops from one thought to another, taking us away from an awareness of the present moment, and placing our attention in the past or the future. To quieten this, students in Maxwell Cade's classes learned to meditate whilst connected to mind mirror machines. (A number of people have taken the mystery out of meditation by defining it as 'what happens in the gap between thoughts'.) At any time the students could press a button on the mind mirror and freeze the pattern on the screen, opening their eyes to look at it. They soon became able to produce the fifth-state pattern at will, and with the aid of biofeedback, they learned to meditate very much faster than they would have done as traditional students in any of the Eastern traditions.

In fact, some long-term students of these were connected to the equipment, which showed that they did *not* produce the patterns associated with meditation. However, they easily learned to change their brain waves and immediately recognised the difference in their experience. After meditation, students are typically able to maintain the fifth-state pattern for ten minutes or more with their eyes open (as long as their gaze remains defocused), and many can move around, hold conversations, read, and do simple mathematical problems without disturbing it. In describing their experience, they talk of a sense of illumination, bliss, or 'oneness'; and many (like myself) have reported that the ability to produce a fifth state has continued to enrich their lives.

Maxwell Cade called the fifth-state pattern 'the awakened mind'. It includes the beta, alpha, theta and delta frequencies, and is symmetrical between the two hemispheres. (See Fig. 10.7.) This pattern has been demonstrated (without training) by many successful people, and in his book called *The Awakened Mind,* Maxwell Cade says that, 'What is being transformed (in learning to produce a fifth state) is one's level of awareness, not only of external reality but also of oneself. It is, perhaps, like gradually awakening from sleep and becoming more and more vividly aware of everyday reality – only it is now everyday reality from which we are awakening!' It is perhaps not surprising that the best business people and athletes transcend this 'everyday reality', and that it is their enhanced power of perception which underlies their achievements.

My contention is that good riders, like other successful athletes and businessmen, show this fifth-state pattern – or at least that they show a more bilaterally symmetrical, integrated brain-wave pattern than the 'man in the street', with less activity in the beta range. The technology to demonstrate this with a moving horse and rider is not yet available, although rather different monitoring equipment has been used to show the presence of alpha waves in successful weightlifters and in performers of the martial art Kendo. (This was demonstrated in a programme called 'Losing It', which was shown on the British Channel 4 TV series 'Equinox' in November 1997.) I and another dressage rider (along with many successful athletes) have demonstrated it consistently in mental rehearsal. In October 1991 I set up an experiment with Matt Ryan, who subsequently won the gold medal in the three-day event at the Barcelona Olympics in 1992. In front of an audience of over two hundred people he was connected to a mind mirror and asked to mentally rehearse an exceptionally good ride. He showed a very strong, stable, fifth-state pattern.

In 1984 an experiment was done with Linda Tellington-Jones, in which both she and the horse who was receiving her TTEAM touch were wired to mind mirrors. Linda's fifth state was strong and immediate; and after about five minutes the horse took on the same pattern! Originally, the horse's brain activity was primarily alpha waves – and whilst people who take on a fifth-state pattern show more alpha and fewer beta waves than normal, the change in the horse required more beta and less alpha. But this is not surprising, for the horse's everyday state is more of an empty mind, whilst ours is a busy one. He needs more consciousness and a less instinctive response to bring him into balance; we need less beta-consciousness and more of the instinctive, intuitive way of thinking which is characterised by alpha waves.

The experiment leaves us with an unanswered question: might this happen too in riding? Could the skilled rider transmit her brain-wave pattern to the horse? Healers – regardless of the philosophical explanation which they offer for their gift – all show a fifth-state pattern, and transfer this to their subjects during hands-on treatment. (This transfer has even been observed, in experimental conditions, during absent healing.) So we have enough evidence to know that transfer is possible, and if we could do it, riding would become tremendously healing, both for us and our horses.

Whilst I wholeheartedly recommend biofeedback training, the fifth state can be both learned – and put to the test – in the riding arena. One of my more advanced pupils, who rode extremely well on a three-day course recently, found herself in front of her usual trainer, determined to show him how much she had learned. Her riding promptly fell to pieces, and she suddenly realised that she was in the same state that she often got into in the warm-up arena. Doubtless, her breathing and her brain-wave patterns had changed, so her activation pattern was different. But her philosophical stance had changed too: for she was trying to *be there* – to demonstrate how perfect she was – not be 'here', riding her horse in each moment, and solving the problems she was currently facing. By *pretending to have arrived* she had stopped journeying, and had started acting as if her current feeling already matched the perfect feeling she had hoped to create.

In the face of some imagined judgement (which we commonly attribute to dressage judges and trainers, as well as to any observer of our riding) she could not tolerate the discrepancy between the two. In effect, she was going through the motions of riding as most people go through life: on the forehand. Instead of admitting what *is,* we rush ahead of ourselves, trying to be in some imagined state that we think we are supposed to be in. We run away from our flaws and pretend to be perfect; we do not want to go through the process of defining them, and to face the inevitable growing pains of learning their lessons. But we will never bring a horse into balance unless we can balance ourselves. It is by far the most effective way.

Epilogue

The changes within the horse world

I<small>N HIS BOOK</small> *Creativity*, Mihaly Csikszentmihalyi considers not only the creative individual and her new idea, but the domain or area of knowledge in which she operates. Before she can come up with anything new she must first master the existing knowledge within her domain – whether that means understanding the classical roots of riding as well as its present-day writings, or whether it means understanding the mathematics, the philosophy and the experimental discoveries of quantum mechanics. Creative ideas add to a domain, change it in some way, or create a new domain, and very often they evolve as a result of an individual crossing the boundaries of existing domains. So a chemist who studies quantum mechanics and applies its theories to molecular bonding can make a more substantial contribution to chemistry than one who stays within the bounds of that domain.

As well as the domain and the individual, there is also the field – the people whose decisions determine whether or not the new idea is accepted. As Csikszentmihalyi points out, the field can be as a wide as society itself, or as narrow as a few individuals. The entire population of the USA were involved in deciding if New Coke was indeed an improvement on the old; but when Einstein came up with his theory of relativity, only four or five people in the entire world could initially understand it. However, their opinion held enough weight to take him from patent clerk to professor, and to make his name a household word. In general, jurisdiction over a given domain is officially left in the hands of a field of experts, and this field includes anyone who has the right to decide whether a new idea or product is 'good' or 'bad'. As we shall see, in different aspects of the horse world we (the riding public) either exercise that right or defer to others. This has significant consequences.

In different domains, different time scales determine the progress of both ideas and experts. Philosophers and social scientists are working within such a diffuse system of thought that it take years for them to master their domains. Thus their genius peaks late, and by the same token, the field can take many years to assess if a new idea is indeed an improvement worth adding to its knowledge base. In contrast, domains like mathematics are so highly structured that their rules and content can be learned relatively quickly. Hence mathematical genius can peak early, and the field can easily assess if any new innovation is worth adding to its knowledge base.

Riding lies somewhere in between, for its traditional system of thought is only moderately structured. But the recent upsurge of young, world-class riders shows us that even though riding skills can peak late in life, it does not necessarily take a lifetime to become an exceptional rider, and a voice of which the field takes note. Within our domain, competitive success is the most effective route for any individual to become elevated to the status of expert; for it *proves* that her contribution is worth including in the domain. (However, this definition excludes many extremely good riders who do not have the single-mindedness, the money, or the lucky breaks needed to get to the top.) Training as an instructor does not carry the same weight – perhaps rightly so – although this demonstrates how little regard the field has for teaching skills as separate from riding skills. It may also show, however, that training as an instructor rarely develops teaching ability to such an extent that these trained people are perceived by the field as having something extra to offer. This is a situation which I would dearly like to see change.

Researchers who bring in information from other domains have the easiest time making their mark when that domain is itself respected by the riding community. When hard science enters the realms of horse care, it creates data which few laymen can argue with – especially when the protagonists are using sophisticated methods of research. In the new domain of equine biomechanics, the research methods of sport science have been applied to equine locomotion. Data from cameras which shoot 250 frames of film per second is revolutionising our understanding of how the horse moves; force plates and tread mills are allowing us to analyse footfall and lameness as never before. They are also showing that many of our previous naked-eye assumptions were extremely naive. As many of our hallowed presuppositions fall by the wayside, those who do not bow to science could be accused of showing a similar mind-set to members of the 'Flat Earth Society'.

Research which originates in the universities is (in theory at least) knowledge for its own sake; but research which is funded by commercial interest seeks knowledge with the intention of securing competitive advantage. It is in the domain of equine nutrition that the most competitive situation exists, and inevitably, different factions of the market produce various findings which they then translate into competing products. Advertising pitches blind us with science, playing on the guilt we can feel if we are not providing our horses with the best in macronutrients, micronutrients, probiotics and electrolytes. Since the knowledge-gap between us and the researchers is so huge, we can be left scratching our heads and wondering who to believe! In fact, we are likely to be most influenced by the company with the largest advertising budget and not by the company with the best product.

The fact that each product defines itself as *best* is a massive added complication. So without *either* a body which supplies knowledgeable, independent monitoring, *and/or* a huge amount of self-education, how can we possibly judge? (In the UK, the Consumer Association fulfils this monitoring role, publishing results in its monthly magazine *Which?*.) The domain of equine nutrition represents huge commercial interests, and since we must all feed our horses, we cannot easily defer our decisions: we become the non-expert expert, who decides the fate of any new product by wielding the spending power of the consumer.

Less controversial than research within the feed industry is research which was prompted by the needs of the new discipline of endurance riding, and the need for a sensible, ethical approach to the Atlanta Olympic Games. Faced with new competitive demands, the field desperately needed information on the effects of stress on horses – particularly the stress of prolonged hard work in hot, humid conditions. This need was combined with the abilities of creative individuals, who have expanded and updated our knowledge. Within the domain of feeding, however, the need for change has evolved not so much out of ethical considerations, but as a result of new research methods, new production methods, and a competitive market place. Added to this was the need for the large feed companies to maximise their profits through buying as cheaply as possible on the world markets. But the ensuing technological revolution has itself produced the conditions needed to catalyse yet another change. This has been brought about by sceptics who argue that the riding public are a gullible bunch of consumers, who will willingly pay money to feed their horses on synthetic products and the by-products of other industries. Thus the high-tech revolution has spearheaded the 'green revolution' whose products hail themselves as 'natural horse feeds' rather than 'the latest scientific discovery'.

Saddlery and farriery, which are (as yet) less scientific domains, are also inherently controversial, perhaps because so many of us claim the right to sit in judgement. Again, we are the non-expert expert – but we often have no qualms about arguing with saddlers or farriers (regardless of whether they represent the traditional or the *avant garde* viewpoint). Despite the long history of both crafts, their shortcomings have become obvious to the increasing number of riders who are no longer content to rely on the simple guidelines which we have traditionally been taught. This questioning has created conditions in the field which encourage change;

but innovative saddlers and farriers do not have the 'clout' of hard scientists, who can make us shut up and take notice by quoting facts and figures. Instead, forward-thinking farriers and saddlers have the difficult job of making themselves heard above the din of our uneducated certainty – and they operate without the large advertising budgets which could make this a lot easier.

I am sure many of them envy the hard scientists who work in the field of biomechanics, for they not only have the advantage of statistics, they are also carving out such a completely new domain that they do not have peers whose investment in the *status quo* can hold back the acceptance of radical new ideas. Thus saddlery and farriery must vie with complementary medicine for the title of 'most disputed domain within the horse world'.

The stakes rise in the veterinary field, since vets as well as riders are involved in the evaluation of these new/old ideas. Vets commonly feel that only hard scientific evidence can be regarded as proof of their validity, and this prompts many equestrians and complementary practitioners to feel that the veterinary profession (like all domains with a strong pre-existing culture) is taking a conservative position in order to protect its own validity and knowledge base. The lay public, however, has no such knowledge base to protect. We – in contrast to the vets – do not need scientific proof, and are readily convinced by anecdotal evidence.

Since people practising within the complementary domain rarely have the time, money, means or knowledge to conduct research, they are unlikely ever to satisfy the criteria of the veterinary community. (The British veterinary community is much more closed-minded in this regard than the American.) Yet complementary medicine has caught on on both sides of the Atlantic. We, the consumers, have voted with our feet – actually breaking the law in some cases – to bring our horses possible alternatives to drug therapy, and/or the low-grade pain which characterises the life of the 'walking wounded'. Over recent years, creative individuals at the forefront of the field have been in the right place at the right time; but those who were around twenty years ago probably feel as if they have pushed a boulder to the top of a hill. At last, they have reached the top.

Keeping up to date with the plethora of new information in the fields of fitness, feeding, saddlery, farriery, dentistry and complementary medicine is (as I know to my cost through my research for *For the Good of the Horse*) more than enough to keep one person occupied. If one or more of these fields particularly interests you, you will be up to your neck in the information which has resulted from the recent explosion of knowledge. For as I pointed out in *For the Good of the Horse*, more has been written about micronutrients in the last five years than in the previous two hundred! The irony is that every time you invest your energy in learning and studying a certain domain, you have withdrawn your interest from another area which you could have studied: this is the 'opportunity cost' of your endeavour. As the years go by and knowledge proliferates, it becomes progressively harder for people to become well versed in the information contained within more than one domain. Thus it becomes more difficult to create the new insights which arise from crossing boundaries.

....

Ideas whose time has come

Within any domain or culture, many more creative changes vanish than are ever implemented. Thus I am in great awe of Caprilli, who many in the Italian cavalry must have thought of as 'that idiot who keeps falling off'. The forward seat was his answer to his personal crisis, and amazingly (given that his credentials stemmed from his failure to ride well within the old paradigm), he managed to convince the field of his own generation to adopt it. His predicament reminds me of my own – although I am certainly *not* proposing a radical new way of sitting. The information which I offer to the field is of a different logical level, for it concerns new ways of *talking about and understanding* the way that good riders have always sat and used their bodies.

New approaches within the domain of teaching and rider biomechanics are only just beginning to reach the stage of 'ideas whose time has come' (and I do indeed feel as if I have been pushing a boulder uphill for the last twenty years). For when the horse world meets a domain which does not have scientific credentials – and which is not already known to it – the ideas which evolve from the meeting do not have automatic credibility.

Thus Monty Roberts has done tremendously well in gaining rapid acceptance for his 'advance and retreat' method of starting horses in a round pen. He has in effect, taken the UK by storm – and he now appears to be doing the same in America. In Europe he (and the Western riding tradition that he comes from) is a tremendous novelty; in America he is one of a number of trainers who have spoken out against the traditional brutality of that culture, and who work in similar ways.

Years of ridicule close to home prompted him to keep his method a secret, until interest from the Queen gave him a platform on which to demonstrate his techniques. They were then given wide publicity in the British press, and shown in demonstrations around the country. Whilst sceptics have scratched their heads and exclaimed that 'No one can do that with an unbroken horse. It must be a con!', his method has appealed to the common person, who could see each horse in the round pen going through the steps which Monty had predicted. Thus the various stages in his map of the human/horse interaction were lived out before everyone's eyes. Most people saw this as a demonstration of their validity; those who did not may well have had a pre-conceived mind-set which closed their eyes to the possibility.

Whilst British experts within the established hierarchy have not shown out-and-out acceptance of the method, they have not rejected it either. As the custodians of knowledge who are faced with a dramatic change in their domain, they are undoubtedly not in an easy position. But with no guidance from on high, the riding public have been free to take on the status of expert (in a domain where cause and effect is much more clear cut and immediately obvious than it is in saddlery or farriery). People have felt free to make up their own minds.

The British and American riding cultures are different enough for Monty's work to be *less* threatening to specific individuals here than it will be there. British trainers have not worked in similar enough ways to squabble over the details of the method (as the American experts may well do). But since his knowledge has its roots in a completely different domain, and since no forerunners have paved the way, it is more of a threat to the culture as a whole. Monty faces different issues on each side of the Atlantic; and given the success he has already had, it is easy to forget the *forty years* during which his techniques were ridiculed (on the rare occasions on which he dared to show them). It is also easy to forget that his early public demonstrations led to even more ridicule. But this has gradually been replaced by dismissal, and then acceptance – but with an attitude of 'Well, of course, it's obvious. In fact, it's just what I've always done myself ....'

This negation of difference deletes and distorts *both* the rigour of Monty's understanding *and* the superficiality of his acceptors' (and I am sure that this will be an even more prevalent response to Monty's work in America). It gives individuals within the existing culture a way to accept the new ideas without losing face. I should perhaps be grateful that I am beginning to hear those same words myself – in response to which I smile sweetly, and say 'Really?' I then (so far) have resisted the temptation to ask my supporter to demonstrate her skills.

....

The designated experts

I and my work are not so unique as Monty's work appears from this side of the Atlantic Ocean. For contributions to teaching methods have been made not just by myself, but by others with a knowledge of sports psychology, bodywork, coaching skills, martial arts, biofeedback, human anatomy, and other associated domains. We have not yet found the same platform as Monty – who has been able to invite large audiences to sit in judgement over his method. But when we stimulate enough public interest, we will be similarly judged on our merits. In the other domains within riding, however, the punters' role as expert has less validity – and feeding, farriery and saddlery are such complex domains that cause and effect are rarely so immediately obvious, and one's eyes and ears cannot judge so readily. But despite this, people rarely defer to more experienced opinion (and put themselves through the trauma of deciding whose opinion they should defer to!). They prefer to keep their 'expert' status.

Ironically, the public take much *less* power into their own hands when it comes to their experiences as a pupil. Although some shop around, trying different trainers until they find one who 'fits', many accept what they are given, without appreciating that there *are* other options. Essentially, by becoming pupils, they have defined themselves as powerless – as *the ones who do not know*. Thus the field's designated experts are not its consumers, but its most revered teachers and trainers. At the top of the tree are those who have coached a known, successful competitor, along with the successful competitors themselves, and the most highly qualified instructors. In all fields – and throughout history – it has proved particularly hard for the bringers of new information to make any impact at all on a domain if they are not personally known and appreciated by its experts (and I am sure Monty Roberts feels a huge debt of gratitude to the Queen). Without this, they are easily dismissed and ridiculed – and as Mihaly Csikszentimihalyi points out 'a domain cannot be changed without the explicit or implicit consent of a field responsible for it.'

Since the two routes of examination training and competitive success give two distinct groups of designated experts, this gives two possibilities of acceptance or rejection. The field as a whole has surrendered the right to decide about new ideas in riding and teaching to its two sets of experts – although more public exposure to new methods may change this in time. It is a tragic irony that the experts are so busy riding horses from dawn to dusk that they are the *least* likely of all riders to spend time reading, and to expose themselves to new information!

Thus the designated experts often have *less* access to new information than the masses. Beyond this, they are likely to be the most conservative voice within the domain. The bottom line is that domains – like all cultures – can only survive in their existing form if they eliminate most of the new ideas proposed by their members. Furthermore, the experts (be they known trainers or successful competitive riders) work from the presuppositions of the talented, so their learning has not been compromised by what is unspoken or badly described in our traditional map of riding. Since it has worked for them, they are unlikely to see why it should not work for everyone. From their perspective, the fault lies not in the map, but in the individuals who have no talent.

Experts who are armed with innate talent never need to ask the 'how' questions about riding which yield procedural knowledge. Without the need to ask those questions, the experts do not appreciate that our traditional map or paradigm leaves many issues unaddressed, for it answers only the 'what' questions which yield declarative knowledge. It is because of this lack of procedural knowledge within our existing paradigm that 'how' questions are rarely permitted within the riding arena. Pupils are discouraged from asking them – both by tradition, and by short-tempered replies which cast doubt on the enquirer's sanity!

It is the riders experiencing a 'how' crisis who have the most compelling reasons for updating our map of riding. But by definition, they are not the experts. What the field does not appreciate, however, is that each individual within it *is* an expert when it comes to her own learning. Seen from a different perspective, the people who struggle the most could be highly valued (rather than marginalised) by the field, since they define the limits of the effectiveness of its teachings. In effect, they fall off the edge of its map, and show us where those edges are. In just the same way, the people who *I* struggle to teach help me define the limits of my own knowledge. Thus the struggling masses have an important voice which deserves to be heard and upheld.

In his seminal book *The Structure of Scientific Revolutions*, Thomas S. Kuhn makes it clear that the emergence of virtually every new paradigm in science was precipitated by a crisis. In this, the old paradigm became so full of inconsistencies, and so unable to explain and predict the workings of nature, that there was a drastic need for change – if only in the minds of a significant few. The crisis which precipitated the emergence of the paradigm described in this book was purely personal. But I was pretty sure well before the final emergence of my 'dark night of the soul' that I was not the only struggling rider in the world. I have since learned – from the other struggling riders who have written to me, or sought me out and transformed their learning – that this was true. Inevitably, these riders were the first to see value in my work: for they had no investment in the old paradigm, and their personal crisis allowed them to surrender it easily. In the same way, it is people with crises created (or at least not solved) by our traditional maps of farriery, saddlery, and medicine who are most open to their new paradigms, and who help to spearhead the revolution.

....

Unless creative ideas have a receptive audience to record and implement them, they vanish. Hence the monthly horse magazines have played a huge part in disseminating knowledge, and building the potential for the

Emergence of new paradigms

field to respond to new ways of thinking. I personally feel that I owe much of my success to my first editor, who had herself struggled with the skills of riding, and who understood my philosophical stance. She also believed in the potential of what was – at that time – a very disorganised manuscript. Although my first book *did* change my life in the ways I hoped it would (and no one chopped my head off in the way I feared they might) I had the naive hope that the headlines would soon read 'Mary Wanless and her small band of dedicated colleagues transform the horse world'. Perhaps one day they will: but Charles Darwin was rather more realistic when he wrote at the end of *Origin of the Species*, 'Although I am fully convinced of the truth of the views given in this volume ..., I by no means expect to convince experienced naturalists whose minds are stocked with a multitude of facts all viewed, during a long course of years, from a point of view directly opposite to mine ... But I look forward with confidence to the future – to young and rising naturalists, who will be able to view both sides of the question with impartiality.'

Similarly, the renowned physicist Max Planck wrote in his *Scientific Autobiography*, 'a new scientific truth does not triumph by convincing its opponents and making them see the light, but rather because its opponents eventually die, and a new generation grows up that is familiar with it.' I certainly do not wish death on those who see no need for change in our traditional paradigm of riding and teaching; but can also see that during the ten years in which my work has been in print, a new generation has begun to grow up, and the horse world has changed. With new paradigms emerging in farriery, saddlery, and medicine, in the ways that we handle horses from the ground, and in the new domain of horse biomechanics, it is time for that climate of change to feed back into riding and teaching. I am doing all that I can to encourage this – by writing, teaching, giving lectures and training teachers. But the seeds of change grow most strongly when they are fed and watered not by creative individuals alone but *by the field itself* – as they have been in these other domains. 'Pupil power' can carry much more weight than you might imagine.

For example, few people appreciate that the Renaissance – and particularly the sudden spurt of artistic activity that took place in Florence in the first twenty-five years of the fifteenth century – did not happen just because an unusually large number of gifted individuals happened to be alive then. Instead, the defining element was the *field*. It was a time of peace and commerce, and Florence was exceptionally rich; but there was also an atmosphere of uncertainty, both within and without the city. Leading citizens responded by deciding to make the city intimidatingly beautiful, and their task of encouraging, evaluating, and selecting works of art caught the interest of the common people. The domain was changing too, with the excavation of Roman ruins allowing the rediscovery of ancient classical methods of building. These solved the problem of how to complete the vast dome over the cathedral of Florence, which had been left open to the heavens for eighty years. Artists were pushed to perform beyond their previous limits, and it was *the task set by the customer along with changes in the domain* that inspired artists like Brunelleschi and Ghiberti. But if they had not been alive then, others would have filled their shoes.

Thus creativity does not just happen within one person, but *within the relationships of a system.* It is this which yields 'ideas whose time has come'. People within the field (that means *you*) have more power than they usually realise – even when they are not the field's designated experts, and do not wield consumer-power as actively as they do when they purchase a product. But buying a service is not so different – and one group of riders influenced their own fate far more actively than most by clubbing together and paying for their trainer to come and learn from me. They voted with their feet, and 'put their money where their mouth was' (and I told part of their trainer's story in Chapter 2.) Very few riders think as creatively as this group, and have the equivalent determination to get the tuition they really want; instead, they passively accept what they are given.

....

I look forward to the time when researchers into equine biomechanics turn their attention to rider biomechanics. I do not think this is far away, and I hope that my work will influence the research questions they attempt to answer. In the history of science, the experiments which follow the proposal of a new paradigm are based on its propositions, and they either ratify or modify it. When more than one new theory is being proposed (as is very often the case) experimental work determines which competing theory is more viable. In hard science, the outcome would normally be narrowed down to one explanation; however, in commercial ventures like equine nutrition, there are too many vested interests for there to be only one outcome.

Future research

In the field of teaching there are currently a number of new approaches – of which only some would profess to be new paradigms. Inevitably those of us involved will each hail our own ideas as best (just as the feed companies define their own products as best); so we cannot be the ultimate judges. As riders begin to feel that they become consumers with wider choices, the market place will exert its influence; but (in theory) the most successful new paradigm will be the one which can answer the most questions – those 'how' questions which I hope riders will insist on finding answers to.

I look forward to these experimental results, and am sure they will validate my premise that riding is a dynamic isometric skill. But as this becomes common knowledge, there are still many dangers ahead. One of my pupils spent her college days training as an opera singer, at a time shortly after the vocal chords had first been examined by laparoscope. She felt that her teachers often substituted statements of scientific fact for teaching, and she felt let down by that process. 'And I'm sure people sang better in the Middle Ages,' she told me, 'when they thought that their vocal chords were in their stomach!' As she discovered, there is no substitute for good communication skills, and the poetic licence that comes with 'it's as if ...' rather than 'research has shown that ...'.

Furthermore, increased scientific knowledge can never put a stop to the processes of deletion, distortion, and generalisation through which knowledge filters down to the masses. These inevitably lead to the hear-say and half-truths which spread confusion, and mis-present the teachings of any school. The statement 'Bear down, feel the pinch and make your thigh bones like iron bars,' is just as full of deletions (and nearly as full of distortions and generalisations) as the statement 'Sit up straight, stretch your leg down, and push your heels down'. In fact, much of this book has been devoted to pointing out the distortions inherent in the popular interpretation of those words.

But within most people – and even within most teachers – there is an inherent desire for these simple platitudes. Few individuals ever invest the time and energy that it takes to become proficient in the theory and practice of any (new or old) domain. Few look beyond the commonly heard half-truths, and glean their knowledge from a viable source. If more people invested wisely in their learning, and were fuelled by a sense both of *what they do not know*, and of *what there is to know*, the world would be a very different place.

Now that really would be for the good of the rider.

Bibliography

Chapter One

Bandler, Richard, and Grinder, John, *The Structure of Magic*, Science and Behaviour Books Inc., USA, 1975.

Grinder, John and DeLozier, Judith, *Turtles All The Way Down*, Grinder, DeLozier Associates, USA, 1987.

Huxley, Aldous, *The Doors of Perception*, Harper & Row Publishers Inc., New York, USA, 1954.

Zaborde, Genie, *Influencing with Ingretrity*, Syntony Publishing, USA, 1983.

Chapters Two, Three, Four and Five

Elson, Lawrence M., and Kapit, Wynn, *The Anatomy Colouring Book*, Harper & Row Publishers Inc., New York, USA, 1977.

Dennison, Dr Paul E., *Switching On*, Edu-Kinesthetics, Inc., USA, 1981.

Dennison, Paul E. PhD, and Hargrove, Gail E., *Personalised Whole Brain Integration*, Edu-Kinesthetics Inc., USA, 1985.

—, *Brain Gym Handbook*, Edu-Kinesthetics Inc., USA, 1989.

German National Equestrian Federation, *The Principles of Riding*, Kenilworth Press, 1996.

Hannaford, Carla PhD, *The Dominance Factor*, Great Ocean Publishers, Virginia, USA, 1997.

Harris, Charles, *The Fundamentals of Riding*, J. A. Allen and Co., London, 1985.

Herbermann, Erik F., *Dressage Formula*, J. A. Allen and Co., London, 1980.

Klimke, Reiner, *Basic Training of the Young Horse*, J. A. Allen and Co., London, 1985.

Müseler, Wilhelm, *Riding Logic*, Methuen, London, 1983.

Podhajsky, Alois, *The Complete Training of Horse and Rider*, George Harrap and Co., London, 1973.

—, *The Riding Teacher*, George Harrap and Co., London, 1973.

Seunig, Waldemar, *Horsemanship*, Doubleday and Co. Ltd, 1976.

Smythe, R. A. and Goody, P. C., *The Horse, Structure and Movement*, J. A. Allen and Co., London, 1975.

Swift, Sally, *Centred Riding*, Heinemann, London, 1985, and Trafalgar Square, USA, 1985.

Wanless, Mary, *Ride With Your Mind*, Methuen, 1987 and Kenilworth Press, 1996, also Trafalgar Square, USA, 1987.

—, *Ride With Your Mind Masterclass*, Methuen, 1991, and Kenilworth Press, 1996, also Trafalgar Square, USA, 1991.

Chapter Six
Bateson, Gregory, *Mind and Nature*, Bantam Books, USA, 1979.
Feldenkrais, Moshe, *The Case of Nora*, Frog Ltd, USA, 1993.
Kandel, Eric R. and Hawkins, Robert H. *The Biological Basis of Learning and Individuality*, Scientific American, September 1992.
Maltz, Maxwell MD, FICS, *Psychocybernetics*, Wiltshire Book Company, USA, 1960.
Sacks, Oliver, *An Anthropologist on Mars*, Vintage Books, USA, 1995.
Sommer, Bobbe PhD, *Psychocybernetics 2000*, Prentice Hall Ltd, USA, 1993.

Chapter Seven
Beaver, Diana, *Lazy Learning*, Element Books, UK, 1994.
Berne, Eric *Games People Play*, Penguin, 1970, USA/UK.
Cason, Richard D. *Taming Your Gremlin*, Harper and Row, USA, 1983.
Csikszentmihalyi, Mihaly, *Flow*, HarperCollins, USA, 1990.
Gallwey, W. Timothy, *The Inner Game of Tennis*, Random House, USA, 1974.
   —, *The Inner Game of Golf*, Jonathan Cape Ltd, 1981.
Gallwey, W. Timothy and Kreigel, Bob, *Inner Skiing*, Bantam Books, 1978.
Harris, Thomas A. MD, *I'm OK - You're OK*, Pan Books, 1973.
John-Roger, and McWilliams, Peter, *You Can't Afford the Luxury of a Negative Thought*, Prelude Press, USA, 1988.
McCluggage, Denise, *The Centered Skier*, Bantam Books, USA, 1983.
Ristad, Eloise, *A Soprano On Her Head*, Real People Press, USA, 1982.
Savoie, Jane, *That Winning Feeling*, J.A. Allen, London 1992, and Trafalgar Square Publishing, USA, 1992.

Chapter Eight
Barlow, Wilfred, *The Alexander Principle*, Arrow Books, London, 1975.
Carrington, Walter, *Riding*, Article in *The Alexander Journal*, No. 14, Autumn 1995,
Dychtwald, Ken, *Bodymind*, Wildwood House, UK, 1979.
Gelb, Michael, *Body Learning*, Aurum Press, UK, 1981.
Hanna, Thomas, *Somatics*, Addison-Wesley Publishing Co. Inc., USA, 1988.
Heller, Joseph and Henkin, William A., *Bodywise*, Wingbow Press, USA, 1991.
Johnson, Don Hanlon, *Bone, Breath and Gesture*, North Atlantic Books, USA, 1995.
Juhan, Deane, *Job's Body, A Handbook for Bodywork*, Station Hill Press, USA, 1987.
Morris, Desmond, *The Naked Ape*, Corgi Books, 1968.
Sacks, Oliver, *A Leg to Stand On*, Harper Perennial, USA, 1987.

Chapter Nine
Anderson, Bob, *Stretching*, Shelter Publications Inc., USA, 1980
Katch, V., Katch, I., and McCardle, W., *Exercise Physiology*, third edition, Lea and Febiger, 1991 USA/UK.

McNaught-Davis, *Developing Flexibility*, Resource Pack, National Coaching Foundation, UK, 1986.

Moore, Gloria, *Isolate and Stretch Effectively*, self-published, c/o Aaron Van Hoven, 4680 Alvarado Ave., Fort Pierce, FL 34946, USA.

Morris, B Mellion, MD, Walsh, W. Micheal, MD., Shelton, Guy L., PT, ATC, *The Team Physician's Handbook*, Hanley & Belfus Inc., USA, 1990.

Pinckney, Callan, *Callanetics*, Arrow Books, 1989, UK.

Sharkey, Brian J., *Coaches' Guide to Sport Physiology*, Human Kinetics Publisher, Inc., USA, 1986.

St George, Francine, *The Stretching Handbook*, Simon and Schuster, Australia, 1994.

Thie, John, *Touch For Health*, T. H. Enterprises, USA, 1987.

Chapter Ten

Cade, C. Maxwell, and Coxhead, Nona, *The Awakened Mind*, Wildwood House, UK, 1979.

Douillard, John, *Body, Mind and Sport*, Crown Trade Paperbacks, USA, 1994.

Fritz, Robert, *The Path of Least Resistance*, Stillpoint Publishing, USA, 1984.

Hardy, Dr Lew and Fazey, Dr John, *Mental Preparation for Performance*, The National Coaching Foundation, UK, 1989.

Hemery, David *Sporting Excellence*, Willow Books, London, 1986.

Houlston, Dr David, *The Social Psychology of Sport*, National Coaching Foundation, UK, 1991.

Loehr, James E., EdD, *The New Toughness Training for Sports*, Penguin Books, USA, 1995.

Millman, Dan, *The Inner Athlete*, Stillpoint Publishing, 1994.

Sasson Edgette, Janet PSY.D, *Heads Up*, Doubleday, USA, 1996.

Wise, Anna, *The High Performance Mind*, G.P.Putnam's Sons, USA, 1995.

Epilogue

Csikszentmihalyi, Mihaly, *Creativity*, HarperCollins Publishers, USA, 1996.

Kuhn, Thomas S., *The Structure of Scientific Revolutions*, The University of Chicago Press, 1962.

Useful Addresses

Bodywork chapter

For a list of Feldenkrais Teachers in the UK contact:

    The Feldenkrais Guild
    PO Box 370
    London N10 3XA

For *Awareness Through Movement* lessons on audiotape contact:

    Garet Newell
    PO Box 1207
    Hove
    E. Sussex BN3 2GG

For information about both teachers and audiotapes in the USA contact:

    The Feldenkrais Guild
    PO Box 489
    Albany, Oregon 97321
    USA

A list of certified Alexander teachers in the UK is available from:

    Society of Teachers of the
      Alexander Technique (STAT)
    20 London House
    266 Fulham Road
    London
    SW10 9EL

A list of certified Alexander Teachers in the USA is available from:

    North American Society of
      Teachers of the Alexander
      Technique (NASTAT)
    3010 Hennepin Avenue South
    Suite 10
    Minneapolis, MN 55408
    USA

Asymmetry chapter

    The Educational Kinesiology
      Foundation
    PO Box 3396
    Ventura, CA 93006
    USA

    Educational Kinesiolgy UK
    The Hendon Natural Health
      Centre
    12 Golders Rise
    Hendon
    London NW4 2HR

Fit and Able chapter

    Touch for Health Foundation
    1174 North Lake Avenue
    Pasadena, CA 91104

    Touch for Health Centre
    Garnet Cottage
    Hunston Road
    Chichester
    West Sussex
    PO20 6NP

    Kinesiology Federation
    PO Box 17
    Woolmer Green
    Knebworth SG3 6UF

The Zen Competitor chapter

Mind Mirror consultants in the UK:

    Isobel Cade
    2 Old Gerden Court
    Mount Pleasant
    St Albans
    Herts
    AL3 4RQ

Mary Wanless
Chapel Plaister Cottage
Wadswick Lane
Box
nr Corsham
Wilts SN13 8HZ

Mind Mirror Consultant in the USA:
Anna Wise
c/o Tools for Exploration
4460 Redwood Hwy, Ste 2-W
San Rafael, CA 94903
USA

RIDE WITH YOUR MIND AIDS TO LEARNING

'The Aids to Learning' catalogue and the items below are available by post from Ride With Your Mind Products, Chapel Plaister Cottage, Wadswick Lane, Box, nr Corsham, Wilts SN13 8HZ, UK. (In the USA, the videotapes are available from Trafalgar Square Publishing, Howe Hill Road, North Pomfret, Vermont 05053 (800 423-4525) and the Gymnasticballs are widely available throughout the USA from physical therapists.)

RIDE WITH YOUR MIND VIDEO MASTERCLASS SERIES

Body Balance: The Basics – Gaining the equilibrium and proper body alignment necessary to establish riding skills which are biomechanically correct.

Rising Trot: Working on the Bit – Developing the correct interaction between rider and the horse, thus establishing the foundation for self-carriage.

Sitting Trot and Canter: Working on the Bit – How to develop correct use of the body and gain a truly independent seat.

Introducing Tempo, Transitions, Lengthening and Shortening of Stride – Tempo and the biomechanics of riding transitions, as well as lengthening and shortening of stride.

MARY WANLESS VIDEO MASTERCLASS SERIES

Symmetry and Circles – Correcting the problems inherent in turning and amplifed by the asymmetries of the rider.

Introduction to Lateral Work – Discover the skills which enable riders to position their own and their horse's body with increasing precision.

Basic Principles ... Advanced Movements – More advanced riders performing advanced movements as they rediscover the basic principles which are the foundation of riding.

A Rider's Guide to Body Awareness – The dynamics of riding explained using dismounted exercises which mimic the biomechanical challenges involved. Also shows some simple stretching exercises.

FURTHER AIDS TO LEARNING

Physioballs (also known as Gymnasticballs) are an invaluable tool for developing balance and stability. Available in three sizes: Pony, Thoroughbred and Warmblood.

Theraband – heavy-duty 3ft loop for strengthening abductor muscles.

Rider's Belt – increases awareness of the pelvic area and helps the rider to learn to 'use her back' effectively. Available in two sizes, small to medium and medium to large.

Index

Page numbers in **bold** denote illustrations

A

Abrahamsen, Trisha 228
acceleration 104-6, 108-9
aerobic exercise 237
Alexander, F.M. 223
Alexander Technique 222, 223, 226-31
alignment
    centre of gravity *see* centre of gravity
    'growing up tall' 38, 41-2, 44, 56, 88, 92
    muscle balance 261
    shoulder/hip/heel alignment 43, 44, 46, 47, 49
    'stretch your leg down' 41, 48, 77, 88, 102, 119, 150
    thigh/calf alignment 48, **48**
    visual feedback 45
    see also bodywork
anxiety 281-2
    cognitive anxiety and physiological arousal 282-3, **282**, 284
    psychological arousal 284
    trait and state anxiety 281, **281**
    worry 282
Applied Kinesiology 259-60
armchair seat 43, 52, 81, 96, **96**
asymmetry 122, 127, 129, 218, 263
    body reading exercise 219-21, **221**
    'C' curve 96, **96**, 130-1, **130**, 132, 133, 136, **143**, 143, 147, 170-1, 221
    conscious asymmetry 132
    diagnosing 132-3
    horse's 127, 129
    injuries and 170, 211
    muscles and 136, 170
    'S' shape **130**, 131, 133, 136, 221
    unconscious asymmetry 132
awakened mind 309-10

B

back
    back pain 43, 212, 267
    horse's ligament system 99, **100**
    stretching **278**
backside
    exercises 245-7, 255
    'square backside' 89, 251, 254
    trochanters 249-50, **249**, 250, 251, **251**, 254
Balkenhol, Klaus 87
Bandler, Richard 18, 23
Barlow, Wilfred 212, 227, 230, 231
bearing down 56, 57, 58-63, **62**, 89, 115
    by the horse 103-4
    solidity and stability 74, 117
    using the Rider's Belt 62-3, **62**
Beaver, Diana 206
Berne, Eric 201
'between hand and leg' 115, **115**
bioenergetics 232
biofeedback 9, 306-7, 309, 311
biomechanics of riding 11, 12, 14, 15, 16, 38, 47, 98, 238, 315, 316, 321
bit
    above the bit 93, 231
    getting the horse onto the bit 94, 98, 115
bodily awareness 37
body image 210-11
body weight
    redistributing 95
    supporting 49-50, 91
bodywork 9, 208-34
    Alexander Technique 222, 223, 226-31
    awareness through movement sessions 225
    becoming 'grounded'/'centred' 219, 234

bodies as print-outs of our thoughts 211
'end-gaining' 230
energetic tradition 232
Feldenkrais Method 170, 222-6, 233
functional integration sessions 224, 225-6
integrative tradition 232-3
manipulative procedures 222
martial arts 12, 41, **41**, 59, 232, 233-4, 234
neck-head-back relationship 227-8, 231
psychological tradition 232
re-education approaches 222-3
stretching 273-5
tension and compression 51, 213-14, 215, 216-17, 218, 219, 226, 227, 296
yoga 232, 233
see also exercises
'both sides on' 137–41, **139**
'bottom walking' 65, 112
brain
    activated neural network density 168-9, 224
    auditory cortex 168
    brain-wave patterns 307-8, **307**, **308**, 309, 310-11
    cerebral cortex 168
    'chunking' information 184, **184**
    goal-striving mechanism 186, 187
    and the homunculus ('little man') 167, **167**, 168
    motor cortex 166
    sensory cortex 166, 167, 176
    see also mindwork
breathing 53, 244-5, 292, 293-4, **293**
breathing down 58
breathing up 58
    diaphragmatic breathing 53, 244-5
    exercise 293-4, **293**

C
'C'-shaped horse 128, 129
'C'-shaped rider 96, **96**, 129, 130-1, **130**, 132, 133, 136, 143, **143**, 147, 170-1, 221
Cade, Maxwell 307, 308, 309-10
calf
    exercise for muscle tone 255-9, 256
    function of 103

muscles 76, **269**, **278**
    thigh/calf alignment 48, **48**
Callanetics 267-8
canter
    plugging in 68
    staying 'with' the horse 65
    transitions 193
    up-and-down movement 61, **61**
Carson, Richard C. 194
centre of gravity 38-9, **39**, 79, 112, 113
    combined rider/horse centre of gravity 114, 115, 118
    in front of the horse 113, **113**, 114, 115
    lowering 52-4
'centred'/'grounded' quality 12, 53, 219, 234
chaos theory 30
Chinese medicine 260
clinic hopping 161-2
'closing the leaks' 53-4, 55, 56, 63, 117, 182, 243-4
co-ordination 227, 238
collagen 216, 217
collection 50, 88, 114
Collins, Joan 274
commitment 71, 74, 157, 158, 160, 280
competition riding 180, 280-311
    and anxiety/stress 280-8
    calming techniques 291-2, 294-5
    cognitive anxiety and physiological arousal 282-3, **282**, 284
    flow experience 300
    loss of form 305
    mastery or winning? 16, 302-4
    mental rehearsal 290-1, 295-6, 297, 310
    performance assessment 300-1
    rigours of 297-8, 304-5
    self-serving bias 301
    simulating competition conditions 298
    toughness, rider's 305
competitive riders 159
complementary health care 259, 315
concentration 73-4, 160, 188, 195
conformation, rider's 87, 97, 247
creativity 312, 321
Csikszentmihalyi, Mihaly 188, 190, 192, 207, 312, 318
cybernetic learning process 155, **156**, 157, 159, **162**

D

Darwin, Charles 320
Das, Ram 190
deceleration 104, 106-7
dedication 160
determination 160
discipline 160
donkeys and mules 70
Dorrance, Tom 129
Douillard, John 294
'downhill horse' 107
downward transitions 118
dressage 88, 112, 180, 234, 286, 301,
    302
  judging 51, 180
  rider's centre of gravity 39, **39**
  seat 96, **96**
  staying in sync with the horse 90
  stirrup length 48
drive theory 284-5, **285**
driving the horse forward 89, 91
'duck paddle' 65, 69
Dychtwald, Ken 233

E

ears
  position 72-3
  pricked ears 71, 72, 73
Edison, Thomas 162-3, 195
endurance riding 190, 314
energy
  exercises 219, 239-44
  Universal Energy 55
energy field 54
equine nutrition 313-14, 315-16
Equus 25
Erickson, Milton 292
evasions 37, 118, 119, 152, 179
event riding 88, 286, 301
exercises 15
  breathing 244-5
  Callanetics 267-8
  'dead leg' exercise 258, **259**
  energy exercises 219, 239-44
  fencing-lunge 151-2, 151, 153
  holding the spine on axis 136-7, **136**
  Ki Aikido exercise 240-2, **241**
  mental rehearsal 275
  muscle tone 255-9, **256**
  'one side on, one side off' 136-40
  pain exercise 67-8, 77, 258
  Pilates Method 266-7
  'popping up' off your seat bones,

correcting 247-55
  'pushing down the plunger' 52-3,
    54-5, 239-40
  'pushing down on the springs' 84,
    84, 88, 261
  spinal stabilisation 261-3, **262**, **263**,
    266
  for spine and backside position
    245-7, **246**
  stretching 273-5
  thighs 102
  using a Gymnasticball/Swissball
    263-4, **264**, **265**, 266, **266**, 275
  warming-up 269-70, 274
  see also bodywork
extension pattern 108, 109, 111, 112

F

farriery 314-15
Fazey, Dr John 284, 287
feedback 7, 161, 195-6, 202
  behaviour/identity distinction 196-7
  biofeedback 9, 306-7, 309, 311
  negative feedback 195
  reading the horse 169, 202
  visual feedback 45, 161, 163-4
Feldenkrais, Moshe 183, 223
Feldenkrais Method 170, 222-3, 233
fencing-lunge exercise 151, **151**, 153
fencing-lunge position 120-1, **121**, 122,
    123, 126
fitness 235-79
  aerobic exercise 237
  cardiovascular fitness 235, 236
fitness training 236-7
flexibility 268, 269
  heart rate 237
  isometric strength 238
  muscular fitness 268
  weight training 237-8, 268-9, 272
  see also exercises
flexion pattern 108, 109, 111, 112, 113,
    135
flow experience 188, 190-1, 192, 193,
    195, 300
flying changes 152
foetal crouch 52, 96, 187, 210, 229, 295
front, rider's, lengthening 80, **80**, 81, 82,
    108, 109
Fuller, Buckminster 213

G

Gallwey, Timothy 192

Gaylord, Mitch 177
Goodwin, Paul 168
Green, Lucinda 306
Grinder, John 18, 23, 292

H
habit patterns 164, 172, 217, 224, 229
half-halts 112, 113, 114, 118, **118**, 119
half-hauls 118, 119
halts 106-7, 113
Harding, Tonya 302
Hardy, Dr Lew 284, 287
Harris, Thomas 201
Hearne, Vicki 202-3, 204
heel position 40, 40, 42, 133
Heller, Joseph 134, 217, 234
Hemery, David 290
Henkin, William A. 134, 217, 234
hip replacements 212
Holderness-Roddam, Jane 235
hollow-backed horse 93-4, 96-7, 103
hollow-backed rider 42, **42**, 43, 44, 52,
    85, 88, 97, 103, 212, 227, 231
homeostasis 172, 173
horse's centre of motion, connecting to
    66
horse's power, containing and directing
    57
horse's tempo, controlling 68, 82, 108,
    109
Huxley, Aldous 19-20

I
inadequacy, sense of 197
independent seat 63
injuries 270-1
    compensating for 170, 211
interactive riding 90-119
internal dialogue 193-5

J
jack-knife 123, **123**, 124, 126, 170
jockeys 235
Johnstone, Lorna 235
joints 269-70
jumping 39-40

K
Kellett, Iris 196-7
Ki Aikido 234, 240, 242
kinaesthetic sensitivity 20-1, 54, 155,
    163
    horse's 204

Klimke, Reiner 50, 79
knees, gripping with 66
Kuhn, Thomas S. 319
Kursinski, Anne 303
Kyrklund, Kyra 79, 283, 302, 306

L
lameness 127
    rider-induced lameness 208
lateral work 140-1, 152
lazy horses 79, 81, 105, 107, 158
learning process
    breakthroughs 178, 179, 179
    clinic hopping 161-2
    communication process 11, 12,
        164-5, **165**
    criticism 22
    cybernetic learning process 178,
        195
    declarative knowledge 154, 180
    experiencing contrasts 173
    facing your emotions 233-4
    feedback *see* feedback
    graph 178-9, **179**
    habit patterns 164, 172
    'learning how to learn' 22
    mental rehearsal 176
    metaphorical use of language 174,
        175
    mirrors, using 163-4
    over-correcting 161
    personal criteria for 'good' 182-3
    repetitions 177-8, 179, 181
    reproducing the 'magical ride' 174,
        192
    skill development 21, 188-9, **189**
    supervised riding 161, 176
    TOTE model 180, 181, **181**, 183,
        184, 230
    'unconscious competence' 177, 183
    'weirdness', feelings of 46, 47, 171-2,
        173
leg aids 69, 70, 74, 123
    tonal quality 74
legs, relaxing 76, 77
Loehr, James E. 305
lunge, riding on the 61
Lyons, John 25, 203

M
McCluggage, Denise 192, 224
'magic spot' 104
Maltz, Maxwell 155-6

mantrap
  spanning 99, 101, 114
  staying out of 90-1, 98
map-making 15-16, 17-32
  consensus map 23, 30, 31
  distortions 22-3, 31
  filtering process 18, 19
  generalisations and deletions 22, 23
  individual variation 18-19, 38
  kinaesthetic map 20, 163
  map of riding 29, 34, 35-6, 38, 163, 185
  mind-sets 25-8, 30, 196
  neurological and genetic constraints 17
  perspectives, altered 24
  redrawing 16, 35, 36, 132
martial arts 12, 41, **41**, 59, 232, 233-4
meditation 232-3, 309
mindwork 185-207
  flow experience 188, 189, **189**, 190-1, 192, 193, 195, 300
  internal dialogue 193-5
  negative thoughts 186-7
  optimal experiences 188
  transactional analysis 201, 206
  see also brain
mirrors, using 163-4
Moore, Gloria 273, 274
Moore, Henry 191
Morris, Desmond 209
Morris, George 159-60
muscle tone 50, 51, 66, 93, 168
  anxiety and 284
  exercise 255-9, **256**
  high muscle tone 50, 51, 55, 59, 93, 99, 153, 231, 236
  increasing 67, 267
muscles
  abdominal muscles 57-8, 58
  abductors 76, 257
  adductors 76, 147, 171, 257, 274, **277**
  asymmetry and 136, 170
  calf 76
  contraction 75, 273
  extensors 210, 261, 275
  externals 77, 103, 147-8, 150, 152
  fascia (connective tissues) 216, 217
  flexors 84, 97, 210, 261, 275
  gluteal 86, 86, 150
  hamstrings 75, 247-8, **248**, 254, 257, 269, 274, **277**
  iliacus 135, **135**, 150

iliopsoas 135, 170
imbalance 84-5, 261, 275
internals 134, 147
isometric use 75, 90, 152, 238, 255, 259
isotonic use 75, 152
latissimus dorsi 147-8, **148**, 149, 150, 151, 152, 153
movement muscles 209-10
muscular fitness 268
postural muscles 209
psoas 134-5, 135, 136, 137, 145, 146, 260, 274, **276**
quadriceps 75, 102, 137, 255, 274, **276**
rider's back **248**
tension 192, 213, 217
tensor fasciae latae 86, **86**, 150, 257, 258
thigh muscles 76, 77, 137
weakness 260-1
muscles, horse's
  back muscles 124-5, **125**, 127, 146, 147, 150, 254
  belly muscles 103, 104

N
nappy horse 114, 134
neck-head-back relationship 227-8, 231, 232
nervous rider 229, 287-8, 295
neuro-linguistic programming 9, 154, 195, 211
Nicholls, David 208

O
O'Connor, Karen Lende 302-4
'one side on, one side off' 138-9, 141, 171
over-correcting 161
over-focused riders 157-8

P
pain exercise 67-8, 77, 258
Parelli, Pat 25
pelvis
  alignment of the 42, **42**, 225
  becoming dexterous with 168
  exercises for 268
  male and female 252, 253
  pelvic wings 130, 135, 150
  positioning on a turn 122, **122**
  shallow pelvis 87, 97

stabilisers **138**, 251
strength and solidarity in 243
Phillips, Captain Mark 187
Pilates Method 266-7
'pinch'/narrowing in 35, 66–8, 76
Pinckney, Callan 267, 268
Planck, Max 320
plugging in 64-89, 93
    connecting to the horse's centre of
        motion 66
    disconnection from the horse 64, 68,
        69
    increasing muscle tone 67
    in trot and canter 65, 68
'popping up' tendency 66, 68, 75, 91,
    247-55
posture 209, 210, 211, 223, 275
    see also bodywork
procedural knowledge 154
propulsive force of the hind legs 61,
    116
psychocybernetics 156
pubic bone
    horse's 103
    rider's 251, 253
push back 94, 96, 97, 116, 200
'push your heels down' 40
'pushing down the plunger' 52–3,
    54–5, 56, 63, 90–1, 117, 239–40

R
Rasmussen, Wayne 271
rein
    halts 106
    lightness into the 91-2
relaxation 50-1, 289
    'dead relaxation' 50-1, 52, 93
    'live relaxation' 50-1, 93
    relaxed alertness 51
    relaxing the legs 76, 77
    research paths 313-14
ribcage displacement 126-7, 128, **128**,
    129, 232
Rider's Belt 62-3, **62**, 89, 94, 243, 327
'rider's bone' 270, 271
riding cultures, British and American
    317
riding 'from back to front' 95
riding 'from front to back' 95
riding partnership 199-200, 202-3,
    204-5
riding-school horses 208-9
rising trot 78-82, **79**, 89, 267

balancing over your feet 78-9, 82
being pushed up 84
lengthening your front 80, **80**, 81, 82
pressure in the stirrups 82
Ristad, Eloise 192, 194
Roberts, Monty 25, 316-17, 318
round-backed rider 42, **42**, 43, 44, 52,
    212
runaway horses 81, 108, 111, 114
Ryan, Matt 310

S
'S'-shaped horse 128, 129
'S'-shaped rider **130**, 131, 133, 136, 221
Sacks, Oliver 208
saddle movement **83**
saddlery 314-15
St George, Francine 237
'sand in his head' 91-2, 94, 107
Sauer, Uwe 271
Savoie, Jane 187
seat bones 65, 67, 97, 267
    equal weighting 120, 131, 133
    exercises for 'popping up' off
        247-55
    'having both sides on' 138, **139**, 171
    pointing down 42, **42**, 67
Sederholm, Lars 95
self-carriage 7
sensory motor amnesia 212-13
shock-absorption 43, 85, 87-8, **87**
sitting deep 91, 167
sitting trot 61, 83-8, 89, 264, **266**
slope, working on a 178
spine
    as a tensegrity mast 214, **215**
    exercises 245-7, **246**, 261-3, **262**, **263**,
        266
    holding on axis 136-7, **136**
    neutral spine 212, 246, **246**, 247, 261,
        265
spiritual perspective on riding 16
spongy buttock syndrome 88
sport psychology 9
startle reflx 210
steering 122, 123, 127
    horse's nose 122, 123, 129
    the wither 129
    see also turns
sternum, horse's 103
stirrups
    length 47, 48, 49, 98, 133
    pressure in 49, 82

straightening a horse 232
stress 280-8
    catastrophe theory 287-8, **289**
    drive theory 284-5, **285**
    eustress 280, 281
    extrovert/introvert continuum 286
    high arousal thresholds 286
    in horses 314
    inverted-U theory 285-6, **285**, 287
    see also anxiety
'stretch up tall' 150
stretching 273-5
    adductor stretch **277**
    assisted stretches 273
    back stretches 275, **278**
    calf muscles **278**
    chest and shoulder **278**
    hamstring stretch **277**
    psoas stretch **276**
    quadriceps stretch **276**
    using Gymnasticballs 275
    when not to 274
supervised riding 161, 176
'switched-off' horse 70, 71-2, 110
'switched-off' rider 73
symmetry 120-53
    asymmetry *see* asymmetry
    functional symmetry 129, 132, 149
    rider 'stuffed and stacked' 143, **143**,
        144-5, **144**, 147, 149-50
spine, holding on axis 136-7, 136
straightness 149

T
T'ai Chi 9, 233
Tai Kwan Do 233
teaching
    new approaches 316, 320, 321,
        322
    or training? 7-8
traditional system 34, 318-19
    see also learning process
Tellington-Jones, Linda 242, 310
tensegrity structure, the body as 213,
    214-15, **214**
tension 51, 214, 215, 218, 219, 226,
    227, 296
texture of the body 51-2
Theraband 257, 272, 327
thighs
    as buffers 99-100, **101**, 102, 103,
        113, 114, 119
    as pivots 100, **101**

exercises for 255-9, **256**, 268
    muscle imbalance 85
    muscles 76, 77, 99, 137, **269**
    strengthening 102, 103, 267
    thigh/calf alignment 48, **48**
    'V' shape 66-7, **67**, 68, 76, 101,
        102, 137, 138, 139-40, 141, 253,
        254
Thoroughbreds 88, 93, 98
Todd, Mark 287
torso
    muscle imbalance 85
    stabilising 86, **86**
Touch for Health 259, 260
transactional analysis 201, 206
triers 158-9, 192
trot
    centre of gravity 79
    rising trot 78-82, **79**, 89, 267
    sitting trot 61, 83-8, 89, 264, **266**
    staying 'with' the horse 65
    up-and-down movement 61, **61**,
        83-4, **83**
turns
    falling in 124, 126
    falling out 124
    fencing-lunge position 120-1, **121**,
        122, 123, 126
    handlebar turns 123
    jack-knife 123, **123**, 124, 126, 170
    lengthening the inside of the horse
        126
    positioning the rider's body 120,
        126
    ribcage bulge 126-7, 128, **128**, 129,
        232
    steering problems 143-4, 145-6
    turning aids **144**, 145-6

U
underside, lengthening 108, 109
Universal Energy 55

V
veterinary science 315
vision
    focused vision 192, 193
    learned phenomena 29-30
    peripheral vision 72, 192
visual feedback 45, 161
visual senses 163

W
walk 61, 78
walk/halt mechanism 106-7
warmblood horses 88, 98
water-ski/motorboat scenario 27, 39, 79, 105, **105**, 106, 107, 108, 109-10, 112
wither 123, 124, 126, 129

Y
yoga 232, 233

Z
'Z' angles 86, 87, **87**, 88, 107, 111, 113, 117, 118, 119
Zaborde, Genie 20

QUOTATION PERMISSIONS/ACKNOWLEDGEMENTS

CHAPTER 1: *The Structure of Magic* © Richard Bandler and John Grinder, by permission of the author and publisher, Science and Behaviour Books Inc., Palo Alto, CA 1.800.547.9982.
Influencing With Integrity © Genie Zaborde, Syntony Publishing, USA.
The Doors of Perception © Aldous Huxley, Harper & Row Publishers Inc., USA.

CHAPTER 5: *The Anatomy Colouring Book* © Wynn Kapit and Lawrence Elson, Harper & Row Inc., New York.

CHAPTER 6: *The Case of Nora* © Moshe Feldenkrais, North Atlantic Press, USA.

CHAPTER 7: *Flow* © Mihalyi Csikszentmihalyi – thanks to Harper & Row Inc., for permission to reproduce the diagram of the flow channel.

CHAPTER 8: *The Alexander Principle* © Wilfred Barlow – thanks to Victor Gollancz in the UK and to A.A. Knopf in the USA.
Bodywise © Joseph Heller and Willian Henkin, thanks to Wingbow Press, California, USA.
Bodymind © Ken Dytchwald, by permission J.P. Tarcher, USA.

CHAPTER 9: *Callanetics* © Callan Pinckney, by permission Random House UK and ICM, New York, USA.

CHAPTER 10: *The Awakened Mind* © C. Maxwell Cade and Nona Coxhead, by permission Element Books, UK.
Thanks to Isobel Cade and Element Books for permission to adapt diagrams from *The Awakened Mind*.
Thanks to the National Coaching Foundation for permission to use diagrams from their handbooks, *Mental Preparation for Performance* by Dr Lew Hardy and Dr John Fazey, and *The Social Psychology of Sport* by Dr David Houlston.